Knowledge-Based Enterprise:
Theories and Fundamentals

Nilmini Wickramasinghe
Illinois Institute of Technology, USA
Coventry University, UK

Dag von Lubitz
Med-SMART, USA & Central Michigan University, USA

IDEA GROUP PUBLISHING
Hershey • London • Melbourne • Singapore

Acquisitions Editor:	Krisitn Klinger
Development Editor:	Kristin Roth
Senior Managing Editor:	Jennifer Neidig
Managing Editor:	Sara Reed
Assistant Managing Editor:	Sharon Berger
Copy Editor:	Larissa Vinci
Typesetter:	Amanda Appicello
Cover Design:	Lisa Tosheff
Printed at:	Integrated Book Technology

Published in the United States of America by
Idea Group Publishing (an imprint of Idea Group Inc.)
701 E. Chocolate Avenue, Suite 200
Hershey PA 17033-1240
Tel: 717-533-8845
Fax: 717-533-8661
E-mail: cust@idea-group.com
Web site: http://www.idea-group.com

and in the United Kingdom by
Idea Group Publishing (an imprint of Idea Group Inc.)
3 Henrietta Street
Covent Garden
London WC2E 8LU
Tel: 44 20 7240 0856
Fax: 44 20 7379 0609
Web site: http://www.eurospanonline.com

Library of Congress Cataloging-in-Publication Data

Wickramasinghe, Nilmini.
  Knowledge-based enterprise : theories and fundamentals / Nilmini Wickramasinghe and Dag von Lubitz, authors.
    p. cm.
  Summary: "This book provides comprehensive coverage of all areas (people, process, and technology) necessary to become a knowledge-based enterprise. It presents several frameworks facilitating the implementation of a KM initiative and its ongoing management so that pertinent knowledge and information are always available to the decision maker, and so the organization may always enjoy a sustainable competitive advantage"--Provided by publisher.
  Includes bibliographical references and index.
  ISBN 978-1-59904-237-4 (hbk.) -- ISBN 978-1-59904-239-8 (ebook)
  1. Knowledge management. I. Von Lubitz, Dag K. J. E. II. Title.
  HD30.2.W523 2007
  658.4'038--dc22
                    2006033748

British Cataloguing in Publication Data
A Cataloguing in Publication record for this book is available from the British Library.

All work contributed to this book is new, previously-unpublished material. The views expressed in this book are those of the authors, but not necessarily of the publisher.

Dedication

For our mothers

Knowledge-Based Enterprise:
Theories and Fundamentals

Table of Contents

Section III: Becoming a Knowledge-Based Enterprise

Section IV: Realities for Knowledge-Based Enterprises

Foreword

Wickramasinghe and von Lubitz begin Chapter IX of this book with a quote from Michael Porter:

The nations that will lead the world into the next century will be those that can shift from being industrial economies based upon the production of manufactured goods to those that possess the capacity to produce and utilize knowledge successfully.

This basic idea is both the reason for and the foundation of this book. Managing knowledge—capturing it, storing it, recalling it, and using it—is the fundamental process that will distinguish between successful and unsuccessful "organizations" of all sizes—from small groups to entire economies—in the 21st century. The authors take this assertion for granted requiring no further comment or proof. We live in a knowledge economy, one where knowledge is *the* critical resource, more important than any of the other traditional economic resources. What must an organization do in order to gain control of and effectively use the knowledge resource?

To answer that question, we should begin by clarifying what we mean by knowledge and the knowledge economy. That is where Wickramasinghe and von Lubitz begin this book. The first three chapters of the book focus on the nature of knowledge, the ways that knowledge is "created," and the centrality of knowledge to organizational performance. Knowledge goes beyond data or information, though these are its fundamental building blocks. Knowledge is not passive and implies the application and *productive use* of information. Knowledge exists in an organization and in its environment, but the organization does not automatically benefit from that knowledge. It must be able to capture the knowledge, represent, store it, and make it available for recall, dissemination, and use. An organization that can capture, store, recall knowledge, and then apply it in relevant situations is at great advantage in today's economy.

The first section of the book concludes by laying out a framework for thinking about knowledge management. The authors choose to adopt a socio-technical perspective as their framework for thinking about knowledge management. In this perspective, three elements are key: people, process, and technology. Understanding knowledge management in any particular setting (organization) requires that we consider all of these elements. Wickramasinghe and von Lubitz discuss all three elements and describe knowledge management approaches focused primarily on the people involved (psycho-social aspects) or the technology employed. They prefer, however, to emphasize the process, and examine how the other elements of the framework impact on each stage in the knowledge management process. The advantages of this approach are that it is broad and context sensitive, and thus can be used to understand the variety and nuance in knowledge management situations across disparate organizations.

The middle portion of the book examines three critical knowledge management infrastructures—the business process infrastructure, the human infrastructure, and the technology infrastructure. *Business* processes are central to the functioning of all organizations, whether they are business organizations or not, and the functioning of these processes is critically dependent on the knowledge available to them. As a consequence, knowledge management can be viewed as the basis for success of these processes.

Knowledge workers are an ever-growing part of modern organizations, and they comprise the critical human infrastructure for knowledge management. The authors identify a range of issues that are important to an understanding of this human infrastructure, including:

- How a knowledge worker's knowledge can be captured and retained;
- Monitoring and controlling knowledge workers' actions;
- Managing change in dynamic environments;
- The organization's culture and how it supports (or fails to support) knowledge management efforts; and
- The role of leadership in assuring the success of knowledge management efforts.

All of these are important aspects of the human infrastructure that should be examined in order to understand knowledge management in any specific situation.

The final infrastructure presented is the technological infrastructure. The authors suggest a three-layer architecture useful for thinking about knowledge management. At the top is the knowledge presentation layer, the *knowledge portal*. In the middle, the *knowledge repository* performs the technical tasks of knowledge management. And, at the bottom, there is a data sources layer, which may include multiple databases as well as other sources. The chapter discusses many specific technologies that may be used to support one or more of these layers.

While the first six chapters present the nuts and bolts of knowledge management, it is the final four chapters that put flesh on this framework and are the most interesting. Chapter VII focuses on the strategic level, reviewing several models related to strategy (e.g., Porter's value chain, competitive forces, and generic strategies frameworks) and identifying areas where knowledge management can support strategy development and execution. The critical message is that while knowledge management can indeed be supportive of an organization's strategic processes, there must be a conscious effort to make this happen.

In Chapter VIII, the authors come back to a theme hinted at several times earlier in the book—that of complexity. They develop an integrative model that pulls together many of the threads presented earlier, and use it to drive home the point that an organization's approach to knowledge management must be context dependent.

Chapter IX focuses on learning and learning organizations. Learning is the key to success, even to survival, in dynamic environments and managing knowledge is fundamental to learning.

Finally, Chapter X presents six brief case studies of knowledge management in real situations. The cases are striking in their variety—by industry, country, objectives, approach, etc. Ranging from agents in real estate brokerages in the United States, to members of multi-disciplinary patient care teams in Australia, to the construction industry in Denmark, these cases help to highlight the universal appeal of knowledge management to support a very wide range of organizations. The approaches taken, types and sources of data, information and knowledge captured, and technologies employed—or in one case the lack of technology employed—differed, but the objective in each case was to harness available knowledge to improve performance. Each context presented its unique challenges and its own implementation issues, and each required that implementation approaches be tailored for that context. The value of these cases is to help us understand the range of situations where knowledge management is appropriate, while appreciating the importance of context and the differences across situations.

Knowledge-Based Enterprise: Theories and Fundamentals is a great starting point for someone who is beginning to explore the field of knowledge management, and provides a comprehensive introduction to this area. The frameworks developed early in the book are followed throughout and help the reader tie together the many pieces of the story. The book is also helpful for someone already familiar with the field precisely because of the consistent organizing frameworks it employs. The case studies are particularly useful for all readers who want to gain an understanding of knowledge management as it is currently being practiced.

Michael J. Ginzberg, PhD
Wilmington, Delaware

Preface

homo cui vivere est cogitare
(Man to whom to live is to think)

- CICERO

Knowledge management (KM) is a nascent, evolving field at the confluence of several management disciplines. One only needs to open a business publication to find articles extolling the benefits of KM. The term KM first began to appear in the management literature only in the late 1980s, while knowledge per se has been important since time immemorial. What then is knowledge management? Is there any substance behind the verbiage and fancy phrases that are so frequently and eloquently offered at keynote addresses, board meetings, and conferences? Some skeptics believe KM to be old wine in new bottles while others are convinced KM is simply just another empty management promise. It is the contention of this book that knowledge management is an important emerging field. Moreover, it is only by embracing knowledge management and becoming knowledge-based enterprises that organizations will find themselves prepared and ready to survive and thrive in a dynamic and extremely competitive business world.

A critical function for all organizations is to have the ability to make rapid decisions. To do this effectively, decision makers require relevant data and information. With the ubiquitous adoption and diffusion of IC^2T (information computer and communications technologies) we have witnessed an exponential increase in information, as well as an increase in the reach and range of business activities, and a corresponding decrease in the operationally acceptable time between the trigger event and decision formulation and implementation. Decision makers are drowning in information overload, and yet must make critical decisions that have far-reaching consequences to their organization under severe time compression. Invariably the result is chaos with decisions that are suboptimal.

The tools, techniques, strategies, and protocols of KM address these problems at their very core. KM focuses on providing quality information and germane knowledge to the decision maker. What ensues is the effective and efficient control of the operational environment so that the organization can not only survive, but thrive and continuously enjoy a sustainable competitive advantage.

A critical issue that permeates much of the economic literature is that concerning the theory of the firm versus the theory of markets. Connor and Prahalad (1996) have extended the idea of the resource-based theory of the firm originally discussed by Coarse (1937) to recognize knowledge-based transactions. In particular, they emphasize that the advantage of a firm in this context is as a unit that is made up of sub-components (people and tools) which together build a knowledge base that enables the organization to operate effectively and efficiently. Moreover, the structuring of the sub-units and activities within the organization should be such that they support the continual acquiring of this knowledge base incurring minimal transaction costs. Hence, a knowledge-based enterprise is one that, irrespective of industry, functions so that it continually applies germane knowledge to any and all its business activities. Knowledge is central to such organizations, while its appropriate application and use are critical success factors. To achieve this goal, knowledge-based organizations must not only understand the fundamental principles of knowledge management but also incorporate the tools, techniques, strategies, and protocols of KM into all areas of their operations.

It must be borne in mind that to become a knowledge-based enterprise requires much more than the chanting of the KM mantra or displaying the organization's KM icon. *Knowledge-Based Enterprises: Theories and Fundamentals* provides an overview of all the key areas within KM. The goal of the book is to open the black box of KM, remove the mystique, replace the rhetoric with reality, and provide the reader with the fundamental principles required for the transformation of an organization governed by the traditional rules of conducting business into a new, dynamic, and responsive knowledge-based enterprise.

Currently, numerous organizations are trying to incorporate aspects of KM in an attempt to address deficiencies within their own organization. Poor performance, ineffective operations, declining market share, or even an attempt to rectify problems with inferior products are matters of concern. However, too many of these measures are attempted without a thorough understanding of what is involved by incorporating KM principles or even a full appreciation of what KM is and is not. It should not come then a surprise that most of the attempts at embracing KM have been futile and unsuccessful. Moreover, this in turn has lead to a disturbing trend in a growing disillusionment with KM and effecting the transition to become knowledge-based.

This book addresses this problem by bringing together all the essential elements of knowledge management, the tools, techniques, strategies, and protocols necessary to create a knowledge-based enterprise. In so doing, it has several differentiating qualities, which set it apart from other books pertaining to KM. First, the book identifies the complex nature of the knowledge construct itself, the underlying dualities that exist when trying to understand knowledge, and its philosophical roots. Few books address this issue and such an omission leaves readers with an incomplete understanding of knowledge, and thus its management can never be totally effective. In addition, the book presents a socio-technical perspective to KM. By offering the key people centric, technology centric, and process centric perspectives to knowledge management it is possible to develop a more in depth appreciation of how to combine all these aspects when incorporating KM into an organization. Another unique feature of the book is that it addresses both macro and micro issues as well as internal and external issues relating to KM. These issues are discussed in conjunction with a presentation of leading theories while insights from practice are provided in the collection of international case studies.

Specifically, the book is divided into four sections. Section I, "Understanding Knowledge," defines the elusive and complex knowledge construct, and clarifies "knowledge economy," how organizations should behave in such an environment, and presents the major theories pertaining to knowledge creation. This is done in three chapters: Chapter I, "Overview of the Networked Knowledge Economy," discusses the "knowledge economy" and contrasts it with previous economies. Chapter II, "Understanding the Knowledge Construct," presents what knowledge is and Chapter III, "Creating Organizational Knowledge," outlines the major philosophical implications connected with the dualities of the knowledge construct.

Section II, "Infrastructures Required to Support Knowledge-Based Enterprises" presents the three fundamental infrastructure blocks essential for any knowledge-based enterprise: human, business, and the technological infrastructures. Chapter IV, "The KM Business Infrastructure" presents the leading theories and techniques to develop a solid business infrastructure, while Chapter V, "The Organization's Human Infrastructure" presents the leading management theories pertaining to various people issues including culture, structure, leadership, and management. Chapter VI, "The KM Technological Infrastructure" discusses the key technologies needed to support and enable any KM initiative. Taken together, this section provides the fundamental socio-technical issues critical for transforming an enterprise into a knowledge-based enterprise. These topics are all subjects that could in themselves be books; however, the goal of this section is to bring all these concepts together so that a complete picture of the essentials for establishing an appropriate infrastructure can be presented concisely and yet completely.

In Section III, "Becoming a Knowledge-Based Enterprise," macro management issues that are significant to knowledge-based organizations are discussed. These comprise of Chapter VII, "KM and Strategy," Chapter VIII, "Managing Knowledge Complexity," and, finally, Chapter IX, "Learning Organizations," which emphasizes the need to apply continuous rather than discrete approaches to knowledge management and the relevance of organizational memory and organizational learning.

The concluding section, Section IV, "Realities for Knowledge-Based Enterprises" presents a compilation of international case studies pertaining to various KM initiatives, which will help to develop an appreciation of the challenges and benefits derived from becoming a knowledge-based enterprise:

- **Case 1:** "IT Platform for Study and E-Collaboration" by Witold Abramowicz, Tomasz Kaczmarek, and Marek Kowalkiewicz discusses a Polish experience of implementing a knowledge sharing and e-collaboration environment.

- **Case 2:** "Distributed Knowledge Networks" by Mogens Kühn Pedersen discusses distributing knowledge in the construction industry in Denmark.

- **Case 3:** "Keller Williams Realty" by Roberta Lamb consists of a discussion of framing a structure for knowledge sharing in the U.S. real estate industry and has a follow up part B that discusses how Keller Williams Realty cemented these KM relationships.

- **Case 4:** "Contingency-Driven Knowledge Management in Palliative Care" by Graydon Davison discusses the role and usefulness of KM in a generally considered "fringe" area of healthcare: palliative care.

- **Case 5:** "Managing Knowledge in Project-Based Organizations" by Jacky Swan, Anna Goussevskaia, and Mark Bresnen discusses the critical role KM plays in project-based organisations in the UK.

- **Case 6:** "Knowledge Management in Practice" by Brian Donnellan, Martin Hughes, and William Golden discusses the need for the tools and techniques of KM in the semiconductor industry in Ireland.

It is our expectation that after reading this book, all readers—executives, middle-level managers, and students—will gain a new appreciation of KM. We hope that those of our readers who have no professional ties to business and its management will also be able to embrace the promise and potential that KM provides not only in the life of organizations but, at a fundamental "gut level" in practically all aspects of our "daily lives." Even shopping involves, at a very basic level, several elements of knowledge management and creation of structure from the chaos of Web or even shelf offerings. Finally, we hope that our professional colleagues will enjoy reading a text presenting a personal view of this new, exciting, and challenging field of KM.

References

Coarse, R. (1937). The nature of the firm. *Economica, 4*, 386-405.

Conner, K., & Prahalad, C. (1996). A resource-based theory of the firm: Knowledge versus opportunism. *Organization Science, 7*(5), 477-501.

Acknowledgments

This book would not have been possible without the cooperation and assistance of numerous people: the contributors, reviewers, our colleagues, students, and the staff at Idea Group Publishing. We are grateful to you all for your support. The authors would especially like to thank Mehdi Khosrow-Pour for inviting us to produce this book, Jan Travers for managing this project, and Kristin Roth for assisting us through the process. Finally, a special thanks to Alina, Nikki, and Varun for their efforts to check that all formatting was correct.

Section I

Understanding Knowledge

Chapter I

Overview of the Networked Knowledge Economy

Introduction

We are not only in a new millennium, but also in a new era. A variety of terms such as the post-industrial era (Huber, 1990), the information age (Shapiro & Varian, 1999), the third wave (Hope & Hope, 1997), or the knowledge society (Drucker, 1999) are being used to describe this epoch. However, irrespective of the term one subscribes to, most agree that one of the key defining and unifying themes of this period is knowledge management. What then is this new concept that creates enthusiasm, stirs skepticism, provokes controversy, and yet promises to be the new way of dealing with ... practically everything?

Knowledge management (KM) is a new and rapidly evolving approach aimed at addressing current challenges to increase efficiency and efficacy of core business processes while simultaneously incorporating continuous innovation. The need for knowledge management is based on a growing realisation by the business community that knowledge is central to organizational performance, and integral to the attainment of a sustainable competitive advantage (Davenport & Grover, 2001; Drucker, 1993). Such a fundamental macro-level shift also has consequent and significant implications upon both meso-level and the micro-level processes throughout organizations. Indeed the assimilation and implementation of knowledge management concepts, tools, techniques, and strategies [i.e., the adoption of knowledge management systems (KMSs)] and subsequent transforming to become a knowledge-based enterprise is not simply attained through the implementation of a Lotus Notes database, rather it requires the correct choice of various tools and techniques to be applied in a coordinated fashion to all organizational operations so that knowledge driven and knowledge generating business process and activities result. In order to make appropriate choices regarding the type of technologies to employ and/or the techniques to adopt, it is first imperative that a thorough understanding of several meso-level elements of the organization is attained. These central elements range from the existing technology infrastructure, organizational structure, and culture and business infrastructure. Moreover, and of equal importance it is necessary to comprehend how these components combine and synchronize to support and facilitate effective and efficient organizational processes which in turn equip the firm to attain its stated business goals, objectives and strategies.

Before we can understand how to appropriately apply the tools, techniques, technologies, and strategies of knowledge management to transform the firm into a knowledge-based enterprise, it is essential first to understand the underlying dynamics of the networked knowledge economy and why knowledge management is so important in this context.

What is the Knowledge Economy?

Economists have categorized the world into three distinct ages—the agrarian age, the industrial age, and now the information age (Persaud, 2001; Woodall, 2000). The hallmark of the information age is the rapid adoption and diffusion of IC^2T (information computer and communication technologies) which has had a dramatic effect on the way business is conducted as well as on the life styles of people. An important consequence of globalization and rapid technological change has been the generation of vast amounts of raw data and information, and the concomitant growth of the capabilities to process them into pertinent information and knowledge applicable to the solutions of business problems. Knowledge has become a major organizational tool in gaining and sustaining competitive advantage.

Traditionally, economists have emphasized land and the associated natural resources, labor, and capital as the essential primary ingredients for the economic enterprise. However, in the Information Age, knowledge is now being considered to be as important as the three original prerequisites. Hence, the new term knowledge economy has emerged. The concept of knowledge economy is often used synonymously (and incorrectly) with "Information Age," and managing knowledge became one of the primary skills organizations needed to acquire in order to survive and prosper (Figure 1).

Figure 1. Impact of IC²T on traditional economic principles to create the knowledge economy and wealth generation

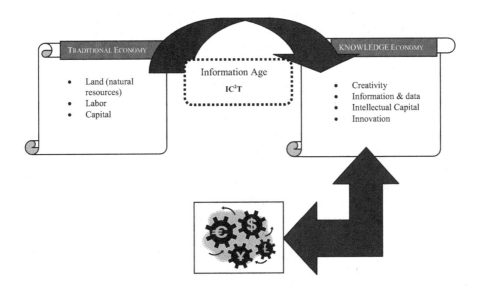

In the knowledge economy, technology plays an integral part in expanding economic potential (Persaud, 2001). Such economic potential is primarily reliant on maximizing the firm's intangible assets and requires the fostering of innovation and creation. To support such initiatives information is required. However, this information serves a dual purpose; it reduces operating costs and also facilitates idea generation and creativity. For example, the use of enterprise-wide systems permits organizations to decrease their transaction costs, which allows them to decrease agency costs. This is because integrated information pertaining to specific tasks and activities can now be acquired in a timely fashion (Wickramasinghe, 2000). Furthermore, information accessed through various shared services modules supports the generation of new and innovative initiatives (Probst, Raub, & Romhardt, 2000; Shapiro & Verian, 1999). Moreover, the continuous collection and analysis of this data and information generated from a variety of transactions throughout the supply chain facilitates idea generation and the rapid design and development of new products, processes, or even new ways to meet requirements.

A cursory perusal of the more popular business press, trade magazines, and even academic literature will serve to highlight the many new terms that have been coined for the information age or knowledge economy. Some of the more prevalent ones include "knowledge-based economy," "borderless economy," "weightless economy," and "digital economy." Irrespective of the term used to describe this epoch, the imperative for organizations is to understand the underlying dynamics of the knowledge economy so that they can structure (or re-structure) themselves accordingly to operate successfully in such a climate or else the terms become meaningless and organizations do not thrive. It is incumbent upon organizations to critically evaluate the rhetoric in order to make the necessary substantive changes required to transform themselves into knowledge-based enterprises.

It is important to note that knowledge, information, and data have always been significant, whether in the agrarian age, industrial age, or information age. The key difference in the knowledge economy or Information Age is that we now have tools in the form of IC²T that support and facilitate large scale data capture and gathering, transforming this data into pertinent information and relevant knowledge as well as the ability to extract and then apply appropriate and germane knowledge to a particular context in a timely fashion. Hence, IC²T have served to dramatically increase the scale and scope of all information processing activities. The facility to communicate information instantaneously across the globe has changed the nature of competition. Information can now be delivered with such speed that companies must develop their knowledge assets to process this information to find solutions to address competitive challenges and problems in a timely fashion. The structure of the knowledge economy emerges from the convergence of computing, communications, and content. The ramifications of this are tremendous and far-reaching, and knowledge management becomes a critical activity for organization in order to enjoy a sustainable competitive advantage.

The knowledge economy offers huge opportunities for small and medium-sized enterprises (SMEs) not only to add value to their existing activities, but also to develop entirely new ranges of innovative products and services, reduce costs, or diversify to new, previously closed markets, etc. Moreover, the advent of ubiquitous Internet connectivity has resulted in a new concept of "idea trade" consequent to the drastically lowered costs of information and its distribution. Companies now sell equity stakes in good ideas and use the capital they raise to realize these ideas, and the competition is based predominantly on the knowledge that now exists in the form of intellectual capital (Persaud, 2001). The pervasive role of knowledge in practically all activities of a nation-state clearly indicates that a country's future economic prospects may depend predominantly on knowledge (Acs, Carlsson, & Karlsson, 1999) and the ability to apply it appropriately. In fact, Michael Porter has noted that the ultimate competitive strength of a nation lies in its ability to maximize its knowledge assets (Porter, 1990).

A company's knowledge assets reside in the creativity of its knowledge workers combined with technological and market know-how (Halliday, 2001). Hence, in the knowledge economy, knowledge, its creation and appropriate use and re-use is inextricably linked to increased profits for the organization, which translates into gaining and sustaining competitive advantage. Realizing the importance of knowledge assets, many companies have changed their original centralized, top-down structure and replaced it by de-centralized, cross-functional teams of individuals motivated by their ownership in the companies (McGarvey, 2001).

The velocity and dynamic nature of the contemporary marketplace has created a competitive incentive among many companies to consolidate and reconcile their knowledge assets as a means of creating value that is sustainable over time. In order to achieve competitive sustainability, many firms are launching extensive knowledge management efforts (Gold, Malhotra, & Segars, 2001). To compete effectively, firms must leverage their existing knowledge and create new knowledge, which serves to grow the extant knowledge base and thereby favorably position them in their chosen markets.

In valuing a company's assets, the key questions in previous economies included: how much real estate or land assets does this company own? What is the value of facilities, plants? How much is the inventory? How many office buildings does the company have at different places? The knowledge economy is based on the application of human "know-how" to everything we create. Thus, human expertise and ideas generate more and more of the total economic value. Central to the knowledge economy is the incorporation of ideas to products and transforming these new ideas into new products. Hence, a large percentage of investment in a knowledge economy is made in R&D.

Managing in the Knowledge Economy with Knowledge Management

In order for organizations to manage and prosper in the knowledge economy, they must embrace knowledge management. Knowledge management deals with the process of creating value from an organisation's intangible assets (Wilcox, 1997). It is an amalgamation of concepts borrowed from several areas including artificial intelligence/knowledge-based systems, software engineering, BPR (business process re-engineering), human resources management, total quality management, and organisational behavior (Wickramasinghe, 1999); thus making KM an extremely inter-disciplinary concept.

Knowledge management is a key approach aimed at solving a myriad of business problems such as competitiveness, decreasing market share, the productivity paradox, information overload, and the need to innovate faced by numerous firms. The premise for the need for knowledge management is based on a major conceptual shift in the business environment where knowledge is now considered to be central to organizational performance (Drucker, 1993). This macro-level shift also has

significant implications upon the micro-level processes of assimilation and implementation of knowledge management concepts and techniques (Swan, Scarbrough,
& Preston, 1999) (i.e., the KMSs that are in place).

The primary objective of knowledge management focuses on the process of creating
value from an organization's intangible assets (Wigg, 1993). Knowledge management can be viewed as transforming data (raw material) into information (finished
goods) and from finished goods into knowledge (actionable finished goods) (Kanter,
1999). To effect these transformations of data into knowledge requires many phases
such as conceptualization, review, consolidation, and action phases of creating,
securing, combing, coordinating, and retrieving knowledge (Wickramasinghe,
1999). In essence then, knowledge management not only involves the production
of information but also the capture of data at the source, transmission and analysis
of this data as well as the communication of information based on or derived from
the transformed data to those who can act on it (Davenport & Prusak, 1998), as
well as the extraction of germane knowledge from this pertinent information (von
Lubitz & Wickramasinghe, 2005).

Definition of Knowledge Management

The process of management is based on transformation of the environment from
the "unknown/uncommon" into "known/common." During the process, the chaotic, disorganized environment changes into a coordinated entity whose activity,
governed by clear rules, results in a constant, predictable, and expected product.
Often depicted as a series of linear events subjected to "if-then" or "when-then"
principle, the process of management consists in reality of integrating and sustaining the integration of several independent "systems" (people, operational divisions,
companies, etc.) into a higher functional unit. Within such a hierarchically higher
unit, the functions of previously independent subcomponents (comprising systems)
become interconnected, coordinated, and mutually dependent to assure execution
of a correspondingly higher task.

Viewed as "systems coordination," successful management clearly depends on access to both historical and real time data and information, and on access to historical
knowledge, all of which must be relevant to the presently managed activities. Since
each system within the managed entity contains (and is defined by) a specific set of
data and information, the process of management requires extraction of this data
and informational content, and their integration into a new set that will characterize
the new, superior structure.

At the outset of the managerial process, each constituent system within the managed environment represents an "unknown" (i.e., its informational content is either
fully or partially enigmatic and needs to be explored). The state of "information

asymmetry" exists, where each system (and thus, the entire environment) contains more hidden information than can be immediately discerned by the managing entity. Hence, the more the managerial entity knows about the systems within the managed environment, the easier it is to integrate them and coordinate their operations into a unified, goal-oriented activity—a "super-system."

The shift of information content from the environment to the managerial entity results in the latter developing the state of "information superiority:" progressively less and less remains in the "unknown/uncommon" domain and more and more becomes "known/common." Since management functions are frequently performed in highly complex, diversified environments consisting of multiple and outwardly unrelated systems, the effective (and successful) management is rarely a linear function. Instead, the involved processes are comparable to the activities of a network hub receiving multiple simultaneous inputs from the periphery, transforming them into multiple actionable (decision) outputs transmitted to the periphery while, at the same time, consolidated information is relayed either to other hubs within the network, or (in a system of pyramid-like up-down organizational structure) to the higher levels within the chain of command. Successful management is therefore contingent both on rapid development of information superiority and on equally rapid transformation of the acquired information into clear and executable decisions. The process of transforming raw data and information, and the fusion of outputs with the pre-existing historical knowledge results in the generation of pertinent knowledge (i.e., knowledge that has direct relevance and applicability to the managerial task(s) at hand). It is this knowledge that forms the essential foundation of all executable decisions made during the process of management. Moreover, the processes involved are equally valid for organizations as varied as manufacturing plants or R&D companies, as much as individuals, teams, or governments.

We define knowledge management as the continuous and ongoing process of an organization or entity to create pertinent information and germane knowledge that can then be applied to facilitate actions, primarily by decision-making. By reducing the information asymmetry to ones favour, knowledge management and more precisely knowledge, enables the decision maker to make better informed, prudent, and sound decisions that in turn lead to successful outcomes for the organization or entity. This holds true whether the organization is a manufacturing plant or R&D company, or the entity is an individual, group, or government.

KM Drivers

The need for, advent, and rapid growth of knowledge management has been fueled by the confluence of three basic changes to the business environment:

1.   The shrinking cycle time for competency-base renewal.

2.   The need to value intellectual capital, driven by the growing economic weight of intangible assets.

3.   The pressure for organizations to contend with the ever increasing volume data and unstructured information.

Driver One: Obsolescence Rate of Competency-Base

The first economic driver in the emergence of KM pertains to the growing speed at which the know-how embodied in the workforce (i.e., the competency-base of an organization) looses currency and relevance. This is intrinsically related to shortening cycle times, the increasing rapidity with which new versions, updates, and/or new technology enter the market and consequently the need for employees to acquire new skills to operate and interact with these new technologies. In addition, it is also related to the entirely new portfolio of competencies that the "knowledge worker" requires in order to develop life-long employability.

The rapid rate of turn over in technology necessitates the demand for life-long learning and training to ensure that employees are familiar with the capabilities and features of the new systems. Moreover, there is a growing need not only to develop a new training infrastructure, but also to redefine the relationship between learning and work. While the education establishment is giving way to an alternative training system composed of corporate universities, adult learning centers, and on-line services, the meaning of training at work is shifting from a support function to the very essence of business development. Hence, establishing what a person has to do in order to add maximum value, what has to be learned, how it can be done best and most expeditiously, how it can be transferred to the right processes and have an impact in terms of business results is a major managerial challenge for organizations. To address such issues in specific contexts has now led to the learning industry becoming one of the fastest growing in the service sector.

The need for continuous learning of the workforce, refinement of intellectual capabilities, and the importance of ensuring the organization is adaptable to the dynamic environment has also served to fuel a growing interest in learning for organizations and transforming ones organization into a learning organization. Like knowledge management, the discipline of organizational learning is also evolving. The two disciplines while sharing much common ground are indeed distinct. More significantly the need for organizational learning necessitates the need for knowledge management and vice versa. The ultimate challenge in organizational learning is to create learning organizations (Senge, 1990). Imperative to such learning organizations is the system of inquiry adopted. These inquiring systems, first identified by Churchman, include the Leibnitzian inquiring organization, the Lockean inquiring organization, the Hegelian inquiring organization, the Kantian inquiring organization, and the Singerian inquiring organization (Churchman, 1971; Courtney, Croasdell, & Paradice, 1998; Courtney, Chae, & Hall, 2000). Irrespective of the specific inquiring system an integral aspect is how organizational knowledge is created, used and managed (Wickramasinghe, 2005).

Driver Two: Emphasis on Intangible Assets in a Company's Market Value

Two converging forces have fueled this shift. One is the growing differential between the book value of a public company and the market value of its stock price. The other pertains to trying to value the growing amount of intangible assets of an organization. Hence, the need to determine the value of intangible capital relative to the total value of a company has sparked significant research efforts to determine the "magic formula." The most notable advance in this area is the balanced score card developed by Kaplan and Norton.

Kaplan and Norton (2001) describe the innovation of the balanced scorecard as follows:

The balanced scorecard retains traditional financial measures. But financial measures tell the story of past events, an adequate story for industrial age companies for which investments in long-term capabilities and customer relationships were not critical for success. These financial measures are inadequate, however, for guiding and evaluating the journey that information age companies must make to create future value through investment in customers, suppliers, employees, processes, technology, and innovation.[1]

The balanced scorecard suggests the need to view the organization from four perspectives:

- The learning and growth perspective.
- The business process perspective.
- The customer perspective.
- The financial perspective.

and to develop metrics, collect data and analyze it relative to each of these perspectives and by doing so get a much more accurate value for the firm.

Unfortunately, most organizations typically ask the wrong questions such as "how do I determine the financial base of my intellectual assets?" The search must focus on not just one of accounting for, but one of developing a consolidated capital base and therefore, one of value-based KM strategy; only then can the value of intellectual assets be fully determined and more accurately captured. This in turn would lead to trying to identify a homogeneous value frame for all forms of capital and their rules of correspondence. In order to do this, we will have to come to terms with the tenets of measurement and value theories. While there have been some developments in this area, most notably within activity based accounting, and some successful organizational initiatives arguably the most effective company to date at accurately valuing its intellectual assets has been the Swedish company Skandia (Probst et al., 2000), there is still much work to be done in this area. Moreover, until the value of intellectual assets can be resolved organizations will continue to struggle to cost justify the benefits of many of their KM initiatives.

Drive Three: Efficiency Pressures to Cope with Massive Information

The final economic driver is concerned with the productivity paradox and the overwhelming flood of data and information faced by most organizations. Inefficiencies associated poor information acquisition, indexing, recording, storage, retrieval, transfer, etc., are significant. The much debated "productivity paradox" in the U.S. economy (relating higher investment in IT technology with relatively poorer results) has less to do with hardware reliability than with lack of process capability (O'Brien, 2005).

Since the late 1990s, software companies had begun to re-label existing or in-development products as "KM solutions" given the growing need for information management not merely data processing (O'Brien, 2005). However, many of these solutions are essentially the same data warehouses, yellow pages, and document taxonomies repackaged. Most of these solutions are based on an attempt to build sufficiently powerful data superstructures in an attempt to process and store the ever-increasing volumes of data (ibid). Irrespective of how large, or how complex, current information systems alone cannot deliver the foundations for KM. This is because KM is much more than a Lotus Notes database (Alavi & Leidner, 2001). Before there is an understanding of what KM is, as well as the establishment of the appropriate structures to support the KM initiative, these systems will never reach their optimal potential (Kanter, 1999).

One of the fundamental problems with the solutions for KM provided by the IT industry is concerned with the issue of what KM is. Knowledge within the IT industry is regarded as "content" (Alavi & Leidner, 2001; Kanter, 1999) and, therefore, treated as "object" (Alavi & Leidner, 2001). Knowledge is seldom seen as a human act, an event, or a happening. Taken as content, it is void of agent and context (human and cultural/organizational factors) and remains a computer operation; hence, the prevailing role of information systems in current "KM solutions" is at best more on the lines of content management than knowledge management (Kanter, 1999). While such packages can be "customized," they do not provide "KM solutions." To provide "KM solutions" it is necessary to depart from existing business processes and then design (or redesign) tools that leverage process capacity as well as embrace a socio-technical perspective (Alavi & Leidner, 2001; Kanter, 1999; Swan et al., 1999; Wickramasinghe, 2003).

To counter the confluence of the impacts of these combined drivers, an even greater need for the adoption and diffusion of knowledge management emerges. However, many of the responses and directions taken by organizations actually exacerbate the problems they face such as information overload, lack of expertise, and exponentially increasing complexity or further increasing of the productivity paradox rather than resolving them (O'Brien, 2005). The academic literature is peppered with numerous examples claiming that KM is a waste of company resources (time and money) and has no benefit at all to the organization (Alavi & Leidner, 2001). However, this is not the fault of knowledge management but rather the superficial understanding of this business strategy and poor implementation of the KM initiative. A strong foundation in KM can only be achieved by becoming a knowledge-based enterprise, not through the spouting of rhetoric and quick fix solutions but rather by making a fundamental changes to the way the organization operates at all levels.

How to Become a Knowledge-Based Enterprise

Implementing a knowledge management system alone does not make an organization a knowledge-based business. For an organization to become a knowledge-based business, several aspects must be considered and addressed concurrently. An organization that values knowledge must integrate knowledge into its business strategy and sell it as a key part of its products and services. To do this requires a strong commitment to knowledge management directed from the top of the organization. Furthermore, knowledge architecture should be designed that is appropriate to the specific organization given its industry and the activities, products or services it may provide. From the knowledge architecture it is important to consider the organizations structure as well as its culture. Does the structure and culture support a knowledge-sharing environment or perhaps a more team focussed, sharing culture needs to be fostered. Then it is necessary to consider the processes of generating, representing, accessing, and transferring knowledge through out the organization and the technology that is required to enable this. Finally, a knowledge-based business should also enable organizational learning to take place so that the knowledge that is captured is always updated and current and the organization is continually improving and refining its product or service. Figure 2 illustrates all the factors required to be a knowledge-based enterprise. What is particularly important to note from this figure is that in a knowledge-based enterprise KM tools, techniques concepts and strategies permeate all aspects of the organisation, its internal activities and external operations. Without such a complete absorption of KM, an organisation will never be truly knowledge-based. Furthermore, a complete absorption of KM is a necessary condition for transforming into a knowledge-based enterprise, however it is imperative the organisation continuously re-evaluates and ensures at all times it is correctly oriented in its environment so that it can operate at an optimal level.

Figure 2. Key factors of a knowledge-based enterprise

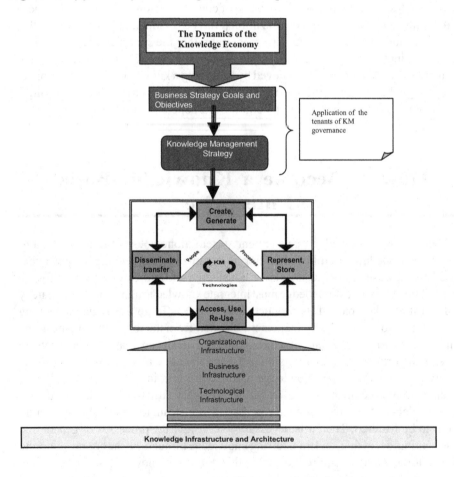

This in turn necessitates continuous examination of all the components that are depicted in Figure 2. The following chapters in this book serve to discuss each of these components in turn so that a full appreciation and understanding of each of the key components can be attained before we put it all together in the final chapter. The collection of case studies at the end of the book helps to illustrate the particular challenges that different organizations have had to contend with as they make their transition to becoming a knowledge-based enterprise as well as how they have overcome these challenges.

Chapter Summary

Knowledge management, in an age where there is an overwhelming amount of information, and perhaps not sufficient resources or understanding to manage all of it, is of critical importance and relevance to all 21st century organizations. KM is not a simple activity, rather it requires thoughtful and careful evaluation of, and understanding of numerous external and internal factors before an organization can even begin to make the transition to a knowledge-based enterprise. We shall expand on each of these factors in the following chapters. The ultimate benefit of KM is the ability of the entity or organization to be able to continually acquire and then apply pertinent information and germane knowledge to actions and decision-making so that successful outcomes may ensue. In this way, the entity positions itself in a state of greater information superiority relative to its environment and thereby, develops a sustainable competitive advantage. As a discipline, KM has a multi-disciplinary nature. This is both strength and a challenge. It is a strength because through the understanding of several interrelated areas it is indeed possible to construct a very robust KM initiative that is not easily replicable, however this is also challenging as it requires great insights and understanding of many areas within the organization and its environment. This explains why so many organizations struggle with the transition to become knowledge-based enterprises and rather grasp for easier alternatives, and also why those who have successfully made the transition are enjoying the fruits of their labors. However, in today's knowledge economy, KM is becoming a competitive necessity rather than a competitive choice and thus it is prudent for all organizations to embrace appropriate KM initiatives and successfully make the transition to knowledge-based enterprises.

References

Acs Z. J., Carlsson, B., & Karlsson, C. (1999). *The linkages among entrepreneurship, SMEs, and the macroeconomy*. Cambridge: Cambridge University Press.

Alavi, M., & Leidner, D. (2001). Review: Knowledge management and knowledge management systems: conceptual foundations and research issues. *MIS Quarterly, 25*(1), 107-136.

Churchman, C. (1971). *The design of inquiring systems: Basic concepts of systems and organizations*. New York: Basic Books Inc.

Courtney, J., Chae, B., & Hall, D. (2000). Developing inquiring organizations. *Journal of Knowledge Management and Innovation, 1*(1).

Courtney, J., Croasdell, D., & Paradice, D. (1998). Inquiring organizations. *Australian Journal of Information Systems, 6*(1).

Davenport, T., & Grover, V. (2001). Knowledge management. *Journal of Management Information Systems, 18*(1), 3-4.

Davenport, T., & Prusak, L. (1998). *Working knowledge*. Boston: Harvard Business School Press.

Drucker, P. (1993). *Post-capitalist society*. New York: Harper Collins.

Drucker, P. (1999). Beyond the information revolution. *The Atlantic Monthly*, 47-57.

Gold, A. H., Malhotra, A., & Segars, A. H. (2001). Knowledge management: An organizational capabilities perspective. *Journal of Management Information Systems, 18*(1), 185-214.

Halliday, L. (2001). An unprecedented opportunity. *Information World Review*, (167), 18-19.

Hope, J., & Hope, T. (1997). *Competing in the third wave*. Boston: Harvard Business School Press.

Huber, G. (1990). A theory of the effects of advanced information technologies on organisational design, intelligence, and decision-making. *Academy of Management Review, 15*(1), 47-71.

Kanter, J. (1999). Knowledge management practically speaking. *Information Systems Management*, Fall.

Kaplan, R., & Norton, D. (2001). *The strategy-focused organization: How balanced scorecard companies thrive in the new business environment*. Boston: Harvard Business School Press.

McGarvey, R. (2001). New corporate ethics for the new economy. *World Trade, 14*(3), 43.

O'Brien, J. (2005). *Management information systems*. Boston: McGrawHill.

Persaud, A. (2001). The knowledge gap. *Foreign Affairs, 80*(2), 107-117.

Porter, M. (1990). *The competitive advantage of nations*. Boston: Free Press.

Probst, G., Raub, S., & Romhardt, K. (2000). *Managing knowledge: Building blocks for success*. Chichester, UK: Willey.

Senge, P. (1990). *The fifth discipline*. New York: Random House.

Shapiro, C., & Varian, H. (1999). *Information rules*. Boston: Harvard Business School Press.

Swan, J., Scarbrough, H., & Preston, J. (1999). Knowledge management--The next fad to forget people? *Proceedings of the 7ᵗʰ European Conference in Information Systems*.

von Lubitz, D., & Wickramasinghe, N. (2005). Healthcare and technology: The doctrine of networkcentric healthcare. *International Journal of Electronic Healthcare* (in press).

von Lubitz, D., & Wickramasinghe, N. (2005). Creating germane knowledge in dynamic environments. *International Journal of Innovation and Learning* (in press).

Wickramasinghe, N. (2000). IS/IT as a tool to achieve goal alignment: A theoretical framework. *International Journal of Healthcare Technology Management, 2*(1/2/3/4), 163-180.

Wickramasinghe, N. (2003). Do we practise what we preach: Are knowledge management systems in practice truly reflective of knowledge management systems in theory? *Business Process Management Journal, 9*(3), 295-316.

Wickramasinghe, N. (2005). The phenomenon of duality: The key to facilitating the transition form knowledge management to wisdom for inquiring organizations. In Courtney et al. (Eds.), *Inquiring organizations: Moving form knowledge management to wisdom*. Hershey, PA: Idea Group Publishing.

Wigg, K. (1993). *Knowledge management foundations*. Arlington: Schema Press.

Wilcox, L. (1997). Knowledge-based systems as an integrating process. In J. Liebowitz & L. Wilcox (Eds.), *Knowledge management and its integrative elements* (pp. 1-30). Boston: CRC Press.

Woodall, P. (2000). Survey: The new economy: Knowledge is power. *The Economist, 356*(8189), 27-32.

Endnote

[1]   Refer to www.balancedscorecard.org

Chapter II

Understanding the Knowledge Construct

Introduction

Central to any in depth understanding of KM is the comprehension of the construct of knowledge itself. Knowledge is a curious construct that exhibits many facets and is difficult to define. In its application to business, numerous synonyms and related terms such as ability, capability, know-how, know-what, core competencies, intelligence, proficiency, and intuition are frequently used to name but a few. Yet, these terms only serve to describe at best few of the facets of knowledge and hence only ever partially substitute its meaning. Debates about what knowledge is and is not have permeated since the discussions of philosophers such as Aristotle, Plato, and Socrates right up to modern times. Such discussions have assisted in shaping the knowledge construct and underscore its complexities.

It is believed this multifaceted nature of the knowledge construct is what gives knowledge its mystique, power, and value (Swan, Scarbrough, & Preston, 1999). Hence, rather than try to provide a concise definition of knowledge, the chapter presents the major facets that constitute the knowledge construct. In this way, not only is the breadth and complexity of knowledge underscored but also its nebulous nature is highlighted. Organizations that implement KM without recognizing the multifaceted nature of knowledge itself are likely at best never to reap the full potential of their KM implementation and at worst experience a serious debacle in their KM initiative (Alavi & Leidner, 2001; Davenport & Grover, 2001).

Historical Understanding of Knowledge

We owe much of our current understanding of the nature of knowledge to the discussions and debates of ancient Greek philosophers including Socrates, Plato, and Aristotle (Maier, 2001; Wickramasinghe, 2005). The knowledge construct itself, its elusive definition as well as trying to define the process of knowing were some of the chief aspects that dominated their thinking. For these ancient Greek philosophers, knowledge was considered to be a homogenous construct that was ultimately representative of the truth (ibid) and the search for knowledge was synonymous with the search for truth. Other notable challenges that served to shape the meaning of knowledge as it is used in the management literature came in the 17th and 18th centuries, when philosophers like Decartes, Leibniz, and Locke began to dispute previous conceptualisations of what knowledge was and developed ideas of knowledge as accurate, provable facts (ibid). In contrast, another group of philosophers, namely Hegel and Kant, defined knowledge as divergent meaning or justified true beliefs (Alavi & Leidner, 2001; Wickramasinghe, 2005). Since the 19th century, many different philosophical schools of thought have emerged and they have all tried to capture the essence of the elusive knowledge construct. Rather than achieve one universally agreed upon meaning, a multiplicity of definitions of the knowledge construct now permeate the literature. Table 1 summarizes these major

Table 1. Multiple perspective on knowledge (Adapted from Wickramasinghe, 2005)

School of Thought	Basic Ideas on Knowledge	Some Proponents
Positivism	Knowledge is gained from the observation of objective reality.	Comte
Constructivism	Knowledge is constructed in our minds thus is not objective.	Erlangen School
Critical Theory	Uses knowledge to integrate the tension between reality of society and the real societal function of science.	Habermas, Horkheimer
Critical Rationalism	All knowledge must be open to empirical falsification before it can be accepted.	Popper
Empiricism	Knowledge can be created from experiments and thus only mathematics and natural sciences can provide secure knowledge.	Locke, Russel
Sociology of Knowledge	Knowledge is a socially constructed reality.	Mannheim, Scheler
Pragmatism	Knowledge represents a local reality based on our experiences.	Dewey

perspectives. What is important to note from the standpoint of KM is that all these perspectives have relevance to any KM initiative and must be carefully considered when designing an organizations KM initiative.

Data, Information, and Knowledge

The concepts of data, information, and knowledge are closely related and more importantly are all necessary components of any KM initiative. In order to design and implement a successful KM initiative, it is vital that not only the distinction between these concepts is clear but also their interrelation.

Data

Data are defined as a series of discrete events, observations, measurements, or facts in the form of numbers, words, sounds, and/or images (Adams, 2001; Becerra-Fernandez & Sabherwal, 2001; Davenport & Prusak, 1998). In organizations much of the useful data are in the form of transaction records, stored in databases, and generated through various business processes and activities. At the moment, organizations generate large amounts of various types of data. These data are typically discrete in form, and thus not very useful. To dramatically increase the usability and usefulness of these data it is necessary to embark upon pre-processing and cleansing activities (Becerra-Fernandez & Sabherwal, 2001). When substantial processing of data occurs, and the processed data are then organized into a context, the data become information. Data then, are simply observation of states, which may have little context associated with it. Furthermore, data are essentially raw materials. They simply exist and have no significance beyond their existence unless processed into a new form—information. Hence, data do not have meaning in and of themselves. Organizations where data are a key focus include insurance companies, banks, statistical organizations, and healthcare organizations. In these scenarios, the data support the core function of record keeping. However, these data are not particularly meaningful or useful for decision-making, a key activity for all organizations. In fact, in the knowledge economy, the most valuable aspect of data is its property of being a raw material for information processing and knowledge acquisition/creation. Hence, from a KM perspective data are valuable for their likely information and knowledge potential.

Information

Information is defined as data that has been arranged into a meaningful pattern and thus has a recognizable shape (Davenport & Grover, 2001; Davenport & Prusak, 1998; Duffy, 2001). Data that has been endowed with relevance and purpose is information. In other words, information is organized and communicated data. Reports created from intelligent database queries result in information. For example, a result reporting on a specific income group in a particular area provides information that can be communicated to the sales force. Technological tools not only enhance the communication capabilities with data but also facilitate the transferring and processing of data into information. Email is perhaps the most pervasive technological tool to communicate information. In transforming data into information five important Cs have taken place (Davenport & Prusak, 1998):

1. **Contextualization:** The purpose surrounding the data collection/gathering is known.

2. **Categorization:** The key units of analysis and key factors relating to the data are known.

3. **Calculation:** Mathematical and/or statistical analyses have been performed on the data.

4. **Correction:** Errors in the data have been corrected or accounted for.

5. **Condensation:** The data have been summarized and distilled.

Currently, organizations are flooded by too much information resulting in the phenomenon of information overload. This can be explained by the theory of bounded rationality developed by Simons (Simons, 1960; Wickramasinghe, Fadlalla, Geisler, & Schaffer, 2003). According to Simons, we can all be rational and make rational decisions but when we experience information overload, we do not have enough mental capacity or cognitive capability to process all the information. In such situations we can only process a sub-set of the information and hence make sub-optimal or (as it would appear to an objective observer) irrational choices. In the knowledge economy the level of information overload, fuelled by increasing use of IC^2T necessitates the further processing of this information into an even more useful and useable commodity; namely, knowledge itself (O'Brien, 2005).

Knowledge

According to the *American Heritage Dictionary*, knowledge can be defined as:

1.   The state or fact of knowing;
2.   Familiarity, awareness, or understanding gained through experience or study; and
3.   The sum or range of what has been perceived, discovered, or learned.

In essence, knowledge is the act or state of knowing gained through the psychological interaction between experience, learning, cognition, and perception of fact and truth. As such, knowledge activities within an organization are largely influenced by the members of the organization and their individualities such as cognition, experience, culture, and expertise, which, at the most fundamental level, are nothing but functions of the chemical processes within the human brain. In practical terms, knowledge is simply the application and productive use of information. According to *Webster's Dictionary*, knowledge is the fact or condition of knowing something with familiarity gained through experience or association. Information embedded and synthesized in the brain is knowledge, which, by its nature, is highly personal and extremely difficult to transfer. While information is descriptive, that is, it relates to the past and the present, knowledge is eminently predictive. It provides the basis for the prediction of the future with a degree of certainty based on information about the past and the present. Knowledge may also be described as a set of models that combine various properties and behaviors within a domain. Knowledge may be recorded in an individual brain or stored in organizational processes, products, facilities, systems, and documents. Knowledge, in its broadest context, is thus the full utilization of information and data, coupled with the potential of people's skills, competencies, ideas, intuitions, commitments, and motivations.

In reality, there exists many possible, equally plausible definitions of knowledge. For the purposes of our understanding, we will focus upon the following definition of knowledge given by Davenport and Prusak (1998, p. 5):

Knowledge is a fluid mix of framed experiences, values, contextual information, and expert insights that provides a framework for evaluating and incorporating new experiences and information. It originates and is applied in the minds of knowers. In organizations, it is often embedded not only in documents or repositories but also in organizational routine, processes, practices, and norms.

In transforming information to knowledge, the role of people is integral. The transformation takes place with a different set of four key C activities (Davenport & Prusak, 1998):

1. **Comparison:** Information in one scenario is compared and contrasted with another.

2. **Consequences:** What implications does the information have for decision-making.

3. **Connections:** How does this bit of information and/or knowledge relate to another.

4. **Conversation:** What do people think of this information.

In the present economy, knowledge is intertwined and embedded in people, processes, technologies, and techniques and leads to the generation of money, leveraging of existing assets, increases in learning and flexibility, increases in power bases, and the realization of sustainable competitive advantages (Bacon & Fitzgerald, 2001; Clegg, 1999; Croasdell, 2001). Knowledge is more relevant to sustained business than capital, labor, or land. Nevertheless, it remains one of the most neglected assets. We believe what is important is to take a holistic view of knowledge which considers knowledge to be present in ideas, judgments, talents, root causes, relationships, perspectives and concepts as well as being stored in the individual brain or encoded in organizational processes, documents, products, services, facilities and systems (Wickramasinghe, 2005). By doing so, organizations open themselves to many possibilities of capitalizing and benefiting from this multifaceted and valuable asset.

For the purposes of completeness, it is important to note that some scholars have challenged the generally accepted, relatively linear transition of data through information to knowledge (Geisler, 2005). Appendix A presents this alternate perspective of knowledge, information, and knowledge systems and thus serves to explain confusions that may exist.

Understanding

A related construct to knowledge and most relevant in knowledge management is understanding. Understanding is an interpolative and probabilistic process (Clegg, 1999). It is cognitive and analytical. It is the process by which one can take knowledge and synthesize new knowledge from the previously held knowledge. The difference between understanding and knowledge is the difference between "learning" and "memorizing" (Ellerman, 1999; Ellinger, Watkins, & Bostrom, 1999; Hammond, 2001). People who have understanding can undertake useful actions because they can synthesize new knowledge, or in some cases, at least new information, from what is previously known (and understood). That is, understanding can build upon currently held information, knowledge, and understanding itself.

Wisdom

It is widely agreed that beyond knowledge lies wisdom. Wisdom is an extrapolative and non-deterministic, non-probabilistic process (Wickramasinghe, 2005). It calls upon all the previous levels of consciousness, and specifically upon special types of human programming (moral, ethical codes, etc.). In the East, wisdom and the notion of taking a holistic approach, be it to healthcare or business practices is significantly more prevalent than in the west (Kienholtz, 2005). In fact, there is a general reticence in the west to delve too deeply into the black box of wisdom (ibid). Integral to wisdom are the processes by which we discern, or judge, between right and wrong, good and bad (Costa, 1995). Wisdom is a uniquely human state (Hammond, 2001; Wickramasinghe, 2005). Wisdom embodies more of an understanding of fundamental principles embodied within the knowledge that are essentially the basis for the knowledge being what it is. Wisdom is thus essentially systemic (Costa, 1995).

Knowledge management offers organizations many strategies, techniques, and tools to apply to their existing business processes so that they are able to grow and effectively utilize their knowledge assets (Granstrand, 2000; Holt, Love, & Li, 2000; Lee, 2000). In essence, knowledge management not only involves the production of information but also the capture of data at the source, the transmission and analysis of this data as well as the communication of information based on or derived from the data to those who can act on it. This rising tide of data can be viewed as an abundant, vital, and necessary resource for creating knowledge (Alberthal, 1995). With appropriate knowledge management techniques, organizations should be able to tap into this resource, channel raw data into meaningful information, and then turn it into knowledge that ultimately leads to enhanced organizational performance.

Figure 1 depicts the generic stages of how data can be organized to a more structured form, information, and how information can then be organized to higher levels of usefulness to the organization; namely, knowledge and, eventually, wisdom. Take the simple example next to illustrate the difference between the key constructs data, information, and knowledge.

1. **Data:** Numbers, say 20, 35 (i.e., two discrete points).

2. **Information:** These numbers represent temperature (i.e., we have added a context to these discrete data points).

3. **Knowledge:** Temperature scale is Celsius (or Fahrenheit) (i.e., not only have we added a context but also a shared meaning and connection). If we are in Celsius context the two temperatures would be quite warm in stark contrast, if we are in the Fahrenheit context the two numbers represent fairly cold temperatures. Thus, as we move from data through information to knowledge

Figure 1. Progression from data to wisdom

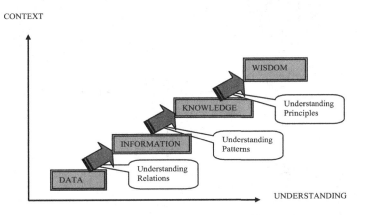

we are increasing the context dependence and understanding dimensions. In addition, Figure 1 shows that for all the transitions understanding is important, be it the understanding of relations, patterns or principles, in supporting and actualizing the transition from one stage to the next. Understanding thus is not a separate level of its own but a necessary requirement from moving through the transitions.

Types of Knowledge

Given the many definitions of the knowledge construct and the divergent philosophical stances as to what knowledge is, it should come as no surprise then that knowledge, unlike data or information, exhibits several types or forms. In order to develop a more complete understanding of the multifaceted nature of the knowledge construct it is necessary to isolate these different types of knowledge that exist.

There are two basic kinds of knowledge (Nonaka, 1994): (1) the kind that is reflected in a person's internal state as well as in that same person's capacity for action and (2) the kind that has been articulated and frequently recorded. Further sub-classification into explicit, implicit, and tacit knowledge is also possible.

Figure 2. Explicit, implicit, and tacit knowledge

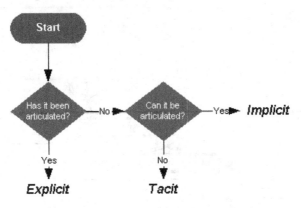

Explicit, Implicit, and Tacit Knowledge

The diagram shown in Figure 2 illustrates the distinctions between explicit, implicit, and tacit knowledge.

Explicit Knowledge

Explicit knowledge is the knowledge that has been articulated and, more often than not, captured in the form of text, tables, diagrams, product specifications, and so on. Nonaka (Nonaka, 1994; Nonaka & Nishiguchi, 2001) refers to explicit knowledge as "formal and systematic" and offers product specifications, scientific formulas, and computer programs as examples. An example of explicit knowledge with which we are all familiar is the formula for finding the area of a rectangle (i.e., length x width). Other examples of explicit knowledge include documented best practices, the formalized standards by which an insurance claim is adjudicated, and the official expectations for performance are set forth in the written work objectives.

Tacit Knowledge

Tacit knowledge is knowledge that cannot be articulated as defined by Polyani (1958, 1966). Polyani (ibid.) used the example of being able to recognize a person's face but being only vaguely able to describe how that is done. This is an instance of pattern recognition. What we recognize is the whole or the gestalt; deconstructing it into its constituent elements in order to be able to articulate them fails to capture its essence. Reading the reaction on a customer's face or changing a golf swing or tennis stroke due to weather conditions prevalent during the game, offers other instances of situations in which we are able to perform well but are unable to articulate exactly what we know or how we put it into practice. In such cases, the knowing is in the doing, a point to which we will return to shortly.

Implicit Knowledge

Knowledge that can be articulated but has not been subjected to this process represents implicit knowledge (Mahe & Rieu, 1998; Onge, 2001). Its existence is implied by or inferred from observable behavior or performance. This is the kind of knowledge that can often be gleaned from a competent performer by a task analyst, knowledge engineer, or other person skilled in identifying the kind of knowledge that can be articulated but has not been articulated yet. In analyzing the task in which underwriters at an insurance company process applications, for instance, it quickly becomes clear that the range of outcomes for the underwriters' work took three basic forms: (1) they can approve the policy application, (2) they can deny it, or (3) they can counter offer. Yet, not one of the underwriters articulated these options as boundaries on their work at the outset of the analysis. Once the outcomes are identified, it becomes a comparatively simple matter to identify the criteria used to determine the response to a given application. In so doing, implicit knowledge has become explicit knowledge.

The explicit, implicit, tacit categories of knowledge are not the only ones in use. Cognitive psychologists sort knowledge into two categories: declarative and procedural (Becerra-Fernandez & Sabherwal, 2001). Some even add strategic as a third category (Figure 3).

Figure 3. Declarative and procedural knowledge (describing vs. doing)

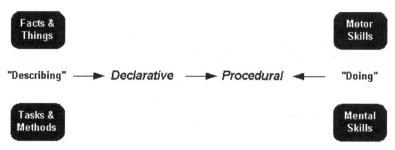

Declarative Knowledge

Declarative knowledge has much in common with explicit knowledge in that declarative knowledge consists of descriptions of facts and things or of methods and procedures (Becerra-Fernandez & Sabherwal, 2001; Roberts, 2000). Being able to state the cut-off date for accepting applications is an example of declarative knowledge. It is also an instance of explicit knowledge. For most practical purposes, declarative and explicit knowledge may be treated as synonymous. This is because all declarative knowledge is explicit knowledge, that is, it is knowledge that can be and has been articulated.

Procedural Knowledge

One view of procedural knowledge is that it is knowledge that manifests itself in the doing of something (Becerra-Fernandez & Sabherwal, 2001; Srikantaiah, 2000). As such, it is reflected in motor or manual skills and in cognitive or mental skills. We think, we reason, we decide, we dance, we play piano, we ride bicycles, we read customers' faces and moods, yet we cannot reduce to mere words that which we obviously know or know how to do. Attempts to do so are often recognized as little more than after-the-fact rationalizations. Another view of procedural knowledge presents it as the knowledge about how to do something. This view of procedural knowledge accepts it as a description of the steps of a task or procedure. The obvious shortcoming of this view is that it is no different from declarative knowledge except that tasks or methods are being described instead of facts or things.

Pending the universal resolution of this disparity, it is necessary to resolve this apparent confusion for ourselves. It is acknowledged that some people refer to descriptions of tasks, methods, and procedures as declarative knowledge and others refer to them as procedural knowledge. One useful solution is to classify all *descriptions* of knowledge as declarative and reserve procedural for application to situations in which the knowing may be said to be in the doing. Figure 3 depicts declarative knowledge connected to "describing" and procedural knowledge to "doing." From such a perspective, it is possible then to view all procedural knowledge as tacit just as all declarative knowledge is explicit.

Strategic Knowledge

Strategic knowledge is a term used by some to refer to "know-when" and/or "know-why" (Stratigos, 2001; Thorne & Smith, 2000). Although it seems reasonable to conceive of these as aspects of doing, it is difficult to envisage them as being separate from the doing. In other words, we can distinguish strategic knowledge only in the describing, not the doing. Consequently, strategic knowledge is probably best thought of as a subset of declarative knowledge instead of its own category. For this reason, we shall not use the term strategic knowledge.

Integration

Figure 4 integrates the diagrams from Figures 2 and 3 to illustrate the "fit" between and among explicit, implicit, tacit, declarative, and procedural knowledge. These relationships are reasonably clear and, with two exceptions, warrant no further discussion. The arrow connecting declarative and procedural indicates that we often develop procedural knowledge or the ability to do something as a result of starting with declarative knowledge. In other words, we often "know about" before we "know how." The implications for knowledge management by having such different and varied types of knowledge are that all must be accounted for and managed.

Figure 4. A framework for thinking about the types of knowledge in knowledge management

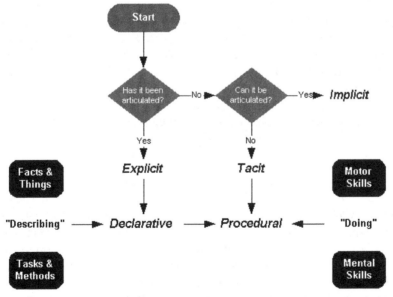

Note: The arrows connecting explicit with declarative and tacit with procedural are meant to indicate the strong relationships that exist between these terms.

Different Facets of Knowledge

The following are the different aspects of knowledge that do not exactly map directly onto any one of the categories of knowledge previously outlined, but rather cross several of them:

1. **Know-how** has an operational orientation. It is mainly action driven and hence pre-dominantly experiential. It is difficult to inherit this type of knowledge from someone else's experience and is essentially synonymous with tacit knowledge.

2. **Know-why** has a causal orientation. It is mainly reflection driven, and therefore based on abstraction. This type of knowledge can be inherited, following someone else's line of reasoning, providing effective communication exists. Know-why has both tacit and explicit components.

3. **Know-when** (and where) has a contextual orientation. It provides the temporal and spatial context for both the *know-how* and *know-why*. It is thus both action and/or reflection driven. An example of the action driven *know-when* is the learning of proper sequencing within an operation while the reflection driven *know-when* is seen in appreciating the environmental context of a causal relationship. Once again, know-when has both tacit and explicit components.

4. **Know-about** has an awareness orientation and includes the three types of knowledge previously discussed. It can be summarized as *"Know-what."* It also contains information about the environmental context of this knowledge so that similarity of problems can be perceived and similar problem-solving approaches adopted, enabling an extension of understanding from the already known to the hitherto unknown. *"Know-about"* contains partial and imperfect knowledge arising from the varying status of the three basic constituents (e.g., pulley was employed well before its functioning principles were understood). Once again, know-about has tacit and explicit aspects.

It is also important to consider the negation aspect of the first three types of knowledge. Thus, *know-how not* represents an aspect of experiential learning where a student learns by making mistakes. This is an important part of operational learning and students who are afraid to make mistakes have to undergo a longer learning cycle. This type of learning is regarded as vital so much so that in case of critical or hazardous systems, computer simulation and virtual reality are increasingly being employed. Thus, a large part of *know-how* knowledge may be derived from learning the *know-how-not* aspect by making mistakes and realizing that the goal isn't achieved through the paths erroneously adopted. On the other hand, *know-why not* seems to logically follow from *know-why* rather than the other way round. It is still possible to learn from mistakes but this requires deeper reflection. Thus, it appears that it is easier to learn from mistakes in a knowledge area that is action oriented which requires relatively less reflection.

Knowledge then is the full utilization of information and data, coupled with the potential of people's skills, competencies, ideas, intuitions, commitments, and motivations. A holistic view considers knowledge to be present in ideas, judgments, talents, root causes, relationships, perspectives, and concepts. Knowledge is stored in the individual brain or encoded in organizational processes, documents, products, services, facilities, and systems. Knowledge is action, focused innovation, pooled expertise, special relationships, and alliances. Knowledge is value-added behavior and activities. Knowledge encompasses both tacit knowledge (in people's heads) and explicit knowledge (codified and expressed as information in databases, documents, etc.). Knowledge is not static; rather it changes and evolves during the life of an organization. What is more, it is possible to change the form of knowledge (i.e., turn existing tacit knowledge into new explicit and existing explicit knowledge into new tacit knowledge or to turn existing explicit knowledge into new explicit knowledge and existing tacit knowledge into new tacit knowledge). These transformations are depicted in Table 2.

Table 2. Knowledge transformations (Nonaka, 1994)

From/To	Tacit Knowledge	Explicit Knowledge
Tacit Knowledge	**Socialization** (Sympathized Knowledge) Where individuals acquire new knowledge directly from others.	**Externalization** (Conceptual Knowledge) The articulation of knowledge into tangible form through dialogue.
Explicit Knowledge	**Internalization** (Operational Knowledge) Such as learning by doing, where individuals internalize knowledge from documents into their own body of experience.	**Combination** (Systematic Knowledge) Combining different forms of explicit knowledge, such as that in documents or on databases.

Knowledge Entities

Our discussion of types of knowledge would not be complete without some mention of knowledge entities. It is observed that learning takes place over a number of topics in a number of subjects over a period of time with progressively increasing depth and/or breadth. This practice indicates that there are levels at which knowledge can be transferred and acquired (Newell, Robertson, Scarbrough, & Swan, 2002; Popper & Lipshitz, 2000). The lowest level would naturally consist of relatively freestanding knowledge entities that are interwoven progressively to produce larger and more complex bodies of knowledge. Thus, knowledge may be viewed as an expanding multi-layered network of interconnected knowledge entities, where the size of the network is indicative of the extent of knowledge while the intensity of the interconnections is indicative of the richness and depth of that knowledge.

The Organizational Knowledge Life Cycle

The knowledge life cycle (depicted in Figure 5) is about knowledge acquisition and creation, knowledge distribution and knowledge application and its use and re-use (Alavi & Leidner, 2001; Hansen & Oetinger, 2001; Levine, 2001). Knowledge activities are centered in human psychological processes such as experience, perception, and emotion. Instead of knowledge being a set of isolated, context-free facts, knowledge is bound up with human intelligence, shaped by social assumptions, and requires active engagement by those involved in the organizational knowledge activity structure. In an organization, there are four major interactive knowledge activities (Wickramasinghe, 2005). The first is knowledge acquisition, which refers to the act of internalizing existing information. The second dimension is knowledge creation, which describes the act of creating new knowledge. The third knowledge activity is knowledge distribution, which is the act of disseminating knowledge throughout the organization. The last knowledge activity is knowledge application, which is the demonstration of knowledge once it is possessed.

The knowledge life cycle suggests that knowledge acquisition is the starting point of all organizational activity. Once an organization acquires existing knowledge, it can use this existing knowledge to create new knowledge (knowledge creation). Organizations can also distribute the existing knowledge to the appropriate members within the organization. If an organization chooses to create new or additional knowledge based on its existing knowledge base, the organization can also distribute that knowledge once it has been created. After the knowledge is distributed and made actionable through the knowledge distribution process, the organization can apply it in the appropriate context. Once knowledge is applied, the results may

Figure 5. The knowledge life cycle (Adapted from Wickramasinghe, 2005)

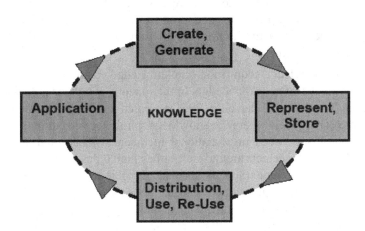

yield additional information that can be used in the *de novo* knowledge creation process. Existing knowledge, as the starting point for organizational knowledge, is the building block of all organizational knowledge.

Although technology can aid in the knowledge activity process, it cannot initiate the knowledge process without the interaction with its human counterparts, who provide the contextual perspectives that are necessary for the relevant generation of knowledge in an attempt to make sense of reality (Swan et al., 1999; Wickramasinghe, 2005). Human and social factors are central in the creation and communication of knowledge.

Knowledge Acquisition/Generation and Creation

Knowledge acquisition is the starting point of the organizational knowledge cycle (Wickramasinghe et al., 2003). Knowledge acquisition is the capture of the existing knowledge through activities such as knowledge transfer, knowledge sharing, observation, interaction, and self-study. The knowledge acquisition activity is responsible for ensuring that the knowledge base required for intelligent problem solving is continually updated and recognizes the relevance of information in the knowledge base for the current problem-solving activity. As such, knowledge acquisition is akin to the act of learning. Knowledge creation/generation, which can be thought of as a sub-set of knowledge acquisition, is concerned with yielding new knowledge from previously existing knowledge. After individuals acquire existing knowledge, this knowledge is then used as a foundation for creating new knowledge. Whether this new organizational knowledge is in the form of innovations, improvements in existing processes, new product designs, or market intelligence and strategic guidelines for the future, it is built on knowledge generated in the knowledge acquisition process.

As distinct from knowledge acquisition, the knowledge creation process focuses only on the formation of new knowledge. In their theory of organizational knowledge creation, Nonaka and Takeuchi (1995) presented a major perspective of the knowledge creation process where the knowledge spiral is created through specific knowledge transfers between organizational members. Nonaka and Takeuchi's (1995) knowledge spiral centers around tacit and explicit types of knowledge. Tacit knowledge is a personal, context specific knowledge that is difficult to formalize and communicate. It includes cognitive patterning, such as mental models and technical knowledge, which is concrete and skill-related, and subjective insights. In contrast to tacit knowledge, explicit, or codified knowledge, suitable for technology and computer manipulation, is transmittable in formal, systematic language expressed in symbols, words, and/or numbers. Tacit knowledge is experientially based and is difficult to communicate. This suggests that tacit knowledge is implicitly learned through the personal interpretation and processing of information based on beliefs, experience, emotions, and all of the subsets of the aspects of human consciousness. Tacit knowledge, as a principal component of knowledge creation, is imperative to the functioning of the knowledge creation process.

In the internalization process, explicit knowledge is converted to tacit knowledge through experiential learning. Experiential learning involves using the senses to interpret the environmental stimuli and create an individual sense of knowledge to respond to the presented reality (Popper & Lipshitz, 2000; Simon, 1999). Interestingly, since sensual learning is essentially neural in nature, technological attempts to simulate our sensual nature include the creation of robots that are embodied, situated agents.

Knowledge creation is central to the organizational knowledge activity cycle. With a reciprocal relationship to knowledge application, it is an essential activity in the innovation process of an organization. Based mainly on the conversion of tacit knowledge, knowledge creation, like knowledge acquisition, is a human based activity set in sociological- and psychological-based tasks. Therefore, information technology is not a vehicle upon which the knowledge creation process is based (Silver, 2000).

Knowledge Representation/Storage

In order for knowledge to be used efficiently and effectively in an organization, it must be represented and stored. In many ways, knowledge representation is closely linked to knowledge creation. However, it is only possible to represent explicit knowledge in databases and knowledge bases. Thus, tacit knowledge that has been created must first be transformed into explicit knowledge before it can be represented. As well as storing the particular knowledge itself it is important to develop knowledge cartographies of where what type of knowledge is stored. We shall elaborate upon this point when we discuss the knowledge architecture and key technologies that facilitate this process in later chapters.

Knowledge Distribution/Use and Re-Use

Knowledge distribution is the third and central activity in the organizational knowledge cycle. In the literature relating to knowledge management and its organizational components, much attention is devoted to knowledge acquisition, knowledge creation, and knowledge application. Although it is important for organizations to acquire existing knowledge and create new knowledge, in order for knowledge to be applied in the quest for competitive advantage, it must be made actionable: it must be distributed through the organization to the individuals responsible for tasks such as innovation, product/process design, or innovation.

The knowledge distribution component interacts with each of the other organizational knowledge activities to optimize and complete the knowledge activity structure within an organization. Similar to the two components that were previously discussed, knowledge distribution is largely a human-based process, although technology plays a major role in facilitating organizational knowledge distribution. Swan et al. (1999) emphasize that organizational knowledge distribution is both social and technical, composed through the interaction between aspects of organizational culture and organizational technology capabilities.

Social processes, such as organizational procedures, hierarchical structure, and social networks affect member interaction within an organization: they are capable of directly enabling or hindering the functions of the knowledge distribution process of an organization. Technological facilitation of knowledge distribution by means of e-mail, bulletin boards, intranets, newsgroups, teleconferencing, data conferencing, and videoconferencing plays the supporting role within the knowledge distribution component. Although designed to support interaction, without interaction itself these technologies are useless. Thus, if organizational members are not encouraged to interact either through individual motivation or deliberate design of organizational culture, interaction will be limited and consequently mitigate organizational distribution of knowledge. Unquestionably, technology is central in the knowledge distribution process. Nonetheless, social processes within the organization are the catalyst for the dissemination of knowledge throughout its internal channels. The success of the organizational distribution of knowledge is directly related to the organizational culture that serves as the framework for interaction.

Knowledge Application

Knowledge application constitutes the last activity in the organizational activity cycle and is predominantly concerned with the utilization and management of knowledge that has been acquired and created by the organization. Most of the literature relating to knowledge management addresses concerns related to the application of knowledge within organizations. The focus of knowledge application relates to how knowledge should be utilized in order to add value to the organization and create an advantageous position. Knowledge application is contextual and perceptive in nature. In order to effectively apply knowledge, one must understand the underlying contexts and operational boundaries, and use the knowledge to create an acceptable answer to the perceived reality of the situation.

Within the business context, computers that possess knowledge in the form of input from human users cannot, at least at present, engage in the knowledge application process in the true form, because they lack the ability to create context and perceive the situation based on their experiences and their interpretation of the external environment. The assessment of the external environment and the creation of a reality are based on a potentially infinite number of combinations of inputs that are based on social, historical, psychological, and cultural. At the moment, computers are best used in the knowledge application process as tools assisting human operators in making value-added decisions.

Why is Knowledge Valuable?

In hyper-competitive environments, the knowledge base of an organization represents one of the principal sources if not the only source of sustainable competitive advantage (Thorne & Smith, 2000; Wickramasinghe & Mills, 2001). As such, this resource must be protected, cultivated, and shared among all members of the organisation. Until recently, companies could succeed based upon the individual knowledge of a handful of strategically positioned individuals. However, when competitors promise more knowledge as part of their services, then competition ceases. Why? Because organizational knowledge does not replace individual knowledge, it complements individual knowledge, making it stronger and broader. Thus, full utilization of the organisational knowledge base, coupled with the potential of individual skills, competencies, thoughts, innovations, and ideas will further enhance the competitive strength of the organization.

Knowledge Assets

Essential knowledge assets comprise knowledge regarding markets, products, technologies, and organizations, that a business owns or needs to own and which enable its business processes to generate profits, add value, etc. (Dixon, 2000; Markus, 2001; Martensen & Dahlgaard, 1999). Knowledge management is not only about managing these knowledge assets but also managing the processes that act upon the assets. These processes include developing knowledge, preserving knowledge, using knowledge, and sharing knowledge. Therefore, **knowledge management** involves the identification and analysis of available and required knowledge assets, and knowledge asset related processes, followed by the subsequent planning and control of actions required to develop both the assets and the processes as needed to fulfill organizational objectives.

Significance of Knowledge Assets

Enterprises are realizing how important it is to "know what they know" and be able to make maximum use of the knowledge (Alberthal, 1995; Davenport & Grover, 2001). This knowledge resides in many different places such as databases, knowledge bases, filing cabinets, and peoples' heads and are distributed right across the enterprise. All too often one part of an enterprise repeats work of another simply because it is impossible to keep track of, and make use of knowledge in other parts. Enterprises need to know:

- What their knowledge assets are; and
- How to manage and make use of these assets to get maximum return.

Most traditional company policies and controls focus on the tangible assets and leave unmanaged their important knowledge assets. Yet, success in an increasingly competitive marketplace depends critically on the quality of knowledge, which organizations apply to their key business processes. For example, the supply chain depends on knowledge of diverse areas including raw materials, planning, manufacturing, and distribution. Likewise, product development requires knowledge of consumer requirements, new science, new technology, marketing, etc.

The challenge of deploying the knowledge assets of an organization needed to create competitive advantage becomes more crucial as

- The marketplace is increasingly competitive and the rate of innovation is rising, so that knowledge must evolve and be assimilated at an ever-faster rate.

- Corporations are organizing their businesses to focus on creating customer value. Staff functions are being reduced as are management structures. There is a need to replace the informal knowledge management of the staff function with formal methods in customer aligned business processes.

- Competitive pressures are reducing the size of the workforce, which holds this knowledge.

- Knowledge takes time to experience and acquire. Employees have less and less time for this.

- There are trends for employees to retire earlier and for increasing mobility, leading to loss of knowledge.

- There is a need to manage increasing complexity as small operating companies are re trans-national sourcing operations.

- A change in strategic direction may result in the loss of knowledge in a specific area.

- A subsequent reversal in policy may then lead to a renewed requirement for this knowledge, but the employees with that knowledge may no longer be there.

What Constitutes Intellectual or Knowledge-Based Assets?

While all information is valuable, not all information is pertinent to any given context (Lesser, Mundel, & Wiecha, 2000). Therefore, individual companies must determine for themselves what information qualifies as intellectual and knowledge-based assets. In general, intellectual and knowledge-based assets fall into one of two categories: explicit or tacit. Included among the former are assets such as patents, trademarks, business plans, marketing research, and customer lists. As a general rule of thumb, explicit knowledge consists of anything that can be documented, archived, and codified, often with the help of information technology (IT). Much harder to grasp is the concept of tacit knowledge, or the know-how contained in people's heads. The challenge inherent with tacit knowledge is to develop appropriate measures figuring out how to recognize, generate, share, and manage this form of knowledge. While IT in the form of e-mail, groupware, instant messaging, and related technologies can help facilitate the dissemination of tacit knowledge, identifying tacit knowledge in the first place is a major hurdle for most organizations.

As discussed by Connor and Prahalad (1996), a knowledge-based firm maximizes its knowledge assets so that it can effect more effective and efficient operations and incur significantly lower transactions costs. It becomes imperative for knowledge-based organizations then to carefully manage their intellectual assets because it is by doing so that they can maximize the benefits of lower transactions costs.

Significance of Knowledge Management Solutions

Knowledge Management encompasses company assets such as competencies, relationships, and information (Moore, 2000; Parent, Gallupe, Salisbury, & Handelman, 2000). Currently, these can exist virtually anywhere in an organization, from the minds of employees, to the back-end database files, or the depths of the document storage warehouse. Put simply, knowledge management (KM) technologies function like a portal, where companies can capture, store, and apply their intellectual capital. But whereas portals merely provide a view of the information, KM technologies provide a Web-based environment for this intellectual capital to be organized, developed, and applied interactively. Ultimately, KM technologies help companies access and cultivate the business knowledge that they seek.

When people leave an organization, a vast amount of training and investment leaves with them. In fact, an estimated 70% to 80% of company knowledge disappears this way. How can businesses in fast-paced markets capture, preserve, and apply this company knowledge? KM technologies help companies in the following ways:

- Identification and promotion of the best business practices.
- Collaborative features streamline project management.
- Rapid access to information- from multiple sources through a single interface.
- No need to reinvent the wheel.

Chapter Summary

This chapter has traced the major philosophical strands that have led to various conceptualizations of what knowledge is. At the heart of these conceptualizations is the underlying tension between knowledge as an objective fact and knowledge as a socially constructed reality having subjective properties. In addition, the connection between knowledge and truth is also discussed. Next we presented the transformations of data to information and then to knowledge. Here we noted that critical to such transformations is the role of understanding. Further, by doing so we were able to define data, information, and knowledge. We highlighted the importance of taking a holistic definition of the knowledge construct because by doing so only then was it possible to fully capture the many nuances of this multifaceted construct and thus realize the true potential of knowledge. We also discussed the major forms of knowledge including but not limited to tacit and explicit, procedural and declarative as well as strategic knowledge and how we can integrate these together to get a more complete whole. Next we presented Nonaka's modes of transformation to show how we can change the form of knowledge from tacit to explicit and vice versa. We also discussed the knowledge life cycle and the four key steps of this life cycle. Finally we highlighted why the knowledge asset is key for organizations today.

References

Adams, K. C. (2001). The Web as a database: New extraction technologies and content management. *www.brint.com, 25*(2), 27-32.

Alavi, M., & Leidner, D. (2001). Review: Knowledge management and knowledge management systems: Conceptual foundations and research issues. *MIS Quarterly, 25*(1), 107-136.

Alberthal, L. (1995). *Remarks to the Financial Executives Institute*, Oct. 23, Dallas, Texas.

Bacon, C. J., & Fitzgerald, B. (2001). A systemic framework for the field of information systems." *Database for Advances in Information Systems, 32*(2), 46-67.

Becerra-Fernandez, I., & Sabherwal, R. (2001). Organizational knowledge management: A contingency perspective. *Journal of Management Information Systems, 18(1),* 23-55.

Clegg, S. (1999). Globalizing the intelligent organization: Learning organizations, smart workers, (not so) clever countries, and the sociological imagination. *Management Learning, 30*(3), 259-280.

Connor, K., & Prahalad, C. (1996). A resource-based theory of the firm: Knowledge versus opportunism. *Organizational Science, 7*(5), 477-501.

Costa, D. (1995). *Working wisdom.* Stoddart, Toronto.

Croasdell, D. C. (2001). IT's role in organizational memory and learning. *Information Systems Management, 18*(1), 8-11.

Davenport, T., & Grover, V. (2001). Knowledge management. *Journal of Management Information Systems, 18*(1), 3-4.

Davenport, T., & Prusak, L. (1998). *Working knowledge.* Cambridge, MA: Harvard Business School Press.

Dixon, N. (2000). *Common knowledge: How companies thrive by sharing what they know.* Cambridge, MA: Harvard Business School Press.

Duffy, J. (2000). The KM technology infrastructure. *Information Management Journal, 34*(2), 62-66.

Duffy, J. (2001). The tools and technologies needed for knowledge management. *Information Management Journal, 35*(1), 64-67.

Ellerman, D. P. (1999). Global institutions: Transforming international development agencies into learning organizations. *The Academy of Management Executive, 13*(1), 25-35.

Ellinger, A. D., Watkins, K. E., & Bostrom, R. P. (1999). Managers as facilitators of learning in learning organizations. *Human Resource Development Quarterly, 10*(2), 105-125.

Geisler, E. (2005). *The structure and progress of knowledge* (in press). Cambridge: Cambridge University Press.

Granstrand, O. (2000). The shift towards intellectual capitalism: The role of infocom technologies. *Research Policy, 29*(9), 1061-1080.

Hammond, C. (2001). The intelligent enterprise. *InfoWorld, 23*(6), 45-46.

Hansen, M. T., & Oetinger, B. V. (2001). Introducing t-shaped managers: Knowledge management's next generation. *Harvard Business Review, 79*(3), 106-116.

Holt, G. D., Love, P. E. D., & Li, H. (2000). The learning organization: Toward a paradigm for mutually beneficial strategic construction alliances. *International Journal of Project Management, 18*(6), 415-421.

Kienholtz, A. (2005). The design and evolution of Singerian inquiring organizations. In Courtney et al. (Eds.), *Inquiring organizations*. Hershey, PA: Idea Group Publishing.

Lee, J. Sr. (2000). Knowledge management: The intellectual revolution. *IIE Solutions, Norcross, 32*(10), 34-37.

Lesser, E., Mundel, D., & Wiecha, C. (2000). Managing customer knowledge. *The Journal of Business Strategy, 21*(6), 35-37.

Levine, L. (2001). Integrating knowledge and processes in a learning organization. *Information Systems Management, 18*(1), 21-33.

Mahe, S., & Rieu, C. (1998, October 29-30). A pull approach to knowledge management. *Proceedings of the 2nd International Conference on Practical Aspects of Knowledge Management*, Basel, Switzerland.

Maier, R. 2001. *Knowledge management systems*. Berlin: Springer.

Markus, L. (2001). Toward a theory of knowledge reuse: Type of knowledge reuse situations and factors in reuse success. *Journal of Management Information Systems, 18*(1), 57-93.

Martensen, A., & Dahlgaard, J. J. (1999). Integrating business excellence and innovation management: Developing vision, blueprint, and strategy for innovation in creative and learning organizations. *Total Quality Management, 10*(4,5), 627-635.

Moore, K. (2000). The e-volving organization. *Ivey Business Journal, 65*(2), 25-28.

Newell, S., Robertson, M., Scarbrough, H., & Swan, J. (2002). *Managing knowledge work*. New York: Palgrave.

Nonaka, I. (1994). A dynamic theory of organizational knowledge creation. *Organizational Science, 5,* 14-37.

Nonaka, I., & Nishiguchi, T. (2001). *Knowledge emergence*. Oxford: Oxford University Press.

Nonaka, I., & Takeuchi. (1995). *The knowledge creating company*. Oxford: Oxford University Press.

O'Brien, J. (2005). *Management information systems*. Boston: McGrawHill.

Onge, A. S. (2001). Knowledge management and warehousing. *Modern Materials Handling, 56*(3), 33.

Parent, M., Gallupe, R., Salisbury, W., & Handelman, J. (2000). Knowledge creation in focus groups: Can group technology help? *Information & Management, 38,* 47-58.

Polyani, M. (1958). *Personal knowledge: Towards a post-critical philosophy*. Chicago: University Press.

Polyani, M. (1966). *The tacit dimension*. London: Routledge & Kegan Paul.

Popper, M., & Lipshitz, R. (2000). Organizational learning: Mechanisms, culture, and feasibility. *Management Learning, 31*(2), 181-196.

Roberts, J. (2000). From know-how to show-how? Questioning the role of information and communication technologies in knowledge transfer. *Technology Analysis & Strategic Management, 12*(4), 429-443.

Silver, C. A. (2000). Where technology and knowledge meet. *The Journal of Business Strategy, 21*(6), 28-33.

Simon, N. J. (1999). The learning organization. *Competitive Intelligence Magazine, 2*(2), 40-42.

Simons, H. (1960). *The new science of management decision*. New York: Harper & Row.

Srikantaiah, T. K. (2000). Knowledge management for information professionals. ASIS Monograph Series, Information Today, Inc.

Stratigos, A. (2001). Knowledge management meets future information users. www. brint.com, *25*(1), 65-67.

Swan, J., Scarbrough, H., & Preston, J. (1999). Knowledge management: The next fad to forget people? *Proceedings of the 7ᵗʰ European Conference in Information Systems.*

Thorne, K., & Smith, M. (2000). Competitive advantage in world class organizations. *Management Accounting, 78*(3), 22-26.

Wickramasinghe, N. (2005). The phenomenon of duality: A key to facilitate the transition from knowledge management to wisdom for inquiring organizations. In Courtney et al. (Eds.), *Inquiring organizations.* Hershey, PA: Idea Group Publishing.

Wickramasinghe, N., Fadlalla, A., Geisler, E., & Schaffer, J. (2003). Knowledge management and data mining: Strategic imperatives for healthcare. *Proceedings of the 3ʳᵈ Hospital of the Future Conference.*

Wickramasinghe, N., & Mills, G. (2001). MARS: The electronic medical record system the core of the kaiser galaxy. *International Journal of Healthcare Technology Management, 3*(5/6), 406-423.

Chapter III

Creating
Organizational
Knowledge

Introduction

Knowledge management (KM) involves processes through which organizations generate value from their intellectual capital and knowledge-based assets. Central to any knowledge management endeavor is the creation of knowledge. Knowledge however, is a multifaceted construct, exhibiting not only many manifestations of the phenomenon of duality such as subjective and objective aspects but also having tacit and explicit forms. It becomes important to keep this in mind when we focus on creating organizational knowledge, or else we may be too limited in our approaches. There are several frameworks that have been developed recently that help us understand what types of knowledge are involved in the process of knowledge creation, and under what organizational structures different types of knowledge are created and applied. These include the people-oriented perspective of knowledge creation as well as the technology-oriented perspective of knowledge creation, which combine the people and technology perspectives and offers the socio-technical perspective of knowledge management. Finally, by taking a process-oriented perspective and incorporating the ideas of Boyd (Barnett, 2004; Boyd, 1976), we have the final and most integrative model for knowledge creation.

The Socio-Technical Perspective for KM

Paramount to knowledge management is the incorporation of the socio-technical perspective of people, processes, and technologies (Alavi & Leidner, 2001; Schultze & Leidner, 2002; von Lubitz & Wickramasinghe, 2005; Wickramasinghe, 2005). This stems primarily from the fact that knowledge itself is a multifaceted construct embedded in people's heads, in processes, and created and generated by means of a wide range of technologies. It is useful to visualise this concept as the KM triad (Figure 1). The significance of the KM triad is to emphasise that knowledge can be created by people and/or technologies and can also be embedded in processes. Thus, to be successful, KM endeavors must always consider these three elements.

Figure 1. The KM triad (Adapted from Wickramasinghe, 2005b)

Figure 2. The primary steps of KM (Adapted from Wickramasinghe, 2005a)

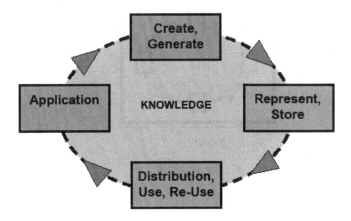

From the KM triad it is possible to analyse the steps involved with KM and their interrelationships. Broadly speaking, knowledge management involves four key stages of creating/generating knowledge, representing/storing knowledge, disseminating/using/re-using knowledge, and applying knowledge which come directly from the KM life cycle (Davenport & Grover, 2001; Davenport & Prusak, 1998; Drucker, 1993; Markus, 2001; Wickramasinghe, 2005), as can be seen in Figure 2.

We can combine these four key steps with the KM triad in Figure 1 to form the KM Diamond. The KM diamond in Figure 3 highlights the importance of the impact of the three elements of KM, namely people, process, and technology on the four steps of knowledge management (creating/generating knowledge, representing/storing knowledge, accessing/using/re-using knowledge, and disseminating/transferring knowledge). In other words, successful KM initiatives require consideration and interactions among all of these components. Ignoring such a holistic perspective is analogous to omitting interaction factors in statistical regression analyses. The main factors (shown in the figure as inward pointing arrows) that impact knowledge (shown as the resultant outward pointing arrows) are people, processes and technology, while the interactions among the constituents are represented by the four key steps of KM and the inner double headed arrows.

Figure 3. The KM diamond (Adapted from Wickramasinghe, 2005b)

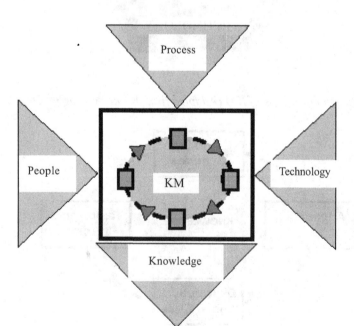

Duality and the Knowledge Construct

As with many concepts in organizational theory, the existence of duality applies when we examine the knowledge construct. Traditionally researchers have turned to Burrell and Morgan's well-established framework of objective and subjective characterizations. A more recent approach using Deetz's four discourses of organizational inquiry also serves to highlight these dualities (Schultze & Leidner, 2002). Let us briefly look at each of these perspectives in turn.

In essence, Burrell and Morgan (1979) brought together two dimensions and four key paradigms that are important to consider when we examine social theory and constructs. The first dimension is that of objective/subjective, where objectivity in this sense refers to an agreement reached by "experts" on what something is or is not, what is observed or not, and/or what has been done or not. Subjectivity, in contrast, is the opposite: there is not necessarily one meaning but in fact, there is discourse and divergence of meaning. The other dimension is that of the nature of society and regulation as opposed to radical change. In trying to understand the dualities with respect to the knowledge construct in and of itself it is the subjective/objective dimension rather than the regulation/radical change dimension that is key. Deetz's framework (Schultze & Leidner, 2002) serves to highlight four discourses with respect to organizational inquiry. Once again, these span two dimensions, the first being the dimension of consensus/dissensus where a consensus approach seeks order while a dissensus orientation recognises conflict and discord. Thus, a consensus orientation toward knowledge would characterise order and equilibrium as the natural state, while a dissensus orientation would characterise conflicting fragmented and divergent views and meanings. The second dimension in this framework is that of emergent vs. a priori. As with the Burrell and Morgan framework (1979), this dimension is less relevant when initially trying to understand the knowledge construct so we leave it for the committed knowledge enthusiasts to pursue this dimension on their own.

In trying to manage knowledge, it is necessary first to understand the binary nature of knowledge; namely its objective and subjective components or consensus/dissensus dimensions. Knowledge can exist as an object, in essentially two forms; explicit or factual knowledge and tacit or experiential (i.e., "know how") (Nonaka, 1994; Nonaka & Nishiguchi, 2001; Polyani, 1958, 1966). While both types of knowledge are important, tacit knowledge is more difficult to identify (and thus manage), although sound management of tacit knowledge can realize greater sustainable competitive advantages to organizations. Of equal importance, though perhaps less well defined, is the realization that knowledge also has a subjective component, and can be viewed as an ongoing phenomenon (i.e., one that is shaped by social practices of communities) (Boland & Tenkasi, 1995; Schultze & Leidner, 2002; Wickramasinghe, 2005). The objective elements of knowledge can be perceived as primarily having an impact on process, while the subjective elements typically impact innovation. Both effective and efficient processes, as well as the functions of supporting and fostering creativity and innovation, are key concerns of knowledge management. Thus, we have an interesting duality in knowledge management that some have called a contradiction (Newell, Robertson, Scarbrough, H., & Swan, 2002; Schultze, 1998; Swan, Scarbrough, & Preston, 1999) and others describe as the *loose-tight* nature of knowledge management.

The *loose-tight* nature of knowledge management comes to being because of the need to recognise and draw upon two distinct philosophical perspectives—the Lockean/Leibnizian stream and the Hegelian/Kantian stream. Models of convergence and compliance representing the *tight* side are grounded in a Lockean/Leibnizian tradition (Malhotra, 2000; Orlikowski, 1992; Wickramasinghe, 2005). These models are essential to provide the information processing aspects of knowledge management, most notably by enabling efficiencies of scale and scope and thus in the language of Burrell and Morgan (1979) supporting the objective view of knowledge management. In contrast, the *loose* side provides agility and flexibility in the tradition of a Hegelian/Kantian perspective. Such models recognize the importance of divergence of meaning essential to support the "sense-making" (Boland & Tenkasi, 1995), subjective view of knowledge management. It is beyond the scope of this chapter to go into an in depth discussion of the specifics of the philosophical background of knowledge management. Nonetheless, a committed knowledge manager should acquire familiarity with the thoughts of Locke, Leibniz, Kant, and Hegel. Wickramasinghe (2003, 2005a, b, c) captured this phenomenon of duality in the Yin-Yang model of knowledge management which is depicted in Figure 4.

Central to the idea of Yin and Yang in Chinese philosophy is the notion of duality and the need for dualities to truly understand the essence of the whole. Figure 4 shows that given a radical change to an environment (such as the introduction of HIPAA and managed care in the U.S. healthcare insurance system) or given a highly competitive environment (such as current e-business environments); an organization's knowledge is a critical survival tool. The Yin-Yang depiction of knowledge management shows that knowledge is required for the organization to be effective and efficient, but also that new knowledge and knowledge renewal are equally necessary. Hence, an organization must incorporate both forms of knowledge in order to truly benefit from knowledge management. It is also important to note that the Yin-Yang model of knowledge management (KM) highlights the Knowledge spiral. The Knowledge Spiral, developed by Nonaka (1994), is central to most of the people-oriented perspectives of knowledge creation. What the Yin Yang model of KM depicts (and what is generally not addressed by other models), is that through the knowledge spiral we can effect a movement between the subjective and objective perspectives of knowledge.

Figure 4. Yin-Yang model of knowledge management (Adapted from Wickramas-inghe, 2003, 2005a, b, c)

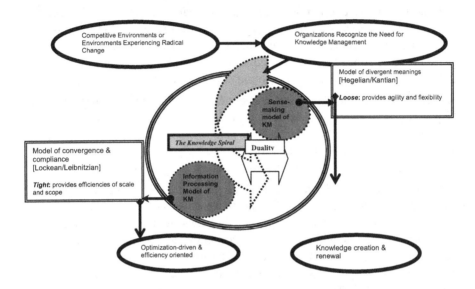

Seemingly trite, the preceding considerations of philosophical perspectives are essential since they provide key insights to the various components of KM initiatives. Moreover, they are the cornerstone of the holistic approach to knowledge creation and their implications must be captured in the development of a meta-framework of knowledge creation. For any organization, the overall effect of a holistic approach to knowledge creation translates ultimately into the attainment of a truly sustainable competitive advantage.

Frameworks for Knowledge Creation

The processes of creating and capturing knowledge, irrespective of the specific philosophical orientation (i.e., Lockean/Leibnizian vs. Hegelian/Kantian), is the central focus of both the psycho-social and algorithmic frameworks of knowledge creation.

The Psychosocial Driven Perspective to Knowledge Creation

Organizational knowledge is not static; rather it changes and evolves during the lifetime of an organization. Unsurprisingly, the form of knowledge itself is also subject to metamorphoses. The existing tacit knowledge converts into new explicit knowledge and existing explicit knowledge into new tacit knowledge, or the subjective form of knowledge transforms into the objective form.

The process of transforming the form of knowledge from one form to another results in the progressively increasing knowledge base as well as the amount and utilization of the knowledge within the organization. This is known as the knowledge spiral (Nonaka & Nishiguchi, 2001). Each transformation causes growth of the overall extant knowledge base of the organization to a new, superior knowledge base.

According to Nonaka (1994), tacit to tacit knowledge transformation usually occurs through apprenticeship type relations where the teacher or master passes on the skill to the apprentice. Explicit to explicit knowledge transformation usually occurs via formal learning of facts, while tacit to explicit knowledge transformation usually occurs when there is an articulation of nuances; for example, as in healthcare if a renowned surgeon is questioned as to why he does a particular procedure in a certain manner, by his articulation of the steps the tacit knowledge becomes explicit. Finally, explicit to tacit knowledge transformation usually occurs as new explicit knowledge is internalised it can then be used to broaden, reframe, and extend one's tacit knowledge. These transformations are often referred to as the modes of socialization, combination, externalization, and internalization respectively (see Chapter II and Table 1).

Table 1. The knowledge transformations identified by Nonaka (Nonaka & Nishiguchi, 2001)

From/To	Tacit Knowledge	Explicit Knowledge
Tacit Knowledge	**Socialization** (Sympathised Knowledge)	**Externalization** (Conceptual Knowledge)
Explicit Knowledge	**Internalization** (Operational Knowledge)	**Combination** (Systematic Knowledge)

Integral to the transformation of knowledge through the knowledge spiral is the creation of a powerful organizational asset—new knowledge. The dictates of the rapidly expanding knowledge-centric economy are such that all processes that effect a positive change to the existing knowledge base of the organization and facilitate better use of the organization's intellectual capital (as does the knowledge spiral) are of paramount importance.

Two other primarily people-driven frameworks that focus on knowledge creation as a central theme are those proposed by Spender and Blackler. Spender draws a distinction between individual knowledge and social knowledge, claiming that each can be implicit or explicit (Newell et al., 2002; von Lubitz & Wickramasinghe, 2005; Wickramasinghe, 2005). Spender's definition of implicit knowledge corresponds to Nonaka's tacit knowledge. However, unlike Spender, Nonaka does not differentiate between individual and social dimensions of knowledge, focusing instead on the nature and types of the knowledge itself. In contrast, Blackler views knowledge creation from an organizational perspective, knowledge can exist as encoded, embedded, embodied, encultured and/or embrained. In addition, Blackler also emphasises the fact that for different organizational types, different types of knowledge predominate and highlight the connection between knowledge and organizational processes.

Blackler's types of knowledge span the continuum of tacit (implicit) to explicit knowledge with embrained being predominantly tacit (implicit) and encoded being predominantly explicit. Correspondingly, the embedded, embodied and encultured types of knowledge exhibit varying degrees of a tacit (implicit)/explicit combination (ibid) (an integrated view of all the three frameworks is provided in Figure 5).

It is important to note that the integrated view does not conflict with the philosophical perspectives discussed earlier or the Yin-Yang model of KM. Consequently, the existence of tacit and explicit knowledge, and even more importantly that of the knowledge spiral itself (the most general of the three psychosocial frameworks) is relevant to both the Lockean/Leibnitzian and Hegelian/Kantian perspectives (Figure 3).

Figure 5 shows that Spender's and Blackler's perspectives complement Nonaka's conceptualization of knowledge creation. More importantly, they do not contradict his fundamental thesis of the knowledge spiral wherein the extant knowledge base is continually being expanded to a new knowledge base, be it tacit/explicit (in Nonaka's terminology), implicit/explicit (in Spender's terminology), or embrained/encultured/ embodied/embedded/encoded (in Blackler's terminology). As has been described, these three frameworks take a primarily people-oriented perspective of knowledge creation. In particular, Nonaka's framework (arguably the most general of the three frameworks) describes knowledge creation in terms of knowledge transformations all of which have been initiated by human cognitive activities. Needless to say that

Figure 5. People driven knowledge creation grid

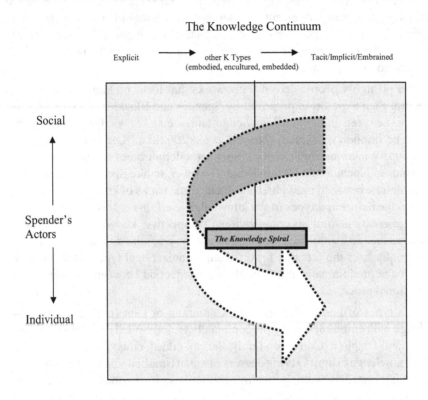

both Spender and Blackler's respective frameworks also view knowledge creation through a primarily people oriented perspective (Figure 5).

The Algorithmic Perspective to Knowledge Creation

In contrast to the previous people-oriented frameworks, knowledge discovery in database (KDD and more specifically data mining) approaches knowledge creation from a primarily technology driven perspective (Adriaans & Zantinge, 1996; Becerra-Fernandez & Sabherwal, 2001; Bendoly, 2003). In particular, the KDD process focuses on how data is transformed into knowledge by identifying valid, novel, potentially useful, and ultimately understandable patterns. KDD is primarily used on data sets for creating knowledge through model building, or by finding data patterns and relationships in data.

Steps in Data Mining

The following steps are typically undertaken in data mining. These steps are iterative, with the process moving backward whenever required (Berry & Linoff, 1997; Cabena, Hadjinian, Stadler, Verhees, & Zanasi, 1998; Chung & Gray, 1999; Fayyad et al., 1996; Holsapple & Joshi, 2002).

1. Develop an understanding of the application, of the relevant prior knowledge, and of the end user's goals.

2. Create a target data set to be used for discovery.

3. Clean and preprocess data (including handling missing data fields, noise in the data, accounting for time series, and known changes).

4. Reduce the number of variables and find invariant representations of data if possible.

5. Choose the data-mining task (classification, regression, clustering, etc.).

6. Choose the data-mining algorithm.

7. Search for patterns of interest (this is the actual data mining).

8. Interpret the patterns mined. If necessary, iterate through any of steps 1 through 7.

9. Consolidate knowledge discovered, prepare reports and then use/re-use the newly created knowledge.

From an application perspective, data mining and KDD are often used interchangeably. Figure 6 presents a generic representation of a typical knowledge discovery process. Knowledge creation in a KDD project usually starts with data collection or data selection, covering almost all steps (see previous and Figure 6) in the KDD process. As depicted in Figure 6, the first three steps of the KDD process (i.e., selection, preprocessing, and transformation) are considered exploratory data mining, whereas the last two steps (i.e., data mining and interpretation/evaluation) in the KDD process constitute predictive data mining.

In practice, the primary tasks of data mining tend to be description and prediction (Alberthal, 1995; Choi & Lee, 2003; Kovalerchuk & Vityaev, 2002; Krzysztof, 2001; McGee, 1997). Description focuses on finding human-interpretable patterns describing the data while prediction involves using some observations or attributes to predict unknown or future values of other attributes of interest. The relative importance of description and prediction for particular data mining applications can vary considerably. The descriptive and predictive tasks are carried out by applying different machine learning, artificial intelligence, and statistical algorithms.

Figure 6. Integrated view of the knowledge discovery process

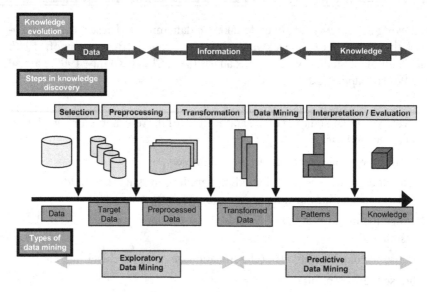

A major goal of exploratory data mining is data cleaning and understanding (Fayyad et al., 1996). Some of the data operations undertaken during exploratory data mining include: sampling, partitioning, charting, graphing, associating, clustering, transforming, filtering, and imputing. Predictive data mining deals with future values of variables and utilises many algorithms such as regression, decision trees, and neural networks (ibid). Predictive data mining also involves an assessment step, which compares different models according to many performance metrics (Figure 7).

Figure 6 shows an integrated view of the knowledge discovery process, the evolution of knowledge from data to information to knowledge and the types of data mining (exploratory and predictive) and their interrelationships. Figure 6 captures all the major aspects connected with data mining and the KDD process and emphasises the significant role of the KDD process to knowledge creation. However, unlike the frameworks discussed above where knowledge is subdivided into various constituent parts, it is important to note that in the KDD process the knowledge component itself is typically treated as a homogeneous block. Figure 6 shows the integrated view of the knowledge discovery process; where the steps of knowledge evolution, the KDD steps as well as the types of data mining are brought together. The figure also indicates the stage at which data changes into information and then knowledge.

Figure 7. Schematic of major data mining approaches for generating knowledge

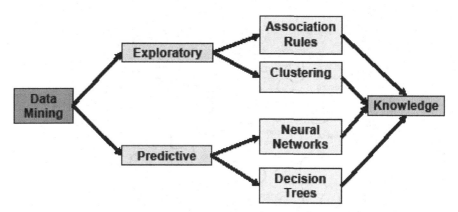

The preceding paragraphs highlighted the key aspects of knowledge creation from both a people, as well as a technology driven perspective. Irrespective of the adopted path of knowledge creation, it is important for effective knowledge creation to realise that knowledge is a multifaceted construct, and knowledge management is a multidimensional approach (consequently the individual steps of knowledge management also should exhibit this multidimensionality).

Given the importance of knowledge management in the knowledge economy, it is indeed useful to combine the people- and technology-driven frameworks into an integrative, all-encompassing meta-framework which will capture the subtle nuances and complexities of knowledge creation, and realize the synergistic effect of the respective strengths of these frameworks.

Business Intelligence and Analytics

Another technology-based sub-specialty connected to knowledge creation is the area of business intelligence and the now newer term of business analytics (Spiegler, 2003; Wickramasinghe, 2003; Wespi, Deri, Kmiec, & Vigna, 2002). The term business intelligence (BI) has become an umbrella description for a wide range of decision-support tools, some of which target specific user audiences. At the bottom of the BI hierarchy are Extraction and Formatting Tools, which are also known as data-extraction tools. These tools collect data from existing databases for inclusion in data warehouses and data marts. The next level of BI hierarchy is known as warehouses and marts. Because the data come from so many different, often incompatible systems with various file formats, the next step in the BI hierarchy is

Figure 8. The umbrella of BI tools

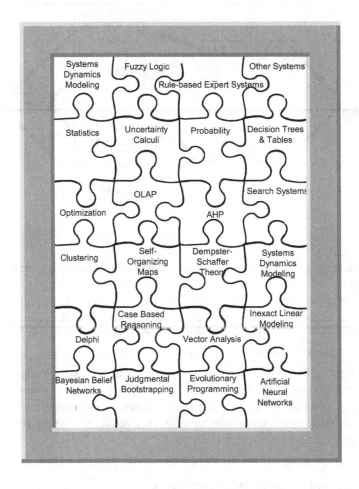

the application of the formatting tools used to "cleanse" the data and convert them all to formats that can easily be understood in the data warehouse or data mart. At the next level of tools resides reporting and analytical tools (known as enterprise reporting and analytical tools). OLAP (online analytic processing) engines such as Oracle Express and analytical application-development tools are used for data analysis and business forecasting, modeling, and trend analysis while Human

Intelligence tools are those assisting in recording human expertise, opinions, and observations for the purpose of creating knowledge repositories. The last category of tools resides at the very top of the BI hierarchy fusing together the analytic and intelligence capabilities with human expertise (Figure 8).

A Socio-Algorithmic Approach to Knowledge Creation

From a macro-knowledge management perspective, the knowledge spiral is the cornerstone of knowledge creation. From a micro-data mining perspective, one of the key strengths of data mining is that of facilitating rapid knowledge creation from vast amounts of data. As noted in the KM triad knowledge management involves the incorporation of people, processes, and technology. Therefore, a framework that integrates the algorithmic approach of knowledge creation (in particular data mining) with the psychosocial approach of knowledge creation (i.e., the people driven frameworks of knowledge creation, in particular the knowledge spiral) would appear to be more reflective of the dynamics involved in knowledge creation. Moreover, such a framework provides a richer and more complete approach to knowledge creation. Consequently not only does it provide a deeper understanding of the knowledge creation process but also offers a knowledge creation methodology that is more adoptable to specific organizational contexts, structures and cultures (Figure 9).

The proposed meta-framework (Wickramasinghe, 2005a, b, c) is equally applicable for exploratory and predictive data mining across the four modes of transformation as well as supporting all BA and BI initiatives. However, we believe that depending on the organizational context and the specific mode of transformation, one type of data mining may in fact be more appropriate and relevant than another. We hypothesise that different data mining techniques are likely to be more suitable depending on which of the four modes of transformation is employed.

The proposed meta-framework incorporates the implications of the various philosophical perspectives of knowledge management. The meta-framework assumptions are consistent with the Lockean/Leibnizian perspective with respect to both the effectiveness and efficiency of knowledge creation, and equally consistent with the Hegelian/Kantian perspectives as they pertain to the need for multiple meanings for knowledge creation. Moreover, the dimensions of consensus/dissensus are also represented through the amalgamation of the strictly structured (i.e., data mining) with a more unstructured approach (i.e., the knowledge spiral) to knowledge creation.

Figure 9 also integrates the specific modes of transformation of the knowledge spiral discussed by Nonaka. These transformations are supported by the integration of

Figure 9. The knowledge product of data mining is deconstructed into its constituent components based on the people-driven perspectives (i.e., Blackler, Spender, & Nonaka respectively) of knowledge creation

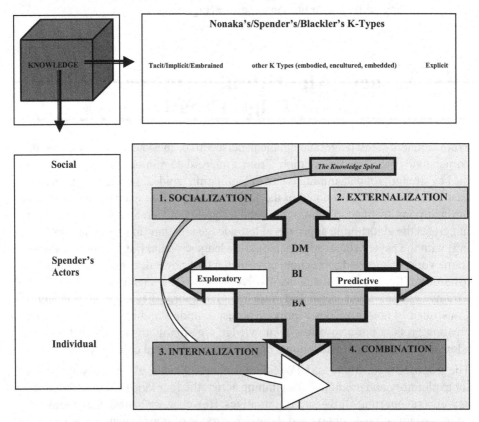

Specific Modes of Transformations and the Role of Technical Approaches such as Data Mining, Business Intelligence and Business Analytics in Realizing Them:
1. Socialization – experiential to experiential via practice group interactions on data mining results
2. Externalization – written extensions to data mining results
3. Internalization – enhancing experiential skills by learning from data mining results
4. Combination – gaining insights through applying various data mining visualization techniques

both the algorithmic techniques and people driven techniques. For example, if we consider the transformation of socialization, which is described in as the process of creating new tacit knowledge through discussion within groups experts, and we then incorporate the results of data mining techniques into this context. These data results provide a structured forum and hence serve to guide the dialogue and consequently the creation of germane knowledge. We note here that such an activity serves to enrich the socialization process without restricting the actual brainstorming activities, and must not be misconstrued as truncating divergent thoughts. In similarity, we can combine the data mining results to the other people-driven modes of knowledge transformation.

Process Centric Perspective of Knowledge Creation

A process-centric approach to knowledge creation is the latest adjunct to the two methods previously described. Process-centric concept of knowledge creation is based on a widely used notion of domain destruction and creation proposed by Boyd (1976). Contrary to either people- or technology-centric models, the process-centric concept is based on destroying the pre-existing domains, selection of their relevant components, then recombining these components into an entirely new domain relevant to the activities within the changed environment. The fundamental assumptions of the process-centric model are based on quantitative physics and mathematical analysis [ibid], but the model also incorporates both people- and technology-centric concepts.

Central to Boyd's idea of destruction and creation is the thesis that in order to cope with our environment we develop mental patterns or concepts of meaning (domains) (i.e., knowledge). However, the world in which we act constitutes an ever-changing environment that demands flexibility of interaction with and response to its continuous and often unpredictable demands. Continual destruction of historically established domains, constructive extraction of their subcomponents, and their recombination into new patterns are fundamental aspects of the response patterns that allows us to be shaped and shape our environment, in a similar fashion to Gidden's structuration theory (Giddens, 1979).

According to Boyd, there are two main ways to approach creating concepts; (1) deduction and analysis—moving from general to specific, or (2) induction and synthesis—moving from specific to general (Boyd, 1976). As time is traversed, be it at an individual level, organizational level or societal level, domains of knowledge are formed to represent observed reality. Destructive deduction is achieved by removing domain boundaries and the disassociation of the previously ordered domain constituent into a chaos. Faced with such disorder the natural propensity is to regain the state of equilibrium and reconstruct order and meaning. The process of reconstituting such order requires induction, synthesis and integration and ends in the construction of a new domain where new commonalities and orderly interrelationships govern the existence of previously disparate parts. The process reflects the fundamental essence of knowledge creation, and the forming of these commonalities and creation of a new domain constitute the principal force that drives increases in the extant knowledge base. However, since the original goal was to re-establish equilibrium, the new domain and the new state of order that it both imposes and represents through the re-establishment of the state of equilibrium of all subcomponents also represents germane knowledge.

Boyd's approach to creation is rooted in mathematics and physics, a novel approach that may, ultimately, provide quantitative foundations of the process. Using Gödel's Theorem (Boyd, 1976) describing incompleteness and inconsistency of ordered systems Boyd demonstrates that "in order to determine the consistency of any new system we must construct or uncover another system beyond it" (von Lubitz et al., 2004). However, the degree of intrusion into the system necessary for the construction of a new one is governed by Heisenberg's uncertainty principle. Hence, the uncertainty values not only represent the degree of intrusion by the observer upon the observed but also the degree of confusion and disorder perceived by that observer.

All natural processes generate entropy, and any closed system is characterized by a progressive increase of its chaos and disorder. Combining Gödel's theorem, Heisenberg's uncertainty principle, and the third law of thermodynamics, Boyd argues that any inward-oriented and continued effort to improve the match-up of concept with observed reality will only increase the degree of mismatch. Hence, we can expect unexplained and disturbing ambiguities, uncertainties, anomalies, or apparent inconsistencies to emerge with the frequency that is proportionate to our efforts to re-establish the order within the system. As a result, rather than reverting to the stability of equilibrium, we will impose an ever-increasing degree of confusion and chaos. Seen from a practical perspective of an organization wishing to survive and thrive in the dynamically changing environment of modern business, any attempt at introspective analysis of its operation that is limited to historical knowledge is doomed to failure and may be the main contributor to the downfall of the organization itself. The only solution available, and the only solution that assures continuous progress is then that proposed by Boyd: a contiguous destruction of old domains, extraction of pertinent subcomponents, and recombination into new domains (Boyd, 1976). The solution also defines the role of the constructor—the more direct involvement in the destruction/creation process, the greater potential for inducing chaos. The creator needs to assume a superior position of providing overall guidance rather than participate in the details of the execution. Inadvertently, we have then arrived at the confirmation of one of the essential rules of operational conduct: micromanagement by superior entities of the organization is one of the most harmful forms of interaction that, rather than inducing order, produce chaos and loss of working potential. Consequently, the level and adequacy of the organization's germane knowledge will suffer and its decline will lead the organization to the rapidly steepening path of self-destruction.

The biologically motivated instinct of survival is a characteristic as much of societies as their functional subcomponents—organizations. More importantly, the exponent of the quality of survival is the measure of how well it fits into the pattern of predetermined survival characteristics (i.e., "survival on our terms") (Boyd, 1976). Thus, for example, the notion of a sustainable competitive advantage for an organization translates into being an active participant in the activities of the selected industry on terms predetermined by the organization. Such terms must allow the organization to continue the sole and complete occupation of its "ecological niche" in a manner that excludes incursion by a competitor. Using military analogy (von Lubitz et al., 2004), the organization's goal is therefore to improve its capacity for independent action that, in turn, allows it the capacity for a flexible response to any emergent threat (ibid). Consequently, individuals and groups must form, dissolve, and reform their cooperative or competitive postures in order to overcome environmental obstacles which may impede or even prevent survival. Knowledge is the primary tool in the development of the appropriate survival strategy and, hence, the goal of knowledge management should be to focus on the knowledge creation effort. New knowledge, as long as it remains inaccessible to the competitor, then becomes one of the most essential weapons in gaining operational superiority, and continuous development of new knowledge—the prerogative for the sustainment of competitive advantage. It is in this context that actions and decisions become of critical importance.

The process centric perspective of knowledge creation and the ability of Boyd's loop to support analysis and consequent action of dynamic operations rapidly, makes it a most important aspect for all knowledge-based enterprises to incorporate into their decision-making activities. Knowledge-based enterprises must continuously operate at optimal efficiency in complex and unstable environments and Boyd's

Figure 10. Process centric perspective of knowledge creation

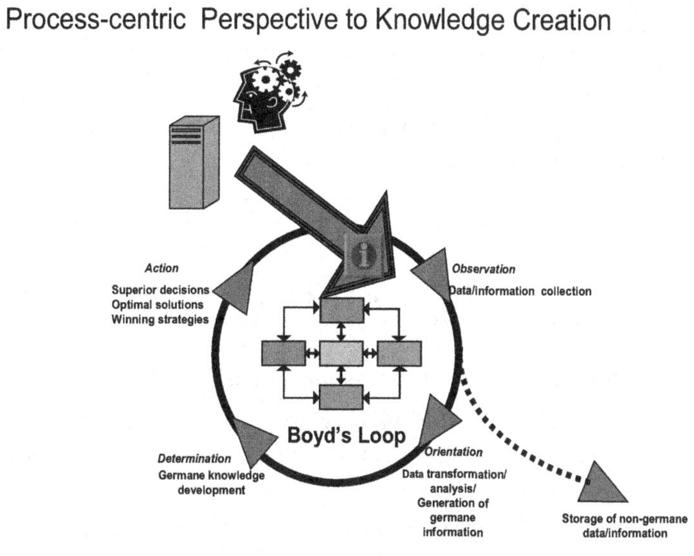

Process-centric Perspective to Knowledge Creation

loop provides a most suitable tool to ensure that at all times rapid decision-making is superior.

Chapter Summary

Any knowledge creation process should start with a clear understanding of the organizational specifics, like the type and the structure of the organization, the dynamics of the people, process, and technology, the multi-dimensional nature of knowledge and the different possible approaches to knowledge creation. The KM Triad and the KM Diamond facilitate such an understanding. Specifically, the KM Triad emphasizes the socio-technical perspectives for knowledge management while the KM diamond emphasizes the impact of the socio-technical perspectives on the four steps of knowledge management and/or knowledge itself.

From the KM Diamond we can see the pivotal role played by knowledge creation, the first step in the KM cycle; since it impacts and simultaneously is impacted by the other steps. Currently two well-established approaches for addressing KM are the algorithmic/technology focused perspective (i.e., data mining and the KDD process) or the psycho-social/people focused perspective (i.e., Nonaka, Spender, & Blacker's respective frameworks). In our opinion, a key limitation is that, taken in isolation, these respective perspectives on knowledge creation present a partial picture of the multifaceted knowledge construct. Given the importance of knowledge creation in the knowledge economy, we believe a more complete picture can be obtained by amalgamating these two perspectives into a unified meta-framework. This is best illustrated by taking a process centric perspective to knowledge creation. Such a meta- framework is of particular value and relevance to enable and facilitate knowledge re-use as it attempts to address a current systemic limitation with respect to knowledge creation.

References

Adriaans, P., & Zantinge, D. (1996). *Data mining*. Addison-Wesley.

Alavi, M., & Leidner, D. (2001). Review: Knowledge management and knowledge management systems: Conceptual foundations and research issues. *MIS Quarterly*, *25*(1), 107-136.

Alberthal, L. (1995, October 23). *Remarks to the financial executives institute*. Dallas, TX.

Barnett, T. P. M. (2004). *The Pentagon's new map.* New York: G. P. Putnam & Sons.

Becerra-Fernandez, I., & Sabherwal, R. (2001). Organizational knowledge management: A contingency perspective. *Journal of Management Information Systems, 18*(1), 23-55.

Bendoly, E. (2003). Theory and support for process frameworks of knowledge discovery and data mining from ERP systems. *Information & Management, 40*, 639-647.

Berry, M., & Linoff, G. (1997). *Data mining techniques: For marketing, sales, and customer support.* John Wiley & Sons.

Boland, R., & Tenkasi, R. (1995). Perspective making perspective taking. *Organizational Science, 6*, 350-372.

Boyd JR COL USAF. (1976). Destruction and creation. In R. Coram (Ed.), *Boyd.* New York: Little, Brown, & Co.

Burrell, G., & Morgan, G. (1979). In search of a framework: Part 1. *Sociological Paradigms and Organizational Analysis,* 1-37.

Cabena, P., Hadjinian, P., Stadler, R., Verhees, J., & Zanasi, A. (1998). *Discovering data mining from concept to implementation.* Prentice Hall.

Choi, B., & Lee, H. (2003). An empirical investigation of KM styles and their effect on corporate performance. *Information & Management, 40*, 403-417.

Chung, M., & Gray, P. (1999). Special section: Data mining. *Journal of Management Information Systems, 16*(1), 11-16.

Davenport, T., & Grover, V. (2001). Knowledge management. *Journal of Management Information Systems, 18*(1), 3-4.

Davenport, T., & Prusak, L. (1998). *Working knowledge.* Boston: Harvard Business School Press.

Drucker, P. (1993). *Post-capitalist society.* New York: Harper Collins.

Fayyad, Piatetsky-Shapiro, Smyth. (1996). *Advances in knowledge discovery and data mining.* Menlo Park, CA: AAAI Press / The MIT Press.

Holsapple, C., & Joshi, K. (2002). Knowledge manipulation activities: Results of a Delphi study. *Information & Management, 39*, 477-419.

Kovalerchuk, B., & Vityaev, E. (2000). *Data mining in finance: Advances in relational and hybrid methods.* Kluwer Academic Publishers.

Krzysztof, J. C. (2001). *Medical data mining and knowledge discovery.* Physica-Verlag.

Malhotra, Y. (2000). *Knowledge management and virtual organizations.* Hershey, PA: Idea Group Publishing.

Markus, L. (2001). Toward a theory of knowledge reuse: Types of knowledge reuse situations and factors in reuse success. *Journal of Management Information Systems, 18*(1), 57-93.

McGee, M. K. (1997, September 22). High-tech healing. *Information Week.*

Newell, S., Robertson, M., Scarbrough, H., & Swan, J. (2002). *Managing knowledge work.* New York: Palgrave.

Nonaka, I. (1994). A dynamic theory of organizational knowledge creation. *Organizational Science, 5,* 14-37.

Nonaka, I., & Nishiguchi, T. (2001). *Knowledge emergence.* Oxford: Oxford University Press.

Orlikowski, W. (1992). The duality of technology: Rethinking the concept of technology in organizations. *Organization Science, 3*(3), 398-427.

Parent, M. R., Gallupe, W., Salisbury, J., & Handelman. (2000). Knowledge creation in focus groups: Can group technology help? *Information & Management, 38,* 47-58.

Polyani, M. (1958). *Personal knowledge: Towards a post-critical philosophy.* Chicago: University Press.

Polyani, M. (1966). *The tacit dimension.* London: Routledge & Kegan Paul.

Schultze U. (1998, December). *Investigating the contradictions in knowledge management.* Presentation at IFIP.

Schultze, U., & Leidner, D. (2002). Studying knowledge management in information systems research: Discourses and theoretical assumptions. *MIS Quarterly, 26*(3), 212-242.

Spiegler, I. (2003). Technology and knowledge: Bridging a "generating" gap. *Information and Management, 40,* 533-539.

Swan, J., Scarbrough, H., & Preston, J. (1999). Knowledge management: The next fad to forget people? *Proceedings of the 7th European Conference in Information Systems.*

von Lubitz, D., & Wickramasinghe, N. (2005). Creating germane knowledge in dynamic environments. *International Journal of Innovation and Learning* (in press).

Wespi, A., Deri, L., Kmiec, Z., & Vigna, G. (2002, October 16-18). Recent advances in intrusion detection. *Proceedings of the 5th International Symposium,* Zurich, Switzerland. Springer Verlag.

Wickramasinghe, N. (2003). Knowledge management and data mining: Strategic imperatives for healthcare. In A. Fadlalla, E. Geisler, & J. Schaffer (Eds.), *Proceedings of the 3rd Hospital of the Future Conference.*

Wickramasinghe, N. (2003). Do we practice what we preach: Are knowledge management systems in practice truly reflective of knowledge management systems in theory? *Business Process Management Journal, 9*(3), 295-316.

Wickramasinghe, N. (2005a). The phenomenon of duality: A key to facilitate the transition from knowledge management to wisdom for inquiring organizations. In Courtney et al. (Eds.), *Inquiring organizations.* Hershey, PA: Idea Group Publishing.

Wickramasinghe, N. (2005b). Knowledge creation. In D. Schwartz (Ed.), *A meta-framework* (pp. 326-335). Hershey, PA: Idea Group Publishing.

Wickramasinghe, N. (2005c). Knowledge creation: A meta-framework. *International Journal of Innovation and Learning* (in press).

Section II

Infrastructures Required to Support Knowledge-Based Enterprises

Chapter IV

The KM Business Infrastructure

Introduction

Knowledge management activities typically span several and often interconnected business processes rather than focus exclusively on a specific business process. In order to fully appreciate how knowledge is embedded within these business processes we must first trace the historical development of information processing as well as several techniques that have developed in the manufacturing arena such as TQM (total quality management), BPR (business process re-engineering), SCM (supply chain management), and CRM (customer relationship management). Central to the understanding of knowledge within business processes is the ability to combine a process-oriented perspective of knowledge (i.e., an organization's ability to learn from—and incorporate data, information, and/or knowledge embedded within) and generate by its processes with a product oriented perspective, or an organization's ability to manage its knowledge asset as an output or valuable byproduct. At first, the difference may appear to be subtle but it is significant and once again relates to the multifaceted, complex nature of the knowledge construct itself. When examining business processes it is also useful to take what is called a "systems thinking" perspective of the organization. By doing so, this enables the identification of knowledge as both product and process. Thus, key management techniques of TQM (total quality management, BPR (business process re-engineering), SCM (supply chain management) and CRM (customer relationship management) are only truly effective when combined with an understanding of how knowledge is embedded within various business processes and by then using this valuable knowledge asset to develop superior processes.

Systems Thinking

What are processes? Basically processes are ordered flows of events. For an organization, processes can represent either the way in which tasks and activities get done (i.e., operational processes), or the way in which work is supported (i.e., management processes). Many processes make up a system and represent ordered flows of events that are necessary so that a specific activity can be executed. For example, a system for an organization might be accounts receivable and payable while the processes that facilitate and enable the activities to occur to support this system include the placement of an order, the issuing of an invoice, the delivery of

Table 1. The five disciplines (Senge, 1990)

Discipline	Practice	Principle	Essence
Systems Thinking	• Systems archetypes • Simulation	• Structure influences behavior • Policy resistance • Leverage	• Holism • Interconnectedness
Personal Mastery	• Clarifying personal vision • Holding creative tension between focusing on result and seeing current reality	• Vision • Creative tension vs. emotional tension • Subconscious	• Being • Generativeness • Connectedness
Mental Models	• Distinguishing data from abstractions of data • Testing assumptions	• Espoused theory vs. theory in use • Balancing inquiry and advocacy	• Love of truth • Openness
Building Shared Vision	• Visioning process • Acknowledging current reality	• Shared vision • Commitment vs. compliance	• Commonality of purpose • Partnership
Team Learning	• Suspending assumptions • Acting as colleagues • Surfacing own defensiveness • Practicing	• Dialogues • Integrate dialogues and discussions • Defensive routines	• Collective intelligence • Alignment

the product, and the receiving of the required payment. The defining of the system or the extent of its boundary is based on judgment. The two central concerns for any system are its reliability and efficiency.

Table 2. Archetypes of systems thinking (Senge, 1990)

Archetype	Description	Management Principle
Balancing Process with Delay	The adjustment of a process due to delayed feedback. If it is not apparent that the feedback is delayed the corrective action maybe too much and thus negatively impact the end result.	In a sluggish system, aggressiveness produces instability. It is thus necessary first to make the system more responsive.
Limits to Growth	A process feeds on itself to produce a period of accelerated growth. Then the growth begins to slow and eventually even reverse itself to accelerate collapse.	Don't push on the growth process without addressing the points of limitation.
Shifting the Burden	A short-term solution is used to correct a problem, with apparently positive results. But this avoids/delays the addressing of the long term corrective action necessary.	Need to focus on the fundamental solution not a temporary fix.
Eroding goals	The long term fundamental goal is forgone due to a shift of focus onto the short term.	Hold the vision.
Escalation	When the advantage of one is seen to depend on the other and thus aggressive action is invoked to keep establishing and re-establishing ones dominance.	Create a win-win scenario.
Success to the Successful	Two or more actives compete for limited resources; the successful one always gets more funding.	Look for the overarching goal for balancing the whole not just excelling in one area.
Tragedy of Commons	Individuals use a common but limited resource solely on the basis on individual needs, which eventually leads to diminishing returns, and then the resource is totally used up.	Manage the common resource through education and self-regulation.
Fixes that fail	A fix, effective in the short term has unforeseen long-term consequences.	Maintain focus on the long term.
Growth and underinvestment	Growth approaches a limit and sufficient investment is not provided.	Hold the long-term vision.

The goal of systems thinking in business is to explore and analyze processes as wholes and understand the inter-relations and inter-connectedness of various processes and thus how they impact on each other. Much of the work of systems thinking has its roots in the ideas of soft systems methodology by Peter Checkland and C. West Churchman's philosophical ideas of the need for systemic thinking (Checkland, 1999; Checkland & Scholes, 1990; Flood, 1999). Peter Senge (1990) in his book, *The Fifth Discipline*, leveraged these ideas in order to define what he believes to be a learning organization. In particular, Senge identified five key disciplines for organizations, the most important being systems thinking. For completeness, Table 1 presents all five disciplines. From the discipline of systems thinking, Senge identified several archetypes that facilitate the diagnosis of problems within systems for organizations. According to Senge, all problems experienced in systems within organizations can be reduced to these archetypes and thus by identifying the archetype relevant to the problem, it is possible to embark upon a resolution. Table 2 lists these archetypes and the potential means for an organization to resolve them. We note that application of the process centric perspective of knowledge creation and especially Boyd's OODA loop principles provides the necessary model to resolve these archetypes and address the specific problems they cause. Of central importance here is that by understanding processes in terms of systems it is possible then to examine their interactions and inter-relatedness and thus their impacts on other aspects of the organization. Once this understanding is achieved then it is possible to change the processes. This not only makes them more effective and reliable but also enables these processes not to have a negative effect on another area within the organization. Systems thinking is about holism and holistic thinking with the underlying premise being that the sum of the parts is indeed less than the whole.

Historical Development of Information Processing

In order to fully appreciate knowledge embedded in processes, it is necessary to trace the historical development of information processing from isolated applications of data base administration in the mid-70's, which focused on technical data integration, to data base integration in the mid-80's, which focused on conceptual data integration (Evans & Wurster, 1999; Shappiro & Verian, 1999). By the late 80's, data management was focusing on enterprise-wide data integration, which, in turn led to information management in the 90s and now has developed into knowledge management. What is important throughout this progression is that the business processes within organizations and their technical counter-parts, work-flow management systems were moving to a focus on information management and ultimately

Figure 1. Integration of people and technological KM perspectives via processes

knowledge management (Davenport & Beers, 1995; Shutub, 1999; Simchi-Levi, 2001). However, in doing so, these processes were in and of themselves generating as well as being sources of embedded knowledge. This phenomenon is what is often referred to as the process view of knowledge. The processes and functions which, were designed primarily to connect the people-oriented knowledge management perspective with the technical-oriented knowledge management perspective, also create and generate knowledge. Figure 1 depicts this. In such a conceptualization as depicted in Figure 1, the goal of knowledge management then is to examine the process, tasks, and functions to not only improve sub-tasks and thereby all tasks, functions, and processes but also ensure that these systems result in heightened effectiveness and reliability. Many management methods such as TQM and BPR, which have tended to develop from manufacturing, have specifically tried to address this (Bashein, Markus, & Riley, 1994; Collier, 1992; Davenport, 1993, 19943; Davenport & Short, 1990).

Business Process Re-Engineering (BPR)

Business process re-engineering (BPR) involves "the fundamental rethinking and radical redesign of business processes to achieve dramatic improvements in critical, contemporary measures of performance, such as cost, quality, service, and speed" (Hammer & Champy, 1994, p. 32). Four key words summarize the major emphases of BPR (Caron, Jarvenpaa, & Stoddard, 1994; Hammer & Champy, 1994):

- **Fundamental:** Since BPR targets basic and key business processes.
- **Radical:** Since BPR requires significant rather than incremental redesign.

- **Dramatic:** Since BPR creates major changes to the current state of the organization.

- **Processes:** Since BPR focuses on redesigning of business processes.

Essential to successful BPR is the analysis of processes, the replacing, and/or redesigning of existing processes to create greater effectiveness and efficiency throughout the organization. Technology is a key enabler of these new processes since it permits companies to re-engineer their business processes and thereby facilitates the design of seamless information flows (Davenport, 1993; Earl, Sampler, & Short, 1995; Weil & Broadbent, 1998). Some of the most dramatic examples of the need and subsequent benefit of BPR are seen in organizations that are transitioning from bricks and mortar to bricks and clicks (i.e., trying to incorporate an e-business component within their existing traditional business structure). In order for these organizations to enter into e-commerce, they require significant changes to their existing processes. The Internet in particular impacts the following:

1. **Coordination:** In performing any process, many sub-processes must take place first and this often requires significant co-ordination of tasks and the Internet by enabling the speedy transfer of information facilitates this greatly.

2. **Content:** The Internet is a very information rich medium that can enable the access to many types of current information such as stock quotes, news, weather, as well as support entertainment such as video games.

3. **Communication:** E-mail primarily enables the sending of messages at any time to many people. By simultaneously impacting coordination, content, and communication the Internet has made it is possible to radically redesign many processes such as new and developing areas of Telemedicine and distance learning (Berwick, Godfrey, & Roessner, 1990; Collins, 1990).

BPR is an important consideration for all organizations, and enables organizations to realize the full benefits of incorporating new technologies. The connection between BPR and knowledge management exists at many levels. Firstly, in the late 80's and early 90s when many large organizations embarked upon elaborate BPR initiatives they assumed that BPR was synonymous with removing people from organizations (Davenport, 1993; Earl et al., 1995). By doing so, much of the intellectual capital of these organizations was removed making them poorly placed in today's knowledge economy. For these organizations, embracing knowledge management then became a strategic necessity so that they could continue to sustain their market presence. Thus, at one level BPR, in particular poor BPR endeavors made KM initiatives even more important. On the other hand, many organizations that are embracing various KM initiatives are also finding that concurrently with such initiatives, it is prudent to simultaneously incorporate some of the principles of BPR as well so that their key business processes are made as effective and efficient as possible. Thus, the knowledge that is either embedded in these processes or generated by these processes is as useful and relevant as possible. Finally, any successful BPR initiative should embrace a process centric view of knowledge to ensure that the pertinent information and relevant knowledge that is both embedded in critical process within the organization and also generated by these processes is in fact captured, stored, used, and reused by the appropriate decision makers.

Total Quality Management (TQM)

Total quality management is an approach to the art of management that originated in Japanese industry in the 1950s and has steadily become more popular in the West since the early 1980s (Collier, 1992; Kaufman, 1991). Total quality is a description of the culture, attitude, and organization of a company that aims to provide, and continue to provide, its customers with products and services that satisfy their needs. The culture requires quality in all aspects of the company's operations with the emphasis on things being done correctly the first time, and defects and waste eradicated from operations. Important aspects of TQM include customer-driven quality, top management leadership and commitment, continuous improvement, fast response, actions based on facts, employee participation, and a fostering of the TQM culture.

Total quality management is a structured system for satisfying internal and external customers and suppliers by integrating the business environment with continuous improvement and breakthroughs with development, improvement, and maintenance cycles, as well as simultaneously changing organizational culture. Pinpointing internal and external requirements allows focus to be placed on the continuous improvement, development, and maintenance of quality, cost, delivery, and morale. Hence, *TQM* is a management philosophy, based upon a set of principles, and supported by a set of proven methodologies and tools. The underlying principles may seem like *common sense*, but they are certainly not common practice. These include:

1. Focusing the organization on satisfying customers needs;
2. Developing and tapping the full human potential of all employees;
3. Involving everyone in efforts to "find better ways";
4. Managing business processes, not just functions or departments;
5. Managing by fact, using reliable data, and information; and
6. Adding value to society, as well as achieving financial goals.

These principles are applied, not as a succession of stand-alone programs, but as an integrated set of systematic, methodical practices designed to create an effective *management system*. Therefore, total quality management (TQM) is an organizational approach to customer satisfaction involving customers, people, and the continuous improvement of processes. TQM is not an end in itself, rather it is an ongoing process. Central to affecting the principles of TQM is diagnosing the current state of the organization and to do this requires pertinent information and relevant knowledge. Further, given the ongoing nature of TQM such knowledge and information must be continually stored and analyzed, thereby making the integration of knowledge management techniques with any TQM initiative an essential component if a truly successful result is to ensue.

Why TQM?

In a global marketplace, a major characteristic that will distinguish those organizations that are successful will be the quality of leadership, management, employees, work processes, product, and service. This means that products must not only meet customer and community needs for value, they must be provided in a continuously improving, timely, cost-effective, innovative, and productive manner. In today's world, two of the most effective and popular "new" management models are lean manufacturing and sSix sigma. Both of these models utilize the basic TQM elements and add some extra refinements to achieve a more robust and powerful system for customer-focused product and service excellence that also focuses on optimizing costs and profits.

Lean Manufacturing

The need for lean manufacturing has arisen to address the problems, which plague numerous countries in North America, Europe, and Japan. After over a decade of downsizing a re-engineering, many of these companies are still searching for sustainable growth and success. Lean thinking manufacturing helps managers to refocus on the essential elements in order to create and foster customer value. Such a refocusing requires the identification of value-creating activities as well as ensuring that the created value flows through the system to the customer (Womack & Jones, 1996). In such scenarios not only are information and knowledge critical to the identification of value-creating activities but the techniques, tools and strategies of KM play a vital role in ensuring superior realization of the tenets of lean manufacturing.

Six Sigma[1]

The concept of Six Sigma was developed by GE. It is a highly disciplined process that helps the company to focus on developing and delivering near-perfect products and services. The word "Sigma" was chosen since it is a statistical term that measures how far a given process deviates from perfection. The central idea behind Six Sigma is that if you can measure how many "defects" you have in a process, you can systematically figure out how to eliminate them and get as close to "zero defects" as possible.

GE began moving toward a focus on quality in the late 80s. This was a very committed initiative which had the full support of the then CEO Jack Welch. The three key elements of quality were the customer, process, and the employee. Now the organization has an embedded culture that focuses on quality and process thinking. Integral to the success of this initiative was the incorporation of techniques and strategies to capture, analyse, use, and re-use relevant information and knowledge to make critical decisions pertaining to ensuring essentially "zero defects." Thus without the incorporating of knowledge management techniques Six Sigma would not have been as successful.

Total quality is the most important, thought provoking revolution in the world of modern management. Many Fortune 500 firms such as IBM, Hewlett-Packard, Motorola, Ford, and GM have committed themselves to total quality management. A sense of quality awareness now exists in many organizations, owing to the international adoption of ISO 9000 as the Quality Standard for the purchase of goods and services. There is, therefore, an enormous demand for quality professionals with the needs of both the private and public sectors. The increasing importance of quality management has prompted more than 30 countries (including China, the U.S., the EEC, and Japan) to adopt the ISO 9000 quality standard for international use. Today, manufacturers of most of the products in world trade are required to meet the ISO 9000 standard.

TQM focuses strongly on the importance of the relationship between customers (internal and external) and supplier. These are known as the *"quality chains"* and they can be broken at any point by one person or one piece of equipment not meeting the requirements of the customer. Failure to meet the requirements in any part of a quality chain has a way of multiplying, and failure in one part of the system creates problems elsewhere, leading to yet more failure and problems, and consequently the situation is exacerbated. The ability to meet customers' (external and internal) requirements is vital. To achieve quality throughout a business, every person in the quality chain must be trained.

Main Principles of TQM

The main principles that underlie TQM are summarized next (Davenport, 1993):

Prevention	Prevention is better than cure. In the long run, it is cheaper to stop products defects than trying to find them.
Zero defects	The ultimate aim is no (zero) defects—or exceptionally low defect levels if a product or service is complicated.
Getting things right first time	Better not to produce at all than produce something defective.
Quality involves everyone	Quality is not just the concern of the production or operations department—it involves everyone, including marketing, finance, and human resources.
Continuous improvement	Businesses should always be looking for ways to improve processes to help quality.
Employee involvement	Those involved in production and operations have a vital role to play in identifying improvement opportunities for quality and in identifying quality problems.

Relevance to Knowledge-Based Enterprises

The principles of TQM, lean manufacturing, and six sigma are too often discussed in isolation and not incorporated into the total KM initiative. Knowledge-based enterprises, however, must pay particular attention to include the key aspects of these techniques and management theories if they are to develop a complete KM initiative that enables them to leverage from their intellectual assets and effect superior operations. If the operations themselves are not efficient and effective, nor do they yield high quality products and/or services a serious problem will ensue; namely the propagation of inefficiencies, errors and faults throughout the system. Thus, the techniques and strategies of KM must be applied in conjunction with other management theories like TQM, lean manufacturing and six sigma, not in isolation. It is for this reason we discuss there theories and principles so as to emphasize the need for a holistic approach.

Enterprise Resource Planning Systems, Supply Chain Management, and Customer Relationship Management

In order to understand supply chain management and customer relationship management and most importantly the relevance of KM in these respective areas, we must first understand the development of enterprise resource planning systems (ERP) and their role especially in e-businesses (Ko, Kirsch, & King, 2005). Concurrently, yet independently of the Web stampede and Internet gold rush, has been the rise of ERP systems. These systems (such as SAP, Baan, Oracle, and PeopleSoft) are steadily and unobtrusively working at reshaping business structure because they attempt to solve the challenges posed by portfolios of disconnected, under-coordinated applications that have outlived their usefulness. ERP systems provide comprehensive management of financial, manufacturing, sales, distribution, and human resources across the enterprise. In addition, they support data "drill down." It is because of these capabilities that ERP systems can address the need for integration particularly across functional departments by overhauling antiquated legacy systems and enabling the uniting of major business processes as well as emphasizing core business processes. The incentives for adopting ERP systems are varied among companies; however, the dominant common thread is the anticipated improvement in IT integrated processes and the business benefits this enables (Kalakota & Robinson, 2001; Norris et al., 2000; Schragenheim, 1999).

Integrating the enterprise has emerged as a critical issue for organizations in all business sectors striving to maintain competitive advantage in today's global environment. Integration not only enables processes to become more efficient and effective, but through integration, it is possible to unlock information and make it available to any user, anywhere, anytime. Traditional thinking has been that if each component of a business process was optimized then the whole process would be optimized. However, now business theorists are recognizing that if a chain of processes is to run at high performance level, each of the individual functional applications must be tightly linked with the other processes around them and thus all processes and sub processes must be considered as a whole. This thinking has given rise to IT supply chain management and the birth of a connected corporation built on a foundation of well integrated enterprise application software; hence a world wide trend to adopting ERP systems.

ERP is the latest in a number of manufacturing and financial information systems that have been devised since the late 1940s to streamline the information flow of goods, from raw materials to finished products (ibid). This flow of information occurs within an enterprise as well as between the enterprise and other entities immediately up and down the supply chain and end users.

From the 1950s to the 1980s, much research was devoted to streamlining the flow of materials (Shutub, 1999). However, the information-centric aspects of business, such as order taking and order fulfillment were sub optimized or defeated by inter-connectivity/communication issues. At this time while the realization was developing for the need for these interconnections, the information and communications technology to enable such a vision was not yet available.

The first steps in systematizing information flow around the manufacturing process were actually taken as early as the 1960s when material requirement planning (MRP) software became available (ibid). Essentially this software enabled the calculation of which materials were required at what manufacturing operation and when they were required. Then the next significant step occurred in the 1980s. At this time efforts were made to make these applications, namely MRP, more robust and better able to generate information based on a more realistic set of assumptions. These efforts culminated in the development manufacturing resource planning (MRPII) (ibid). MRPII represented an enhancement of MRP, adding a layer of sophistication to the basic calculations of MRP but not changing its logic structure. Finally, in the 1990s ERP software emerged (ibid). This software enabled the realization of an integrated supply chain since it provides a "suite" of applications capable of linking all internal transactions. ERP software thus, enables an organization to distribute and access internal information efficiently so that it may be used for decision support inside the company and communicated to business partners throughout the value chain.

ERP is a structured approach to optimizing a company's internal value chain (Simchi-Levi et al., 2000). The software if fully installed across an entire enterprise, connects the components of the enterprise through a logical transmission and sharing of common data. For example when data such as a sale becomes available at one point in the business, it finds its way through the software, which automatically calculates the effects of the transaction on other areas such as manufacturing, inventory, procurement, invoicing and booking the actual sale to the financial ledger. Thus, what ERP really does is organize, codify, and standardize an enterprises business processes and data. The software transforms transactional data into useful information and collates the data so that it can be analyzed. In this way, all of the collected transactional data become information that companies can use to support business decisions.

ERP represents an adaptive technology. Adaptive technologies are those that move earlier technologies forward incrementally. ERP represents an incremental movement from MRP and MRPII. E-business, on the other hand is referred to as a disruptive technology; since, it changes the way people live their lives and do business (Norris et al., 1999). Moreover, in contrast to the incremental evolution of ERP, e-business has made a dramatic impact on the business scene. Some advocates claim that it is the ultimate solution to the information management problems experienced by all organizations. While traditional production management information systems (MRP, MRP II, and ERP) have focused on the movement of information within the enterprise, Web-based technology facilitates movement of information from business to business and from business to consumer, as well as from consumer to business. Thus, the combination of ERP software and Web based technologies, or ERP software that has Web-based capabilities can be a very powerful and essential tool for any organization to collect, and distribute information within and between itself and its key players such as customers and suppliers. In discussing the relationship between e-business and ERP technologies and then identifying the key role for KM, the following key points become important:

1. Most companies need some sort of internal transaction engine to match the internal information flow with the actual flow of goods and/or services. ERP systems provide such an engine.

2. A good e-business operation requires the support of a well-tuned back end system i.e. there must be something behind the Web pages. ERP systems provide such support to streamline all back end functions effectively and efficiently.

3. No one path will lead to success—each company needs to decide on its own strategy, which should be driven primarily by customer, demands, competitive pressure, and the current state of the enterprise and then adopt the technology to support this.

Microsoft, Coca-Cola, Cisco, Hershey Foods, Colgate, and Compaq are a few examples of large companies that have adopted ERP systems, which they believe, have helped them reduce inventories, cycle times, lower costs, and improve overall operations. They identify the key to be that ERP systems work like an information lubricant facilitating the exchange of data among corporate divisions through the unification of key processes. Fujitsu, after a 10 month successful implementation of SAP, is enjoying several benefits from the integration of processes affected by the ERP system such as; 90% reduction in cycle time for quotation from 20 days to 2 days, 60-85% improved on time delivery and 50% reduction in financial closing times from 10 days to 5 days (ibid). Given these tangible benefits, it is not surprising that organizations are now trying to integrate ERP systems with their e-commerce capabilities.

Supply Chain Management

Supply chain management (SCM) involves the adoption of strategies that enable the effective and efficient operation of the logistic network (Birkhead & Schirmer, 1999; Corbett, Blackburn, & Wassenhove, 1999; MacLeod, 2000) (i.e., the integration of suppliers, manufacturers, warehouses, and customers both within and across industries). The issues relating to supply chain management become particularly important in a form of e-commerce that is increasingly becoming more prevalent, namely; business-to-business e-commerce.

Business-to-Business E-Commerce

Business-to-business e-commerce creates new dynamics that differ considerably from those of other e-commerce relationships (Freeman, 1998). Business-to-business (B-to-B) e-commerce solutions frequently automate and impact workflows or supply-chain processes that are fundamental to a business' operations. One of the most challenging areas of Internet-based e-commerce today appears to be B-to-B trading although, ironically it is business–to-consumer e-commerce that receives most public attention. Little is known about B-to-B e-commerce on the net; however, its importance cannot be understated especially given that B-to-B e-commerce is anticipated to grow to at least US$5,330.9 billion by 2007(Kalakota & Robinson, 2001). In addition, it is B-to-B e-commerce that is now driving the demand for ERP systems, given its huge reliance on effective supply chain management. Furthermore, it is B-to-B e-commerce that can benefit most by viewing the integration of e-commerce/ERP systems in the light of a knowledge management perspective.

Supply Chain Management in B-to-B E-Commerce

B-to-B e-commerce essentially replaces the physical processes with electronic ones, creating new models for collaboration with customers and suppliers (MacLeod, 2000). There are many models of B-to–B e-commerce: (1) the supply-oriented marketplace which describes most of the manufacturer driven electronic stores, (2) the buyer-oriented model where large buyers open their own electronic markets and invite potential sellers to bid, and (3) the intermediary marketplace which involves an electronic intermediary company setting up an electronic market place for buyers and sellers. While their clearly exist subtle differences between these models what is of critical importance is that underlying all these models is the need for IT enabled supply chain management to be in place.

IT is an important enabler for effective supply chain management especially with the innovative opportunities coming to the fore with electronic commerce and the Internet. Supply chain management spans the entire organization (with customers on one end and suppliers on the other). The primary goal of supply chain IT is to link the point of production seamlessly with the point of delivery or purchase. By doing so we create an information trail (refer to Figure 2). This information allows planning, tracking, and estimating lead times based on real data as well as enabling us to have knowledge relating to the availability and the status of products and material. Importantly, in IT enabled supply chain management we have the ability to

Figure 2. Information flows through the supply chain

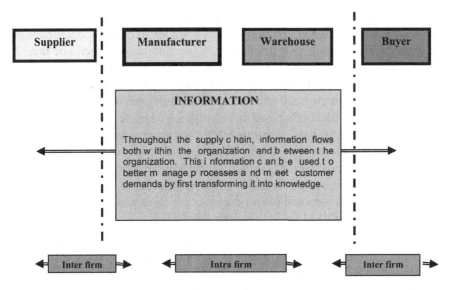

integrate large amounts of information generated anywhere throughout the logistic network in a timely and efficient fashion. This is clearly an advantage, especially given that the impact of e-commerce is to dramatically shrink the dimensions of distance and time. To utilize this information we need to access it, collect it, and analyze it. By having integrating supply chain IT such as ERP systems this not only makes the complex process of supply chain management easier but also enables the generation, storage and utilization of information gathered throughout the logistic network in real time.

Supply channels coordinate the succession of functions required to bring a product from the factory to the customer. One of the impacts of e-commerce is that it dramatically shrinks the dimensions of space and time. In B-to-B e-commerce, this translates into applying excessive pressure on the coordination functions within the supply chain—thus supply chain management becomes critical. Specifically, the technologies associated with e-commerce impact the supply chain in the following ways: (1) eliminate intermediary institutions by substitution or consolidation, using computer and communication technology; (2) do not generally eliminate the intermediary function; and (3) either automate or shift intermediary functions forward or backward, along the supply and marketing chains.

Coupled with these impacts, information, and communication networks are flattening organizations and pushing focus onto their core competencies in order to experience sustainable competitive advantage (Westland & Clark, 2000). The impact of technology on redefining the barriers of time and space is neither new nor unexpected, but the pace and extent of the changes due to the capabilities of the Internet is what has been devastating. Given the growth of e-commerce, it is not surprising that we are now observing a move to more and more B-to-B e-commerce. However, for B-to-B e-commerce to be successful though there needs to be in place robust supply chain management strategies. In a process as complex as supply chain management, systems that not only perform their own function but also facilitate the: (1) collecting of information on each product from production to delivery or purchase point, (2) providing of visibility for all parties involved, (3) accessing of any data in the system from a single point of contact, (4) analysis and planning activities, as well as (5) making of trade-offs based on information from the entire supply chain, are critical. ERP systems have such capabilities. Integrating ERP systems with an organizations e-commerce environment then, offers the enterprise access to several sources of information including: (1) product specifications, prices, sales and history, (2) customer sales history and forecasts, (3) supplier product line and lead times, sales terms, and conditions and (4) product process capacities, commitments and product plans, which should lead to strategic advantages.

Supply chain management involves the adoption of strategies that enable the effective and efficient operation of the logistic network (i.e., the integration of suppliers manufacturers, warehouses, and customers both within and across industries). Given that we now operate in a global environment, the location of various components of the logistic network could feasibly span many continents throughout the world thus making co-ordination, communication as well as effective and efficient operations very challenging.

Supply Chain Integration

In offering e-commerce solutions, organizations face tremendous logistics and supply-chain challenges (Ceri & Bongio, 2000; Cox, 2000). With increasing pressures to enable products to market faster and more efficiently than ever before, organizations need real-time, Web-centric, collaborative logistics technology to increase efficiency by connecting to all their supply-chain partners to achieve the ultimate goal of maximizing shareholder value. Collaborative logistics is the new evolution in supply-chain management because it expands visibility and control beyond the walls of an organization by connecting the company to all elements of the supply chain. The integration of the supplier into the organizational structure adds value to the organization's customers. As price competition ceases to be a global force, the supplier's role will be to add value not just to reduce costs. Customers and suppliers will work together and form inter-organizational teams that will facilitate improved communication between organizations and increase the rate of learning. Benefits will be gained from the effects of sharing mutual experience and knowledge that will result in the whole chain becoming better aligned with the customer's requirements and objectives.

The Reverse Value Chain

Traditionally, information systems were developed based on inward business value chains, which were high value-added internal activities of organizations and their core competencies (Rowley, 2000; Schoonmaker, 2001; Schumacher, 2001; Sharma, Gupta, & Wickramasinghe, 2005; Webb & Gile, 2001). This method of information system development was effective for integrating the internal business processes since it focuses on core business processes, which is the "right" end of a value chain that weaves itself through the structure of a company and out into the marketplace. Unfortunately, this method of looking at only one end of the value chain—in terms of how to leverage core competencies—too often leads to a set of processes that do not create value for customers. Companies typically focused on their own core competencies and too often were blindsided if customer requirements shifted in a direction counter to the way their core competencies are aligned. Therefore, traditional information systems although creating many automation benefits, are still lacking in improving the customer end of the value chain. By reversing the value chain (i.e., taking a customer as apposed to the traditional inward focus) many e-commerce revolutionaries have gained a competitive edge.

In traditional reengineering activities, management would leverage the core competency through a set of efficient business processes so as to bring a well-defined set of products and services to market (i.e., products and services that best use the core competencies of the organization). Next identification of the sales and distribution channels that best served the market were addressed. Using this approach, management would build value around a process and push the firm's competency to the market in an efficient manner.

By building value around the process, companies were efficiently pushing products and services to market. However, the rigid processes the applications demanded provided static efficiencies in a dynamic world. With the dynamics of the new economy, business processes must be flexible, and it may be necessary to outsource what were once core competencies to organizations better able to perform these tasks.

Customer Relationship Management (CRM)

CRM stands for customer relationship management. It is a strategy used to learn more about customers' needs and behaviors in order to develop stronger relationships with them (Talley & Mitchell, 2000; Timmers, 1999; Turban et al., 2000; Westland & Clark, 1999). Undoubtedly, good customer relationships are at the heart of business success. There are many technological components to CRM, but thinking about CRM in primarily technological terms is a mistake. The more useful way to think about CRM is as a process that will help bring together various of information about customers, sales, marketing effectiveness, responsiveness and market trends. CRM is a business strategy that integrates people, process, and technology to enhance relationships with customers, partners, distributors, suppliers, and employees to maximize revenue growth and market share. CRM is a comprehensive initiative that provides seamless coordination among sales, marketing, service, field support, and all other customer-facing functions.

CRM has evolved since its earliest manifestation, originally driven by an inside-out focus, through three phases of evolution: technology, integration, and process. Recently we have seen a major leap forward to a fourth phase: customer-driven CRM—an outside-in approach that has intriguing financial promise.

1. **Technology:** In its earliest incarnation, CRM meant applying automation to existing sales, marketing, support and channel processes as organizations attempted to improve communications, planning, opportunity, and campaign management, forecasting, problem solving, and to share best practices (Birkhead, 1999). To some degree, it worked. However, automating poorly performing activities or processes rarely improves the quality of the outcome. Consequently making the quality of the return on investment (ROI) meager—if measurable at all. Although the promise of the technology existed, few organizations were realizing the pinnacle of performance. The metric of success was increased efficiency in sales, marketing, support, and channel processes.

2. **Integration:** By developing cross-functional integration, supported by data warehousing and shared roles and responsibilities, organizations began to create a customized view of the customer. Support issues, Web hits, sales calls, and marketing inquiries started building a deeper understanding of each customer and allowed aggressive organizations to adapt their tactics to fit individual needs. Integration focused around two primary components (KPMG, 2001):

    •   **Make it easier to do business with the seller:** Instead of operational silos that inhibited superior customer relationships, the organization as a whole took ownership and responsibility for customer satisfaction. With a single view of the customer, it was much easier for anyone to respond to sales opportunities or impending support issues and take appropriate steps. Expected benefits are to improve retention and lower support costs.

    •   **Predictive modeling:** Data mining of an aggregate of corporate knowledge and the customer contact experience was used to improve operational and sales performance. By applying complex algorithms to a history of purchasing or inquiry characteristics, it became practical to predict the demands of individual customers. Up-selling, cross-selling, even the ability to preempt potential problems, was now possible for all customer-facing representatives. Expected benefits are to have better cross-selling/up-selling and improved product offerings or delivery.

3. **Process:** By rethinking the quality and effectiveness of customer-related processes, many organizations began to eliminate unnecessary activities, improve outdated processes, and redesign activities that had failed to deliver the desired outcomes. Then, by re-creating the process through an understanding of the capabilities of the technology, the outcomes were more predictable and the promises for a meaningful ROI more substantial and realistic. The metrics for success became the improved effectiveness in serving the customer.

Thus far, almost everything about CRM has focused on improving the effectiveness and efficiency of the seller's organization (Bickert, 1997; Chen & Jeng, 2000; Hymas, 2001; Meltzer, 2002). Organizations have evolved from sales representatives working from paper notebooks, or a card system, to a tightly integrated network that sees movement in sales activity, predicts product demand on manufacturing, and manages the logistics of complex teams to serve the buyer and seller. Marketing, support services, channel management, revenue management, resource allocation/management, forecasting, manufacturing, logistics, and even research and development have all seen the benefits of a well-designed CRM strategy.

What is the Goal of CRM?

The idea of CRM is that it helps businesses use technology and human resources to gain insight into the behavior of customers and the value of those customers (Chablo, 2000; Dewan, Jing, & Seidmann, 1999; Jiang, 2000; Marshak, 1999; Yaman, 2001). It can help business to:

1. Provide better customer service.
2. Make call centers more efficient.
3. Cross sell products more effectively.
4. Help sales staff close deals faster.
5. Simplify marketing and sales processes.
6. Discover new customers.
7. Increase customer revenues.

CRM continues to be the most vibrant, critical, and evolving technology category in today's market. CRM today is no longer only concerned with enterprise software. Rather, today's CRM is a flexible solution where you can mix software, hosted services, and other components to meet your specific business needs. It goes beyond sales, marketing, and customer service applications into business intelligence, analytics, hosted applications, mobile capabilities, and much more.

No doubt, today's most serious business and technology challenges are surrounding:

- Acquiring and retaining customers.
- Customer loyalty.
- Increasing customer profitability.

Addressing these challenges is imperative to any company's success. In order to succeed in today's competitive environment, one needs to understand the business and technology challenges that support customer acquisition, retention, and loyalty. With a focus on CRM, one will be able to leverage every resource within company to satisfy customers and develop lasting and rewarding customer relationships.

Role of Knowledge Management

In all ERP initiatives and especially in relation to supply chain management and customer relationship management, the timely access to relevant information and superior knowledge is critical. Not only does such information and knowledge facilitate well functioning processes but it is also through the ability to access required information and knowledge that critical decisions such as effective ordering of stock or identifying and supporting customer needs can be made. Thus, ERP systems provide the technology to enable organizations to effect efficient supply chains and effective customer relations but it is the knowledge and more specifically the application of this knowledge in making sound decision-making that ensures the full added value benefits. This makes the incorporating of the techniques of knowledge management in such initiatives a critical success factor in enterprise integration.

Enterprise Integration

As we have already discussed, business-to-business e-commerce is now driving much of the ERP demand. In fact, it is providing the opportunity to bring these two, once disparate IT developments, together. Some people go as far as to claim that ERP is now the backbone of e-business because it provides the enterprise-wide application software that enables a centralized repository of information for the massive amount of transaction detail generated.

We are currently observing the development of three distinct architectures for integrating e-commerce with ERP systems (Afuah & Tucci, 2003; Barsky & Ellinger, 2001). These include (1) the inside-out approach, (2) the outside-in approach, and (3) the open electronic cart.

Figure 3a. Architectures of integrating e-commerce with ERP systems: The inside-out approach

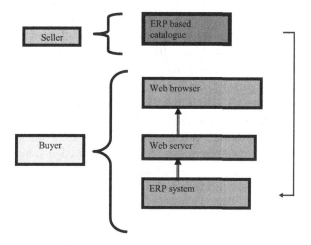

Figure 3b. Architectures of integrating e-commerce with ERP systems: The outside-in approach

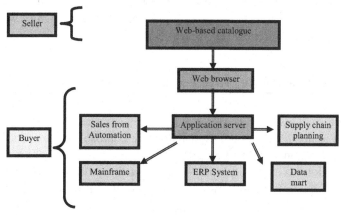

The inside-out approach involves extending the ERP application systems to users through a Web interface (refer to Figure 3a). This configuration enables companies to distribute ERP transaction capabilities to a wide audience of Web users without requiring that they load any specific client software.

The outside-in approach uses a robust software or application server such as Lotus' Domino or Microsoft's Enterprise Server to integrate multiple systems into an e-business solution (refer to Figure 3b).

In the open electronic cart approach, the buyer has a shopping cart that resides on the buyers PC. Items from multiple sources can then be stored by the buyer in this electronic cart. The order too can be made and stored in this cart. Because the electronic cart has an open file format the ERP system can be easily interfaced.

Integrating supply chain management through ERP and connecting this with the B-to-B e-commerce activities is critical for organizations operating in a B-to-B e-commerce environment. Irrespective of the architecture adopted, the integration of e-commerce and ERP systems is enabling a massive information repository to result. However, the full value of this integration is not, as yet being realized. The information that is being gathered throughout the logistic network is causing information overload and a burden, rather than an asset that can be managed to enable the organizations to achieve a strategic advantage. The full benefits and ultimate sustainable competitive advantage can only be realized if these integrated systems are viewed as knowledge management systems and knowledge management takes place. It is by applying knowledge management techniques that it becomes possible for organizations to maximize this information asset and thus achieve a sustainable competitive advantage.

ERP as the Backend of E-Business

The integrated ERP system should form the hub of the e-business providing support to existing business strategies, opening the door to new strategic opportunities, adding greater customer value, and creating tightly coupled relationships with trading parties (Barsky & Ellinger, 2001). We depict this in Figure 4.

Enterprise-Wide Integrated E-Commerce Portal

E-commerce is not just a virtual storefront for online transactions anymore. We need only to look at the demise of the myriad dot com companies as evidence. Today's e-commerce solutions need to have all facets of their businesses online, from customer interactions to extended supply-chain management with trading partners. A few years ago, e-commerce platforms were focused primarily on handling transac-

Figure 4. ERP as the backend of e-business

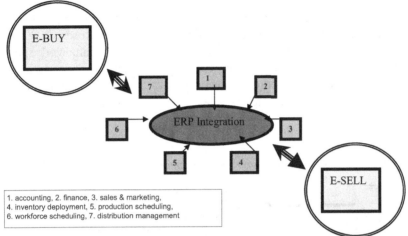

tions and managing catalogs. Buying and selling over the Web was still a novel concept, and the e-commerce application providers offered limited functionality. Today, businesses are demanding more than just online transaction support. An essential component of fully fledged e-businesses is an enterprise-wide e-commerce portal that helps them to build relationships with customers; be it in a business-to-business (B-2-B), business-to-consumer (B-2-C), or online marketplace model (Meister, Patel, & Fenner, 2000). The corporation must have the enterprise portal, an integrated software which can house its databases, file servers, Web pages, e-mails, ERP (enterprise resource planning), and CRM (customer relationship management) systems accessible to all its constituents.

Developing such an integrated enterprise-wide e-commerce portal to support B2C and B2B electronic business models is one of the major challenges for software developers. It requires integration of many technologies including Web modeling languages, data content, interface tools, content delivery tools, messaging technologies, etc., to combine in one integrated storefront (Ceri & Bongio, 2000). The e-commerce portal should be able to support complete multimedia formats and should be automatically enabled for WAP (wireless application protocol) to allow mobile shoppers to buy anytime, anywhere (Talley & Mitchell, 2000). Further, it should support all Web scripting languages. The e-commerce portal should have the ability for different users to access a wide range of information and services in a customized fashion between its employees, customers and partners; and where the content and services comprise the information resources, products, and services of the enterprise (Rosen, 2000). Currently, most applications do not communicate with each other, resulting in significant reduction in the flow of critical information, which impacts productivity and ultimately the bottom line.

Framework for Enterprise-Wide E-Commerce Portal

As organizations develop enterprise-wide e-commerce portals we believe hat KM must play a key role (von Lubitz & Wickramasinghe, 2006; Rosen, 2000). We highlight this in the framework we present in Figure 5. Our framework specifically emphasizes integration of the many disparate e-commerce systems. Such an Enterprise-wide e-commerce portal is intended to offer a single focal centralized point for linking to a collection of applications, and a method for initiating processes

Figure 5. Framework for enterprise-wide e-commerce portal

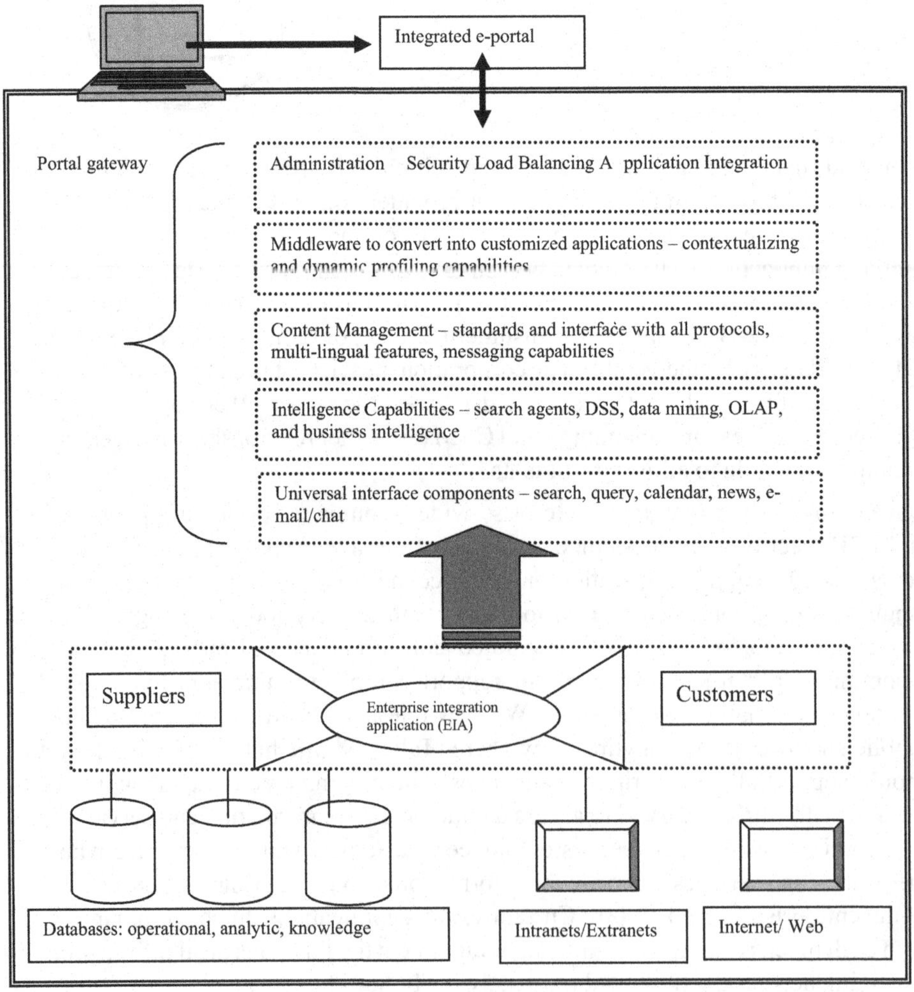

that transcend multiple systems. In an integrated portal, users can go to one place and perform searches across disparate repositories such as a Lotus Notes database, Microsoft Exchange public folders, Web sites, file systems, databases, and a collection of other repositories (Ceri & Bongio, 2000; Hille, 2001; Retter & Calyniuk, 1998; Stehle, 2001). Portal's core functions include e-mail, group calendaring and scheduling, shared folders/databases, threaded discussions, and custom application development to support B2C and B2B business models. Furthermore such a portal should include all of the following capabilities: (1) workflow and routing of documents; (2) discussion threads; (3) User-chat sessions; (4) dynamic group and team creation; (5) interactive collaboration, including video, voice, and application sharing; (6) cross-repository searching; (7) business intelligence; (8) CRM; (9) discussion threads; (10) document management; (11) e-mail; (12) ERP; (13) online chats; (14) personal and group calendar; (15) reporting; (16) sales-force automation. All of these capabilities can be grouped into broad categories such as database design, messaging technologies, supply chain, multilingual content, security solutions, electronic payment systems, content management, middleware and knowledge management and thus the framework evolves as depicted in Figure 5.

Current Web pages in general and especially current medical Web-portals and on-line databases such as Medline provide the decision maker with voluminous information that he/she must then synthesize to determine relative and general relevance; i.e., they are passive in nature. In contrast, we suggest that a "smart" portal (Figure 4.6a) that enables the possibility to access the critical information rapidly is more useful and should be the future of portal design (von Lubitz & Wickramasinghe, 2006). Sequential knowledge generation is achieved by the decision maker initiating a search from the smart portal and receiving the necessary germane knowledge pertaining to that request, where this germane knowledge is generated by utilizing the intelligence capabilities of the smart portal (Figure 6b) and hence provides assimilated and synthesized information that is relevant and structured in a useable fashion to the decision maker. Thus, the smart portal is active and provides the decision maker or effector with relevant data, information, and knowledge so he or she does not need to determine the relevance of relative pieces of information and knowledge rather only needs to apply the knowledge and information to make a sound decision.

Other design elements unique to the smart portal (Figures 6a and 6b) include the ability to navigate well through the system (i.e., the smart portal must have a well structured grid map to identify what information is coming from where, or what information is being uploaded to where). In order to support the ability of the smart portal to bring all relevant information and knowledge located throughout the system to the decision maker there must be universal standards and protocols that ensure the free flowing and seamless transfer of information and data; the ultimate in shared services. Finally, given the total access to the system provided by the smart portal to the decision maker it is vital that the highest level of security protocols

Figure 6a. Smart portal

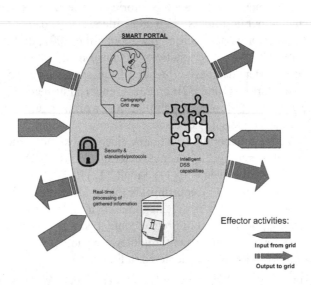

Figure 6b. Intelligence capabilities of the smart portal

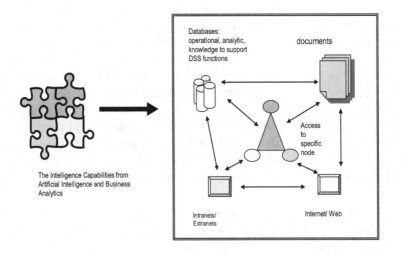

are maintained at all times; thereby ensuring the integrity of the system at all times. The smart portal provides us with a vision of the future and serves to underscore the confluence of ERP, e-business, and knowledge management. Moreover, it is important to stress that while ERP and e-business techniques are necessary for its correct functioning, it is through the incorporation of the techniques of knowledge management that the true power of the portal can be realized.

Chapter Summary

The myriad business processes together constitute the business infrastructure of an organization. Current management initiatives such as TQM, BPR, SCM, and CRM are aimed at trying to ensure these processes are more effective and efficient. Contemporaneously, growth in B-to-B ecommerce is necessitating even faster and hyper efficient and effective flows of information, while the advent of ERP has necessitated re-evaluation of traditional "back-end" business functions. Organizations spend millions of dollars trying to design and develop more effective and suitable business process however, without an understanding the role of knowledge in these processes or the utilization of the data, information and knowledge generated by various business processes, all attempts at making business processes will be sub-optimal. The tools and techniques of knowledge management must be applied in conjunction with any or all these initiatives before organizations can maximize the full benefit of their business infrastructure and ensure that they are in fact designing and implementing value-adding process. All initiatives such as TQM, BPR, SCM, and CRM will never be truly successful unless they incorporate knowledge management.

References

Afuah, A., & Tucci, C. (2003). *Internet business models and strategies*. Boston: McGrawHill.

Barsky, N. P., & Ellinger, A. E. (2001). Unleashing the value in the supply chain. *Strategic Finance, 82*(7), 32-37.

Bashein, B. J., Markus, M. L., & Riley, P. (1994). Preconditions for BPR success: And how to prevent failures. *Information Systems Management, 11*(2), 7-13.

Berwick, D. M., Godfrey, A. B., & Roessner, J. (1990). *Curing health care: New strategies for quality improvement*. San Francisco: Jossey-Bass Publishers.

Bickert, J. (1997). Cohorts II: A new approach to market segmentation. *Journal of Consumer Marketing, 14*(4-5), 362-380.

Birkhead, B. (1999). *Behavioral segmentation systems: A perspective.* Macon Consulting Ltd. Retrieved from http://www.crm-forum.com/library/macon/macon-002/brandframe.html

Birkhead, N., & Schirmer, R. (1999). Add value to your supply chain. *Transportation & Distribution, 40*(9), 51-60.

Caron, M., Jarvenpaa, S. L., & Stoddard, D. B. (1994, September). Business reengineering at CIGNA Corporation: Experiences and lessons learned from the first five years. *MIS Quarterly*, 233-250.

Ceri, S. P. F., & Bongio, A. (2000). Web modeling language (WebML): A modeling language for designing Web sites. *Computer Networks, 33*(1-6), 137-157.

Chablo, E. (2000). *The importance of marketing data intelligence in delivering successful CRM.* SmartFOCUS Ltd. Retrieved from http://www.crm-forum.com/library/ven/ven-017/ven-017_clean.htm

Checkland, P. (1999). *Systems thinking, systems practice.* Chichester, UK: Wiley.

Checkland, P., & Scholes, J. (1990). *Soft systems methodology.* Chichester, UK: Wiley.

Chen, Y. T., & Jeng., B. A. (2000). Customer segmentation mining system on the Web platform. *America's Conference on Information Systems*, Long Beach, CA. Omnipress.

Collier, J. C. (1992, August). Becoming empowered through TQM. *Quality Digest*, 29-34.

Collins, A. (1990, May/June). Quality control as a model for education: It would improve our output. *Engineering Education*, 470-471.

Corbett, C. J., Blackburn, J. D., & Wassenhove, L. N. V. (1999). Partnerships to improve supply chains. *Sloan Management Review, 40*(4), 71-82.

Cox, J. (2000). E-commerce changing the face of databases. *Network World, 17*(31), 38.

Davenport, T. H. (1993). *Process innovation.* Boston: Harvard Business School Press.

Davenport, T. H. (1994, July). Reengineering: Business change of mythic proportions? *MIS Quarterly*, 121-127.

Davenport & Prusak. (1998). *Working knowledge.* Boston: Harvard Business School Press.

Davenport, T. H., & Beers, M. C. (1995). Managing information about processes. *Journal of Management Information Systems, 12*(1), 57-80.

Davenport, T. H., & Short, J. E. (1990, Summer). The new industrial engineering: Information technology and business process redesign. *Sloan Management Review*, 11-27.

Dewan, R., Jing, B., & Seidmann, A. (1999). One-to-one marketing on the Internet. The *20ᵗʰ International Conference on Information Systems*, Charlotte, North Carolina. Omnipress.

Earl, M. J., Sampler, J. L., & Short, J. E. (1995). Strategies for business process reengineering: Evidence from field studies. *Journal of Management Information Systems, 12*(1), 31-56.

Evans, P., & Wurster, T. (1999). Strategy and the new economies of information. In D. Tapscott (Ed.), *Creating value in the networked economy*. Boston: Harvard Business Press.

Flood, R. (1999). *Rethinking the fifth discipline*. London: Routledge.

Freeman, L. (1998, January). *Net drives B-to-B to new highs worldwide*. NetMarketing.

Hammer, M., & Champy, J. (1994). *Re-engineering the corporation*. Sydney: Allen & Unwin.

Hille, E. (2001). The 10 rules for evaluating an e-mail management solution. *Customer Inter@Ction Solutions*, 19(8), 50-54.

Hymas, J. (2001). *Online marketing: Segmentation and targeted customer strategies for the Web*. Macon Consulting Ltd. Retrieved from http://www.crm-forum.com/library/macon/macon-008/brandframe.html

Jiang, P. (2000). Segment-based mass customization: An exploration of a new conceptual marketing framework. *Internet Research*, 10(3), 215-226.

Jones, G. (2001). E-mail management technologies: A purchaser's primer. *Customer Inter@Ction Solutions*, 19(8), 56-59.

Kalakota, R., & Robinson, M. (2001). *e-Business 2.0*. Boston: Addison Wesley.

Kaufman, R. (1991, December). Toward total quality "Plus." *Training*, 50-54.

Ko, D., Kirsch, L., & King, W. (2005). Antecedents of knowledge transfer from consultants to clients in enterprise systems implementations. *MIS Quarterly*, 29(1), 59-85.

KPMG. (2001). *Customer relationship management: Delivering value through sales, marketing, and services*. KPMG Consulting. Retrieved from http://www.kpmgconsulting.com/library/pdfs/c2103_CRMWP.pdf

MacLeod, M. (2000). Language barriers. *Supply Management*, 5(14), 37-38.

Marshak, R. T. (1999). The many faces of marketing automation. Complementary - not competitive - technologies. *E-Business Strategies & Solutions*, 28-31.

Meister, F., Patel, J., & Fenner, J. (2000). E-commerce platforms mature. *Informationweek, 809,* 99-108.

Meltzer, M. (2002). *Segment your customers based on profitability.* Applied Management Technologies. Retrieved from http://www.crm-forum.com/library/art/art-160/

Norris, G. et al. 2000. *E-business and ERP, Pricewaterhousecoopers.* Chichester, UK: John Wiley & Sons.

Retter, T., & Calyniuk, M. (1998). *Technology forecast.* Pricewaterhouse.

Rosen, M. (2000). Enterprise portals: A single point of access to corporate data. *Software Magazine, 20*(5), 22-24.

Rowley, J. (2000). The reverse supply-chain impact of current trends. *Logistics and Transport Focus, 2*(6), 27-31.

Schoonmaker, M. (2001). Opinion: Rosettanet standards provide full e-biz process architecture, Ebn; Manhasset; Issue 1253, pp. PG 43, Mar 12.

Schumacher, E. (2001). Collaborative logistics. *Traffic World, 265*(8), 29.

Senge, P. (1990). *The fifth discipline.* New York: Random House.

Shappiro, C., & Verian, H. (1999). *Information rules.* Boston: Harvard Business School Press.

Sharma, S., Gupta, J., & Wickramasinghe, N. (2002). *A framework for designing the enterprise-wide e-commerce portal for evolving organizations.* Electronic Commerce Research, submission.

Shutub, A. (1999). *Enterprise resource planning.* Boston: Kluwer Academic Publishing.

Simchi-Levi, D., et al. (2000). *Designing & managing the supply chain.* Boston: Irwin McGraw-Hill.

Stehle, D. (2001). System performance depends on middleware. *Material Handling Management, 56*(2), ADF4-ADF6.

Talley, B., & Mitchell, L. (2000). Which product should you choose to quickly develop a database-driven commerce site? *InfoWorld, 22*(38), 82.

Timmers, P. (1999). *Electronic commerce.* Chichester, UK: John Wiley.

Turban, E. et al. 2000. *Electronic commerce.* Upper Saddle River, NJ: Prentice Hall.

von Lubitz, D., & Wickramasinghe, N. (2006). Networkcentric healthcare: The entry point into the network (forthcoming). In A. Tattnall (Ed.), *Encyclopaedia of Portal Technology and Applications.* Hershey, PA: Idea Group Publishing.

Webb, J., & Gile, C. (2001). Reversing the value chain. *The Journal of Business Strategy, 22*(2), 13-17.

Weil, P., & Broadbent, M. (1998). *Leveraging the new infrastructure*. Boston: Harvard Business Press.

Westland, C., & Clark, T. (1999). *Global electronic commerce*. Cambridge: MIT Press.

Womack, J., & Jones, D. (1996). *Lean thinking*. New York: Simon-Schuster.

Yaman, B. (2001). Web systems management means managing business processes. *Communications News*, *38*(5), 14.

Endnote

[1]   Refer to http://www.ge.com/sixsigma/ for complete details on Six Sigma at GE.

Chapter V

The Organization's Human Infrastructure

Introduction

The integral component of the organizational infrastructure is its people. Without people, even a virtual organization could not function. People give any organization life, purpose, and its "raison d'être." This is even more true when we focus on knowledge management. Ultimately, whatever the type of knowledge (e.g., tacit or explicit) with which we are concerned with, organizational knowledge cannot exist without people (Boland & Tenkasi, 1995; Swan, Scarbrough, & Preston, 1999). In the knowledge economy, the knowledge worker, a term coined to describe an expert decision maker who has significant autonomy, has a critical role to the success, growth, and sustainability of the organization (Beckman, 1999; Cortada, 1998).

People within an organization are influenced by the culture and structure of the organization (Martin, 1992)—its microenvironment. In order for knowledge management to be embraced and flourish in an organization the underlying culture and structure of that organization must be clearly understood. Further, it is important to understand the leadership and management style of the organization (Senge, 1996). Thus, key elements that together form the unit level of the organization's human infrastructure include the issues of culture, structure, leadership, and management, and team dynamics. If special attention is not paid to these components, the KM initiative will be doomed to failure.

Knowledge Workers

In the knowledge economy, knowledge workers are considered the most valuable resource. Reich (1992) argues that it is only through the working together of knowledge workers that true competitive advantage can ever be achieved. The term "knowledge worker" was first coined by Peter Drucker in the 1960s (Cortada, 1998; Drucker, 1993, 1999). More recently in the 1990s, Drucker and others have repeatedly noted that we have entered a period where the basic resource is knowledge and the knowledge worker is to play a central role in organizations (Cortada, 1998; Drucker, 1993, 1999; Wickramasinghe & Ginzberg, 2001; Wigg, 1993). The most significant distinguishing aspect of knowledge workers is their ownership of the means of production (i.e., their expertise and knowledge) (Wickramasinghe & Ginzberg, 2001).

The rise of the knowledge worker in the current workforce is primarily due to the fact that since the 1990s, this type of worker has been a key employee in the business world and most job growth in developed nations has been for people with these skills (Davenport & Prusak, 1998; Drucker, 1993, 1999). While the existence of knowledge workers is not unique to the knowledge economy, the important difference between knowledge workers in previous ages, as apposed to knowledge workers in the knowledge economy, is that they did not dominate the work force as they do today (Probst et al., 2000). Furthermore, it is only now in the knowledge economy that we have a knowledge worker, Bill Gates, as the wealthiest man in the world (Allee, 1997; Probst et al., 1998; Scott Morton, 1991).

Apart from talent, intelligence, training, and often extensive expertise required in execution of their professions, the majority of knowledge workers share other distinctive characteristics (Kanter, 1999; Wickramasinghe & Ginzberg, 2001): they constitute the most valuable asset to the organization and their work activities are complex, non-repetitive and, hence, typically difficult to evaluate (Kanter, 1999; Wickramasinghe & Ginzberg, 2001). Hence, knowledge workers are identified as possessing specialized skills and training that have taken time and considerable investment to develop. In addition, the knowledge worker plays a key role, since the decisions [primarily unstructured decisions (Wickramasinghe, 2003)] made by him or her have a significant impact on the organization in which he or she is employed. Knowledge work can be defined as non-repetitive, non-routine work that entails substantial levels of cognitive activity (Wickramasinghe & Ginzberg, 2001). Thus, knowledge work is challenging and non-routine, or it can be described as relating to the solving of non-programmed tasks or unstructured decisions. Knowledge workers then can be defined as a select subset of employees who own the means of production (i.e., their knowledge (ibid.)). They possess specialized skills and training, which they have acquired by investing significant resources (time, money) for their education. In addition, knowledge workers are empowered and have the autonomy to make decisions that have far reaching consequences for the organization for which they work (ibid.).

Knowledge workers are not a homogeneous group. For example, if we think about professionals such as doctors and lawyers as distinct from researchers as distinct from high level executives, while they all fall into the definition of knowledge workers, since they possess specialized skills and training, which they have acquired by investing significant resources (time, money) for their education, they are empowered and have the autonomy to make decisions that have far reaching consequences for the respective organization for which they work, yet they are different and distinct too. They have a different set of specialized skills and are differentiated into subcategories through their specialized skill sets. It is possible then to sub-divide knowledge workers into four basic types (Snowden, 2002): (a) integrators who operate in a complex domain such as managers, (b) pathfinders who operate in a complicated domain such as professionals, (c) dividers who operate with the unknown domain such as researchers and scientists, and (d) catalysts who operate in the chaotic domain such as artists and philosophers.

Capturing Knowledge from Knowledge Workers

An important area of knowledge management is concerned with the capturing of knowledge from experts or knowledge workers. The captured critical knowledge is primarily tacit (Nonaka, 1991, 1994; Wickramasinghe & Mills, 2001) and to be of use to the organization at large it must be transformed and then stored in repositories for later use and re-use thereby increasing organizational memory (Alavi, 1999; Liebowitz, 1999; Maier & Lehner, 2000). In particular, this requires the transferring of problem-solving expertise from a knowledge worker or expert source to a repository or a program (Alavi & Leidner, 1999; Alavi & Leidner, 2001; Borghoff & Pareschi, 1998) as well as fostering a knowledge sharing culture (Bock, Zmud, Kim, & Lee, 2005; Wasko & Faraj, 2005). To do this systematically, a process by which the expert's thoughts and experiences are collected must be invoked. Typically, in such a process of knowledge extraction and capture, a knowledge developer collaborates with an expert to convert expertise into a coded program.

Capturing how experts know what they know is the key goal in such a process. Thus, knowledge developers focus on how experts approach a problem, look beyond the facts or the heuristics, re-evaluate how well they understand the problem domain, and how accurately they are modeling it (ibid.). Curiously, the sequence is largely similar to the four stages of the OODA Loop: Essentially, they are tracing through an expert's ability to outline the four steps of the OODA Loop: observation, orientation, determination, and action. To extract this information, knowledge developers usually interview experts using a variety of interview techniques including structured, semi-structured, and unstructured interview methods (Wickramasinghe, 2003). Generally, the choice of the expert is made based on some of the following criteria such as peers and co-workers regard for the expert's decisions, "who is the person called" (i.e., the expert is consulted) every time there is a problem, the person who exhibits an exceptional quality in explanations and knows when to follow hunches and in all cases (or more often than others) a correct or appropriate solution ensues.

In extracting knowledge from experts, it is possible for the knowledge developer to use a single expert or multiple experts (Kelly, 1990; Malhotra, 2000). The advantages of using a single expert include ease and cost minimisation. In general, it is ideal to have a single expert when building a simple KM system or if the problem is in a restricted domain, since it facilitates the logistics aspect of coordinating arrangements for knowledge capture, and problem-related or personal conflicts are easier to be resolved (ibid.). However, the shortcomings of such an approach include: (1) that the expert's knowledge is not easy to capture, (2) single experts provide only a single line of reasoning, which makes it difficult to evoke in-depth discussion of the domain, and (3) not all expert knowledge resides with the single expert (ibid.). Thus, an important trade-off in knowledge extraction can be best summarized as a cost or convenience versus quality or depth of knowledge. We note that such a choice must be made prudently and the limitations with either scenario need to be considered carefully.

Table 1. Case illustration of knowledge extraction from expert

---

Case Illustration:

In an iron ore processing plant, Smelt Best in the Mid-West of the US, Bob was the chief engineer who had managed the emission flows to be within EPA requirements for many years. But Bob was at retiring age and thus left the company. When Bob left, the emission flows went out of control and the company was having major problems in trying to calibrate the mix of gases in order to bring the emissions under control. This scenario was presenting a huge problem to the company. They decided to send a knowledge developer, Tyg, who had no expertise in the processing of iron ore but was well trained in the disciplines of AI and Computer Science, to extract the critical knowledge from Bob so they could store this within the organization and develop an appropriate system to handle this problem. Through a series of questions, structured, semi-structured, and unstructured as well as the running of small tests that took several weeks it was discovered ultimately how the various gases could be controlled and the order of the smelting process so that EPA emission levels were met at all times. The task was not easy since Bob would just carry out certain functions without having a solid foundation of why he did something when he did--truly reflective that Bob had acquired this knowledge over years of experience. Tyg then developed an intelligent knowledge management system based on Bob's tacit knowledge and explicit knowledge of key industry facts to address the problem of emissions for Smelt Best.

Whereas in the case of multiple experts the primary advantages include: (1) the fact that complex problem domains benefit from the expertise of more than one expert and (2) working with multiple experts stimulates interaction and the listening to a variety of views which allows the knowledge developer to consider alternative ways of representing the knowledge, while the major drawbacks include: (1) coordination and scheduling difficulties, (2) disagreements and/or divergent opinions, and 3) confidentiality issues (Kelly, 1990; Malhotra, 2000; Snowden, 2002). Table 1 illustrates the process taken from a real-life case vignette where the names of the company have naturally been changed. The material point to note from this case vignette is Bob's tacit knowledge, which went unnoticed while he was employed but was in fact the critical skill that kept the emission levels within appropriate EPA levels. This scenario is very common for many organizations and thus makes the capturing and recording of expertise (tacit knowledge) of a knowledge worker a key activity in an organization's KM initiative.

Monitoring and Control of Knowledge Workers

Monitoring and control of its workforce is an important consideration for all organizations. The task becomes more complex in the context of the knowledge worker given that this employee has unique expertise and typically must be monitored by those who do not possess equivalent expertise. The key still lies in trying to align the goals of knowledge workers with those of the organizations for which they work. This requires an expansion of the fundamental tenets of classical agency theory, a well-known economic theory that is concerned with goal alignment into the scenario of a knowledge worker agent (Wickramasinghe, 2000).

From a classical economic perspective, a firm is a unified entity that seeks to maximise profit. Classical agency theory however shows that this is not necessarily the case (Jensen & Meckling, 1973, 1992). The theory describes the firm as consisting of agency relationships between a principal or manager and an agent or employee. The key being that the principal requires the agents to carry out certain tasks. In doing so it cannot be guaranteed that the decisions made by the agents will be aligned with the goals of the principal. Therefore the principal needs to guard against sub-optimal behaviour and the divergence between the agent performing activities which do not facilitate the achievement of the principal's goals. In attempting to align the goals of the agent with those of the principal, the principal must incur some costs referred to as agency costs (Jensen & Meckling, 1973, 1992; Wickramasinghe, 2000). Agency costs consist of monitoring costs, residual loss, and decision information costs

A monitoring activity is considered to be an activity conducted by the principal such as direct monitoring, as well as other methods of evaluating performance or even ways to limit the tasks the agent performs, to ensure that the outcomes are as the principal would desire (ibid.). Thus, the monitoring costs are the costs associated with performing the monitoring activities. By incurring monitoring costs, goal-aligned behaviour increases. Residual loss represents the loss to the principal despite trying to align goals (ibid.). As residual loss increases goal alignment decreases. The relationships between goal alignment and monitoring and residual loss are depicted in Figure 1.

Decision information (DI) costs are defined as the costs associated with moving localized information from the agent to the principal so that the principal can make a sound decision (ibid.). As the information moves up to the principal, the DI cost increases and goal alignment increases. This relationship is depicted in Figure 2.

In order to achieve a high level of goal alignment, principles have the option of incurring higher levels of monitoring or increasing the decision information costs. However, in the case of a knowledge worker agent who has autonomy to make

Figure 1. Goal alignment, monitoring costs, and residual loss (Adapted from Wickramasinghe, 1999)

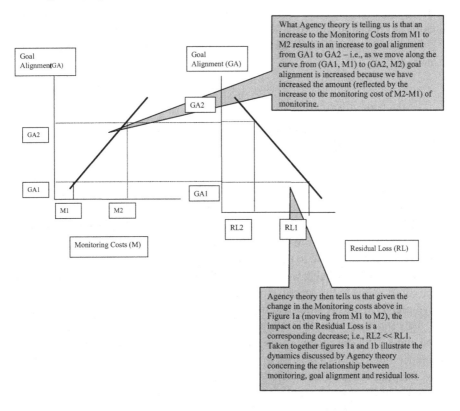

Figure 2. Goal alignment and decision information costs (Adapted from Wickramasinghe, 1999)

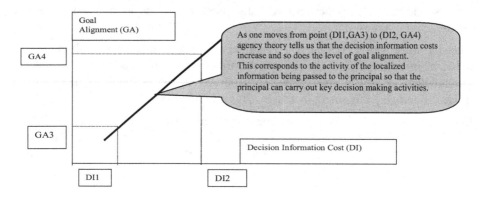

decisions, the decision right is with the knowledge worker agent (i.e., he or she makes the key decisions. In terms of the three costs previously mentioned, this means that (Wickramasinghe, 2000; Wickramasinghe & Ginzberg, 2001; Wickramasinghe & Lamb, 2002):

1.   The decision information cost is low.[1]
2.   Goal aligned behaviour is low.
3.   Residual loss is high.

There are two ways to address the problem of low goal aligned behaviour with simultaneous high residual loss (ibid.), which is both significant and has wide spread implications for the organisation: (1) Move the decision-making to the principal. However the major problem with this approach is that it is the knowledge worker agent who has the expertise to make the decision not the principal. (2) Increase the monitoring of the knowledge worker agent. Clearly, the second choice is preferable and the solution lies in the careful structuring and design of technology. Essentially an asymmetry of information exists between principal and knowledge worker agent. This indicates that IS/IT (information systems /information technology) in general and KMS (knowledge management systems) in particular can be used as a tool connecting these two players by aiding decision-making and communication. Figure 3 depicts the scenarios. Wickramasinghe (2000), and then Wickramasinghe and Lamb (2002) have conducted research that demonstrates that the shift in the monitoring cost curve from M to M' in Figure 3 is as a direct result of self-monitoring behaviour induced and enabled by the IS/IT/ and/or KMS (such results have been confirmed by studies conducted by Coombs, Knight, and Willmott (1992). The role of self-monitoring in increasing goal aligned behaviour of knowledge workers is critical; and the enabling role of KMS in particular, has far reaching consequences on managing knowledge workers.

Scenario 3 in Figure 3 depicts the situation after the implementation of significant technology that has the potential to enable and induce "self-monitoring" behavior. What we see is an increase in goal alignment and a decrease in the residual loss without a corresponding increase in the monitoring costs (as agency theory would predict) rather as a result of the shift to the monitoring cost curve in Figure 3b

Figure 3. Agency theory for the knowledge worker (Adapted from Wickramasinghe, 2000; Wickramasinghe & Ginzberg, 2001; Wickramasinghe & Lamb, 2002)

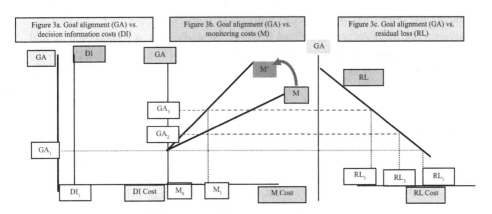

In the context of a knowledge worker agent the DI cost is fixed and low; say DI1 (as in Figure 3a), from this agency theory tells us that the corresponding level of goal alignment will also be low – GA1. We then have the following possible scenarios depicted in Figures 3b and 3c:

<u>Scenario 1</u>: no monitoring (i.e., base case) – Total cost $(TC_1) = DI_1 + RL_1 + M_0 = TC_1$ and GA_1

<u>Scenario 2</u>: monitoring with minimal KMS (i.e., no or little knowledge management systems)
$$Total cost (TC_2) = DI_1 + M_1 + RL_2 = TC_2 \text{ and } GA2 > GA1$$

<u>Scenario 3</u>: substantial KMS (i.e., the practices with the respective billing/practice management systems)
$$Total cost (TC_3) = DI_1 + M_1 + RL_3 = TC_3 \text{ and } GA_3 >> GA_2$$

Thus the impact of substantial KMS enabling self monitoring is that $GA_3 >> GA_2, GA_1$; $TC_3 << TC_2, TC_1$

Furthermore, the shift in the curve M to M' represents the role of self monitoring in effecting a higher level of goal alignment (GA_3) – we can represent this mathematically by the change in the gradients of the two functions (M and M':

Gradient of curve $M = (GA_2 - GA_1) / (M_1 - M_0)$
Gradient of curve $M' = (GA_3 - GA_1) / M_1 - M_0)$

Gradient (M') - Gradient $(M) = $ *self monitoring cost* which is at least in part borne by the knowledge worker agent from M to M'. This shift is attributed to the technology induced self-monitoring behavior of the knowledge worker agent. Thus, for the same amount of monitoring performed by the principal (M_1) we have a higher level of goal alignment (GA_3) and also a decrease to the residual loss (RL3). This is clearly in contradiction to what is predicted by agency theory because agency theory does not consider that monitoring costs could be borne by the agent; or that in complex organizations, the agent might be a member of the collective principal entity.

Expanding Agency Theory

In order to explain this apparent paradox (in conditions of low monitoring by the principal the knowledge worker agent exhibits high goal aligned behaviour on the implementation of significant IS/IT) and thereby enhance agency theory, it is necessary to incorporate the power-knowledge concept developed by Foucault (1980; Townly, 1993). Foucault's work is complex and taken at face value might appear to have little relevance to knowledge workers or their practices of self-monitoring. However, the three recurring themes in his work, namely, power, knowledge, and subjectivity provide an appropriate venue to understand the underlying dynamics of the occurrence of self-monitoring within the context of a knowledge worker agent

The Amalgamation of the Power-Knowledge Dynamic with Agency Theory

Foucault believed that knowledge (which is gained through information) plays a pivotal role in the altering of power relations (Rabinow, 1984). In his schema, Foucault identifies three modes of objectification of the subject: (1) dividing practices, (2) scientific classifications, and (3) subjectification (ibid). The third mode, which is of interest to us, concerns the "way a human being turns him or herself into a subject" in particular "… the person initiates an active self-formation" (ibid., p. 11). Foucault proposes that the third mode occurs because the person has knowledge or the access to knowledge and can use this to achieve a more powerful position or at least impact the existing power relation in a positive manner. An essential component in this dynamic is the role of "technologies of normalization" which play a "…key role in the systematic creation, classification and control…" ibid., p. 21).

Returning to the early discussion of the break down of agency theory in the context of a knowledge worker agent performing self-monitoring, it becomes possible to analyze this through the lens of Foucault to better understand and explain the occurrence of the voluntary self-monitoring behavior enabled by the technologies. It is this behavior that has resulted in the shift of the monitoring curve in Figure 3b, Scenario 3c.

The principal implemented the technology in order to achieve better, more effective, and efficient operations and managerial control. These technologies however, enabled the knowledge worker agent to begin to perform self-monitoring activities (i.e., the agent turned him or herself into the subject and enacted processes of self-formation as Foucault would predict). This behavior resulted in an attempt (on the part of the knowledge worker agent) not to lose power or perceived power in the existing principal knowledge worker agent relationship. This was only possible because of the enabling role of the technology. The observed behavior is even more understandable when we remember that these agents are knowledge workers and thus the very reason for their role is the specialized, idiosyncratic knowledge that they possess. Hence, when they feel that this knowledge is threatened or they believe that their role is being diminished they actively try to regain or defend their power via enacting a power/knowledge dynamic as Foucault would predict [and was evidenced in the form of performing self-monitoring in prior studies (Wickramasinghe & Lamb, 2002)].

The enhancement of agency theory with Foucault's power/knowledge concept provides us with a useful mechanism to understand and explain the breakdown of agency theory in the case of a knowledge worker agent. More importantly, it underscores the role of technology, especially knowledge management systems, in facilitating the achievement of a higher level of goal alignment.

Organizational Considerations

Many factors must be considered when thinking about people issues. These range from how people react and relate to the technologies they must use, to how they operate within the organization (Ginzberg, 1978). In dynamic environments, organizations must continually change and adapt. Some of these changes are incremental while others are dramatic (Evans & Wurster, 1999). Embracing knowledge management for most organizations represents a significant change to many areas including the organizational culture and structure as well as the way people within the organization go about their tasks so that they maximize the benefits of a sound knowledge management approach (Huber, 1990). To effect change smoothly and as easily as possible it is necessary to invoke change management techniques (Ginzberg, 1978).

Change Management

Change management, the systematic approach to ensuring the successful absorbing of a new technology or initiative in an organization with minimal disruption, requires considering many aspects at both the macro level—taking an overall view of the organization, and the micro level—taking a view that considers individuals within a department or group (Ginzberg, 1978). Underlying any change management effort should be a consideration of the Lewin/Schein model unfreeze, move, and refreeze (ibid.). Thus, what the organization wants to do regarding change management is unfreeze a current state problem or process, make the necessary changes, and move to the desired process or solution and then refreeze so these changes will become the way the organization operates (refer to Figure 4) (i.e., a desired future state).

In structuring the actual change or moving stage, seven key factors are identified as follows: the nature of the change (i.e., is it radical or incremental), the process, the roles of all people involved, resistance to change, commitment, culture, and synergy (Ginzberg, 1978; Wickramasinghe & Ginzberg, 2001). The key for any organization going through change management is to exhibit resilience. Figure 5 depicts these seven aspects of change and at the center is resilience because all these factors contribute to making the organization more resilient to endure the change process successfully. Another important aspect pertaining change concerns developing a clear vision of the desired future state. Without such a clear vision it is difficult to achieve the new robust structures and appropriate behaviors, this will result in poor structures, and inappropriate behaviors will be preserved when the "refreeze" stage takes effect (Ginzberg, 1978). In addition, it is essential that organizations are flexible, develop structured approaches to managing ambiguity, engage change rather than defend it, and most importantly be positive (Ginzberg, 1978). Integral to facilitating appropriate change management is unsurprisingly the need for strong leadership and appropriate management (Hedlund, 1990; Mintzberg, 1989). Any

Figure 4. Lewin-Schein theory of change

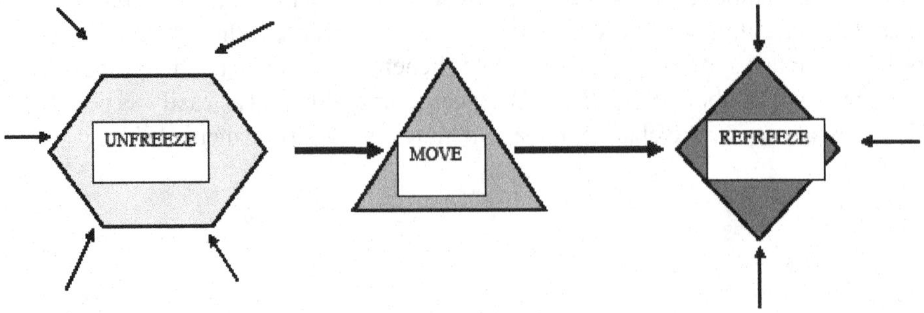

Figure 5. The seven key factors of change

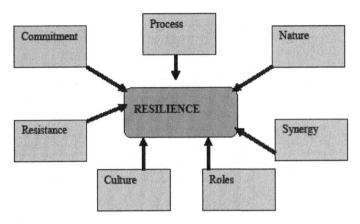

change management must be driven from the top. In the knowledge economy change is a necessity and knowledge-based organizations must acquire the skills to embrace and endure change effectively and efficiently to be successful.

Organizational Culture and Structure

Organizational culture and structure have been shown to play a significant role in facilitating or hampering any knowledge management initiative (Martin, 1992; Robey & Azevedo, 1994; Schein, 1996). If we look at the endeavors of some of the main consulting companies to launch their respective knowledge management initiatives during the late 1980s and early 1990s, we can see that a significant amount of senior management effort, time, and resources were assigned to fostering the appropriate sharing culture and flexible supportive structure that would enable the four key steps of knowledge management to ensue (Wickramasinghe, 2003). Table 2 highlights some of the key aspects that confronted three of the Big 5 consulting firms at this time.

Culture

Let us now examine organizational culture and its relevance to KM. Culture and more specifically organizational culture, is another complex construct like knowl-

Table 2. Summary of consulting companies respective culture and structure dimensions[2]

Factors	Case 1	Case 2	Case 3
Environment	• 1995 management consulting industry was estimated to be 40 billion dollar industry worldwide and 50% of this was in the U.S. • Cases 1, 2, & 3 part of Big 6. • Three industry trends included (i) growth, (ii) integration of services, (iii) globalization. • Recruitment and retention of people was proving to be challenging. • Market innovation was becoming essential for consulting companies. • Clients were expecting value added products and services at competitive prices. • Mergers and acquisitions that had occurred meant there was a need to consolidated knowledge, techniques, standards, and approaches across the globally dispersed offices of these firms.		
Culture	• Considered a pioneer in its ability to leverage its own intellectual capital. • While culture is collegial—historical performance evaluations had discouraged information sharing. • Lacks a strong sharing culture to support knowledge management.	• Diverse culture—due to many partnership mergers. • Of the three cases most individualistic—traditionally performance was based/rewarded on individual performance. • Minimal sense of a sharing culture.	• Always had a strong sharing culture. • Had strengths in its design, development, and implementation of computer systems--made adoption of KMS easy. • Had a history of developing "methods" and "techniques" hence much support for KM methods and many existing methods and techniques incorporate KM perspectives.
Structure	• Has three separate key centers in the U.S. to support distinct aspects all relating to knowledge including methodologies and technology tools, research and analysis as well as knowledge base administration and finally research initiatives and executive roundtables. • Emphasis on team based learning. • Organized around lines of business and geographic areas.	• Re-structured along lines of business a change from a geographic/functional structure. • Established knowledge centers and new expanded organizational roles • Focusing on their human resource asset. • Fusion between internal processes, systems, and technologies was critical. • The three dimensional structure of geographic areas, lines of business, and functions enabled the matrix search strategy for their KMS.	• Organized by industries it serves and competencies necessary to provide services. • Set up role & responsibilities for KM (e.g., 200 people full time KM managers). • Emphasis on cross functional teams such as comminutes of practice and competency groups.

edge itself (Martin, 1992; Robey & Azevedo, 1994). As we come into contact with organizations, we are subject to formal and informal codes of behaviors, norms, rituals, stories about what happens within the organization, tasks, and jargon (ibid.). Organizational culture can be defined as the pattern all these attributes make. We can use the metaphor of a jigsaw puzzle to illustrate our meaning most effectively. If we think of the various aspects of an organization that we encounter as the pieces of the jigsaw puzzle, then the picture we get by fitting all these separate pieces together represents the organizational culture. Some essential questions should come to mind regarding organizational culture including: (1) should it be a source of harmony within an organization, (2) is it homogenous or do sub-cultures exist, and (3) can it be changed. It is these three questions that have a significant bearing on the successful adoption and embracing of knowledge management within an organization and must be understood in the context of an organization before it launches its KM initiative.

Organizational culture, by providing a sense of shared meaning and a set of appropriate norms, practices, and behaviors for the organization, should lead to a certain level of harmony (ibid.). However, an organizational culture can be both stifling and supportive depending on the specific situation. To understand this we need to first understand the major types of organizational cultures. The three generally recognized types of culture in the social sciences literature (ibid.) include

- **Integration:** Where all manifestations of organizational culture are supportive and thus there is no ambiguity.

- **Differentiation:** Where there exists divergences in cultural beliefs, norms etc at some level and only within a sub-culture can consensus be evidenced.

- **Fragmentation:** Where ambiguity is the essence of the organizational culture.

We capture these differences in Table 3, as well as note their impact to a knowledge management initiative. From this, we can see that the culture irrespective of whether it is integration, differentiation, or fragmentation can either facilitate or hamper any knowledge management initiative. What is important then is how to foster the appropriate culture. To do this we actually must focus on the pieces of the jigsaw puzzle (i.e., what are the norms, practices, beliefs, behaviors, etc.) that are important for fostering a knowledge management initiative.

In order to understand the requirements of a culture that is supportive of any knowledge management initiative, it is useful to examine the key knowledge issues at different goal levels within an organization. The three important goal levels include (Wilcox, 1997)

Table 3. Perspectives of culture

Perspective	Integration	Differentiation	Fragmentation
Consensus / Dissensus	Consensus	Consensus only in sub-culture	Dissensus
Manifestations	Consistent	Inconsistent	Complex—neither all consistent nor all inconsistent
Ambiguity	None	Outside subculture	Focus on it
Impact on KM	Good if culture supportive of KM	Good if many sub-cultures are supportive of KM	Good if it forms a focus for ambiguity

1.   **Normative:** Knowledge goals pertain to the general vision of the company policy.

2.   **Strategic:** Knowledge goals pertain to long-term projects aimed at realizing the vision and intent of the company.

3.   **Operational:** Knowledge goals pertain to the daily activities within the company.

Table 4 identifies these and their impact to knowledge management.

In order to be flexible and adaptive, businesses in the knowledge economy are particularly stifled by large hierarchical organizational structures. Furthermore, it is often important for businesses to be sharing knowledge throughout the organization; hence, a sharing, collaborative team-based culture is most appropriate. Changes to culture and structure typically take time but one should not overlook the importance of acquiring or altering these components in order to become a successful organization. One of the best examples of strong commitment to foster a sharing culture and thereby engage in implementing a dramatic cultural change

Table 4. Key knowledge issues and their implications for organizational culture

Goal level	Structures	Activities	Behaviors
Normative	Company charter • How does this impact KM.	Company policy • Knowledge vision, mission statements, and identification of critical areas for knowledge.	Company culture • Sharing of knowledge, innovative spirit, and level of communication.
Strategic	Organizational structures • Conferences, reporting, R&D organization, experience groups, and management support systems (i.e., technologies such as Lotus Notes, EIS).	Programs • Cooperation, building core competencies, information provision.	Approach to problems • Orientation to knowledge goals, problem-oriented knowledge identification.
Operational	Organizational processes • Control of knowledge flows. Deployment processes • Knowledge infrastructure, supply of knowledge.	Tasks- knowledge projects • Build expert databanks, introduce appropriate knowledge-based systems.	Performance and cooperation • Knowledge sharing, knowledge in action.

occurred in the consulting companies when they embraced knowledge management (Wickramasinghe, 2003). This was certainly no easy task, but the benefits have been significant, in fact the respective knowledge management implementations would not be successful had it not been for the culture changes that took place. It is particularly important in the current climate, where speed and time are so critical, for organizations to be cognizant of necessary changes to culture and structure, and ensure these take place in order to facilitate key business process and maximize their knowledge management initiatives.

The introduction of technology into an organization or the change to a new technology platform can result in altering the roles of people within the organization and their relative power. Tasks might become richer and more challenging or may require less skill and become more routine. Changes in power structures and roles by the introduction of technology and consequent effects to the organization are best exemplified in the classic case study by Markus (1983), which discusses the introduction of an information system in the Golden Triangle Corporation. The result was that the system impacted the jobs of various accountants in the corporation, making some jobs richer (for the financial accountants) and others more routine (for the divisional accountants). By doing so, the system affected the relative power of two departments within the corporation. The combination of these two impacts led to many resistance issues connected with the system. The key lessons to be learned from this case study include understanding the impact of the technology on all interested parties in the organization and ensuring resistance is minimal if at all by effecting appropriate change management strategies in conjunction with the implementation of the system. Given the significant reliance on technology, in particular knowledge management systems, for most organizations in a knowledge economy, this becomes of even greater importance.

Structure

One of the best known taxonomies of organizational structures or typologies is Mintzberg's typology of organizational configurations (Mintzberg, 1989). Mintzberg identifies seven major typologies: (1) entrepreneurial, (2) machine, (3) professional, (4) diversified, (5) innovative, (6) missionary, and (7) political (ibid.):

1. **Entrepreneurial organizations** are described as "simple, characterized, above all, by what it is not: elaborated. ... typically it has little or no staff, a loose division of labor, and a small managerial hierarchy. Little of its activity is formalized, and it makes minimal use of planning procedures or training routines. In a sense, it is a non-structure..." (Mintzberg, 1989, p. 117).

These organizations are generally small and designed to take advantage of opportunities presented, or created, by a dynamic yet relatively simple environment.

2. **Machine organizations** are described as containing "... highly specialized, routine operating tasks, very formalized communication throughout the organization, large-size operating units, reliance on the functional basis for grouping tasks, relatively centralized power for decision-making, and an elaborate administrative structure with a sharp distinction between line and staff" (Mintzberg, 1989, p. 133).

These types of organizations are structured for control, with task coordination derived from highly standardized work practices that carry little discretion in decision-making for the operators and line first-line managers and where the division of labor is never blurred.

3. **Professional organizations** are described as ones where "work is complex, requiring that it be carried out and controlled by professionals, yet at the same time remains stable, so that the skills of those professionals can be perfected through standardized operating programs. The structure takes on the form of *professional* bureaucracy, which is common in universities, general hospitals, public accounting firms, social work agencies, and firms doing fairly routine engineering or craft work. All rely on the skills and knowledge of their operating professionals to function; all produce standardized products or services" (Mintzberg, 1989, p. 174).

These types of organizations are found in complex, relatively stable environments that require processes that must be learnt over long periods and can produce standard outcomes, although the processes themselves are often too complex to be standardized in their application.

4. **Diversified organizations** are described as "not so much an integrated identity as a set of semi-autonomous units coupled together by a central administrative structure. The units are generally called *divisions* and the central administration, the *headquarters*." Divisions "are created to serve distinct markets and are given control over the operating functions necessary to do so, ... Each is relatively free of direct control by headquarters or even of the need to coordinate activities with other divisions ... There *is* a headquarters, and it has a series of roles that distinguish this overall configuration from a collection of independent businesses providing the same set of products and services" (Mintzberg, 1989, pp. 155-156).

These organizations are typically large and the diversification is driven by the need to address multiple markets.

5. **Innovative organizations** are described as having "... highly organic structure, with little formalization of behavior; specialized jobs based on expert training; a tendency to group the specialists in functional groups for housekeeping

purposes but to deploy them in small project teams to do their work; a reliance on teams, on task forces, and on integrating managers of various sorts in order to encourage mutual adjustment, the key mechanism of coordination, within and between these teams; and considerable decentralization to and within these teams, which are located at various places in the organization and involve various mixtures of line managers and staff and operating experts" (Mintzberg, 1989, p. 1999).

These organizations are found in complex, relatively dynamic environments where the requirement is for flexibility in structure so that different forms of expertise can be drawn together quickly to address problems and situations directly.

6. **Missionary organizations** are described as having "a very special culture—a richly developed and deeply rooted system of values and beliefs that distinguishes a particular organization from all others" (Mintzberg, 1989, p. 221).

    Within these organizations, the identification between organization and the people who work there is so strong that it can be used as a mechanism for coordinating activities, in place of the direct supervision that is found in machine organizations, for example.

7. **Political organizations** are described as ones where the internal system of politics "reflects power that is technically illegitimate...in the means it uses, and also sometimes in the ends it promotes. In other words, political power in the organization (unlike government) is not formally authorized, widely accepted, or certified. The result is that political activity is usually divisive and conflictive, pitting individual or groups against the more legitimate systems of influence and, when those systems are weak, against each other" (Mintzberg, 1989, p. 238).

    These organizations contain conflict, between competing units or individuals, which arise from the effort to gain and maintain power.

Three other generic organizational structures (Hedlund, 1990; Huber, 1990) believed to be important include: (1) the hierarchical structure (here the emphasis is on the level or position within the organization), (2) the functional structure (here the emphasis is on a particular business area, e.g., accounting or marketing), and (3) the departmentalized structure (here both level and function are of equal consideration). These are depicted in Figure 6(a) through (c). Irrespective of the typology or specific organizational structure knowledge management is useful for all structures, however it is important to understand the particular organization structure before initiating and implementing any new KM initiative.

Finally, given the high degree of specialization required by knowledge workers in a knowledge economy we are seeing more and more the emergence of multidisciplinary

Figure 6. Typical organizational structures

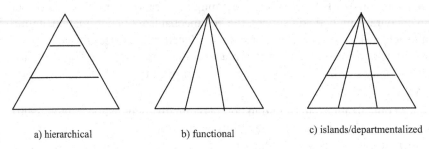

a) hierarchical   b) functional   c) islands/departmentalized

or cross functional teams, and even virtual communities as a preferred structure (Cortada, 1998). In a team or group dynamic scenario, the key to maximising the tacit knowledge is to view the group as a collaborative intelligence rather than a collection of intelligence. Moreover, it is important to understand the comfort zones of every member as well as their respective strengths and weaknesses so that projects can be designed to take advantage of the whole team and each member's expertise (Rubenstein & Geisler, 2003). Hence, two broad concepts become important (ibid.):

1. **Team building:** Requires creating a congenial work environment, improving communications and building strong relationships and trust between all team members.

2. **Team learning:** Requires looking outward to build knowledge while simultaneously looking inward to create alignment between the new knowledge and existing expertise.

Figure 7 depicts two views of teams within organizations. Figure 7(a) shows the more traditional view where knowledge worker teams are made up of people from the same horizontal layer, while figure "b" demonstrates the more emerging make up of cross functional or multi-disciplinary teams which are viewed as a vertical slice taken from all levels of the organizational structure. Figure 7(b) represents the structure that supports more successful adaptation of KM technologies, learning structures and processes in the organization as well as the better use of the intellectual capabilities of the organization.

Figure 8 depicts the key dynamics that take place within team structures, especially multi-dimensional or cross-functional team dynamics. Essentially, the respective

Figure 7. Shifting perspective from viewing knowledge workers at horizontal levels to a cross-functional perspective

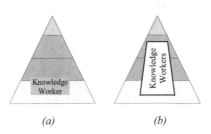

(a)   *(b)*

knowledge that is brought to the team by each individual knowledge worker impacts the innovative function and quality of the process or project and this in turn leads to the creation of new knowledge and hence increases the individual's extant knowledge base as well as the team's knowledge base (ibid.). Once team structure is selected, teams should strive to achieve the highest possible outflow of ideas: quality, knowledge, and innovative ideas. Quality ideas are based on quantitative measures of improving processes, such as cost and time. In contrast, knowledge ideas are concerned with unstructured data as well as structured data analysis. Finally, innovative ideas are those that are unusual even abnormal initiatives that will lead to fundamental process improvement beyond quality and knowledge ideas.

Using creative and innovative thinking methods, individual and team profiles must be established and stored in profile databases (Cortada, 1998; Rubenstein & Geisler, 2003). One individual may become a member in more than one team. Team members are dynamically transferred between teams based on performance analysis of the individual as well as teams, such as communication, politics, lack of harmony among team members, and incongruence between member profiles. Once individual and team profiles based on innovation and creativity techniques have been established, team membership selection, composition, and transfer should be conducted dynamically so that team and individual satisfaction and performance should be maximized. It is necessary for organizations to perceive that knowledge and innovation generation requires commitment across the organization; this in turn will lead to teams being formed around critical processes. Each team/individual must be given the chance to suggest new ideas to their own team as well as other teams. Members of any team may be invited to meetings of any other teams, if needed. This will then create what is called a circular team organization (Figure 8).

We note that probably the ultimate type of cross-functional team would be a community of practice. The notion of a community of practice is becoming more prevalent in the literature and even practice particularly because of its impact on learning and innovation and thus knowledge creation and impact more generally to knowledge

Figure 8. Knowledge generation within team dynamics

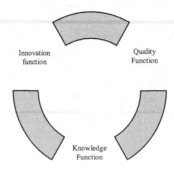

management (Alavi & Leidner, 2001; Allee, 1997; Wickramasinghe, 2003). Given its strong connection with learning and innovation, we shall return to a discussion of community of practice in our chapter on Organizational Learning.

Management and Leadership

Management

The final area of consideration with respect to the organization's human infra-structure pertains to management. Management must recognize the challenges and opportunities presented to the firm in a knowledge economy and then decide and develop internal and external strategies to respond to the environment in which the firm operates (Mintzberg, 1989; Senge, 1996). Simply put, management must "make sense" of the environment and chart the organization's course. This involves not only looking after what already exists, be it existing products or services, but also looking ahead and into the future to grasp new opportunities (ibid.). Managerial roles typically differ at different levels of the organization with senior manage-ment focusing primarily on long-term strategic level decisions about products and services. Middle management then focuses on how to carry out the plans and goals of senior management while operational managers are concerned with monitoring the day-to-day activities of the firm (Mintzberg, 1989). It is necessary that all these areas are functioning smoothly and in an appropriate and meaningful fashion so that the organization can be successful. Peter Senge (1996) has often noted that no significant change can occur unless it is driven from the top. This is certainly true for knowledge management. By examining companies that have embraced knowledge management successfully, we can see that one common underlying theme is strong leadership and top management commitment for the knowledge management initiative under way, in particular there is a high correlation between successful KM initiatives and top management support. We can categorize leaders into three groups, which essentially correspond to levels within an organization; namely, Local Line Leaders, Executive Leaders, and Internal Net-workers (Hedlund, 1990). Irrespective of the level of leadership, the leader must perform many roles for the KM initiative to succeed including but not limited to being a creator of corporate culture, facilitator, coach, sustainer, change agent, pathfinder, empowering knowledge workers, and aligning key areas so that a consistent KM vision and strategy ensue. Table 5 captures the major KM roles.

Table 5. The people positions in knowledge management

Leadership	Roles	Individuals	Collectives
CKO	**Subject matter specialist**	**Knowledge sponsor**	Network and community
Senior knowledge manager	**Knowledge broker**	**Knowledge worker**	Team
Local Line Managers	**Boundary spanner**		Work group
Internal net-workers	**Knowledge sponsor**	**Knowledge skeptic**	
	Community manager		
	Coach		
	Author		
	Mentor		
	Coordinator of KM		
	Subject matter specialist		

Leadership

Leadership is a process by which a person influences others to accomplish an objective and directs a group or organization in a cohesive and coherent fashion (Blake & Moulton, 1985). To do this, leaders apply various skills and abilities such as knowledge and expertise, beliefs, values, and ethics, known collectively as leadership skills (ibid.).

Bass (1989, 1990) identifies three distinct categories of leaders: Some people are "natural" leaders, others rise to the occasion during a crisis or important event, and the third category relates to people who through promotion and seniority find themselves in leadership roles. The tenets of transformational leadership—the need to embrace personal transformation from a "member of the troop" to its leader, the need to learn new skills, and the requirement to apply the learned skills in the process of leading pertain most strongly to the third group. Ultimately, however, it is the dynamic leadership that fosters innovation and entrepreneurship (Bjerke & Hultman, 2003; Gudergan & Gudergan, 2004; Llorens-Montes, Garcia-Morales, & Verdu-Jover, 2004; Sharma, Gupta, & Wickramasinghe, 2005). The term "dynamic leadership" seems to define a fairly obvious form of action: a forceful, sweeping approach that solves problems in a visionary manner, the "I am in charge here" of General Haig following the shooting of President Reagan. In reality, the process is much more complex, difficult, extremely demanding, and requires far more than a dynamic personality and the willingness either to charge or to be in charge.

Leadership becomes the essential operational factor when organizations, be it small work teams or major international corporations, face unstable environments, where change is unpredictable, the actors within the "action space" change, where the rules of competition are in constant flux, and where good ideas of the past turn into suicidal concepts of the current reality. In many ways, this is the situation of today—new competitors entered many formerly stable markets and changed the rules almost at will, rapidly developing technology transformed traditional concepts and practically instantaneous access to information resulted, at least in some activities (e.g., banking) in decision cycles lasting seconds rather than days or even months. The present environment of business is clearly demanding but what is less evident is the fact that unless the leader devises and implements measured responses to the *current* challenge in a manner that will address its *future* transformation, the chosen solutions will fail. They will fail since their underlying assumption is the static nature of the challenge and that its characteristics remain constant over the near future. The solutions devised under such a conceptual umbrella will fail because the leader fails to recognize the inevitable truth that while solutions to the perceived change are being devised, the environment might have already transformed into something new and entirely different. The latter problem is the continuing dilemma of IT managers—hardware and software required to cope with the increasing operational requirements demand continuous and substantial expenditure. On the other hand, the tempo of technology development is such that within a very short time, the "leading edge" becomes "legacy." Thus, in order to retain operational competitiveness, the organization may spend vast amounts of funds in maintaining modern IT infrastructure. But, funds being a finite resource, it may be necessary to shift their allocation and reduce the support of R&D, which, in turn, may adversely affect competitiveness on the market.

A good example is provided by the recently reported losses of General Motors caused by rapidly escalating healthcare costs. Maintaining a high level of employee healthcare benefits is unquestionably welcome by the workforce and enhances its stability. On the other hand, with foreign manufacturers benefiting from socialized healthcare, the costs of benefits incurred by GM shift the profitability balance toward the negative side and, almost incredibly, force the automotive giant to the brink of bankruptcy. The company leadership is thus faced with a number of choices starting from lobbying for national healthcare services to actually declaring bankruptcy and shutting down. In more general terms, leaders operating within complex and changing environments face the essential dilemma: is it better to wait and observe the transformational trends of the field or join the battle and attempt to steer the change in the required direction by being directly involved in the process of the change itself? Either approach can be deadly as demonstrated by almost countless examples not only from business but also from politics, education, war, medicine, or any other field where leadership is essential to progress and good leadership is not necessarily the equivalent of success.

One does not need to look far. Even the best local bookshop, led by the most insightful management and beloved by its loyal customers will wither under the impact of an international bookselling chain. And yet, some magnificent little bookshops have survived despite rubbing shoulders with giants, and their survival has been the result of close observation of the nature and characteristics of the ongoing transformation within the operational space. Such a transformation may be extremely rapid and, as we have already discussed in the preceding chapter, the leader needs to be prepared and ready to direct the organization and its people successfully in order to maintain the organization's competitive position in its industry. Failure or slowness to respond, lack of direction, unfocused responses (or responses focused on irrelevant aspects of the environmental pressure), organizational inflexibility or adherence to the rule of "it is not done this way here" usually result in severe and detrimental consequences for the organization. Speed, precision, and adequacy of action, anticipation of future changes, and flexibility of response are the principal leadership challenges (Bolman & Deal, 1991; Kouzes & Posner, 1987). The reader may recall in this context the essential aspects of Boyd's OODA loop discussed earlier, and the fact that implementation of OODA loop-based training and (subsequently) thinking greatly facilitates acquisition, development, and implementation of these cardinal operational attributes of a leader.

Operationally, all actions of a leader must be formulated, defined, and executed with the "winning strategy" in mind (Sahay, Mohan, & Maini, 2004). However, it must be emphasized that "winning" may at times signify nothing else but a graceful retreat that assures future return to battle. Too often great leaders are penalized by presiding over "organized defeats" which form the backbone of future victories (remember Churchill and the evacuation of the British Expeditionary Force at Dunkirk?). It must be remembered, however, that all *executed* actions will have an impact on the operational environment (Figure 9) which may be highly complex and contain both the immediate subject of these actions as well as many less indirectly influenced entities and systems of entities. Thus, unless environmental diversity and the wide range of potential impacts of one's own strategy on the environment are carefully considered, evaluated, and incorporated into that strategy, the response of the environment to the proposed actions may be far more complex than originally assumed, and the results adverse rather than promoting the original intentions (Porter, 1980, 1985). It is then necessary to reconfigure the next set of actions in such a way that the subsequent stage of interaction with the environment opens again the unobstructed path to the predetermined objective. The pattern of action-counteraction-restructuring-new action is a cyclical process.

Although organization A interacts only with B, the latter interacts with C (stippled arrow) and indirectly with D. As close collaborators, C and D form their own "micro operational universe" (oval denoted by a broken line). Firm D has two satellite divisions (x, y), one of which (x) affects negatively "C" whose lowered performance

Figure 9. Complexity of interactions within the operational universe

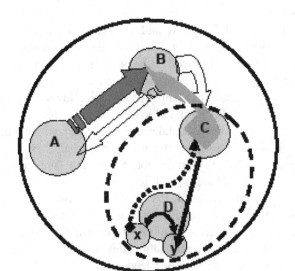

impact B. Consequently A is also negatively affected (downward stippled arrow). In complex operational spaces, influences that are least obvious may be the most destructive cycle progressing along the time axis and characterized by three cardinal attributes: complexity, speed, and direction of movement (von Lubitz & Wickramasinghe, 2006 and Figure 10). We are once again reminded of Boyd's OODA loop (refer to Chapter I).

Note that in the context of leadership theory, the concept of the OODA loop has another significant function: it facilitates understanding the critical role of the mistakes made during the initial data collection (e.g., selective or biased selection, rejection of "non-conforming" data as necessarily false, etc., conducted at the observation stage of the loop) that precedes (or at least should do) every decision made by the leader. Of equal importance are the errors made during the subsequent orientation stage of the loop (such subjective analysis of data/facts based on preconceived notions, influence of personal bias, inflexibility, etc.). Errors made at these two stages of the leadership process have the cardinal impact on everything that follows (i.e., the determination and action stages of the loop.). Analysis of the loop progression clearly indicates that with each subsequent action cycle, correction of errors committed at the earliest stages demands increasingly larger resources and removes them from where they should be otherwise committed—at the centre of action, at the time and place where concentration of effort will assure maximum success. Uncorrected errors compound at each new revolution of the loop and exponentially increase the chance of failure. Probably the best example of "leadership loop failure" was the disastrous response of state and federal authorities to hurricane Katrina in August 2005. The response to Hurricane Wilma (its shortcomings notwithstanding) shows how application of Boyd's loop-based leadership can lead to positive outcomes in situations demanding flexible, ongoing, and dynamic response to the continuously but unpredictably changing operational environment. Clearly, to assure efficiency of action, the interval separating each individual stage of the loop must be as short as possible, particularly when interacting with highly fluid, ultra-complex systems such as military or healthcare information. Hence, leadership procrastination in exploration of the action environment and early threat detection and identification are among the most powerful determinants of success. Knowledge management and IC^{2}T are the most effective tools in averting such delays by facilitating rapid, reliable, and in many instances automated sampling of the environment involving collection of multi-source data, their manipulation, analysis, and classification into larger information/germane knowledge entities. Consequently, decision supporting outputs are faster, more situation/operational environment-relevant and, most importantly, allow a robustly elevated rate of stimulus-response cycle (operations "inside the loop"). Ultimately, by increasing reaction relevance and speed, effective use of IC^{2}T and KM facilitates leadership's goal-oriented manipulation of the operational environment and also increases both the level (accuracy) and predictive range of responses to environment induced pressures.

Figure 10. Action cycle and its variables: Time, direction, and cycle revolution speed

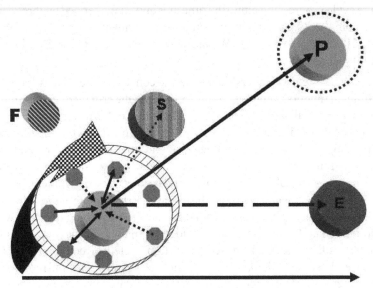

The significance of appropriate use of IC^{2}T and KM tools is underlined by the fact that under most circumstances the dynamic is highly heterogeneous and consists of a wide range of direct and indirect interrelated subcomponents.

Every organization (large disc) interacts directly or indirectly with a number of other entities (small polygonals) existing within the same operational space (barrier-like oval). Some of these interactions may have beneficial results (solid short arrows) while others may be detrimental (short stippled arrows), and some are uni- while other bi-directional. The environment is unstable and chaotic and only a clear perception of the existing complexities aided by the speed of the action cycle (curved arrow--see below) will allow the organization progress successfully to its goal (P). Some organizations whose leadership is unable to respond to the unpredictable patterns of interactions within the operational space will fail entirely (F). Others will be greatly suppressed by the competitors and their development will stagnate (S). One group will develop a state of equilibrium with the environment (E) which will allow its members a state of "undistinguished survival." Only those organizations whose leadership is capable of active exploitation of the environment and of flexible response to its pressures will thrive in the chaotic operational space.

The consequences of our interactions with the environment are never unidirectional. In reality, interaction with one or several constituents of the environment will elicit responses of synergy or retaliation or even fail to elicit any immediate response at all. Consequently, progress may either slow down or accelerate, causing perturbations in the forthcoming revolutions of the OODA cycle. The most important aspect of operational business environments is their inherent instability (our interaction with them upsets the state of equilibrium) and unpredictability (every interaction with the environment has a potential to elicit its unforeseen changes.) Thus, one of the principal attribute of successful leadership is to conduct the activities of one's own organization in a manner that will minimize the element of opponent induced unpredictability while, and at the same time, increasing their destabilization. The latter will not be achieved through the mere increase in the complexity or frequency of multiple interactions with the already complex environment. The emerging chaos may, actually, lead to the destabilization of one's own organization). Instead, unbalancing the opposition is best attained through the elevation of the speed of one's own action cycle, and by giving it a precise direction of movement to be followed during a predetermined interval (von Lubitz & Wickramasinghe, 2006). Unpredictability of the environment that indirectly supports the hostile intents of the opposition can be reduced through an increased rate of information extraction from within this environment. The process is, as indicated above, governed by the speed of the action cycle (ibid.) that, in many ways, can be enhanced through the efficient use of fused IC^2T and KM. In summary then, the principal function of a leader operating in a complex, changing, and unpredictable environment is to impose as rapidly as possible the state of persisting dominance within the action space. Once such dominance is firmly established, the leader must execute the dominant thrust that will definitively end all opposing influences. Occupation of the action space vacated by the opposition is the ultimate goal of the "winning strategy." It must be remembered, however, that the goal of a leader is not to vanquish and destroy. Instead, the "winning strategy" associated with good leadership establishes a "win-win" environment for all protagonists. It allows them to thrive but in a manner that, while beneficial to all partners, ultimately assures undivided support for the dominant entity's interests.

Implications for Knowledge-Based Enterprises

Peter Drucker (1999) noted that arguably the most important issue for organizations is to manage their knowledge workers because it is through an organization's knowledge workers that ultimate success is achieved. The key asset for knowledge-based enterprises is its intellectual capability. This is determined by the knowledge workers in the organization. The need for strong leadership and careful management is vital if this asset is to be fostered and its benefits fully maximized. However, this is in an of itself a complex task and requires the careful consideration of many of the preceding topics discussed in this chapter, including an appreciation of the culture and structure within the organization and how to effect appropriate change management so that the best utilization of the organizations human infrastructure ensues. Thus, another important aspect on which knowledge-based enterprises must continually focus is how to ensure effective leadership and management is in place that serves to foster one of its most important assets, its knowledge workers.

Chapter Summary

"To conceive of knowledge as a collection of information seems to rob the concept of all of its life ... Knowledge resides in the user and not in the collection. It is how the user reacts to a collection of information that matters" Churchman (1971, p. 10). Churchman is clearly underscoring the importance of people in the process of knowledge creation and its management. In fact, without people it would not be possible to have organizational knowledge as we know it. Thus, the human infrastructure is without a doubt integral to the successful embracing of any KM initiative and must be given careful consideration. We have isolated and discussed in turn the key aspects that together make up the vital human infrastructure. However, it must be stressed that the human infrastructure must be well balanced (i.e., all areas must be considered as well as their interaction) and fit the specific organizational context if the KM initiative is to be supported and successful.

References

Alavi, M. (1999). *Managing organizational knowledge*. Working Paper.

Alavi, M., & Leidner, D. (1999). Knowledge management systems: Issues, challenges, and benefits. *Communications of the Association for Information Systems, 1*(5).

Alavi, M., & Leidner, D. (2001). Review: Knowledge management and knowledge management systems: Conceptual foundations and research issues. *MIS Quarterly, 25*(1), 107-136.

Allee, V. (1997). *The knowledge evolution*. Boston: Butterworth-Heinemann.

Bass, B. (1989). *Stogdill's handbook of leadership: A survey of theory and research*. New York: Free Press.

Bass, B. (1990). From transactional to transformational leadership: Learning to share the vision. *Organizational dynamics, 18*(3), 19-31.

Batio, C., (2001). SuperCargo Ships, MBI Publ. Co. (Osceola, WI), 7-96.

Beckman, T. (1999). The current state of knowledge management. In J. Liebowitz, (Ed.), *Knowledge management handbook*. New York: CRC Press.

Bjerke, B., & Hultman, C. M. (2003). A dynamic perspective on entrepreneurship, leadership, and management as a proper mix for growth. *International Journal of Innovation and Learning, 1*(1), 72-93.

Blake, R. R., & Moulton, J. S. (1985). *The managerial grid III: Key to leadership excellence*. Houston: Gulf Publishing Co.

Bock, G., Zmud, R., Kim, Y., & Lee, J. (2005). Behavioral intention formation in knowledge sharing. *MIS Quarterly, 29*(1), 87-111.

Boland, R., & Tenkasi, R. (1995). Perspective making perspective taking. *Organization Science, 6*, 350-372.

Bolman, L., & Deal, T. (1991). *Reframing organizations*. San Francisco: Jossey-Bass.

Borghoff, U., & Pareschi, R. (1998). *Information technology for knowledge management*. Berlin: Springer-Verlag.

Churchman, C. (1971). *The design of inquiring systems: Basic concepts of systems and organizations*. New York: Basic Books Inc.

Coombs, R., Knight, D., & Willmott, H. (1992). Culture, control, & competition: Towards a conceptual framework for the study of information technology in organizations. *Organization Studies, 13*(1), 51-72.

Cortada, J. (1998). *The rise of the knowledge worker*. Boston: Butterworth-Heinemann.

Davenport, T., & Prusak, L. (1998). *Working knowledge*. Boston: Harvard Business School Press.

Drucker, P. (1999, October). Beyond the information revolution. *The Atlantic Monthly*, 47-57.

Drucker, P. (1993). *Post-capitalist society*. New York: Harper Collins.

Evans, P., & Wurster, T. (1999). *Blown to bits*. Boston: Harvard Business School Press.

Foucault, M. (1980). *Power/knowledge: Selected interviews and other writings by Michael Foucault, (1972-77)*. Harvester: Gordon Brighton.

Ginzberg, M. (1978, May). Steps towards more effective implementation of MS and MIS. *Interfaces, 8*(3).

Gudergan, G. P., & Gudergan, S. P. (2004). Learning to strategise innovative services: The role of systems dynamics. *International Journal of Innovation and Learning, 1*(3), 227-239.

Hedlund, G. (1990). A model of knowledge management and the N-Form corporation. *Strategic Management Journal, 15*, 73-90.

Huber, G. (1990). A theory of the effects of advanced information technologies on organizational design, intelligence, and decision-making. *Academy of Management Review, 15*(1), 47-71.

Jensen, M., & Meckling, W. (1973). Theory of the firm: Managerial behavior, agency costs, and ownership structure. *Journal of Financial Economics, 3,* 305-360.

Jensen, M., & Meckling, W. (1992). Specific and general knowledge, and organizational structure. In L. Werin & H. Wijkander (Eds.), *Contract economics* (pp. 251-291). Blackwell.

Kanter, J. (1999, Fall). Knowledge management practically speaking. *Information Systems Management.*

Kelly, R. (1990). Managing the new workforce. *Machine Design, 62*(9), 109-113.

Kouzes, J. M., & Posner, B. Z. (1987). *The leadership challenge.* San Francisco: Jossey-Bass.

Liebowittz, J. (1999). *Knowledge management handbook.* London: CRC Press.

Llorens-Montes, F. J., Garcia-Morales, V. J., & Verdu-Jover, A. J., (2004). The influence on personal mastery, organizational learning, and performance of the level of innovation: Adaptive organization versus innovator organizations. *International Journal of Innovation and Learning, 1*(2), 101-114.

Maier, R., & Lehner, F. (2000). Perspectives on knowledge management systems theoretical framework and design of an empirical study. *Proceedings of 8th European Conference on Information Systems (ECIS).*

Malhotra, Y. (2000). Knowledge management & new organisational forms. In Y.

Malhotra (Ed.), *Knowledge management and virtual organizations.* Hershey, PA: Idea Group Publishing.

Markus, L. (1983). Power politics and MIS implementation. *Communications of the ACM, 26*(6), 430-444.

Martin, J. (1992). *Cultures in organizations: Three perspectives.* Oxford: Oxford University Press.

Mintzberg, H. (1989). *Mintzberg on management.* New York: The Free Press.

Nonaka, I. (1991). The knowledge creating company. In Harvard Business Review on Knowledge Management, 1998. Boston: Harvard Business School Press.

Nonaka, I. (1994). A dynamic theory of organizational knowledge creation. *Organization Science, 5,* 14-37.

Porter, M. (1980). *Competitive strategy.* New York: Free Press.

Porter, M. (1985). *Competitive advantage.* New York: Free Press.

Probst, G. et al. (2000). *Managing knowledge building blocks for success.* Chichester, UK: Wiley & Sons.

Rabinow, P. (1984). *The Foucault reader*. New York: Pantheon Books.

Reich, R. (1992). *The work of nations*. Vintage Books.

Robey, D., & Azevedo, A. (1994). Cultural analysis of the organizational consequences of information technology. *Accounting Management and Information Technology, 4*(1), 22-38.

Rubenstein, A., & Geisler, E. (2003). *Installing and managing workable knowledge management systems*. Westport, CT: Praeger Publishers.

Sahay, B. S., Mohan, R., & Maini, M. (2004). Strategies for building a sustainable competitive advantage. *International Journal of Innovation and Learning, 1*(3), 209-226.

Schein, E. (1996). Leadership and organizational culture. In Hesselbein et al. (Eds.), *Leader of the future*. San Francisco: Jossey Bass.

Scott Morton, M. (1991). *The corporation of the 1990s*. New York: Oxford University Press.

Senge, P. (1996). Leading learning organizations, the bold, the powerful, and the invisible. In Hesselbein et al. (Eds.), *Leader of the future*. San Francisco: Jossey Bass.

Sharma, S. K., Gupta, J. N., & Wickramasinghe, N. (2005). A framework for building learning organizations in the 21st century. International Journal of Innovation and Learning, 2(3), 261-273.

Snowden, D. (2002). Complex acts of knowing: Paradox and descriptive self-awareness. *Journal of Knowledge Management, 6*(2), 100-111.

Swan, J., Scarbrough, H., & Preston, J. (1999). Knowledge management: The next fad to forget people? *Proceedings of the 7th European Conference in Information Systems*.

Townly, B. (1993). Foucault, power/knowledge, and its relevance for human resource management. *Academy of Management Review, 18*(3), 518-545.

von Lubitz & Wickramasinghe, (2006). Dynamic leadership in unstable and unpredictable environments. *International Journal of Innovation and Learning* (in press).

Wasko, M., & Faraj, S. (2005). Why should i share? *MIS Quarterly, 29*(1), 35-37.

Wickramasinghe, N. (1999). *Using IS/IT as a tool to achieve goal alignment in the case of the knowledge worker in the healthcare industry*. Unpublished dissertation, Case Western Reserve University.

Wickramasinghe, N. (2000). IS/IT as a tool to achieve goal alignment: A theoretical framework. *International Journal Healthcare Technology Management, 2*(1/2/3/4), 163-180.

Wickramasinghe, N. (2003). Do we practise what we preach: Are knowledge management systems in practice truly reflective of knowledge management systems in theory? *Business Process Management Journal, 9*(3), 295-316.

Wickramasinghe, N., & Ginzberg, M. (2001). Integrating knowledge workers and the organization: The role of IT. *International Journal Healthcare Quality Assurance, 14*(6, 7), 245-253.

Wickramasinghe, N., & Lamb, R. (2002). Enterprise-wide systems enabling physicians to manage care. *International Journal Healthcare Technology and Management, 4*(¾), 288-302.

Wickramasinghe, N., & Mills, G. (2001). MARS: The electronic medical record system the core of the Kaiser Galaxy. *International Journal Healthcare Technology Management, 3*(5, 6), 406-423.

Wigg, K. (1993). *Knowledge management foundations*. Arlington: Schema Press.

Wilcox, L. (1997). Knowledge-based systems as an integrating process. In J. Liebowitz & L. Wilcox (Eds.), *Knowledge management and its integrative elements*. New York: CRC Press.

Endnotes

[1]   Classical agency theory also discusses a bonding term. This has no impact on self-monitoring or the use of KMS and thus, it is not discussed here. For a more complete discussion, refer to Wickramasinghe and Wickramasinghe and Lamb

[2]   Data from table was derived from Wickramasinghe (2003).

Chapter VI

The KM Technological Infrastructure

Introduction

To compete in the current dynamic business environment, organizations have to develop an ability to strategically use the knowledge assets already inherent within them as well as the new intellectual capital they create daily. As mentioned previously, knowledge management is an area that is not always easily defined, since it is broad and spans various disciplines. The field encompasses the use of management levers, techniques, methods, collaborative concepts, as well as the use of various information computer and communications technologies (IC^2T). However, it is difficult to imagine robust and effective KM initiatives taking place in the Information Age without a solid technology infrastructure supporting them. The development of such a robust infrastructure requires special attention to be paid to critical aspects, including the architecture from which the infrastructure is developed, as well as the interconnecting of the various possible IC^2T and their support of specific KM steps.

Knowledge Architecture

Architecture, specifically the information technology architecture, is an integrated set of technical choices used to guide an organization in satisfying its business needs (Weill & Broadbent, 1998). Typical information technology architectures contain policies and guidelines covering hardware and software considerations, communications and network issues, guidelines pertaining to data usage and storage, as well as applications and their functions (Wickramasinghe & Davison, 2004). Similarly, the knowledge architecture outlines key aspects of knowledge including its form, how it is captured, and transferred throughout the organization (Wickramasinghe, 2003; Wickramasinghe & Davison, 2004). Underlying the knowledge architecture (refer to Figure 1) is the recognition of the binary nature of knowledge; namely its objective and subjective components (Wickramasinghe, 2003). The knowledge architecture is designed to enable all the multiple facets of the knowledge construct to be represented within its overarching structure.

The knowledge architecture recognizes the different yet key aspects of knowledge; such as knowledge as an object and a subject, and thus provides the blue prints for the design of an all encompassing knowledge management system (KMS), in the same way the IT architecture defines the design for any IT system (Weill & Broadbent, 1998; Wickramasinghe, 2003). Clearly then, the knowledge architecture is defining a KMS that supports both objective and subjective attributes of knowledge and requires a solid KM infrastructure to be developed in order to actualize such a KMS.

The pivotal function underlined by the knowledge architecture is the flow of knowledge. The flow of knowledge is fundamentally enabled (or not) by the knowledge management system. Given the importance of knowledge, systems are being developed and implemented in organizations that aim to facilitate the sharing and integration of knowledge (i.e., support and facilitate the flow of knowledge). Such systems are called knowledge management systems (KMSs) as distinct from transaction processing systems (TPSs), management information systems (MISs), decision support systems (DSSs) (Alavi & Leidner, 1999; Lee & Yang, 2000; Persaud, 2001), and executive information systems (EISs) (Alavi, 1999). For example, companies of note that have specifically implemented KMS include Cap Gemini Ernst & Young, KPMG, and Accenture (Davenport & Hansen, 1999; Wickramasinghe, 2003). In fact, the large consulting companies were some of the first organizations to realize the benefits of knowledge management and plunge into the knowledge management abyss (Davenport & Prusak, 1998). These companies treat knowledge management with the same high priority as they do strategy formulation, an illustration of how important knowledge management is viewed in practice (Wickramasinghe, 2003). Essentially, these knowledge management systems use combinations of the following technologies: the Internet, intranets, extranets, browsers, data warehouses, data filters, data mining, client server, multimedia, groupware, and software agents

Figure 1. Overview of the knowledge architecture (Adapted from Wickramasinghe & Mills, 2001)

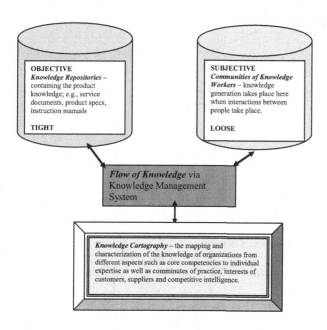

to systematically facilitate and enable the capturing, storing, and dissemination of knowledge across the organization (Alavi, 1999; Davenport & Prusak, 1998; Kanter, 1999). Unlike other categories of information systems, knowledge management systems can vary dramatically across organizations (Alavi & Leidner, 1999; Laudon & Laudon, 1999). This is appropriate if we consider that each organization's intellectual assets, intangibles, and knowledge should be to a large extent unique and thus systems enabling their management should indeed support these unique qualities and hence differ. Given the high level of the conceptual overview of the knowledge architecture presented in Figure 1, a detailed yet generic KM architecture that could be used for knowledge capture, creation, distribution, and sharing in any organization is shown in Figure 2. In particular, it is important to note that such a generic KM architecture consists of 3 main layers; namely, the data source layer, the knowledge management layer and the knowledge presentation layer (Liebowitz, 1999), all of which are consistent with the high level overview of the knowledge architecture

Figure 2. Generic KM architecture

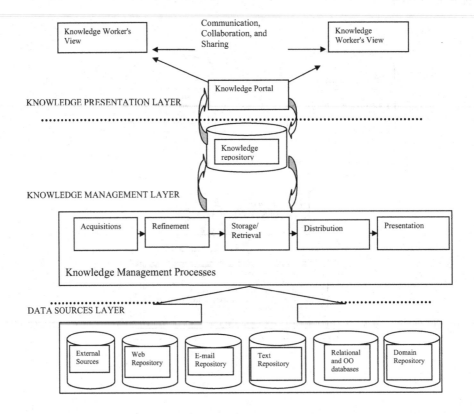

since they are flexible yet robust enough to support both the subjective and objective aspects of the knowledge construct. In many ways the most complex layer, the knowledge management layer, plays a key role in the design of an appropriate and effective KM architecture. Figure 3 provides a drill down view of the major tools, techniques, and technologies that make up this layer. Once again, we emphasize that even with the knowledge management layer we do not merely have technologies but also incorporate people and techniques. The KM infrastructure then helps to actualize and support the blue prints established by the KM architecture, and also highlight the interactions required at the human/technology interface (Duffy, 2000, 2001; Wickramasinghe, 2003; Wickramasinghe & Davison, 2004).

Figure 3. Knowledge management layer tools, techniques, and technologies

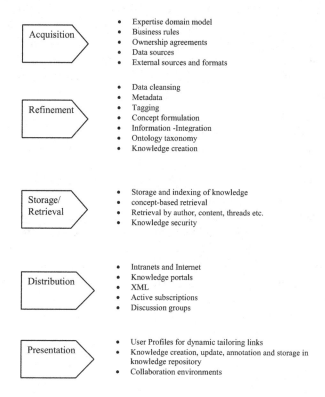

Acquisition
- Expertise domain model
- Business rules
- Ownership agreements
- Data sources
- External sources and formats

Refinement
- Data cleansing
- Metadata
- Tagging
- Concept formulation
- Information -Integration
- Ontology taxonomy
- Knowledge creation

Storage/ Retrieval
- Storage and indexing of knowledge
- concept-based retrieval
- Retrieval by author, content, threads etc.
- Knowledge security

Distribution
- Intranets and Internet
- Knowledge portals
- XML
- Active subscriptions
- Discussion groups

Presentation
- User Profiles for dynamic tailoring links
- Knowledge creation, update, annotation and storage in knowledge repository
- Collaboration environments

Establishing a Knowledge Management Infrastructure

The business world is growing increasingly more competitive and the demand for innovative products and services has become greater than ever before. In this period of creativity and ideas, the most valuable resources available to any organization are human skills, expertise, and relationships (Drucker, 1988, 1993, 1999). KM is about capitalizing on these precious assets (Duffy, 2001). Currently, most companies do not capitalize on the wealth of expertise in the form of knowledge scattered across their levels (Gold, Malhotra, & Segars, 2001; Halliday, 2001). However, information centers, market intelligence, and learning are now converging to form knowledge management functions. A KM infrastructure, in terms of tools and technologies (hardware as well as software), needs to be established so that knowledge can be created from any new event or activity on a continual and systematic basis (Duffy, 2000; Wickramasinghe, 2003).

The KM infrastructure forms the foundation for enabling and fostering knowledge management, continuous learning, and sustaining an organizational memory (Drucker, 1999; Ellinger, Watkins, & Bostrom, 1999; Hammond, 2001; Holt, Love, & Li, 2000; Lee & Hong, 2002). An organization's entire "know-how," including new knowledge, can only be created for optimization if an effective KM infrastructure is established (Wickramasinghe & Davison, 2004). Specifically, the KM infrastructure consists of social and technical tools and techniques, including hardware and software that should be established so that knowledge can be created from any new events or activities on a continual basis (Duffy, 2000, 2001; Wickramasinghe & Davison, 2004). In addition, the KM infrastructure will have a repository of knowledge, a system to distribute the knowledge to the members of the organization, and a facilitator system for the creation of new knowledge (Wickramasinghe & Davison, 2004). Thus, a knowledge based infrastructure will foster the creation

Figure 4. Five key elements of the knowledge management infrastructure (Adapted from Wickramasinghe & Davison, 2004)

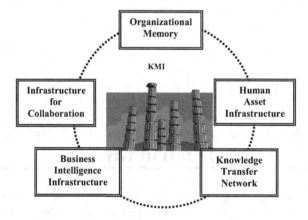

of knowledge, and provide an integrated system to share and diffuse the knowledge within the organization (Srikantaiah, 2000), as well as offer support for continual creation and generation of new knowledge (Wickramasinghe, 2003). A knowledge management infrastructure contains, at least, the elements displayed in Figure 4 and described in Table 1.

Table 1. Elements of the knowledge management infrastructure

Element of the Knowledge Management Infrastructure	Description
Infrastructure for Collaboration	The key to competitive advantage and improving customer satisfaction lies in the ability of organizations to form learning alliances; these being strategic partnerships based on a business environment that encourages mutual (and reflective) learning between partners (Holt et al., 2000). Organizations can utilize their strategy framework to identify partners and collaborators for enhancing their value chain.
Organizational Memory	Organizational memory is concerned with the storing, subsequent accessing, and replenishing of an organization's "know-how" which is recorded in documents or in its people (Maier & Lehner, 2000). However, a key component of knowledge management not addressed in the construct of organizational memory is the subjective aspect (Wickramasinghe, 2003).[1] Organizational memory keeps a record of knowledge resources and locations. Recorded information, whether in human-readable, electronic form, or in the memories of staff is an important embodiment of an organization's knowledge and intellectual capital. Thus, strong organizational memory systems ensure the access of information or knowledge throughout the company to everyone at any time (Croasdell, 2001).
Human Asset Infrastructure	This deals with the participation and willingness of people. Today, organizations have to attract and motivate the best people; reward, recognize, train, educate, and improve them (Ellinger et al., 1999) so that the highly skilled and more independent workers can exploit technologies to create knowledge in learning organizations (Thorne & Smith, 2000). The human asset infrastructure helps to identify and utilize the special skills of people who can create greater business value if they and their inherent skills and experiences are managed to make explicit use of their knowledge.
Knowledge Transfer Network	This element is concerned with the dissemination of knowledge and information. Unless there is a strong communication infrastructure in place, people are not able to communicate effectively and thus are unable to effectively transfer knowledge. An appropriate communications infrastructure includes, but is not limited to, the Internet and intranets for creating the knowledge transfer network as well as discussion rooms, bulletin boards for meetings, and for displaying information.
Business Intelligence Infrastructure	In an intelligent enterprise, various information systems are integrated with knowledge-gathering and analyzing tools for data analysis and dynamic end-user querying of a variety of enterprise data sources (Hammond, 2001). Business intelligence infrastructures have customers, suppliers, and other partners embedded into single integrated system. Customers will view their own purchasing habits, and suppliers will see the demand pattern, which may help them to offer volume discounts etc. This information can help all customers, suppliers and enterprises to analyze data and provide them with the competitive advantage. The intelligence of a company is not only available to internal users but can even be leveraged by selling it to others such as consumers who may be interested in.

Knowledge Management Infrastructure Design

Knowledge management facilitates the following processes (Alavi & Leidner, 1999; Marshall & Prusak, 1996; Wickramasinghe, 2003):

1. **Generation of knowledge:** Creating new, tacit knowledge.

2. **Access of knowledge:** Accessed easily by people inside or outside the firm.

3. **Transfer of knowledge:** Transferred formally through training or informally through social contact.

4. **Representation of knowledge:** Represented by recorded, explicit knowledge that is easy to utilize.

5. **Embedding of knowledge:** Automating the use of knowledge in a decision-making process.

6. **Facilitation of knowledge:** Developing cultures and policies that support knowledge sharing.

It is important that management reviews the knowledge processes to determine which is best suited to the company's business strategy since not all processes are as important or relevant for every KM initiative. We shall now examine more closely the technologies and technological infrastructure issues that support each of these processes. We emphasize that technology should not be viewed in isolation; rather it is important that both technological and organizational considerations are made in tandem when developing an appropriate KM infrastructure.

In choosing and designing a knowledge management infrastructure, an important consideration is to first address the organization's process needs: generation of knowledge, access of knowledge, transfer of knowledge, representation of knowledge, embedding of knowledge, and facilitation of knowledge (Davenport & Klahr, 1998; Duffy, 2000; Orlikowsky, 1992; Schultz, 1998; Swan, Scarbrough, & Preston, 1999). From this, the next steps should concentrate on identifying the necessary technological and organizational infrastructures that will support these processes. Table 2 summarizes these major infrastructures that support knowledge management.

Infrastructures that Support the Generation of Knowledge

Technology assists in the generation of knowledge by allowing people to freely exchange ideas by using tools such as electronic networks and groupware. Marshall

Table 2. Key knowledge management processes and related infrastructures

KM Process	Information Technology Infrastructures	Organizational Infrastructures

Generation of knowledge	• Electronic networking
	  • Internet
	  • Intranets
	  • Extranets
	• Groupware
		• Human experts and knowledge workers

Access of knowledge	• Data warehouses • Online databases • Knowledge repositories • Expertise directories	• Accessibility of human experts
Transfer of knowledge	• Data mining • OLAP	• Formal training • Apprenticeships • Informal socialization • Formal socialization
Representation of knowledge	• Knowledge maps	• Knowledge centers • Document management centers
Embedding of knowledge	• Decision support systems • Intelligent agents	
Facilitation of knowledge flow	• Electronic networking • Groupware	• Top management leadership • Rewards and incentives • Succession policies

and Prusak (1996) explain that the generation of new knowledge takes place in a social setting where people can openly discuss, argue, and challenge prevailing theories. Technology tools that support the generation of knowledge revolve around expediting communication. For example, a new product development team needs to facilitate communication among many different departments including research, engineering, marketing, and finance.

Electronic networking is perhaps the greatest tool for generating knowledge (Kanter, 1999). The Internet allows geographically distant people to communicate and share information easily and cheaply by using standard protocols. Intranets on the other hand, allow the effortless sharing of confidential information among employees and security levels can easily be set for each employee allowing access only for those who need to know or for all employees. Some of the most useful application of intranets have been to support and encourage peer-to-peer knowledge sharing and its applications (Dixon, 2000). Companies can also use extranets, which are designed to offer clients or suppliers access to needed company information. In an increasingly linked and just-in-time environment, accurate and timely information sharing among partners is increasingly important to support rapid decision-making.

Another popular communication tool is groupware, software specifically designed to support teamwork. In a university setting for example, WcbCT offers a portal for students and instructors to quickly access documents and communicate through e-mail and bulletin boards. Key features of groupware that make it particularly useful for supporting the KM steps are that it allows every team member to have access instantly to the same body of information and that it is possible to support each other as well as support simultaneous changes made to this information.

Infrastructures that Support the Access of Knowledge

KM companies assist employees in accessing knowledge. Knowledge access is often facilitated by technology, including data warehouses, online databases, and knowledge repositories. In large companies, knowing every employee and his or her specialty nears impossibility. Designing a space in which employees may seek the specific knowledge that they require is the goal of creating access. The physical librarian at the reference desk was once the starting point for many research questions. Today, much of the librarian's job as the key to knowledge and the library's function of a warehouse of information is automated.

Data warehouses have contributed greatly to the knowledge management movement. They store snapshots of operational data such as sales, inventory, and customer information. Many larger companies now have ten to twenty years of transactional data with which they can assess their relative current position or upon which they can build future models. For example, Tandem Computers has designed a data warehouse to which many systems can report, making it possible to assess key numbers (e.g., sales data and financial data that come in from disparate locations) to the one place (Marshall & Prusak, 1996).

Online databases often refer to external information databases such as Lexis-Nexis, which provides access to published news and research. However, online databases may also refer to internal databases. A best practices database can offer solutions to common and not so common problems. For instance, help desks often create best practice databases to better serve customers.

Knowledge repositories usually refer to postings of reports on past projects. The Big 6 consulting firms develop repositories of client proposals, leads, white papers, presentations, and many other documents that consultants all over the globe produce (Kanter, 1999).

Though much of the knowledge management literature refers to accessibility of knowledge through technology, the accessibility of human experts is also of critical importance. Cross, Parker, Prusak, and Borgatti (2001) explain that knowing who knows what, gaining timely access, willingly sharing knowledge rather than dumping information, and feeling safe in asking for information facilitate the access of tacit knowledge, knowledge in the expert's head. Companies often create electronic expertise directories to help employees find needed contacts and mentors.

Infrastructures that Support the Transfer of Knowledge

Transferring knowledge usually begins with the distribution of written reports. Transferring knowledge also includes training employees to interpret the reports and educating employees about the structure of the organization and to whom they should go for specific knowledge (Marshall & Prusak, 1996). Transferring data may also include techniques for transforming inert data into usable information.

Data mining and OLAP (online analytic processing) permit companies to analyze the jumble of data stored in data warehouses. For example, grocery stores use rule induction to produce information on who buys what and what products are purchased together. Information is gathered via a shopping card. Information based on shopping card usage may be used to target promotional offers (e.g., coupons given to customers at the register) to particular customers. Mathematical models and cheap computing power allow quick, in-depth analysis of large volumes of historical data.

Many more organizational, rather than technological, structures facilitate the transfer of knowledge. Formal training and apprenticeships are a tried and true method of transferring knowledge to new employees or to employees who are working towards a promotion. New KPMG employees undergo rigorous training in the Internet and KPMG's internal knowledge Web (Kanter, 1999).

Informal socialization includes discussions at the water cooler, casual exchanges over lunches among colleagues, and any other unstructured event that allows the sharing of ideas. With the demand for increased output and the globalization of many businesses, fewer opportunities exist for serendipitous information exchange.

Formal socialization attempts to create opportunities for knowledge exchange may include group meetings or knowledge fairs. A common knowledge fair might include employees from research and development and from marketing with the expectation that their knowledge would combine with synergy to create new product ideas.

Infrastructures that Support the Representation of Knowledge

Representation of knowledge is often determined by a department that organizes and sets standards for what knowledge is retained and in which format it is to be retained. Often a knowledge center or a document management center will oversee the presentation of knowledge. First, the company faces a policy choice of which knowledge is important and worth storing. Second, the knowledge center must decide on the best way of presenting information (e.g., a text document, a database, a media clip, a hyperlinked document). Third, the knowledge center should consistently manage its documents to eliminate obsolete documents and create ease of use. Access to these documents is often through a document repository.

Companies with large numbers and varieties of documents may design knowledge maps (Kanter, 1999). A knowledge map is a visual display of captured knowledge that allows an information seeker to follow paths from one source of stored information to another. Often a knowledge map is a hyperlinked hierarchy of topics that represents documents residing on a server.

Infrastructures that Support the Embedding of Knowledge

Infrastructures that support the embedding of knowledge are primarily technological. These tools are complicated—computerized checklists and decision trees—that aid in decision-making. Marshall and Prusak (1996) explain that automating knowledge in the form of computerized controls works best when the inputs and outputs are factual and not based on biases or uncertain interpretations. When knowledge facts are embedded in an automated checklist, front line employees can use the experience and knowledge of their peers. However, facts do change; management should take care to keep the facts that aid decision-making current.

Decision support systems are designed to help decision makers make an informed choice based on the outcomes of past decisions. For example, Partners HealthCare designed a decision support system to help doctors prescribe the best medication to its hospital patients (Davenport & Glaser, 2002). In this case, the decision support system accessed patient records and databases of drug characteristics to suggest the drug and dosage that best helped the patient and best lowered hospital costs. The 700-bed hospital estimates that it saved $1 million by preventing adverse drug reactions in patients.

Intelligent agents are software packages that save time and effort by embedding commands or knowledge in computer processes. A simple example is sophisticated e-mail software. The software may allow the user to create rules for directing mail to different folders or automatically scheduling meetings based on the information in the e-mail message (Kanter, 1999). Spreadsheets are another example of embedded knowledge. Excel's statistical package can calculate in seconds what it would take a person, days to calculate.

Infrastructures that Support the Facilitation of Knowledge

The facilitation of knowledge is primarily supported by culture, top management leadership, and rewards and incentives. The culture of a company is the primary social infrastructure for the sharing of knowledge. In a knowledge management environment a sharing culture should be cultivated. Competitive environments often prevent the sharing of knowledge. Some highly competitive firms are endeavoring to change their cultures. For example, Salomon Brothers has asked its stock traders to think more like a stockholder than a stock trader. Top management leadership and human resource policy have the most influence on a company's culture.

Top management leadership, primarily leadership by example, can be a strong influence on the exchange of knowledge. Do the top leaders themselves share information throughout the company? Does the company have an open-book policy? Jack Welch is known for his policy on being number one or two in the market and for his policies on promotion, including his emphasis on the criteria that an employee must demonstrate being a team player before he or she can warrant promotion (Slater, 1999).

Rewards and incentives support behavior and companies should oversee compensation systems to influence positive behavior (Davenport & Prusak, 1998). For instance, stock traders who are paid based on the volume of trades, in general, focus on increasing volume rather than on what would benefit the company or the customer. In such scenarios, companies should also consider implementing policies that compensate employees for sharing usable knowledge. Perhaps an employee could earn a small bonus every time a document he or she posted is accessed.

In a knowledge company, developing succession policies becomes crucial for knowledge retention. When an employee retires or is downsized, the company usually loses the tacit knowledge that is only known by the individual. Lesser and Prusak (2001) suggest four tactics for minimizing the loss of departing employees: (1) when layoffs are under consideration, think instead about reducing the salary of all employees; (2) devise practices to capture the knowledge of employees on the verge of retirement; (3) pay departing employees a bonus for training their replacement; and (4) encourage experienced employees to work with new employees.

Knowledge Management Tools and Techniques

Knowledge management tools encompass the technologies and techniques of collaborative computing and the soft issues of teamwork, cooperation, and group dynamics. Companies increasingly recognize knowledge management's potential to unlock corporate information resources—both implicit and explicit—as they seek to improve business practices and processes, deliver innovative products and services, and gain competitive advantage. Internet technologies provide the necessary connectivity and interoperability, offering a low-cost, standardized, future-proof, backward-compatible network infrastructure—a so-called intranet. However, adoption of an intranet as a corporate communications conduit is still insufficient. Companies must develop and optimize internal information sources to realize their growth potential, tap external knowledge sources—including joint-venture partners, strategic alliances, and university sources—to improve or expand their capabilities, and provide all participants in the value chain with a framework for understanding, participating in, and improving the company's operations and profit growth potential.

Knowledge-management tools help companies enhance knowledge creation and encourage its proliferation throughout the enterprise. Knowledge-management tools enable the collection, coordination, and distribution of information and knowledge so that team members can collaborate effectively in pursuit of a common goal. Although some analysts dismiss the term knowledge management as hyperbole, the underpinning technologies of workflow systems, conferencing tools, and electronic meeting support systems, harnessed by corporate intranet and extranet systems, have already taken root within many organizations. Only through the creation of networks of knowledge—both within and between companies—can organizations remove barriers of distance and time between distributed groups, increase quality and productivity, and facilitate competitiveness within the expanding global marketplace. The major KM tools and techniques can be thought of in different ways and it is important at all times not to lose focus of either their impacts or their technological capabilities. It is useful to think of the major KM tools and techniques in terms of their social and community role in the organization be it in (1) the facilitation of knowledge sharing and socialization of knowledge (production of organizational knowledge); (2) the conversion of information into knowledge through easy access, opportunities of internalization and learning (supported by the right work environment and culture); (3) the conversion of tacit knowledge into "explicit knowledge" or information, for purposes of efficient and systematic storage, retrieval, wider sharing, and application. In doing so, it brings to the forefront their role in specific aspects and components within the knowledge management layer of the generic KM architecture in Figure 2. Another useful approach to consider regarding KM tools and techniques is to group them in relation to those that capture and codify knowledge and those that share and distribute knowledge. Such a conceptualization tends to emphasize their underlying technical capabilities.

KM Tools and Technologies that Capture and Codify Knowledge

There are various tools that can be used to capture and codify knowledge. These include databases, and various types of artificial intelligence systems including expert systems, neural networks, fuzzy logic, genetic algorithms, and intelligent or software agents.

Databases

Databases store structured information and assist in the storing and sharing of knowledge. Knowledge can be acquired from the relationships that exist among different tables in a database. For example, the relationship that might exist between a customer table and a product table could show those products that are producing adequate margins, providing decision-makers with strategic marketing knowledge. Many different relations can exist and are only limited by the human imagination. These relational databases help users to make informed reliable decisions, which is a goal of knowledge management. Discrete, structured information is still managed best by a database management system. However, the quest for a universal user interface has led to the requirement for access to existing database information through a Web browser.

Data Mining Techniques

The exponential increase in information, primarily due to the electronic capture of data and its storage in vast data warehouses, has created a demand for analyzing the large amount of data generated by today's organizations so that enterprises can respond quickly to fast changing markets. These applications not only involve the analysis of the data but also require sophisticated tools for analysis. Knowledge discovery technologies are the new technologies that help to analyze data and find relationships from data to finding reasons behind observable patterns. Such new discoveries can have profound impact on designing business strategies. Thus, data mining techniques, and the newer techniques of business intelligence and business analytics, which basically combine the major data mining techniques with key business objectives, drivers, and outcomes critical to the generation of knowledge from data assets, dominate the technical tools for deriving knowledge from an organizations data assets. Four key data mining techniques include (Fadlalla & Wickramasinghe, 2005):

1. Decision tree;
2. Clustering;
3. Neural networks; and
4. Association rule.

Figure 5. Major techniques of data mining

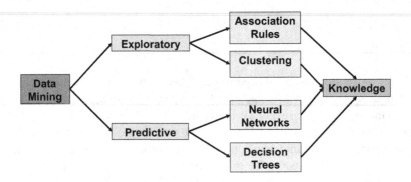

While we acknowledge there are numerous data mining techniques, we focus on these techniques since they are some of the major techniques currently used in most data mining initiatives; the first two techniques are used for exploratory data mining, the latter two techniques are used for predictive data mining (Figure 5). We will first outline the major steps involved in data mining in order to achieve the final goal of knowledge creation, before we describe each of the previous data mining techniques.

Data mining is the non-trivial process of identifying valid, novel, potentially useful, and ultimately understandable patterns from data (Fayyad, Piatetskey-Shapirio, Smyth, & Uthurusamy, 1996). Data mining algorithms are used on databases for model building, or for finding patterns in data. When these patterns are new, useful, and understandable, we say that this is knowledge discovery. How to manage such discovered knowledge and other organizational knowledge is the realm of knowledge management.

As discussed in Chapter III, data mining is a step in the broader context of the knowledge discovery process that transforms data into knowledge. Figure 6 shows the knowledge discovery process, the evolution of knowledge from data through information to knowledge (Fayyad et al., 1996) as well as the types of data mining (exploratory and predictive) and their interrelationships. Data issues that data mining helps us wrestle with include huge volumes of data, dynamic data, incomplete data, imprecise data, noisy data, missing attribute values, redundant data, and inconsistent data. Furthermore, data mining offers a wide variety of models to capture the characteristics of data and to help knowledge discovery including summarization, clustering/segmentation, regression, classification, neural networks, rough sets, association analysis, sequence analysis, prediction, exploratory analysis, and visualization.

Figure 6. Data mining and the KDD process

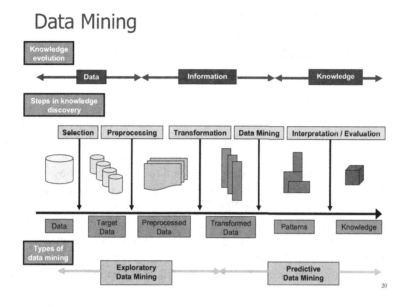

As can bee seen in Figure 6 the data extracted from the large pool of data is not the final outcome intended. It typically contains a significant amount of erroneous information that should be excluded prior to inputting the correct data to be processed by the data mining algorithms; thus, data goes through the following process steps before being used for any decision-making or prior to any of the previous techniques being utilized effectively (Fadlalla & Wickramasinghe, 2005; Fayyad et al., 1996).

1. **Selection:** Selecting the data according to some criteria (e.g., all those people who are suffering from heart attack).

2. **Preprocessing:** This is the data cleansing stage where certain unwanted information is removed which may slow down queries.

3. **Transformation:** The data is not merely transferred across but transformed in that overlays may be added.

4. **Data mining:** This stage is concerned with the extraction of patterns from the data. It includes choosing a data-mining algorithm, which is appropriate to search a particular pattern in the data.

5.   **Interpretation and evaluation:** The patterns identified by the system are interpreted into knowledge by removing redundant or irrelevant patterns, and translating the useful patterns into terms that can be understood by users.

Let us now examine more closely the four key data mining techniques.

Decision Tree (Fadlalla & Wickramasinghe, 2005; Fayyad et al., 1996)

In critical decision situations, mistakes are undesirable and costly. Thus, data mining techniques are used to find the most pertinent information and data to facilitate superior decision making. The decision tree technique achieves this by closing the gap between the facts and real understanding. Decision tree represents the knowledge or the available information in tree-like form and then a method for treatment is selected. The decision is usually made on the choices of outcomes. Decision trees are built through recursive partitioning, which is splitting the data into partitions and subsequently splitting it further (refer to Figure 7). All the information is first used to determine the structure of the tree. The critical aspect in decision tree mak-

Figure 7. Data mining resulting in the decision tree—each path from the tree root down represents a rule (i.e., a type of pattern) (Adapted from Fadlalla & Wickramaisngeh, 2005)

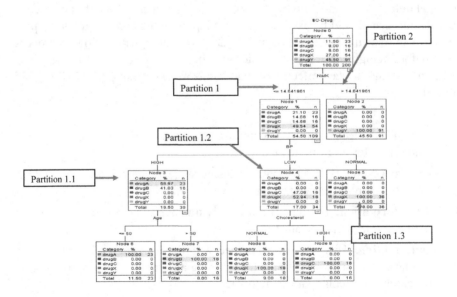

ing is the location of the initial split. This split has a binary positioning in the field. The first splitter is found because it is important to decide a single class, which predominates. Then the reduction of diversity is done.

The diversity in the tree decides the probability of a certain symptom occurring from the given set. If there are just two probabilities, the condition is the simplest since the probability of one is minus the other. Then the second splitter is again divided depending upon the choices after the initial node. This continues until the outcome can no longer be subdivided and is labeled as a leaf node. If there is just one decision to be made, such a node is removed. The best solution of the splitter is determined and a leaf node is made (Figure 5 depicts this). The second part of decision tree making is the pruning of the excess and unnecessary nodes. Excess leaves make the performance of decision tree analysis less efficient. The pruning method allows the tree to grow deep and find ways to prune off the branches that fail to generalize. Pruning is important to ensure the highest quality outputs at all times.

Consequences of Choosing the Decision Tree Technique

Each partition in the decision tree is a test of a single variable. The interrelation between the variables can never be found from the decision tree.

Advantages of the Decision Tree Technique

*   The decision tree as a whole is a graphical representation since visually the tree structure itself supports the location of the correct split or accurate decision.
*   The model of the decision tree helps in reasoning and can be used to examine and justify a decision choice.

Disadvantages of the Decision Tree Technique

The decision tree variables cannot predict a continuous response variable. Specifically, all the splits are dependent on the previous splits. Hence, the model has high order interactions. The decision tree cannot discover a single rule based on the ratio when two values are given rather a new variable has to be defined to specify a simple rule. The shortcoming of decision tree is in the way it handles the numeric input variables which sometimes leads to loss of the information. The decision tree first groups all the information and then categorizes which may lead to loss of information.

Clustering (Fadlalla & Wickramasinghe, 2005; Fayyad et al., 1996)

In the study and treatment of chromosomal and DNA related problems for example, the clustering technique is important. This technique is a type of undirected data mining. The purpose of undirected data mining is to find the structure as a whole (i.e., there are no target variables which are to be predicted but the clusters are formed and grouped together) and then the decision is made using decision tree or neural network techniques. This is a relatively primary tool, typically used merely to study all the possible conditions before more refined and confirmatory analysis takes place.

Clustering is a classification technique, which enables us to find specific factors such as the likelihood of a patient recovering from cancer. Clustering can also be used for maintaining the records for patients in terms of their height, weight, or other historic variables. The most frequently used method for clustering is k-mean. This is a geometrical method, which uses the average location of all the members from the particular cluster. The whole field is divided into numbers and then these numbers are normalized. The value of each field is interpreted as the distance from the origin along the corresponding axis. Here the centers are initially defined and then adjusted using predefined algorithms. To start a clustering session, a random set of centers are chosen which are then adjusted by adding to and removing centers during the analysis processes. The clustering technique is dependent on the two main criteria:

1.   The cluster must be homogeneous (i.e., membership within a group must be as similar as possible).

2.   Each group or cluster must be mutually exclusive (i.e., two groups should be as distinct as possible).

In most cases, clusters are usually mutually exclusive but in some instances, they may be overlapping, probabilistic or have hierarchical structures. In k-means, a data point is assigned to the cluster, which has the nearest centriod (i.e., the nearest mean). Clustering requires the data to be in numeric form since it works by assigning the cluster points accordingly. This process of assigning points to clusters continues until points stop changing positions (i.e., cluster hopping) and their boundaries become stable.

Consequences of Choosing the Clustering Technique

Clustering is one of the less rigorous data mining techniques used in exploratory data mining and is often classified as undirected data mining (Kudyba & Hoptroff, 2001). This is because the analyst seeks to discover hidden relationships in the data without directing the analysis. The approach combines computer algorithm techniques and statistical measures to identify like groups or clusters and enables the analysis to quickly and accurately mine through large volumes of data.

Advantages of Clustering

- The main strength of clustering is that it is an undirected knowledge discovery technique.

- The clustering can be used as a preparatory technique for other data mining techniques such as decision trees or neural networks.

- The outcome of clustering can be visually represented and hence easily understood.

- Creating clusters reduces the complexity of the problem by sub-dividing the problem space into more manageable partitions.

- The more separable the data points the more effective the clustering effort becomes.

Disadvantages of Using Clustering

- Clustering represents a snap shot of the data at a certain point in time and thus may not be as useful in highly dynamic situations.

- Sometimes the clusters generated may not even have a practical meaning.

- It is possible not to spot the cluster sometimes since you do not know for what you are looking.

- Clustering can be computationally expensive.

Neural Networks (Fadlalla & Wickramasinghe, 2005; Fayyad et al., 1996)

The technique of neural networks is modeled after the human brain and normally consists of many input nodes, one or more hidden (middle) layer nodes and one or more output nodes. The input and output nodes relate to each other through the hidden layer. The input layer represents the raw information that is fed into the network. The hidden layer represents a computational layer that transforms the inputs coming from the input layer into inputs to the output layer. The behavior of the output layer depends on the activity of the hidden layer where the weights between the hidden and output layers are used as a reconciliation mechanism to help minimize the difference between the actual and desired outputs.

The outcome of a neural network is improved through the minimization of an error function (i.e., namely the difference between a desired output and an actual output value). The most widely used algorithm that is used to minimize this error function is known as back propagation. Each input pattern is evaluated individually and if its value exceeds a predetermined threshold, then a pre-specified rule fires (i.e., is activated) whereby its outcome is fed forward to the next layer. The firing rule is an important concept in neural networks and accounts for the high flexibility of the technique since the rule determines how one calculates whether a subsequent neuron (node) should fire for any given input pattern.

The most important application of neural networks is pattern recognition. The network is trained to associate specific output patterns with input patterns. The power of neural networks comes into play in its predictive abilities (i.e., associating an input pattern that has not previously been classified with a specific output pattern). In such cases, the network will most likely give the output that corresponds to a pre-classified input pattern that is least different from the new input pattern.

Neural networks are mainly used in the medical sciences in recognising disease types from various scans such as MRI or CT scans. The neural networks learn by example and therefore the more examples we feed into the neural network the more accurate its predictive capabilities become. Neural networks can process a large number of medical records each of which includes the information on symptoms, diagnoses, and treatments for a particular case. The use of neural network as a potential tool in medical science is exemplified by its use in the study of mammograms. In breast cancer detection, the primary task is detection of tumorous cells in the early stages. The best probability for a successful cure of this disease is in its early detection. Therefore, the power of neural networks lies in that they could be used to detect minute changes in tissue patterns (a key indicator of the existence of malignant cells) that are often difficult to detect with the human eye.

Advantages of Neural Networks

- Neural networks are good classification and prediction techniques when the results of the model are more important than the understanding of how the model works.
- Neural networks are very robust in that they can be used to model any type of relationship implied by the input patterns.
- Neural networks can easily be implemented to take advantage of the power of parallel computers with each processor simultaneously doing its own calculations.
- Neural networks are very robust in situations where the data is noisy.

Disadvantages of Neural Networks

- The key problem with neural networks is the difficulty to explain its outcome. Unlike decision trees, neural networks use complex non-linear modeling that does not produce rules and hence it is hard to justify ones decision.
- Significant preprocessing and preparation of the data is required.

- Neural networks will tend to over-fit the data unless implemented carefully. This is due to the fact that the neural networks have a large number of parameters, which can fit well into any arbitrary data set.

- Neural networks require extensive training time unless the problem is small.

Association Rule Mining (Fadlalla & Wickramasinghe, 2005; Fayyad et al., 1996)

Association rules are used to discover relationships between attribute sets for a given input pattern. Such relationships do not necessarily imply causation, they are only associations. For example, an association rule that can be derived from medical data could be that 80% of the cases that display a given symptom are diagnosed with a similar condition and hence improves diagnostic capabilities. These patterns (associations) are not easily discovered using other data mining techniques. The support of an association rule is the percentage of cases, which include the antecedent of the rule, while the confidence of the association rule is the percentage of cases where both the antecedent and the consequence of the rule are displayed. Only rules whose support and confidence exceed predetermined thresholds are considered useful. The classic algorithm used to generate these rules is the apriori *algorithm*.

Advantages of Association Rule

- The association rules are readily understandable.
- Association rules are best suited for categorical data analysis.
- It is widely used in hospitals to maintain patient's records.
- The outcomes are easy to interpret and explain and thus easy to use in the aiding of decision-making.

Disadvantages of Association Rule Mining

- Generate too many rules and sometimes these are even trivial rules.
- The association rules are not expressions of cause/effect rather they are descriptive relationships in particular databases, so there is no formal testing to increase the predictive power of these rules.
- Insight, analysis, and explanation by healthcare professionals are usually required to identify the new and useful rules and thereby achieve the full benefits from such association rules.

The exponential increase in information, primarily due to the electronic capture of data and its storage in vast data warehouses, has created a demand for analyzing the large volumes of data so that enterprises can respond quickly to fast changing markets. These applications not only involve the analysis of the data, but also require sophisticated tools for analysis. Knowledge discovery technologies, in particular the techniques of data mining, are the essential technologies that help to analyze data, find significant relationships between data and then help to find reasons behind observable patterns. Such new discoveries can have a profound impact on designing business strategies. With the massive increase in data being collected and the demands for intelligent applications like customer relationship management, demand planning and predictive forecasting, the knowledge discovery technologies have become necessities to providing a high performance and feature rich intelligent application servers. A knowledge-based economy is heavily reliant on such information technology, knowledge sharing, as well as intellectual capital and knowledge management, to maximize the true potential of data assets.

We now briefly review some other key technologies connected with knowledge capture and codification.

Case-Based Reasoning Applications (Kolodner, 1991; Slade, 1991)

Case-based reasoning (CBR) represents a general paradigm for reasoning from experience and has two main objectives: (1) trying to understand, using scientific means the nature of intelligence and human thought; and (2) trying to develop technological intelligence that "mirrors" human intelligence. Problem solving requires knowledge while memory is the repository for this knowledge thus making the representation and storage of knowledge critical for CBR. Hence, applications combine narratives and knowledge codification to assist in problem solving. Descriptions and facts about processes and solutions to problems are recorded and categorized. When a problem is encountered, queries or searches point to the solution. CBR applications store limited knowledge from individuals who have encountered a problem and found the solution and are a useful means of transferring this knowledge to others.

Expert Systems (Buchanan & Shortliffe, 1984; Leonard-Barton & Sviokla, 1988)

Expert systems represent the knowledge of experts and typically query and guide users during a decision-making process. They focus on specific processes and typically lead the user, step by step, toward a solution. The level of knowledge required to operate these applications is usually not as high as for CBR applications. Expert systems have not been as successful as CBR in commercial applications but can still be used to teach knowledge management.

CAD/CAM (Laudon & Laudon, 1999)

CAD/CAM (computer-aided design/computer-aided manufacturing) systems are a combination of hardware and software that enable engineers and architects to design everything from furniture to airplanes. In particular, CAD/CAM systems allow an engineer to view a design from any angle with the push of a button and to zoom in or out for close-ups and long-distance views. In addition, the computer keeps track of design dependencies so that when the engineer changes one value, all other values that depend on it are changed accordingly.

Using I-Net Agents: Creating Individual Views from Unstructured Content (Duffy, 2001)

The world of human communication and information has long been too voluminous and complex for any one individual to monitor and track. Agents and I-net standards are the building blocks that make individual customization of information possible in the unstructured environment of I-nets. Agents will begin to specialize and play a more significant role than current general purpose search engines and "push" technologies.

Two complementary technologies have emerged that allow us to coordinate, communicate, and even organize information, without rigid, one-size-fits-all structures. The first is the Internet/Web technologies that are referred to as I-net technology and the second is the evolution of software agents. Together, these technologies represent the new-age building blocks for robust knowledge architectures, designed to help information consumers find the knowledge they are looking for in the manner in which it is required. The Web and software agents make it possible to build sophisticated, well performing information brokers designed to deliver content, from multiple sources, to each individual, in the individual's specific context and under the individual's own control. The software agents supported with I-net infrastructure can be highly effective tools for individualizing the organization and management of distributed information.

Distributed Hypertext Systems (Hammond, 2001)

Distributed hypertext systems have been concerned with the generating and leveraging of organizational knowledge for more than a dozen years. Theodor Holm Nelson coined the term "hypertext" in the 1960s, and his writings about representation, access, and management of knowledge, embodied in his vision for Project Xanadu—a global "docuverse" that pre-figured the World Wide Web, are useful for managing information and knowledge.

KM Tools and Technologies that Share and Distribute Knowledge

Computer networks provide an effective medium for the communication and development of knowledge management. The Internet and organizational intranets are used as a basic infrastructure for knowledge management (Alavi, 1999; Wickramasinghe, 2003). Intranets are rapidly becoming the primary information infrastructure for enterprises. An intranet is basically a platform based on Internet principles accessible only to members of an organization/community. The intranet can provide the platform for a safe and secure information management system within the organization, help people to collaborate as virtual teams, crossing boundaries of geography and time. While the Internet is an open-access platform, the intranet, however, is restricted to members of a community/organization through multi-layered security controls. The same platform, can be extended to an outer ring (e.g., dealer networks, registered customers, online members, etc.), with limited accessibility, as an extranet. The extranet can be a meaningful platform for knowledge generation and sharing, in building relationships, and in enhancing the quality and effectiveness of service/support.

The systems that are used to share and distribute knowledge include (Wickramasinghe & Lichtenstein, 2005): e-mail, group collaboration systems, groupware, intranets, extranets and the Internet, document management systems, geographic information systems (GIS), which involve digitized maps coupled with powerful computer and software that permit the superimposition and manipulation of various types of demographic and corporate data on maps, Help desk technologies, and even office systems such as word processing, desktop publishing, and Web publishing. The computer-supported collaborative work (CSCW) community addresses issues of shared development of knowledge and its relevant technologies including group decision support systems, groupware such as Lotus Notes and Netscape's Collabra Share as well as the more recent developments in corporate intranets and extranets which are likely to increase the level of IP-based technologies and replace or complement proprietary products like Lotus Notes.

Finally, the numerous KM tools and technologies can also provide the systems that integrate various legacy systems, databases, ERP systems, and data warehouse to help facilitate an organization's knowledge discovery process (Acs, Carlsson, & Karlsson, 1999; Wickramasinghe, 2005). Integrating all of these with advanced decision support and online real time events enables an organization to understand customers better and devise business strategies accordingly. Such a holistic focus on the various KM tools and technologies is achieved when one tries to actualize knowledge discovery through technologies. Creating a competitive edge is the goal of all organizations employing knowledge discovery for decision support; however, the specific mix of technologies may vary. Organisations need to constantly seek information and turn this information into needed knowledge that will enable better decisions to be made which in turn will generate greater revenues, or reduce costs, or increase product quality and customer service. Knowledge discovery provides unique benefits over alternative decision support techniques, as it uncovers relationships and rules, not just data. These hidden relationships and rules exist empirically in the data because they have been derived from the way the business and its market work, and represent important and germane knowledge for the organization.

Table 3. A summary of various tools and technologies available for knowledge management

Technologies & Tools	Description	KM Steps Supported
E-mail	While e-mail appears to be a simple innocuous communication tool, especially in geographically disparate organizations, e-mail plays a major role in enabling KM initiatives to take place.	Knowledge Creation/Generation Knowledge Representation/Store Knowledge Use/Re-use Knowledge Application
Groupware	Groupware is a class of software that helps groups of colleagues (*workgroups*) attached to a local-area network organize their activities. There are three basic components of groupware: a Knowledge base—technically, a data repository of any kind; Workflow—a set of rules describing the activity in which a group of people participates and therefore defining the scope of collaboration process; and Collaboration—a process of exchanging messages between group members.	Knowledge Creation/Generation Knowledge Representation/Store Knowledge Use/Re-use Knowledge Application
CAD/CAM	Acronym for *computer-aided design*. A CAD system is a combination of hardware and software that enables engineers and architects to design everything from furniture to airplanes. CAD systems allow an engineer to view a design from any angle with the push of a button and to zoom in or out for close-ups and long-distance views. In addition, the computer keeps track of design dependencies so that when the engineer changes one value, all other values that depend on it are automatically changed accordingly.	Knowledge Creation/Generation Knowledge Representation/Store Knowledge Use/Re-use Knowledge Application

Table 3. continued

Technologies & Tools	Description	KM Steps Supported
Data Mining	Data mining is the process of analyzing databases to uncover new and valuable information, usually in the form of previously unknown relationships between variables.	Knowledge Creation/Generation
BI/BA tools	Business intelligence (BI) refers to the ability to collect and analyze huge amounts of data pertaining to the customers, vendors, markets, internal processes, and the business environment.	Knowledge Creation/Generation
Expert systems	An expert system is regarded as the embodiment within a computer of a knowledge-based component from an expert skill in such a form that the system can offer intelligent advice or take an intelligent decision about a processing function. Expert systems are computer-based programs which are designed to record human expertise (knowledge), and then to be able to apply this knowledge to applications in a certain domain.	Knowledge Creation/Generation Knowledge Use/Re-use Knowledge Application
Distributed hypertext systems	*Distributed hypertext systems* have been concerned with the generation and leveraging of organizational knowledge for more than a dozen years. Theodor Holm Nelson coined the term "hypertext" in the 1960s, and his writings about representation, access, and management of knowledge—embodied in his vision for Project Xanadu, a global "docuverse" that pre-figured the World Wide Web—are useful for managing information and knowledge.	Knowledge Creation/Generation Knowledge Representation/Store Knowledge Use/Re-use Knowledge Application
Document management	*Document management* systems originally were primarily concerned with providing online access to documents stored as bit-mapped images. Document management technology—already in widespread use in large, information-intensive companies—is likely to become an integral part of virtually every "intranet" in one form or another. XML and its parent technology, SGML (standard generalized markup language), provide the foundation for managing not only documents but also the information components of which the documents are composed. This is due to some notable characteristics of XML data.	Knowledge Representation/Store Knowledge Use/Re-use Knowledge Application

Table 3. continued

Technologies & Tools	Description	KM Steps Supported
Geographic information systems	*Geographic information systems*, a term associated with knowledge management is used as a graphic tool for *knowledge mapping*. Known by the acronym GIS for short, the technology involves a digitized map, a powerful computer and software that permits the superimposition and manipulation of various kinds of demographic and corporate data on the map.	Knowledge Representation/Store Knowledge Use/Re-use Knowledge Application
Help desk technology	*Help desk technology* is primarily concerned with routing requests for help from information seeker to the right technical resolution person within an organization	Knowledge Creation/Generation Knowledge Representation/Store Knowledge Use/Re-use Knowledge Application
Intranets	*Intranets*—intra-corporation networks that use the Internet's IP (Internet Protocol) standard—not only permit sharing of information, but they also view the organization's information (including structured resources like relational databases as well as unstructured text) through Web browsers like Internet Explorer and Netscape Navigator.	Knowledge Creation/Generation Knowledge Representation/Store Knowledge Use/Re-use Knowledge Application
Concept mapping	*Concept mapping* seems to be rooted primarily in educational techniques for improving understanding, retention, and as an aid to writing. A concept map is a picture of the ideas or topics in the information and the ways these ideas or topics are related to each other. It is a visual summary that shows the structure of the material the writer will describe.	Knowledge Creation/Generation Knowledge Representation/Store Knowledge Use/Re-use Knowledge Application
Semantic networks	*Semantic networks* are often closely associated with detailed analysis of texts and networks of ideas. One of the important ways they are distinguished from hypertext systems is their support of semantic typing of links, for example, the relationship between "murder" and "death" might be described as "is a cause of." The inverse relationship might be expressed as "is caused by." Semantic networks are a technique for representing knowledge.	Knowledge Representation/Store Knowledge Use/Re-use Knowledge Application

Table 3. continued

Technologies & Tools	Description	KM Steps Supported
Hypertext (an expanded semantic network)	*Hypertext*, known to most people these days by its implementation in the World Wide Web, is sometimes described as a semantic network with content at the nodes. But the content itself—the traditional document model—seems to be the driving organizational force, not the network of links. In most hypertext documents, the links are not semantically typed, although they are typed at times according to the medium of the object displayed by traversing the link.	Knowledge Creation/Generation Knowledge Representation/Store Knowledge Use/Re-use Knowledge Application
Information modeling	*Information modeling* is concerned with precise specification of the meaning in a text, and in making relationships of meaning explicit—often with the objective of rapid and accurate development of new software applications for business requirements. Some of the essence of information modeling is expressed in the following definition: "The process of eliciting requirements from domain experts, formulating a complete and precise specification understandable to both domain experts and developers, and refining it using existing (or possible) implementation mechanisms."	Knowledge Creation/Generation Knowledge Representation/Store Knowledge Use/Re-use Knowledge Application
Conceptual indexes	*Conceptual* (or "back-of-the-book") *indexes* are rarely discussed in the same breath as hypertext, conceptual maps, and semantic networks—perhaps because indexers themselves sometimes relish the aura of "black art" surrounding indexing—but the connection is fundamental. Conceptual indexes traditionally map key ideas and objects in a single work. An index is a structured sequence—resulting from a thorough and complete analysis of text—of synthesized access points to all the information contained in the text. The structured arrangement of the index enables users to locate information efficiently.	Knowledge Creation/Generation Knowledge Representation/Store Knowledge Use/Re-use Knowledge Application

Table 3. continued

Technologies & Tools	Description	KM Steps Supported
Metadata	*Metadata* is simply information added to a document (or a smaller unit of information) that makes it easier to access and re-use that content. It's also referred to as simply "data about data." You'll find metadata in many different forms, including key words in a software help system, the document profile information attached to documents in a document management system, and the classification information in a library card catalog.	Knowledge Representation/Store Knowledge Use/Re-use Knowledge Application
*S*ymbolic *K*nowledge *A*cquisition *T*echnology (SKAT)	SKAT develops an evolving model from a set of elementary blocks, sufficient to describe an arbitrarily complex algorithm hidden in data, instead of routine searching for the best coefficients for a solution that belongs to some predetermined group of functions. Each time a better model is found, the system determines the best regression parameters for that model.	Knowledge Creation/Generation Knowledge Use/Re-use Knowledge Application
Web Based Groupware Portal	Tools and business utilities including: e-mail, group calendaring, group scheduling, group discussion, instant messaging, instant conferencing, knowledge management, file management.	

The Intelligence Continuum

The intelligence continuum (Wickramasinghe & Schaffer, 2005) is a collection of key tools, techniques, and processes of the knowledge economy (i.e., including data mining, business intelligence/analytics, and knowledge management). Taken together it represents a powerful system for refining the data or raw material stored in data marts and/or data warehouses and thereby maximizing the value and utility of these data assets for any organization. In essence, the intelligence continuum serves to apply a combination of various tools and technologies already discussed. Its advantage over applying various technologies separately and in an ad hoc fashion is that it provides a systematic approach to analyzing an organization's data assets and facilitates the development of predictive measures, so that the future state can be enhanced (Wickramasinghe & Schaffer, 2005).

Figure 8. The intelligence continuum (Adapted from Wickramasinghe & Schaffer, 2005)

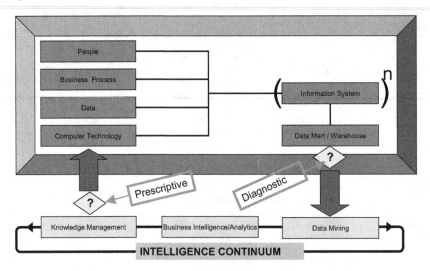

The first component is a generic information system, which generates data that is then captured in a data repository. In order to maximize the value of the data and use it to improve processes, the techniques, and tools of data mining, business intelligence and analytics and knowledge management must be applied to the data warehouse. Once applied, the results become part of the data set that are reintroduced into the system and combined with the other inputs of people, processes, and technology to develop an improvement continuum. Thus, the intelligence continuum includes the generation of data, the analysis of these data to provide a "diagnosis" and the reintroduction into the cycle as a "prescriptive" solution (Figure 8). The construction of the intelligence continuum and its subsequent use, however, requires an organization to possess a well-developed KM architecture and infrastructure, as well as a clear KM directive.

Implications for Knowledge-Based Enterprises

The myriad of technologies that can support and enable any KM initiative continues to grow exponentially. The transformation into a knowledge-based enterprise should not however be considered to be synonymous with the incorporation of the latest or even greatest technologies. Rather, it should be viewed as the careful construction and judicious design of an appropriate IT platform, established through the development of a sound IT infrastructure and enabling IT architecture, that facilitates and supports effective operations at all times. The intelligence continuum serves to underscore this key issue since the activities of diagnose and prescribe hold true irrespective of the particular technologies. The choice of technologies should be context dependent.

Too often organizations fall into the trap of blindly adopting the latest technology as a panacea for their current problems such as declining productivity, poor quality, or information overload. Such an approach is particularly dangerous for knowledge-based organizations as they must at all times have pertinent information and germane knowledge readily accessible. Under this type of scenario however, not only will knowledge-based organizations suffer similar problems faced by all organizations that indiscriminately apply technology solutions but more importantly they detract from their sustainable competitive advantage of effecting superior operations by maximizing their knowledge assets at minimal transaction costs. This in turn leads to dramatic failures and contributes to disillusionment with KM.

Chapter Summary

This chapter provides a comprehensive overview of the major technologies used in knowledge management. However, for an organization to enjoy the full potential of any of these technologies it is essential to first develop a KM architecture from which an appropriate, robust KM infrastructure can be constructed. The application and adoption of the intelligence continuum represents a highly sophisticated set of KM tools and technologies that is required in hypercompetitive environments that have established a sound KM initiative. By adopting these techniques and strategies, organizations will be able to truly embrace knowledge discovery solutions and thereby maximize their implicit knowledge assets and hence become knowledge-based enterprises.

References

Acs, Z. J., Carlsson, B., & Karlsson, C. (1999). *The linkages among entrepreneurship, SME's, and the Macroeconomy*. Cambridge: Cambridge University Press.

Alavi, M. (1999). Managing organizational knowledge, Working Paper.

Alavi, M., & Leidner, D. (1999). Knowledge management systems: Issues, challenges, and benefits. *Communications of the Association for Information Systems, 1*, Paper #5.

Boland, R., & Tenkasi, R. (1995). Perspective making perspective taking. *Organizational Science, 6*, 350-372.

Buchanan, B., & Shortliffe, E. (1984). *Rule-based expert systems.* Reading, MA: Addison-Wesley.

Croasdell, D. C. (2001). IT's role in organizational memory and learning. *Information Systems Management, 18*(1), 8-11.

Cross, R., Parker, A., Prusak, L., & Borgatti, S. P. (2001). Supporting knowledge creation and sharing in social networks. *Organizational Dynamics, 30*(2), 100-120.

Davenport, T. H., & Glaser, J. (2002, July). Just-in-time deliver comes to knowledge management. *Harvard Business Review*, 5-9.

Davenport, T. H., & Hansen, M. T. (1999). *Knowledge management at Andersen Consulting.* Harvard Business School Case, 9-499-032.

Davenport, T. H., & Klahr, P. (1998). Managing customer support knowledge. *California Management Review, 40*(3), 195-208.

Davenport, T., & Prusak, L. (1998). *Working knowledge.* Boston: Harvard Business School Press.

Dixon, N. (2000). *Common knowledge: How companies thrive by sharing what they know.* Boston: Harvard Business School Press.

Drucker, P. (1993). *Post-capitalist society.* New York: Harper Collins.

Drucker, P. (1999, October). Beyond the information revolution. *The Atlantic Monthly*, 47-57.

Drucker, P. F. (1988, January-February). The coming of the new organization. *Harvard Business Review*, 1-19.

Duffy, J. (2000). The KM technology infrastructure. *Information Management Journal, 34*(2), 62-66.

Duffy, J. (2001). The tools and technologies needed for knowledge management. *Information Management Journal, 35*(1), 64-67.

Ellinger, A. D., Watkins, K. E., & Bostrom, R. P. (1999). Managers as facilitators of learning in learning organizations. *Human Resource Development Quarterly, 10*(2), 105-125.

Fadlalla, A., & Wickramasinghe, N. (2005). Realizing knowledge assets in the medical sciences with data mining: An overview in creating knowledge-based healthcare organizations. In N. Wickramasinghe, et al. (Eds.), *Creating knowledge-based healthcare organizations* (pp. 164-177). Hershey, PA: Idea Group Publishing.

Fayyad, U., Piatetskey-Shapirio, G., Smyth, P., & Uthurusamy, R. (1996). *Advances in knowledge discovery and data mining*. Menlo Park. CA: AAA Press/The MIT Press.

Gold, A. H., Malhotra, A., & Segars, A. H. (2001). Knowledge management: An organizational capabilities perspective. *Journal of Management Information Systems, 18*(1), 185-214.

Halliday, L. (2001). An unprecedented opportunity. *Information World Review,* (167), 18-19.

Hammond, C. (2001). The intelligent enterprise. *InfoWorld, 23*(6), 45-46.

Holt, G. D., Love, P. E. D., & Li, H. (2000). The learning organization: Toward a paradigm for mutually beneficial strategic construction alliances. *International Journal of Project Management, 18*(6), 415-421.

Kanter, J. (1999, Fall). Knowledge management practically speaking. *Information Systems Management*.

Kolodner, J. (1991). Improving human decision-making through case-based reasoning. *AI Magazine*, 52-68, summer.

Kudyba, S., & Hoptroff, R. (2001). *Data mining and business intelligence*. Hershey, PA: Idea Group Publishing.

Laudon, K., & Laudon, J. (1999). *Management information systems* (6th ed.). Upper Saddle River, NJ: Prentice Hall.

Lee, C. C., & Yang, J. (2000). Knowledge value chain. *Journal of Management Development, 19*(9), 783-793.

Lee, S. M., & Hong, S. (2002). An enterprise-wide knowledge management system infrastructure. *Industrial Management & Data Systems, 102*(1/2), 17-25.

Leonard-Barton, D., & Sviokla, J. (1988). Putting expert systems to work. *Harvard Business Review*, March/April, 91-98.

Lesser, E., & Prusak, L. (2001). Preserving knowledge in an uncertain world. *MIT Sloan Management Review, 43*(1), 101-102.

Liebowittz, J. (1999). *Knowledge management handbook*. London: CRC Press.

Maier, R., & Lehner, F. (2000). Perspectives on knowledge management systems theoretical framework and design of an empirical study. *Proceedings of 8th European Conference on Information Systems (ECIS)*.

Marshall, C., & Prusak, L. (1996). Financial risk and the need for superior knowledge management. *California Management Review, 38*(3), 77-101.

Orlikowsky, W. (1992). The duality of technology: Rethinking the concept of technology in organizations. *Organizational Science, 2*(3), 398-427.

Persaud, A. (2001). The knowledge gap. *Foreign Affairs, 80*(2), 107-117.

Schultz, U. (1998, December). *Investigating the contradictions in knowledge management*. Presentation at IFIP.

Slade, S. (1991). Case-based reasoning: A research paradigm. *AI Magazine*, Spring, 42-55.

Slater, R. (1999). *Jack Welch and the GE way*. McGraw Hill.

Srikantaiah, T. K. (2000). Knowledge management for information professional. ASIS Monograph Series, Information Today.

Swan, J., Scarbrough, H., & Preston, J. (1999). Knowledge management: The next fad to forget people? *Proceedings of the 7ᵗʰ European Conference in Information Systems*.

Thorne, K., & Smith, M. (2000). Competitive advantage in world class organizations. *Management Accounting, 78*(3), 22-26.

Weill, P., & Broadbent, M. (1998). *Leveraging the new infrastructure*. Cambridge: Harvard Business School Press.

Wickramasinghe, N. (2003). Practicing what we preach: Are knowledge management systems in practice really knowledge management systems? *Business Process Management Journal, 9*(3), 295-316.

Wickramasinghe, N., & Davison, G. (2004). Making explicit the implicit knowledge assets in healthcare. *Health Care Management Science, 7*(3), 185-196.

Wickramasinghe, N., & Lichtenstein, S. (2005). Supporting knowledge creation with e-mail (in press, forthcoming *International Journal of Innovation and Learning*).

Wickramasinghe, N., & Mills, G. (2001). Integrating e-commerce and knowledge management: What does the Kaiser experience really tell us? *International Journal of Accounting Information Systems, 3*(2), 83-98.

Wickramasinghe, N., & Schaffer, J. (2005). Creating knowledge driven healthcare processes with the intelligence continuum (in press *International Journal of Electronic Healthcare* (IJEH)).

Endnote

[1]   Knowledge as a subjective component primarily refers to an ongoing phenomenon of exchange where knowledge is being shaped by social practices of communities (Boland & Tenkasi, 1995), in the tradition of a Hegelian/Kantian perspective where the importance of divergence of meaning is essential to support the "sense-making" processes of knowledge creation (Wickramasinghe & Mills, 2001).

Section III

Becoming a Knowledge-Based Enterprise

Chapter VII

KM and Strategy

Introduction

Given that knowledge has now emerged as a key resource for organizations, knowledge and its management then naturally have significant strategic implications. In order to understand the connection between knowledge and strategy and thereby the strategic value of KM, we first need to understand some key frameworks and models that facilitate the analysis of organizations and their environments. These include the frameworks of Porter; namely his generic strategies, competitive forces model, and value chain model respectively and McFarlan's strategic grid. In addition, we show that these frameworks are particularly useful in identifying how KM can facilitate organizations to maximize their competitive advantages. By understanding these key strategy models, it is possible then to fully appreciate how KM can and should be incorporated into an organization's strategy design.

Generic Strategies

The origins of the word strategy can be traced back to the ancient Greek word "strategós"; however strategy was first embraced in business policy by the development of the SWOT (strengths, weaknesses, opportunities, threats) framework (Maier,

2001). Essentially the goal of strategic management is to find a "fit" between the organization and its environment that maximizes its performance (Hofer, 1975). This describes the market-based view of the firm and was predominantly developed and pushed by the frameworks of Michael Porter. The first of Porter's famous frameworks is the generic strategies framework.

The use of technology and knowledge must always enable or enhance the businesses objectives and strategies of the organization. This is particularly true for 21st century organizations where many of their key operations and functions are heavily reliant on technology and the demand for information and knowledge is critical. A firm's relative competitive position (i.e., its ability to perform above or below the industry average is determined by its competitive advantage). Porter (1980) identified three generic strategies that impact a firm's competitive advantage. These include cost, focus, and differentiation. Furthermore, Porter himself notes that two and only two basic forms of competitive advantage typically exist:

1. Cost leadership and
2. Differentiation.

Firms can use these two forms of competitive advantage to either compete across a broad scope of an industry or to focus on competing in specific niches; thereby, leading to three generic strategies. Porter (ibid) notes that firms should be cautious about pursuing more than one generic strategy; namely cost, differentiation, and focus. We depict the generic strategies in Figure 1. For example, if a cost leadership

Figure 1. The generic strategies

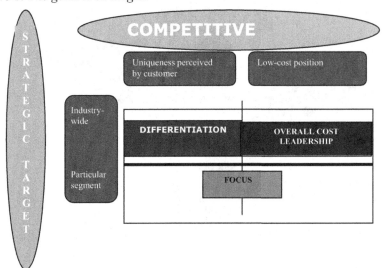

strategy is adopted it is unlikely that a firm can also maintain differentiation since it would not be possible to pursue simultaneously the costly capital investment or maintain high operating costs required for differentiation and thus in the long run the firm would have a confused strategy which leads to failure.

Industry Analysis

In order to design and develop one's strategy, an organization should first perform an industry analysis. Porter's five forces or competitive forces model is most useful (Lewis et al., 1993; Porter, 1980, 1985, 2001). Figure 2a depicts this model while Figure 2b illustrates how the model can be used in the airline industry, for example United Airlines. Essentially, Porter has taken concepts from microeconomics and modeled them in terms of five key forces that together outline the rules of competition and attractiveness of the industry. The forces are as follows:

1.   **Threat of new entrant:** A company new to the industry that could take away market share from the incumbent firms.

2.   **Threat of substitute.** An alternative means that could take market share from product/service offered by the firms in the industry.

Figure 2a. Porter's competitive (five) forces model

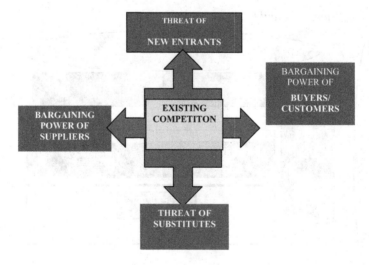

3. **Bargaining power of buyers:** The strength of buyers or groups of buyers within the industry relative to the firms.

4. **Bargaining power of suppliers:** The strength of suppliers relative to the firms in the industry.

5. **Rivalry of existing competition:** Relative position and market share of major competitors.

The collective strength of these five forces determines the attractiveness of the industry and thus the potential for superior financial performance by influencing prices, costs, and the level of capital investment required (Porter, 1985). Once a thorough industry analysis has been performed, it is generally easier for a firm to determine which generic strategy makes most sense to pursue and enables the firm

Figure 2b. Porter's competitive (five) forces analysis for United Airlines

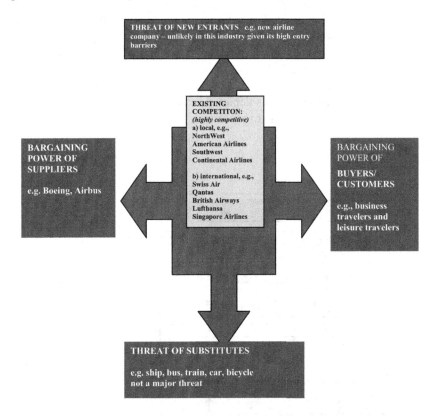

to exploit most of its core competencies in its existing environment. Thus given the complementary nature of these models it is important to use them together.

Internal Analysis Porter's
Value Chain Model

In addition to understanding the industry structure and key external activities, firms must also understand their business processes and key internal operations. In particular, firms need to identify their capabilities. A useful model or framework to use here is Porters' Value Chain Analysis (Porter, 1985). In order to examine a firm's capabilities, some classification of the firm's activities is required and this is primarily what the value chain provides. Figure 3 depicts the value chain. From this we can see five primary functions including inbound logistics, operations, outbound logistics, sales and marketing, and service, and four secondary functions; namely, administration and management, human resources, technology, and procurement. By analyzing each of these factors in turn, it is possible for the organization to identify areas where value can be added; and thereby, enable the business to achieve a sustainable competitive advantage. The value chain is a key tool for any type of organization. More importantly, incorporating KM into both the primary and secondary activities depicted in the value chain will facilitate the achievement of added value to the organization and in turn the achievement of a

Figure 3a. The value chain

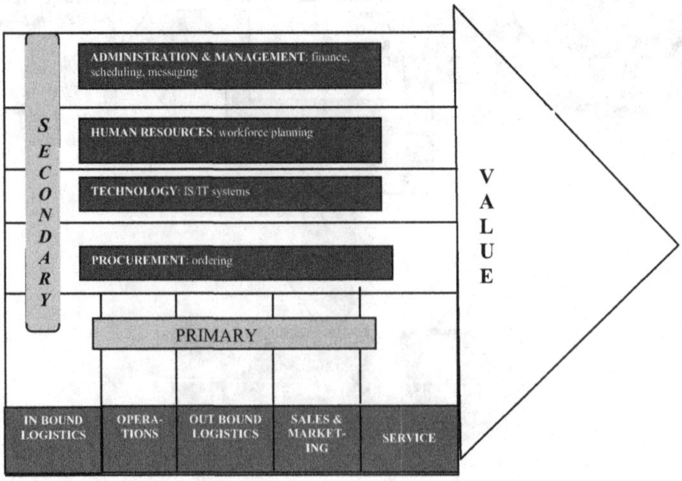

Figure 3b. Value chain analysis for Dell

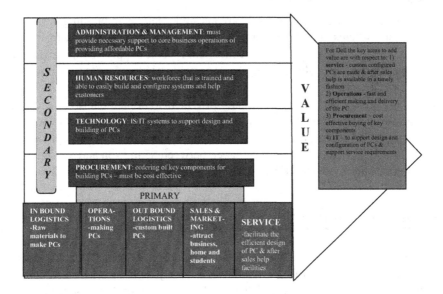

sustainable competitive advantage. For instance, embracing such KM tools as data mining and BA/BI will not only enhance service, sales, and marketing possibilities for the firm but also enable better administration to take effect as well as increase the value of the IT portfolio of the firm.

The Reverse Value Chain

The value chain, which we discussed in the preceding section, typically starts from the firm end to the customers. The reverse value chain means we must start look-ing at the value chain from the customer end. In the 21st century, as organizations increasingly resort to e-commerce with so many online shop fronts, it is difficult to compete only on price, product features, and/or advertising/promotion. Under-standing customer needs, offering additional services such as supporting customer search, product selection, and placement of orders, quick delivery, and logistics are important factors for achieving a competitive advantage. Well-executed automatic replenishment and reverse logistics programs such as product defects (recall), cus-tomer dissatisfaction (exchange), returns (damage), and redistributions (seasonal and excess inventory) enable companies to differentiate themselves from their competi-tors (Barsky & Ellinger, 2001; Porter, 2001). Automatic replenishment programs

(ARPs) create value by substituting information on inventory that reduce overall stock levels in the distribution channel.

Many organizations around the world are taking initiatives in building Web-based information systems that report information about reverse logistics to improve customer service. These companies realize that reverse supply chain management would help in creating value for customers as well as help in containing costs. The explosion of e-commerce has some online retailers reporting return rates as high as 50%. Many retailers are hiring third-party providers to implement reverse logistics programs designed to retain value by getting products back in the most expeditious manner so they can be speedily redistributed and customers can be kept satisfied. Kmart, for example reports that it has saved between $5 million and $6 million per $1 billion in sales by outsourcing reverse logistics (Barsky & Ellinger, 2001).

Web-Based Information Systems and Supply Chain

Web-based information systems provide the opportunity for customers, suppliers, third party partners, and organization to work closely together on a single communication medium (Afuah & Tucci, 2003; Corbett, Blackburn, & Wassenhove, 1999; Kalakota & Robinson, 2001). An effective supply chain improvement program depends on customer demand and competitor practices being collected and analyzed. This process allows businesses to make supply chain decisions in functions including services offered, use of a third party logistics provider, and amount/placement of inventory. Competitive advantage can be achieved through benchmarking and competitor intelligence focused on supply chain functions such as transportation, warehousing, purchasing, and customer service (Birkhead & Schirmer, 1999).

Web-based information systems should help to integrate the reverse value supply chain. Reverse logistics is the up stream flow of goods in which all supply-chain actions occur in reverse; moving goods from their typical final destination for the purpose of recapturing value, or proper disposal. Information regarding reverse logistics including processing returned merchandise due to damage, seasonal inventory, restock, salvage, recalls, and excess inventory, as well as packaging and shipping materials from the end-user or the reseller will help organizations to reduce the cost of logistics and would improve data management (Rowley, 2000).

Traditionally, information systems were developed based on inward business value chains, which were high value-added internal activities of organizations and their core competencies. This method of information system development was effective for integrating the internal business processes since it focuses on core business processes, which is the "right" end of a value chain that weaves itself through the structure of a company and out into the marketplace (Yaman, 2001). However, this method of looking at only one end of the value chain—in terms of how to leverage core competencies—too often leads to a set of processes that does not create value for customers. Companies typically focused on their own cores competencies and thus could be blindsided if customer requirements shift in a direction counter to the way core competencies are aligned. Therefore, the traditional information systems though creating many automation benefits are still lacking in improving the other end of the value chain (i.e., the customer). By reversing the value chain, many e-commerce revolutionaries have gained a competitive edge, and may potentially conquer their industries (Webb & Gile, 2001).

In traditional reengineering activities, management would leverage the core competency through a set of efficient business processes so as to bring a well-defined set of products and services to market (i.e., products and services that best use the core competencies of the organization). Next, identification of the sales and distribution channels that best served the market were addressed. Using this approach, management would build value around a process and push the firm's competency to the market in an efficient manner.

By building value around the process, companies were efficiently pushing products and services to market. However, the rigid processes the applications demanded provided static efficiencies in a dynamic world. With the dynamics of the new economy, business processes must be flexible, and it may be necessary to outsource what were once core competencies to organizations better able to perform the task (Webb & Gile, 2001).

McFarlan's Strategic Grid

The Strategic Grid is essentially a contingency model that underscores two key dimensions for determining the relative strategic positioning of an organization with respect to its competitors (Applegate, Austin, & McFarlan, 2003). The Strategic grid consists of two axes: (1) an assessment of a firm's business portfolio ranging from low to high, and (2) a vertical axis that determines the strength of a firm's IT portfolio, again ranging from low to high. Figure 4 depicts the Strategic Grid. An organization is considered to be "strategic" if it rates high with respect to both its technology portfolio and business portfolio. If an organization rates low on either or both its business portfolio or technology portfolio respectively (i.e., is in the support quadrant of the grid), the adoption of KM tools, technologies, and techniques can effect a transition to the prize position of "strategic" in this grid. This is because firstly, pertinent information and germane knowledge area required for diagnosing the existing deficiencies within the business (and/or IT) portfolio and then pertinent information and germane knowledge are equally necessary to prescribe the correct remedy and support the required decision-making that must take place. Hence, we can see that the power of KM lies in its ability to effect the transition to the strategic

Figure 4. McFarlan's strategic grid

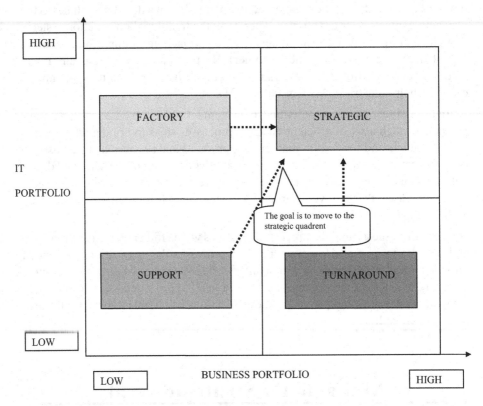

quadrant by impacting both the business portfolio and/or the IT portfolio for the firm. Conversely, without such an incorporation of the techniques of KM it is highly probable that suboptimal decisions will be made and inappropriate changes would be made to either (or both) the business portfolio and IT portfolio thereby making the transition to the desired strategic quadrant less likely.

Designing a KM Strategy

A competitive management strategy typically incorporates four main components including (a) the goals of the organization, (b) an external analysis of the market, (c) an internal analysis of the market, and (d) what gives the firm its competitive advantage. Taken together, these components and the respective analyses that they generate are central components to the design of a firm's own unique and hopefully sustainable competitive advantage. We have already presented the tools for analyzing both the external and internal environments; namely Porter's competitive forces model and value chain. It is now necessary to learn how to assemble the various pieces of the puzzle in order to design a complete strategy.

In formulating any strategy, the first step is to select the company's goals and match the organization's abilities and market opportunities. Information plays a critical role in strategy formulation (Barney, 1991; Evans & Wurster, 1999). Information regarding the external and internal analyses, derived from using models such as Porter's competitive forces and value chain, enables the manager to perform this task. Figure 5 depicts the main components of strategy from a market-based perspective and how they fit together. From Figure 5, it is important to note that the external analysis and internal analysis are both impacted and in turn, impact the goals of the firm, while KM has most impact on the attainment of competitive advantage.

As already discussed, the most important aspect of competitive advantage is that it must be sustainable. There is general agreement in the management literature that KM is not only integral to enterprise, corporate, business, or functional area strategy, but is key to the creation of economic value and sustainable competitive advantage (Blumentritt & Johnston, 1999; Boisot, 1998; Earl, 2001; Earl & Scott, 1999; Zack, 1999). However, the incorporation of KM into the overall strategy design for an

Figure 5. Key components of a market-based view of formulating a competitive strategy

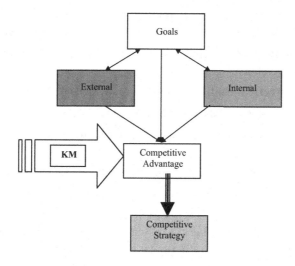

organization is generally done inadequately in practice (Maier, 2001). One reason for this is that the market-based view of strategy design, which reached its pinnacle with the development of Porter's models (ibid), is excellent for determining external and internal analyses but tends to neglect what is required for an organization to create and integrate sustained competitive advantages based on unique resources. It is interesting to note that even Porter himself in later discussions (Porter, 1996) underscores the importance of the inclusion of an organization's resources, in particular KM, as both a necessary and sufficient pre-requisite for attaining a sustainable competitive advantage (Alavi, 1999; Davenport, 2003; Davenport & Prusak, 1998; Grant, 1996).

The limitations with the market-based view of strategy have resulted in the development of the resource-based perspective. In particular, the work of Wernfeldt (1984) has played a significant role in establishing this new paradigm for strategy. Fundamental to the resource-based view of strategy (Figure 6) is that success through competitive advantage is determined by the existence of organization-specific resources. Furthermore, in a dynamic or competitive market where specific products and/or services change quickly, key organization resources and capabilities are more enduring (Barney, 1991; Zack, 1999). Such organizational resources include both tangible and intangible assets such as, but not limited to, core capabilities (Leonard-Barton, 1992), dynamic capabilities (Teece, Pisano, & Shuen, 1997), financial resources, and physical resources. In order to be capable of generating sustained competitive advantages, these resources must have the following characteristics (Maier, 2001):

1.   **Scarce:** Competitors cannot easily obtain rare resources.

2.   **Competitively superior/valuable/relevant:** Thus, resources enable organizations to create value for their customers or are perceived as value creating.

3.   **Multi-purposeful:** Core competencies must provide potential access to a wide variety of unique skills.

4.   **Non- or imperfectly imitable:** Cannot be replicated easily.

5.   Non-substitutable-resources cannot be easily substituted.

6.   **Non-transferable:** The more difficult it is to purchase the more sustainable the resource.

7.   **Durable:** The longevity of the competitive advantage lies in the durability of the resource.

By incorporating KM and knowledge as a resource in organizations (Blumentritt & Johnston, 1999; Earl, 2001; Grant, 1996)—taking a knowledge-based view of the

Figure 6. Key components of resource-based view of formulating a competitive strategy

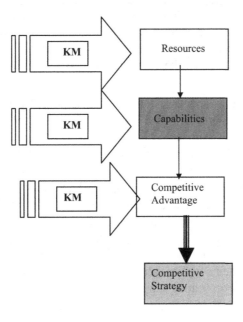

firm—KM and knowledge become incorporated into strategy design at all levels in the resource-based perspective as can be seen in Figure 6. This serves to underscore the importance of KM in strategy design. Some have noted that a pure resource-based view of strategy over compensates for the missing components of a market-based view and thus both external market position factors coupled with internal resources are key for sound strategy design (Spender, 1994). Such a perspective underpins a knowledge-based view (Maier, 2001). Essential to actualizing a knowledge-based strategy is the need to perform a knowledge-based SWOT analysis (i.e., an in depth examination as to how the existing strengths and weaknesses can be enhanced with KM techniques, technologies, and tools) and then used to maximize opportunities and diminish threats; together with identifying which knowledge is a unique and valuable resource, which knowledge processes represent unique and valuable capabilities and how these resources and capabilities support a firm's product and market positions (Davenport & Prusak, 1998; Zack, 1999).

Competitive Advantage and
Value Creation

In trying to obtain a competitive advantage and thereby create value, three areas must be considered; namely, customer value, supplier value, and the value of the firm. All three can be described in quantitative terms as shown in Table 1 (Spulber, 2003).

To attract customers, a firm must create customer value that is at least as great as that offered by competitors. Therefore, what becomes important then is for the firm to develop ways and means to create such value. This becomes an area where KM and the tools and technologies of KM can be especially useful; notably the incorporation of KM driven CRM or the reverse value chain as discussed in earlier chapters. Companies also create value for their suppliers including but not limited to (1) parts and components manufacturers, (2) manufacturers of capital equipment, (3) wholesale product sellers, (4) service providers, and (5) technology licensing and R&D. As with customer value, it is logical for a firm to create supplier value that is at least as great as the competing alternatives. Once again, KM has a key role in enabling firms to increase their supplier value. By embracing the many tools and technologies of KM such as incorporating supply chain management with KM, data mining, and BA and/or BI tools and techniques, as well as other Internet based KM technologies, the organization's intangible assets become more useful and thereby valuable. The final component of value, the value of the firm, is represented by the total value created, net of customer value and supplier value, or in other words the present value of customer revenues minus the present value of payments to suppliers and the costs of using the firm's assets (Spulber, 2003). Consequently, the firm tries to increase its value by trying to capture a greater market share and thereby increasing both supplier and customer value, which in turn increases its own value. Creating greater value is typically accomplished in three ways: (1) operating more efficiently, (2) providing greater benefits to customers by improving products and services, and (3) developing innovative transactions that offer new value to the market. Once again, the tools, technologies, and techniques of KM that we have

Table 1. The value components

Customer Value = customers' willingness to pay for the firm's product or service – asking price of the firm's product or service
Supplier Value = bid price offered by the firm – supplier costs
Value of the firm = asking price – bid price – cost of the firm's assets
Value created by firm = customer value + supplier value + value of the firm *or* customer willingness to pay – supplier costs – cost of the firm's assets

discussed in preceding chapters are relevant, such as the techniques of data min-ing, BI/BA, and Internet-based KM technologies, and can enable more efficient operating, improve services, and products as well as facilitate the development of innovative transactions that offer new value to the market.

Value-Driven Strategy

Value driven strategy is a method for choosing the appropriate goals and strategies (Spulber, 2003). Central to this technique is the evaluation of goals and strategies based on whether or not they increase the firm's total value. The total value of the firm is represented by the present value of the firm's economic profits over the long term. What is particularly important to keep in mind here is that the company's goals and strategies should make the best match between the organization's abili-ties and market opportunities. The basic components of the value driven strategy are depicted in Figure 7.

Evaluating Organizational Abilities and Market Opportunities

Having a good idea of the market opportunities is critical to evaluating a company's organizational capabilities. Traditional accounting techniques value an organization's capabilities in terms of quantitative factors such as appraising the company's resources and assets. However, a key area of importance in today's knowledge economy is the value of the organization's intangible resources and assets, its intellectual and human capital. An organization's intangible assets in particular can increase their value significantly by embracing the tools, techniques, and technologies of KM.

In contrast, evaluating the marketing opportunities for a company involves an external assessment of potential customers, suppliers, competitors, and partners.

Figure 7. Components of value-driven strategy

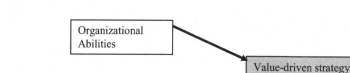

While it is more complex, KM can still have a key role to play here. In particular, the tools and technologies of KM such as data mining, BA/BI, and Internet-based technologies can play a critical role in facilitating better evaluations and thus better decision-making. Moreover, as environments are dynamic not static these tools and technologies can also facilitate the continuous revising and updating of these evaluations so that the value-driven strategy is more up to date.

Incorporating KM into the Strategic Vision

In a knowledge economy, a key source of sustainable competitive advantage and profitability lies in how a company creates and shares its knowledge (Allee, 1997; Davenport & Prusak, 1998; Earl, 2001). The benefits of incorporating KM into strategy design can take many forms and occur at many levels (Alavi, 1999; Allee, 1997; Davenport & Prusak, 1998). It can help reduce the costs of producing goods and services and thereby help an organization compete on the basis of price. Alternatively, the incorporation of KM techniques and tools can help an organization enhance or differentiate its service offerings. This unique aspect of KM; namely that it can facilitate an organization to increase its competitive advantage at many levels is due to the complex nature of the knowledge construct and thus makes it imperative in a knowledge economy that KM is indeed incorporated into an organizations strategic vision. By incorporating KM into the strategic vision, this ensures that knowledge is given the high priority it needs and that this vital knowledge resource will be managed rather than being entrusted to serendipity (Holsapple & Joshi, 2002). Furthermore, the incorporation of KM into the strategic vision enables the firm to achieve the vision and realize its value proposition (Davenport, 2003). Thus, it is necessary to have a framework to formulate a KM strategy. We depict such a framework in Figure 8.

Specifically, Figure 8 brings together the key elements of KM; namely the technological infrastructure, human infrastructure and business infrastructure, in other words the resources within the organization and how they impact the development of the KM strategy and KM strategic vision. Furthermore, it is important to emphasize that such a process is iterative and should be continuous; hence the use of double arrows to reflect this in Figure 8.

An in-depth study by Wickramasinghe (2003), which analyzed the KM initiatives at various consulting companies found that key to the success of the respective KM initiatives was the fact that KM was articulate and incorporated within the strategic vision. Table 2 highlights some other important findings with respect to KM and strategy from this study.

Figure 8.

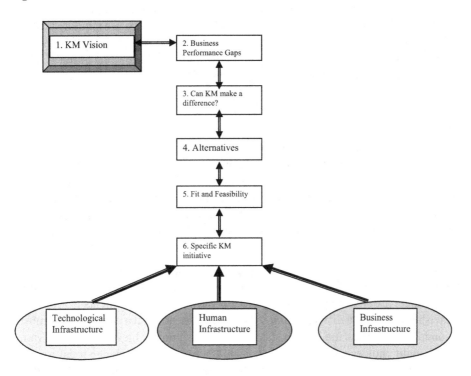

Table 2. KM and strategy

KM and Strategy in Practice
KM articulated in strategic vision
KM supported from the top
All aspects of strategy design incorporated KM
All strategy discussions included the need for KM and how KM would help realize the goals and objectives of the organization
Development of internal and external KM focus

These findings are reflected in other organizational examples that have also had success with their KM initiatives. Buckman Laboratories for example embarked upon a KM initiative in the late 1990s (HBS, 2003). Their success and significant sales growth was attributed mostly to their KM system K'Netix, while the success of K'Netix can be seen to be the result of the drive and support from top management and the incorporation of KM into the strategic vision. We see similar success in the many consulting companies' respective KM initiatives KPMG (HBS, 1997), American Management Systems (HBS, 1998) and Andersen Consulting (HBS, 2002) as well as Du Pont's AI system (1995). Thus, the connection between a successful KM initiative, strong leadership and top management support and the articulation of KM as part of the strategic vision is necessary but not sufficient for ensuring success.

Knowledge management strategies should aim to set forth the criteria for choosing what knowledge a firm intends to pursue, and how it will go about capturing and sharing that knowledge (HBS, 1997). As a rule, a good starting point is to decide the kind of value the company intends to provide and to whom (suppliers, customers, etc.). Only then can knowledge and KM in particular begin to be articulated within a strategic vision and key questions as to what is the relevant knowledge, who are the key people and how to actualize such an approach can they be addressed.

It is important to realize that the knowledge requirements for different types of firms will by definition be different. For example the knowledge requirements for a low cost producer are significantly different to the knowledge requirements from a firm that wishes to pursue a differentiated strategy. This means that a strategy audit must be conducted to assess the current state of the firm's knowledge and its gaps. From such an audit choices can then be made as to the required knowledge to be sought after and obtained. Earl (2001) develops this idea further by identifying three distinct schools of knowledge management. These include (1) Technocratic—since the KM strategy is largely focused on the use of technologies and information systems. Within this broad category, however, Earl (2001) identifies three sub-categories: (a) systems—for example Xerox's knowledge-based systems, (b) cartographic—for example AT&T's online directories of the location of expertise, and (c) engineering—for example HP's Intranet and knowledge-base that focus on improving designs and areas for continuous improvements. (2) Economic—where the KM initiative explicitly creates revenue streams from the exploitation of knowledge and intellectual resources, with one such example being Dow Chemicals. (3) Behavioral which again has three sub-categories: (a) organizational, which tries to foster communities of practice, such as the oil companies Shell and BP Amoco, (b) spatial, where the design of open spaces is to encourage discourse and the sharing of knowledge—for example British Airways, and (c) strategic, which sees KM as a key dimension of competitive strategy—such as Unilever. It is important to note that incorporating KM as part of the strategic vision is as important to all these schools of KM for truly effective and successful KM initiatives to be realised.

Implications for Knowledge-Based Enterprises

For knowledge-based enterprises to leverage their knowledge assets and thereby effect superior operations it is essential that KM forms an integral element of their strategic vision, strategic intent, and business strategy. In this way, KM is not considered as an after thought or side issue but is always kept as a central consideration. This in turn enables the organization to draw on its knowledge base with confidence that at all times germane knowledge and pertinent information are available and accessible to support critical thinking and rapid decision-making. Hence, not only will the organization be sure to attain a higher level of value and sustainment of its competitive advantage but of equal importance it will also reap the full benefits afforded to it by lower transactions costs (Kogut & Zander, 2003).

Chapter Summary

In order to develop appropriate strategies organizations need to adopt models and frameworks. In this chapter, we presented three important models developed by Michael Porter: (1) the generic strategies model, (2) the competitive forces model, and (3) the value chain model. We also discussed how these models can be used to enable a sound analysis of the micro and macro business environments to result. Following this, we discussed the need to also consider the reverse value chain for an e-business (i.e., to understand the impacts from the customer's and supplier's perspectives respectively). We then noted the implications for competitive advantage afforded to organizations by incorporating the tools, techniques, and technologies of KM. Finally, we presented McFarlan's strategic grid and identified that the embracing of KM tools, techniques, and technologies is a necessary but not a sufficient condition for enabling any organization to transition to the strategic quadrant of this grid. These frameworks and models then make up the key tools for any organization to develop an effective KM strategy.

To create a sensible strategy it is also important to consider how strategy design should be embarked upon. In so doing, a market-based perspective tends to be the choice. However as it has serious limitations with respect to designing a sustainable competitive strategy, a preferable approach can be found in the development of the resource-based perspective and/or the knowledge-based perspective. From such a perspective, it is possible to identify the role of KM in creating value to customers, suppliers and thereby increasing the value of the firm. Such a value driven strategy has two distinct components namely, market opportunities and organizational capabilities and the role of KM in each of these, in particular the tools and technologies of KM such as BI/BA, data mining and Internet–based tools. This then shows how the infrastructures human, business, and technological intrinsically relate to the KM strategy and hence must be developed and designed with a particular focus on their ability to enable, support, and effect a clear KM strategy.

References

Afuah, A., & Tucci, C. (2003). *Internet business models and strategies*. Boston: McGraw Hill.

Alavi, M. (1999). *Managing organizational knowledge*. Working Paper.

Allee, V. (1997). *The knowledge evolution*. Boston: Butterworth-Heinemann.

Applegate, L., Austin, R., & McFarlan, F. (2003). *Corporate information strategy and management*. Boston: McGraw Hill Irwin.

Barney, J. (1991). Firms resources and sustained competitive advantage. *Journal of Management, 17*(1), 99-120.

Barsky, N. P., & Ellinger, A. E. (2001). Unleashing the value in the supply chain. *Strategic Finance, 82*(7), 32-37.

Birkhead, N., & Schirmer, R. (1999). Add value to your supply chain. *Transportation and Distribution, 40*(9), 51-60.

Blumentritt, R., & Johnston, R. (1999). Towards a strategy for knowledge management. *Technology Analysis and Strategic Management, 11*(3), 287-300.

Boisot, M. (1998). Knowledge assets: Securing competitive advantage in the knowledge chains. *Sloan Management Review, 40*(4), 71-82.

Corbett, C. J., Blackburn, J. D., & Wassenhove, L. N. V. (1999). Partnerships to improve supply chains. *Sloan Management Review, 39*(3), 61-72.

Davenport, T. (2003). The director's cut. Accenture Document.

Davenport, T., & Prusak, L. (1998). *Working knowledge*. Boston: Harvard Business School Press.

Earl, M. (2001). Knowledge management strategies: Toward a taxonomy. *Journal of Management Information Systems, 18*(1), 215-233.

Earl, M., & Scott, A. (1999). Opinion: What is a chief knowledge officer? *Sloan Management Review, 40*(2), 29-38.

Evans, P., & Wurster, T. (1999). Strategy and the new economies of information. In D. Tapscott (Ed.), *Creating value in the networked economy*. Boston: Harvard Business Press.

Grant, R. (1996). Toward a knowledge-based theory of the firm. *Academy of Management Executive, 17*(1), 109-122.

HBS (Harvard Business School). (1995). "Du Pont' Artificial Intelligence Implementation Strategy." 9-189-036.

HBS (Harvard Business School). (1997). "A Note on Knowledge Management." 9-398-031.

HBS (Harvard Business School). (1997). "KPMG Peat Marwick U.S.: One Giant Brain." 9-397-108.

HBS (Harvard Business School). (1998). "American Management Systems: The Knowledge Centers." 9-697-068.

HBS (Harvard Business School). (2002). "Knowledge Management at Andersen Consulting." 9-499-032.

HBS (Harvard Business School). (2003). "Buckman Laboratories (A)." 9-800-160.

Hofer, C. (1975). Toward a contingency theory of business strategy. *Academy of Management, 18*(4), 784-810.

Holsapple, C., & Joshi, K. (2002). Knowledge management: A threefold framework. *The Information Society, 18*, 47-64.

Kalakota, R., & Robinson, M. (2001). *E-business 2.0*. Boston: Addison Wesley.

Kogut, B., & Zander, U. (2003). A memoir and reflection: Knowledge and an evolutionary theory of the multinational firm 10 years later. *Journal of International Business Studies, 34*, 505-515.

Leonard-Barton, D. (1992). Core capabilities and core rigidities: A paradox in managing new product development. *Strategic Management Journal, 13*, 111-125.

Lewis, G. et al. (1993). *Australian strategic management*. Upper Saddle River, NJ: Prentice Hall.

Maier, R. (2001). Knowledge management systems. Berlin.

Porter, M. (1980). *Competitive strategy*. New York: Free Press.

Porter, M. (1985). *Competitive advantage*. New York: Free Press.

Porter, M. (1996). What is strategy? *Harvard Business Review, 74*(5-6), 61-78.

Porter, M. (2001). Strategy and the Internet. *Harvard Business Review, 79*, 62-78, March.

Rowley, J. (2000). The reverse supply chain. Impact of current trends. *Logistics and Transport Focus, 2*(6), 27-31.

Spender, J. (1994). Organizational knowledge, collective practice and penrose rents. *International Business Review, 3*(4), 353-367.

Spulber, D. (2003). *Management strategy*. Boston: Irwin McGraw-Hill.

Teece, J., Pisano, G., & Shuen, A. (1997). Dynamic capabilities and strategic management. *Strategic Management Journal, 18*(7), 509-533.

Webb, J., & Gile, C. (2001). Reversing the value chain. *The Journal of Business Strategy, 22*(2), 13-17.

Wernfeldt, B. (1984). A resource-based view of the firm. *Strategic Management Journal, 5*(2), 171-180.

Wickramasinghe, N. (2003). Do we practice what we preach: Are knowledge management systems in practice truly reflective of knowledge management systems in theory? *Business Process Management Journal, 9*(3), 295-316.

Yaman, B. (2001). Web systems management means managing business processes. *Communications News, 38*(5), 14.

Zack, M. (1999). *Knowledge and strategy*. Boston: Butterworth-Heinemann.

Chapter VIII

Managing Knowledge Complexity

Introduction

As discussed throughout the preceding chapters, knowledge is not a simple construct. Rather, knowledge is a complex structure that is neither static nor homogenous in its make up. Further, germane knowledge is highly context dependent; hence, germane knowledge in the context of a hospital setting would be significantly different to germane knowledge in the context of a manufacturing company. Thus, once we have developed an appreciation of all the component parts required for a successful knowledge management initiative, we must then focus on the whole, the complexity of knowledge, and its management. In so doing, it will only then be possible to make the whole truly greater than just the sum of the parts.

The launching place for managing knowledge complexity lies in the construction of an integrative model for organizational knowledge management. Such a model, which we present, serves primarily to identify the key components that have been discussed individually in preceding chapters. In addition, our model highlights the interaction effects these components have on each other when they are combined. This in turn, underscores the importance of developing synergies, strategies, tactics, and techniques to facilitate the success of the knowledge management initiative. In trying to ensure the success of the knowledge management initiative, it also becomes vital to develop an appreciation for several other areas that at first may appear to be unrelated or irrelevant but are in fact critical in the achievement of a successful outcome. These areas include the need to be prepared and ready, the vital role of training and, in particular, the use of simulation in establishing both the appropriate levels of intellectual preparedness and readiness, and the ability to think critically and to make rapid yet sound decisions. Combined, the construction of an integrative organizational model of knowledge management, as well as the development of the key synergies, strategies, tactics, and techniques, form the key success factors for any knowledge management initiative.

An Organizational Model for KM

Figure 1 presents an organizational model of knowledge management. Any holistic knowledge management initiative should begin with an understanding and evaluation of the dynamics of knowledge economy, and how these impact the organization under consideration. The resultant findings from such an evaluation will serve to form inputs into the organizational model of knowledge management that will in turn help to develop the respective business and specific knowledge management strategies that the organization should adopt.

Chapter I highlighted many of the key aspects that drive today's knowledge economy, while Chapter VII provided frameworks and tools that focused at the industry level to help with the evaluation of the external dynamics, and also the subsequent development of the primary issues on which the organization should focus. We have already stated that the key drivers of today's knowledge economy include (a) the need to maximize the intellectual capital of an organization, (b) the emerging realization that knowledge has become one of the most important sustainable competitive advantages, and c) the fact that knowledge is now considered as essential to an organization as the traditional economic inputs of land, labor, and capital. These three drivers, coupled with the findings from applying the frameworks discussed in Chapters VIII and IX (such as Porter's five forces model and the strategic grid), enable an organization to understand the dynamics of knowledge economy as it relates to its own industry. From here, it is then necessary for the organization to identify its relative strengths and weaknesses when compared to its competitors in a given industry.

Based on such an evaluation, the organization must then shape its business strategy, goals, and objectives. Implementation of this approach satisfies the requirements of the first two steps of Figure 1. The business strategy combined with the organization's goals and objectives then shapes the specific knowledge management strategy required by that organization. For example, integral to Ernst and Young's knowledge management strategy is the transition of the organization toward a truly knowledge based business (Chard, 1997). In contrast, Du Pont's knowledge management strategy

Figure 1. Organizational model of knowledge management

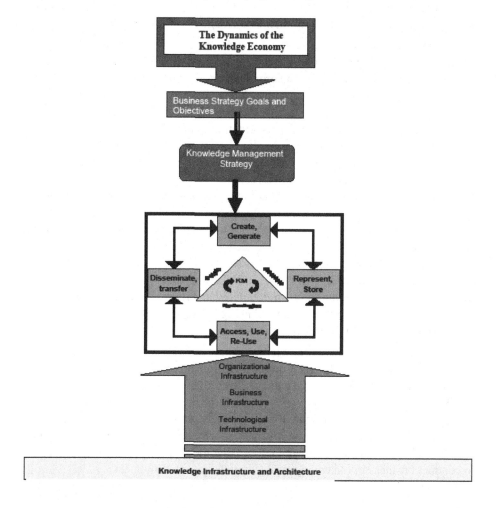

is concerned with the capture of knowledge and its delivery to a specific site (Keil, 1988). The consulting company, KPMG (now known as Bearing Point), based its knowledge management strategy on three key components: (1) selection of the best products and services, (2) development and delivery of the best solutions, and (3) helping clients manage and effectively use their knowledge (Alavi, 1997). In all three examples, the respective knowledge management strategies were derived and formulated after a detailed analysis of the dynamics of the pertinent external environment, the way business was conducted, and organizational goals and objectives. It is important to note here that some organizations often incorporate their knowledge management strategy as a part of their business strategy. Hence, steps 2 and 3 of

Figure 1 may actually be combined. This was indeed the case for KPMG but not for either Ernst and Young or Du Pont, who chose to keep their respective business strategies distinctly separate from their knowledge management considerations.

Once the knowledge management strategy has been developed, it is then necessary to focus on how to make such a strategy operational. For this to happen success-fully, several components within the organization must work together in sympathy in order to implement the formulated knowledge management strategy (Figure 8.1.) The focus of the practical approach must concentrate on four key steps of knowledge management: creation/generation, representation/storage, access, /use/ re-use, and dissemination/transfer (discussed in detail in Chapter III), as well as the incorpora-tion of a socio-technical perspective (i.e., the continuous consideration of people, process, and technology). It is imperative to always keep in mind that the three components (people, process, and technology) are interconnected, thus a change in process, for example, will also impact both the people and technology components. Further, in order to achieve a well-coordinated knowledge management initiative, it is necessary that the people, process, and technology components not only support and facilitate each other but are also consistent, and enable the four key steps of knowledge management. Chapters IV, V, and VI discussed each of these components (people, process, and technology) in detail. What Figure 1 tries to underscore is that this triad of people, process, and technology is central in the development of a robust knowledge management approach for any organization.

Finally, the four major steps of knowledge management can only be truly efficient if they are supported by the organization's knowledge infrastructure, and architecture. For this to happen, the knowledge management initiative, and more specifically the four key steps must be designed to leverage off the primary sub-components of the organization's infrastructure; namely, the business infrastructure, the technology infrastructure, and the organizational infrastructure (see the bottom section of Figure 1). When all of this occurs, we can then say that the organization is fully prepared to conduct business in today's dynamic knowledge economy.

Prepared vs. Ready

Singapore was fully prepared. The city and the island were stocked with supplies and ammunition. The mood was optimistic despite the increasing danger of war with Japan. The back of Singapore—the major outpost of the British Empire—was protected by an almost impenetrable jungle and swamps crossed by a few, easily defendable roads. The sea approaches were covered by two 15-inch ex-battleship guns that could decimate the approaching invasion fleet. In addition, HMS "Prince of Wales" and HMS "Repulse," a modern battleship and an aging but fast, well-armed battle cruiser, and their destroyer escort provided distant cover of the sea-lanes. It was a pity the promised aircraft carrier was detained by repairs following its grounding in the Bahamas. Still, it was also widely known that the Japanese air force was truly not up to snuff. Bombing the defenseless Chinese cities was a totally different thing from attacking a well protected, major military base or trying to sink modern, fast warships capable of unrestricted evasive maneuvering in the open sea. On the December 7, 1941, Singapore was as prepared against invasion as any place could ever be. But was it truly ready?

The Japanese landings took place at Kota Baru, well over 500 miles north of the city. On December 10, the battleship and the battle cruiser were at the bottom of the sea, both sunk by the Japanese airplanes. The bombing of airfields and supremacy of the Japanese aircraft and pilots in the air quickly decimated the Royal Air Force, while the Japanese Army moving with unprecedented speed arrived at the back-door of the fortress by the end of January. Crossing the Johor Strait separating Singapore from the mainland at night and during low tide, the Japanese invaded the city. On February 15, 1942, 90,000 British, Australian, and Indian troops under command of General Sir Arthur Percival capitulated. Lieutenant General Bennett, the commanding officer of the Australian forces participating in the defense of the city stated subsequently: "The whole operation seems incredible: 550 miles in 55 days—forced back by a small Japanese army of only two divisions, riding stolen bicycles and without artillery support."

What relation is there between this seemingly irrelevant recapitulation of history and the process of knowledge management and operations of knowledge workers? Section 1 presented an integrative organizational model of knowledge management that, if faithfully implemented, will enable any organization to be prepared to conduct business in modern, dynamic knowledge economy. However, is this necessarily the same as being ready? The distinction may appear subtle but it has far-reaching implications for all organizations, and the analogy to one of the critical moments of the Second World War helps to understand it.

Singapore was *prepared*. The fortress, held to be the "Gibraltar of the East" was believed to be impregnable. With 90,000 superbly trained troops, many of whom were already battle hardened veterans, aircraft at local airfields to protect its skies, naval forces to defend distant sea approaches, shore installations providing local defense, the jungle and the swamps guarding the back door, and finally a strait in the back whose shallow depth prevented the use of landing craft on the northern shore of the island, Singapore appeared a bastion that could not be invaded by even the strongest force (Barber, 2003). Singapore had everything that a conventional military wisdom considered necessary to stop any attack, and then serve as a launching platform for a decisive and winning counter attack. Yet, when the Japanese invasion arrived, Singapore turned out to be the fortress that was not *ready*. Using light and highly mobile units fighting with unprecedented and demoralizing savagery, the Japanese attacked from the inland. Their air force proved superior to the aging planes of the RAF and rapidly eliminated both air and naval defenses. Shore-based artillery arcs of fire were restricted to the sea approaches only: the guns were useless against an attack coming from across the Johor Strait. The depth of the Strait itself, insufficient for the operation of landing ships, did not affect small craft and rubber boats used to transfer Japanese infantry to the opposite shore.

Amazingly, while many of the factors that ultimately contributed to the fall of Singapore were known to the Allies, they were entirely disregarded. Allied intelligence provided definitive warnings of the imminent Japanese attack. The mobile nature of Japanese style of warfare has been observed during the conflict in China that also demonstrated the singular resilience of Japanese infantry, and its ability to operate in austere environments. The superiority of the Japanese Zero fighter was known, as much as the unhesitant and precise use of bombers against both sea and land targets. Overconfidence and disdain of the Japanese as highly capable, relentless fighters by Allied politicians and military commanders (despite illustrious military history of Japan) pushed the *available information* aside, and prevented its consolidation into *useful (germane) knowledge* whose practical and timely application could have averted the subsequent disaster.

The Japanese, on the other hand, were both *prepared* and *ready*. The Japanese General Staff understood well the Allied approach to warfare—after all, many of its members were trained in the West. The Japanese were also fully aware of the dismissive and supercilious attitude of the Allies, and, while offended by it, they were also fully prepared to exploit Allied conceit and excessive confidence. Converting carefully gathered information into the knowledge of the likely Allied responses, the Japanese were able to select resources necessary for the exploitation of Allied weaknesses. The Japanese were prepared. They were also ready: while the initially weak Allied response was unexpected, it did not confuse Japanese commanders (it is interesting to note that one of the explanations given for the chaos following Operation Iraqi Freedom was the unanticipated speed of the invasion and the consequent lack of clear action plans for the period immediately following the fall of Baghdad). Instead, using unconventional movement and distribution of resources, the Japanese compounded confusion (and even panic) in the Allied camp. The readiness for action, manifested in the Japanese flexibility to respond to the unexpected threats (e.g., the unexpected appearance of heavy British naval task force) combined with the effective use of operational feints allowed them to retain initiative firmly, consistently, and at all times. Consequently, the Japanese retained superiority at all *critical points* of action—the principal attribute that allowed them to by-pass all irrelevant elements and concentrate on the strategically important objectives (Alexander, 2002).

Basic Rules

Underlying the scenario previously described are some very important basic rules. They are nothing but common sense, and all have been mentioned countless times in countless textbooks, scientific papers, pamphlets, and speeches. Yet, the equally commonplace disregard of these basic rules has led to spectacular failures in politics and business (Barnett, 2004; Stiglitz, 2003). Let us, therefore, examine them more closely and see how they relate to the context of KM.

- **Contempt** for the opposition prevents *objective assessment* of its strengths and weaknesses—the two essential elements that are critical for the development of present and future strategies for organizational success and inter-organizational competition. Failure in the objective assessment of these two elements allows the opposition to conceal its critical assets to be used as the "secret surprise weapons" at the most critical stages of the competitive process. Consequently, the initiative shifts rapidly from the "strong" entity to the entity that was perceived as weak and incapable of offensive action. The sudden emergence of such "threats" is the common source of confusion and disarray that necessitates either a drastic modification of the original strategy, unexpected relocation of resources, or, in the worst cases, abandonment of what could have been a lucrative interaction. *Objective assessment* of the opposition is the most significant step to precede every business operation based on the exploitation of perceived competitive advantages.

- **Disregard of pertinent information** prevents generation of knowledge that is pertinent to the interaction(s) among potential partners or competitors, whether this occurs within own organization, between organizations, or, on a global scale, among competing nations (Barnett, 2004). It must be emphasized that *pertinent information* is not always obvious. Thus, when entering into competition on design and manufacture of an aircraft, it is not enough to know the design and manufacturing strengths and weaknesses of the competitor. The elements such as the political support of the opposing company resulting in state subsidies, the stability or loyalty of its workforce, the extent and strength of internal vs. external subcontracting, or the future operational stability of the principal customers may play a much more significant role than the present capability of the competitor to design and build the required airplane.

- **Pertinent information is not equal to pertinent knowledge** since pertinent information represents merely aggregation of structured data, grouped into readily perceived, understood, and coherent categories. *Pertinent (germane) knowledge* represents, on the other hand, the ability to use information as the essential tool in the interaction with, and the response to the competitor's moves. It is thus the sum total of all information *plus* the ability to implement it constructively and purposefully in the continuously changing environment of interactions between the two competitors. Pertinent knowledge can be thus compared to a complete, ready to use weapon that consists of several subcomponents (e.g., tacit knowledge, explicit knowledge, pertinent information, etc.) which can be applied at a specific time, in a specific context, and to attain specific gains that will assure the ultimate victory. To be truly effective, pertinent knowledge of the organization must also include understanding of the extent of the competitor's pertinent knowledge—a task that is difficult to perform and can be accomplished only through the objective assessment and extrapolation of the competitor's known profile and mode of operation. Like all intelligence gathering operations, the result of all subsequent analyses will be an "actionable extrapolation." As such, the result is predictive rather than factual, and will be subject to modifications depending, in turn, on the continuous gathering of pertinent information (intelligence, see Barnett, 2004)

- **Preparedness is not the equivalent of readiness**, a fact the reader should be able to realize from the example of the conquest of Singapore. However, in order to make sure the distinction is clear, let us define both concepts (von Lubitz, Carrasco, Levine, & Richir, 2004):

Preparedness is defined as the availability (prepositioning) of all resources, both human and physical, necessary for the management of, or the consequences of, a specific crisis event or event complex.

Readiness is defined as instantaneous ability to respond to a suddenly arising major crisis (e.g., sudden slow-down in the manufacturing supply chain) based on the instantaneously available human and materiel countermeasure resources that may or may not be prepositioned for crisis-related mobilization.

As we can see, preparedness is based on the anticipation of the event, its possible ramifications (consequences) within the organization, and its impact on customers. Readiness, on the other hand, is based solely on the immediate capability to contain the crisis through the initiation of correct response to the event or event complex that either contains its adverse consequences, or exploits possible advantages that such an event may suddenly present. In other words, while development of preparedness is typically the responsibility of the upper layers of management (a strategic task), the development of appropriate readiness (tactical task) is the domain of both the upper *and* the middle/lower management. It is the latter who, most commonly, are the first to encounter events that may have a substantial impact on the organization as a whole. These considerations also indicate that:

- **Preparedness not founded on broadly-based knowledge is useless.** The development of appropriate preparedness is predominantly a strategic task requiring intimate knowledge of several aspects of the organization, its operational structure, and its customers (Figure 1.) It also requires knowledge of peripheral fields that frequently include politics, national culture within which the organization operates, and even history—the example of Singapore contains lessons that can be applied to almost any business operation! The knowledge required for the development of preparedness is both explicit and tacit, since only such combination allows the critical perspective necessary for correct anticipation of the events that may have a major impact on the organization and its activities.

- **Readiness not based on pertinent knowledge is useless.** Unquestionably, every employee of a company should know how to behave in the case of fire, or (hopefully) be able to correctly administer basic life support. Pertinent knowledge constitutes the foundation necessary for the correct initiation of life-saving procedures in the event of a specific and clearly defined crises. Likewise, a stockbroker who notices sudden fluctuations in the trade of a typically steady stock does not need to know the foundations of the telecommunication platform that allows continuous tracking of that particular stock but must intimately know the fluctuation patterns of the market, the triggers of such fluctuations, their characteristics, etc. Coping with the sudden and unpredictable event requires the background of pertinent (or germane) knowledge that will dictate the nature of the subsequent response. Hence, readiness is context dependent. It is worth noting that while readiness requires a high degree of specialist professional knowledge, the development of preparedness depends on, and demands a much broader knowledge basis. Thus, one of the inevitable consequences of progressing up the management ladder is the need not only for the continuous learning within one's own profession, but also a vigorous expansion of ones intellectual horizons and increasingly higher familiarity with the domains that were formerly disregarded as irrelevant. Trivial as this observation may appear, the failure to increase one's own and organizational knowledge base led to many easily avoidable business failures. Unfortunately, trivia are the most rapidly forgotten knowledge element despite the fact that they are based on nothing else but application common sense to real life dilemmas. It is worth to note that common sense has been consistently considered the principal foundation of good and successful business!

- **Readiness is the most essential tool in response to, and containment of, an unexpected threat.** While intuitively obvious, the practical development of readiness is not an easy task. Possession of knowledge is not equivalent to the ability to employ it under the stress of less-then-routine circumstances. In other words, the fact that an appropriate knowledge basis exists is not automatically equivalent to the existence of readiness. Thus, while it is a commonly known fact that oil is lighter than water and therefore will float on water, emergency rooms world over are filled with patients suffering often quite severe burns resulting from the attempts to put out flames in the frying pan by splashing water onto the burning oil. Car manufacturers pay billions in damages to the victims of faulty car design despite the fact that undergraduate engineering students would fail their exams if they suggested similar approach. There are countless examples of failures to initiate an immediate and correct response to a threat, and all of them indicate that while germane knowledge is essential for the development of readiness, possession of germane knowledge is simply not enough

- Readiness is the most essential tool in exploitation of suddenly emerging weaknesses of the opposition—another superficially banal point whose disregard may be extremely costly. Competition is based on the exploitation of the weaknesses of other organizations operating within the same environmental niche. It is, as it were, a biological phenomenon—all species compete for resources, and one of the safest forms of competition is the ability to occupy environments that other species find inhospitable or even hostile. Business competition is based on similar principles but its cycles are vastly shorter. Hence, readiness to respond to suddenly perceived weakness of the competitor opens new doors for expansion of one's own market share, profits, operational diversification, etc. Consider the following example (Conway's History of the Ship: The Shipping Revolution). Most of the goods transported globally are moved aboard ships. However, the most expensive part of the process is not the transport itself but the delays caused by on- and off-loading operations. Ships make money while in passage, not while tied to a pier. The cargo handling operations would be vastly shortened if the cargo could be preloaded into a container, and the container, rather than individual palletized items, loaded aboard the waiting vessel. The concept is simple and intuitive. Yet, only Malcolm Mclean had the vision of implementing it in practice, and his SeaLand Inc., became the world's first company devoted to containerized transoceanic transport. Today, the traditional freighters with their forest of complicated masts and rigging became an almost museal rarity. The pertinent knowledge of the shipping business that McLean acquired during his life as a truck driver and the owner of a trucking company served as the foundation for his readiness to exploit the weakness of the shipping business that, in turn, revolutionized the industry.

The mere fact of possessing knowledge is not enough. It is similar to having a picture hidden in a vault rather than displayed on the wall. Knowledge needs to be applied to specific tasks in order to transform itself from a purely intellectual facet of life into a highly productive tool essential for the conduct of practically any meaningful human activity whose purpose is to produce tangible results.

Assume, for a moment, that you are about to leave your hotel for an interview whose success may result in a job that has always been the dream of your life. You are fully prepared—you have all pertinent facts (knowledge) in your head, your attire is superb, your accessories clearly indicate that you have the expected "class." You twist around while donning your jacket and the front button of your blouse or shirt pops off. No matter how much you try, the front opens at every move and reveals your underwear. Instead of looking as a walking example of elegance, you appear scruffy and a little unkempt. That, considering the intensity of the competition, may cost you the job. Everything counts. What do you do? Your readiness to respond to this seemingly trivial event may have a bearing on the rest of your life.

The simplest thing to do is to sew the button back on. However, it vanished under the bed and finding it will cost you time that you do not have. You can change your shirt. Unfortunately, you have only one that is immaculately pressed. The next best thing is to remove the lowermost button on your shirt, the one that will be hidden by the waist of your skirt or trousers—only you will be aware of the transgression. Then, if you have a needle and thread, put this button in place of the missing one. If you do not have the required tools, ask the concierge and do not forget to mention the need for haste. Your available time is getting shorter and shorter. Once you have all tools set and ready, do you have the pertinent knowledge of sewing buttons on your shirts? Rather amazingly, a vast number of men do not. The resulting attempts may be either futile, or result in the appearance that is only marginally better than that produced by the entirely missing button.

In the preceding example, you have both the knowledge necessary to respond to the crisis and the willingness to initiate a meaningful corrective response. Yet, the outcome is still a disaster. What you do not have is training in the practical application of such knowledge (and, rather unbelievably, several articles and book chapters have been devoted to the knowledge of replacing buttons that suddenly went awry!) Thus, while the experience supported by broad-based knowledge is the necessary foundation for the development of meaningful preparedness, training is the most essential aspect of developing readiness.

Role of Training

There is another way of solving the button dilemma. Realizing you cannot do a decent job of replacing the button, you call the hotel's desk and ask for a maid to help you. That may raise a few eyebrows and could make you look like a fool. On the other hand, the dilemma has a far greater dimension: do you prefer to be viewed by the hotel staff as a person incapable of replacing the missing shirt buttons or risk an irretrievably lost chance of getting the job of your life merely because you will be viewed as the scruffiest among all the applicants. Clearly, the job is far more important. But, if you get the job and become the president of a global-reach corporation, there is a chance a tabloid will dig up the "button story" and run a campaign (stirred by a competitor) aimed at ruining you by showing you as an utterly incompetent and dangerous fool. In the current social atmosphere where all dirty tricks are used in order to gain advantage, a newspaper article like the one suggested would certainly be one of those. A tiny insight in your past, as innocuous as it can be yet sufficiently illustrative to offer a suitable pretext to those who need it in order to launch a vicious attack at you. You begin to run through the range of all possible disaster permutations a missing shirt button may cause, all of them nasty, while the time is ticking away. Your readiness to "go to wars" collapses, and when you finally arrive at the interview, the wall of total confidence is shaken. Moreover, you lost some of your initially unassailable advantage: subconsciously, you make sure the replaced button appears "just right," you fidget, and your uncertainty gets noticed. Your interviewer neither knows nor cares about the reasons for your nervousness but assigns you "minus points." After all, if you cannot calmly and competently handle a simple job interview, how will you behave during major negotiations, where composure and a clear head are the most important psychological resources at your disposal? You fail and do not get the job. Why? The only weapon you did not have in your armory was training! You were not trained in making instantaneous choices, selecting the most direct path to contain the consequences of an adverse event, you were not trained in eliminating non-essential attributes of the novel situation that you are forced to cope with. You were not trained to apply the knowledge you have under the circumstances that diverged from the expected. *You were not trained to think under pressure!*

People are critical to the success of any knowledge management initiative. In order to help the "knowledge workforce" work smarter rather than merely harder, it is important that appropriate training is implemented. Knowledge is an entirely useless intellectual ballast if it can not be employed meaningfully and constructively. Moreover, all knowledge that you have is, essentially, historical. Why? Simply, because it is a body of understanding based on the analysis of the past, of all information brought to our attention by the events that took place *until this very moment but not a moment ahead in time.* Thus, proper use of knowledge as a solution to all forthcoming events is based on extrapolation, on a careful (which does not mean slow!) analysis of all pertinent characteristics of the evolving scenario, on defining similarities to the past events, characterizing the differences and isolating entirely novel elements, visualizing all interrelationships among the individual subcomponents, and then making appropriate decisions. It is a long list of actions, some of which must be performed concurrently, others sequentially. Yet, you might have noticed that, while performing all these analytical steps and using historical knowledge, you are also creating a new addition to the existing knowledge. Your response to a novel environment, whether correct or not, provides another tiny brick to the collective body of organizational (or even human) knowledge. The extant knowledge base of the organization has grown, albeit in tiny increments, and may find its use in the future. Thus, by acting in the present, you have contributed to the historical knowledge, and, at the same time affected the future. Paradoxical as it may seem, our actions affect several points along the time axis, and their future relevance may be substantial, even if, at the time they are executed, most or maybe even all of these actions appear trivial. Thus, to avoid potential disasters, it is critical that all responses, particularly to novel situations, are as correct as they can be.

While it is desirable that all actions that we execute are correct, in reality plenty of mistakes are always committed. Yet, mistakes have a potent educational function—objective—rather than punitive analysis of failure is the best way of avoiding similar failures in the future. Since any failure, even if based on a most honest error, may have extraordinarily severe consequences, it is in the best interest of any organization to introduce preventive measures that will limit the occurrence of "adverse events." The best preventive measure is training. It is simply the best method to equip all members of any organization with tools limiting the occurrence of failure. Training allows combination of theoretical knowledge with its practical implementation. It is a simple concept, lauded by "organizational consultants" and leadership experts, and also a frequently neglected aspect of organizational life whose real significance is best exemplified by, once again, looking at the "military way of life."

As complex and technology-oriented modern armed forces may be today, the rifle is still the ubiquitous companion of every infantryman. The new recruit learns everything about it. He knows its characteristics, knows how all components fit together, how it fires. The recruit learns and acquires profound knowledge of the application of this inseparable companion of life. But the rifle can be used in a multitude of vastly different situations. It can represent an element of authority while on guard duty, it is a life saving device while in a firefight conducted from a foxhole, or serves as an instrument of instantaneous aggression during urban combat. In all these situations, the rifle is handled differently, yet expertly, and even if its application is shifted from one situation to another without conscious thinking, it is done smoothly, immediately, and appropriately to the situation. The art of using the rifle is acquired through incessant training during which knowledge transforms into action that, while appearing automated, is simply the result of experience in practical applications of the pre-existing body of knowledge.

Training can have many practical forms. Sometimes the term is misapplied to theoretical education—a seminar on sales techniques or marketing is often called "training." Yet, the latter represents nothing but a static transfer of knowledge from the master to the student. The training element, the practical application of that knowledge is entirely missing despite the occasional role-playing that may be included in the seminar.

Training is entirely practical; it facilitates acquisition and refinement of tacit knowledge by transferring the student from the theoretical world of explicit knowledge to the practical world of its application. It is the stage where knowing is transformed into doing. Thus, the main purpose of training is to familiarize the student not only with the routine uses of the acquired knowledge but also with the unexpected or the entirely unknown, and make the student realize that, while the exact circumstances may vary, most of the situations from the past have very many elements that are identical to the presently encountered ones. The knowledge foundation that the student already has is, typically, more than sufficient to deal with the sudden change in the operational environment. Training habituates to such changes, and habituation to the challenges imposed by the change is the fundamental tool required for addressing its consequences both rapidly and correctly, but more importantly, in a manner that assures positive outcomes.

Training has to be realistic (it does not make much sense to train an accounting analyst in coping with the complex issues of the supply chain—although a certain amount of knowledge of how such a chain works may be of a great help in understanding its financial aspects, thereby helping in the execution of analyst's duties!) While realistic, training also has to be challenging, expose the trainee to novel situations, and have a context of relevance. It will be a waste of time to train a law student working as a summer clerk in adding paper to the photocopying machine. Training the same student to be able to clear a jam of the machine may, on the other hand be a blessing when a court petition needs to be delivered in a hurry! The reader surely recalls the moments of panic when the photocopier jammed at the end of the day and nobody at the office knew how to deal with it.

Training must also incorporate the entire body of knowledge appropriate to the role and functions of the trainee within the parent organization. It has to be relevant, and relevance can be attained only through the exposure of the trainees to the specific, well-defined situations that require specific and well-defined solutions. Today, many of the training seminars deal with issues presented at a level so general that the contents become entirely meaningless. The value of such training is vastly inferior when viewed in the context of the resources put into organizing it, the expectations of its outcomes, and the practical applicability of the "lessons learned."

Training must develop the capability to summarize the pertinent elements of a novel situation or environment, and then analyze them in the context of the already existing knowledge. The resultant analysis provides the foundation for the subsequent decision-making process. Summarizing novel facts is a comparatively easy task since everything that has not been encountered previously is, by definition, new. The only effort at this stage is therefore a coherent extraction of novel elements from the surrounding mass of the already experienced elements, followed by a systematic organization of the new factors that is based, for example, on their potential or perceived significance. Analysis of the new elements is, however, a much more complex procedure. It demands confronting the new with the pre-existing body of knowledge, determination whether the new is genuinely new or merely a variation of the already known elements, followed by the definition of the existing interrelationships and the potential impact of these interrelationships on the immediate operational outcomes, extrapolation of the impact of such outcomes on the future actions, and, ultimately, the definition and commitment to the appropriate actions both imminent and the future ones. The synthesis/analysis cycle may be comparatively "slow" (measured in days or weeks), as seen in positioning the organization within the fluctuating environment of transoceanic shipment of crude oil. It may be also be extremely rapid as, for example, during an airliner cockpit emergency where minutes may separate recovery from a catastrophic loss of the aircraft.

Finally, training has to incorporate stress. In normal life, upper layers of management experience stress quite frequently and in many forms. It can be either physical (sleep deprivation caused by transoceanic travel) or emotional (coping with issues to which there are no good solutions, and the only available approach is selecting the least damaging one, then facing the consequences of one's choice). Many studies have shown significant decrease of performance and ability to solve complex problems under stress, and sometimes the execution of even simple tasks can be compromised. Airline crews, physicians, soldiers, business executives, and many other professionals are prone to such degradation. On the other hand, members of the military Special Forces are capable of solving often very complex tasks involving active extraction and practical implementation of a wide range of previously acquired knowledge in a seemingly stress-impervious manner. Interestingly, while the physiological effect of mental or physical stress is essentially similar to all, the intensity of Special Forces training creates much greater physical endurance and enhances psychological reserves that allow normal intellectual functions under the circumstances that rapidly degrade performance of the untrained personnel. It is, of course, nonsensical to expect the president of a major company to be a commando. On the other hand, when training potential business leaders, it is important to incorporate in their education not only the body of necessary knowledge but also train them in its use in the adverse environments that demand critical thinking and decision-making under stress. It is a simple thing to make a critical business decision while contemplating all its repercussions in the comfort of one's office, and with the ready access to the pool of broad-based knowledge accumulated within one's own organization. It is a completely different feeling, when the decision has to be made immediately, in a potentially adversarial environment of the negotiating table, immediately after a transoceanic flight, and using a foreign language as the only means of communication with the negotiation partners!

Simulation

Frequent training is particularly significant for the retention and consolidation of the acquired knowledge, and for the development of expertise in its flexible utilization (Lary, Pletcher, & von Lubitz, 2002). Yet, and often as a cost-cutting or time-saving measure, the frequency of training is swept aside as an insignificant factor in contributing to the overall efficiency of doing business despite the fact that several studies consistently show very rapid deterioration of unused knowledge and skills. It may be a fact very close to the heart of many readers to know that only six months after the end of the training, students retain only about 50% of skills and knowledge of advanced cardiopulmonary life support (ACLS). It is for this very reason that many healthcare organizations reduced inter-training intervals from up to two years down to 6-12 months between mandatory refresher courses. Maybe not enough, but surely a vast improvement compared to the past when refresher training was not even considered as valuable.

How can simulation be of use in training? Until very recently, when one wanted to test preparedness and response readiness in case of a major failure at the car production line there were only two choices: either shut down the line in order to pretend that such event occurred or conduct the entire evolution on paper. Shutting the production line, even for a very brief period, can be prohibitively expensive. Doing the exercise on paper is, on the other hand, as unrealistic as anything can be. In order to conduct the exercise involving physical shutdown, a series of preparatory notices needed to be distributed. Consequently, everybody working at the line knew precisely the nature and time of the event that was about to happen and everyone treated it as a "fake." Consequently, the response was amazingly predictable and the exercise treated as a managerial joke that caused more trouble than it was worth. The delays that the shut-down imposed had to be caught up with, the disruptions were very costly, and the practiced remedial actions almost surreal. After all, it was difficult to pretend replacement of a "burnt out" electrical motor when the motor was simply turned off. At the word "Repaired!" the switch was flipped to its "on" position, and everything worked smoothly again. Paper exercises produced even worse results: paper could not accommodate full complexity of the event, the exercise could not involve the entire staff of the line, and the resulting "remedial" actions were, consequently, not only theoretical but frequently entirely useless.

Simulation is an ancient concept: the game of chess is nothing but a highly stylized simulation of warfare. However, aviation was the first to adopt simulation in the mid-twenties as a routine training tool. Ever since then, countless pilots were subjected to the claustrophobia of the Link-trainer cockpit in which they learned the secrets of instrument flying. Today, the sophistication of flight simulators has reached the level of life-like reality and simulator-based training made pilots not only better but also safer: only the simulator allows training the crews in responding to the events that may have potentially fatal consequences. Albeit much later, medicine took to simulation with equal eagerness. Today, particularly in the USA, there are hardly any medical or nursing students who did not have exposure to High Fidelity Patient Simulators—highly computerized mannequins that can behave like humans, and that respond to procedures and drugs in the same way a sick human patient would. Virtual reality is used with an ever increasing frequency in surgeon training, surgery planning, and in individual procedure training. Computer-based simulations of hospital operations begin to find their way as both training and operations-testing tools. In addition to using simulation to train its pilots, armed forces of the world are employing simulators of often great sophistication and complexity to train operators of tanks, ships, or even as tools in complex exercises involving several units operating within large geographical areas. Simulation of manufacturing processes, plant maintenance operations, shipping, and port operations, etc., gains rapid popularity as the means to greatly increase the efficiency of all involved processes (Brandon-hall.com, 2002; Rouse & Boff, 2005; Strategy Dynamics, 2004; Yardley, Thie, Schank, Galegher, & Ripose, 2003). The most important attribute of simulation is, however, not the honing of eye-hand coordination but its ideal suitability for the development of critical thinking and rapid decision-making. And the development of critical thinking and rapid decision-making are among the most important outcomes for any knowledge management initiative.

The OODA Loop

What is "critical thinking?" What is "decision-making?" Both terms acquired the highly respectable patina as the principal constituents of business/management/education/ leadership dictionary filled with virtually meaningless but highly popular terms (incidentally, "virtual" is also part of the collection!) Yet, both activities are the essential ingredients of the daily life. They are, as a matter of fact, the essential tools of survival and constitute the integral elements of what is known as the "common sense." It is worth noting that both activities are closely related to each other: critical thinking, unless accompanied by decisions and their implementation (i.e., action) is a patently futile exercise. Making a decision without prior analysis of the essential characteristics of the event that requires making such decision is, obviously, a foolhardy approach to problem solving. It thus appears that critical thinking and decision-making consist of two sub-elements each:

- **Critical thinking:** Summary and analysis.
- **Decision making:** Selection of action and implementation of action.

Observe, however, that once you implement action, it will induce a series of consequences whose potential ramifications will induce another stage of critical thinking followed by a new stage of action selection and action implementation. The circle will revolve again, and continue to revolve (at least theoretically) into infinity. The intuitively simple process turns out to be quite complex, and misstep at any of its constituent stages may lead to quite irreversible consequences. Clearly, when dealing with the task of peeling a potato, the task is simple, and the consequences limited. Or are they?

CRITICAL THINKING AND DECISION MAKING IN POTATO PEELING PROCESS

Critical Thinking:

Summary stage

- Select appropriate type and size of the potato.
    - Large potato unavailable.
    - Small potato available but has plenty of "eyes."
- Select appropriate peeling tool.
    - Potato peeler blunt and useless.
    - A kitchen knife is sharp but rusty in places.

Analysis stage

- The potato is too small but will have to do, the peeler will not peel the potato but the knife is sharp enough and will work well*).

Decision making:

Action selection stage

- Rinse the potato in hot water to remove dirt, surface bacteria, and eventual chemical residue**).
- Peel the potato using available tools (i.e., potato and knife).

Action-implementation stage

- Execute the rinsing procedure.
- Execute peeling***.

Let us now look at the consequences of peeling the potato on the next revolution of the thinking-decision circle:

- *: Your potato is small and by using a large knife, you make the process unwieldy. Hence, you increase the risk of accidentally cutting yourself.
- **: Rinsing the potato in hot water will remove dirt. However it will have a very limited effect on the bacteria (you would need boiling water, not merely hot tap water). If any chemicals are present, their amounts will be small. Some will rinse away during a perfunctory wash. Some will not.   If you are concerned about, for example, pesticide contamination, the chemicals will be incorporated in the flesh of the potato. Rinsing will have no effect on these compounds.
- ***: The knife was too large, the potato too small, and its surface too slippery. You cut yourself with the rusty part of the knife's edge, and the cut was deep. You rinsed the cut under water (it hurt!) and then put a dressing on it. Few days later, the fingers became swollen and very painful. You applied topical antibiotic. After few more days your entire palm and then the forearm became swollen, discolored, and you noticed purplish streaks running along its surface. You finally went to the local emergency room (you did not happen to have health insurance and had problems finding the hospital whose ER would take you). The physician told you that you have a very serious infection, and that it probably spread through your body. You will need a fairly serious treatment that may involve surgical cleaning of the infected finger and a lengthy antibiotic treatment.

As you can see, even a very simple task, if not approached without some forethought, may lead to potentially serious or even deadly consequences. What then, if the problem relates to the operations of a major international company and you happen to be its CEO? The nature of your thinking and the type of decisions you will make may affect the lives of thousands of employees, may affect the entire way business is done, and—if the importance of your organization is high enough within the national economy—there may be political consequences that, in turn may impact other nations as well. Your responsibility is huge and your decisions must be absolutely correct. If you are wrong, it will be completely futile to admit sheepishly in front of TV cameras that the fault is yours and you take the full blame! Nobody really cares at that stage. The disaster has already occurred!

Clearly, critical thinking and decision-making are, for the most part, quite instinctive. However, the complexity of the involved processes increases exponentially with the complexity of the addressed problem since the knowledge database that needs to be employed in the process of summarizing and analyzing increases, and the number and range of the ramifications resulting from the interplay of all subcomponents increase as well. Hence, the number of all possible decisions that can be made and that are relevant to the solution of the problem increases as well. On the other hand, once the decision has been made, the range of available actions decreases sharply since there is only a limited number of appropriate and correct actions that will executing the selected decision. Some of these processes can be reduced to the level of algorithm-based approaches. The latter are best exemplified by the procedures involved in the treatment of an unconscious patient where actions are guided by a series of "yes-no" rules: does the patient have a pulse? Yes. Is the patient breathing? No. Is the patient's airway obstructed? Yes. Clean the airway. Is the patient breathing? No. Provide artificial ventilation. And so on … in very complex environments such highly structured solutions break down frequently. There are too many possibilities. The individual sub-stages of the process may cross over into each other and produce further complexities. Yet, solutions to the presenting problems need to be found and, quite frequently, they must be found very rapidly.

The process of critical thinking and decision-making has been analyzed and subsequently formalized by the late Col. John Boyd, USAF (Boyd, 1987) who presented the results in the form of the famous "Boyd Briefing" given to countless politicians, military officers, and businessmen. Boyd's major achievement was the observation that essentially any form of human activity can be broken into four main subcomponents interacting with each other in a sequential, loop-like manner—the OODA Loop (Figure 2).

Originally aimed at the war fighting community, implementation of the OODA loop completely changed many aspects of modern combat. Soon after its inception, the loop found rapidly its practical applications in disciplines as diverse as business, transportation, and medicine (Richards, 2004). Today, although its creator is largely unknown to the majority of its users, OODA loop is a widely used tool, and even the colloquialism of "being kept inside the loop" derives from Boyd's loop.

The loop is based on a cycle of four critical and interrelated stages: observation followed by Orientation, then by decision, and finally action. The cycle revolves both in time and space. Observation and Orientation stages of the loop are its critical aspects at which the plurality of implicit and explicit inputs determines the sequential decision and action steps. The outcome of the latter affects, in turn, the character of the next initiation point (observation) in the forward progression of the rolling loop (Figure 2). The orientation stage specifies the characteristics and the nature of the "center of thrust" (Boyd used the German expression "Schwerpunkt") at which the most significant activity is to concentrate and which, in turn, determines the specifics of the sequential stages (determination and decision—the definition of action to be

Figure 2. The OODA Loop by John Boyd

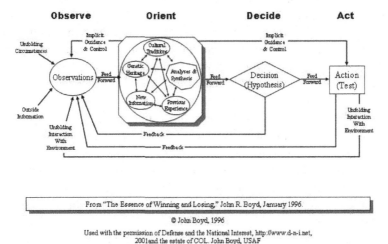

From "The Essence of Winning and Losing," John R. Boyd, January 1996.

© John Boyd, 1996

Used with the permission of Defense and the National Interest, http://www.d-n-i.net, 2001 and the estate of COL. John Boyd, USAF

> Two aspects of the loop are striking: its multidimensional complexity and its dynamic nature that encompasses both time and space. The deceptively simple Loop represents arguably the best depiction of the complexity of interactions and interrelationships involved in critical thinking and decision-making processes, and how actions based on these processes together with other external inputs affect the environment, and hence—the next revolution of the loop. Importantly, all actions within the loop are simultaneous—action does not interrupt observation or decision does not relieve from the need to orient. Contrary to the commonly committed error, OODA loop does not represent a linear process developing along the time axis but a process that develops simultaneously within the operational sphere where time is but one of the constituent elements.

taken, and action—its specific execution). However, the progression of the loop is not linear—a commonly made error in the interpretation of its progression. It does not merely roll along the time axis—the stages within the loop are simultaneous, delicately intertwined, and balanced. Action does not interrupt observation, or decision does not halt orientation. The domain of the loop is thus multidimensional, and embraces all constituents of the environment within which the loop revolves. Time is only one of those elements.

Outwardly, the OODA loop appears almost banal. In reality, it provides the essential framework for knowledge-based, multidimensional critical thinking and decision-making whose operational consequence—*Action*—is executed in real time, and determines the operational tempo and direction of the entire process. Unsurprisingly, practical implementation of OODA loop as one of the pivotal elements in the current doctrine of network-centric operations led to significant changes in many aspects of modern warfare and business. It also works in very simple situations and, if you wish, you may apply the loop to the analysis of the highly unfortunate potato-peeling event. If you do it correctly, you will realize that a much safer course of action was to boil the potato. After cooling, its skin would then peel off easily without the need for a knife. Moreover, whatever bacteria would have been lodged in the surface of the potato would be killed by protracted exposure to the boiling water. There is also a possibility that at least some of the noxious chemicals would be rendered harmless by heat-induced denaturation!

Implementation of Boyd's OODA loop-based training rapidly develops the art of critical thinking and decision-making. Importantly, it also provides the ideal solution to the dilemma of training these skills in a manner consistent with their practical use within a constantly changing environment of multiple situational inputs that are, in turn, characterized by their own temporal and physical instability (operational chaos or "fog of war" of von Clausewitz, 1994).

The dynamic nature of the OODA paradigm makes it a pre-eminently suitable readiness development tool in the context of the frequently fluid business operations. However, the commonly employed pattern of training prevents such implementation. As already mentioned, today's "training" is based predominantly on didactic lectures or seminars that quite effectively eliminate the very active nature Observation and Orientation stages by predetermining their characteristics—in fact there is not much to observe or to orient, and everything is offered by the instructor. As a result, both stages are entirely static and the course of the sequential steps (determination/decision and action) is enforced *a priori*. The result is a rigid, algorithmic training structure whose implementation produces be at best inconclusive and, at worst, entirely misleading lessons.

The latest advances in simulation technology and the rapid development of network-centric operations philosophy provide more than merely a tool allowing implementation of effective OODA loop-based training in the development of the essential critical thinking and decision-making skills. Simulation also allows practicing these skills under stress since simulation offers the possibility of practically unlimited manipulation of time and resource factors. It also permits ready introduction of "confounding elements" such as spurious or misleading information, sudden change in critical factors, interference by competing organizations, etc. Thus, the world opened by introduction of simulation as a training tool provides the necessary richness and variety of texture that are needed to practice critical thinking and decision-making in a real life-like environment. The very same richness serves as the ideal platform for the OODA loop based development of skills.

Simulation and OODA loop are the complementary tools of the most advanced form of training through which both speed and accuracy of action in critical and rapidly evolving environments can be developed. It also allows rapid testing of "what-if" scenarios, and, equally importantly, practical testing of theoretical assumptions. Hence, in a rather indirect manner, the fusion of the two components into a single training concept serves as a tool in the development and consolidation of new elements of knowledge that, at the same time, allows gathering of experience in practical applications of this knowledge. It is in the context of such experience that the value of combining the synthetic environment with Boyd's loop becomes eminently clear. Gathering experience in real life can be a protracted and often quite a bloody process. Gathering the same experience in a simulated environment is not only bloodless but also fast. Thus, the practical results of simulated experience can be applied to real life operations with equal rapidity. It is this type of training, one that combines simulation with OODA loop-based critical thinking and decision-making skills that allows an airline pilot who flew a specific aircraft type only in a simulator to sit in the cockpit and fly confidently and safely a real airliner with a full load of passengers.

The Generalist

Today, the world is based on specialization. If you scan announcements of vacancies, the potential employers look for specialists whose functions are commonly described in very specific and narrow terms. The knowledge and experience that are required are very specific. At times, even the personal characteristics are outlined by quite specific norms. Several agencies specialize in finding specific candidates for specific jobs. However, there is an agency where none of these rules apply—the armed forces. Can you imagine an ad saying, "A presentable person, with infantry training, combat experience, experience of armor warfare, and solid managerial/ leadership skills is required to assume the position of a commanding officer of an armored infantry division at the rank of brigadier general. Salary commensurate with experience?"

Armed forces all over the world accept people with practically no experience of the military and through a long process of education and training, convert them into specialists. However, at some stage of every military officer's life a transition occurs. The officer is transferred to a series of staff duties of ever-increasing complexity, where the original specialization is less and less important but overall experience, and the total sum of the general knowledge assumes predominance. If you look at the Pentagon today, you will find many of such officers. Those who once upon the time commanded infantry units, ships, or flew airplanes are now in charge of the development of ultra-complex information management systems, direct global logistic operations, and manage multi-billion weapons procurement programs. Life-long service and experience combine with the acquisition of further education in frequently non-military fields that converts such officers from narrow specialists into broad-based generalists.

In civilian life, it is almost unconceivable that a specialist in acoustic design will become the marketing executive at a fashions house. Yet, in the armed forces, it is not an uncommon event that an infantry general commands a task force providing medical assistance in another country as a part of the recovery from devastation caused by an earthquake. The general has enough knowledge and command experience to be able to provide overall direction of the involved operations—to provide leadership. His staff, consisting of specialists in logistics, medical affairs, infrastructure development, security, public relations, etc., will develop and execute the specific aspects of the overall plan of action. The general does not need to be intimately familiar with the minute aspects of all the involved components. He must, however, be aware of the general nature of the processes involved in the conduct of all involved activities that, cumulatively, will assure a positive outcome at the end of the operation. The general is a generalist capable of combining the contents of several independent domains into a completely new one that addresses the issues posed by the problems the general is tasked to solve. The general must both *create* the new process and then *lead* its execution.

In a seminal yet formally almost unknown paper, *Destruction and Creation*, Boyd analyzed the process of creating new knowledge showing that it can be created only through the preceding process of destruction. The existing knowledge is domain-oriented. It may be centered on drug design, accounting, aeronautical engineering, or theatre. It is, nonetheless, strictly limited to the sphere in which it is practically employed. Thus, creation of new knowledge can be attained only by the "destruction" of domain barriers and the imaginative selection of suitable constituents belonging to the range of previously well defined and circumscribed domains, followed by reassembly of these constituents into an entirely new entity (i.e., the process of creation). Boyd's briefing contained a simple but striking example of this approach. Assume that you have the domains of a toy tank, a motorboat, a bicycle, a tub, and an Alpine resort. Is there anything preeminently useful that could be created by using the principle of destruction and creation?

- Take the concept of tracks from the toy tank.
- Take the motor from the motorboat.
- Take the handle bars from the bicycle.
- Take the tub.
- Take a pair of skis from the Alpine resort.

Combine all these constituents creatively, what you get is a

SNOWMOBILE

Consisting of

- **Tracks:** Concept taken from the toy tank.
- **Small engine:** Concept taken from the outboard of motor boat.
- **Steering handles:** Concept taken from the bicycle.
- **Hull:** Concept taken from the inverted tub that hides the engine, transmission, etc.
- **Steering skis:** Concept taken from the Alpine resort.

Simple, isn't it? If you look at the history of creation, many concepts have been developed by the combination of outwardly entirely unrelated ideas. However, in each case, the creator had to be in possession of sufficiently broad knowledge to be able to perceive application of individual domain components into an entirely new entity. Stated differently, what has been entirely missed by a specialist preoccupied with the contents of own domain, has been noticed and utilized by a generalist who, by combining several disciplines, was able to perceive the existence of functional relationships that could not be perceived by the observer capable of only a narrow view.

Increasingly higher level of responsibility within an organization requires an increasingly more sophisticated level of knowledge and the ability to use it flexibly. At the level of upper management, professional knowledge constitutes merely a background, a grounding in the art of knowledge application, rather than the predominant tool. Instead, the ability to extract pertinent elements from several, vastly separate and independent pools of knowledge becomes increasingly essential (Bloom, 2002; d'Epiro & Desmond Pinkovish, 2001; Murray, 2003). Thus, the progression up the ladder of responsibility is accompanied by the gradual change of a specialist into a generalist. Unfortunately, it is the change that is neither facilitated by the current education and training system nor, with the salutary exception of the military, the world of business operations. Maybe, the principal reason why there are a number of splendid generals but significantly fewer splendid chief executives is the fact that the military insists on the development of a generalist attitude together with the increase in rank and seniority! There are many attributes commonly ascribed to the most prominent leaders of business such as Bill Gates, Donald Trump, or Jack Welch: visionaries, leaders, managers extraordinaire. One attribute has never been applied—all of them are also superb generalists able to perceive, extract, and combine constructively the individual elements of distinctly separate knowledge domains.

In his analysis of creation, Boyd pointed out that the creator is also an observer whose interactions with the observed system are subject to the Uncertainty Principle of Heisenberg stating that the greater degree of intrusion by the observer upon the observed system, the greater the degree of disorder within that system that the observer perceives. Combining this concept with the Second Law of Thermodynamics and Gödel's Proof that true statements or concepts existing within the system cannot be deduced from the postulates that make up this system; Boyd argued that "… uncertainty and disorder can be diminished by the direct artifice of creating a higher and broader more general concept to represent reality." Boyd's postulate represents a completely new idea of the principles underlying creation of new knowledge where, out of disordered and often conflicting, separate domains, and entirely new and ordered entity can be formed. The postulate also hints at the role of the consultant—the ultimate knowledge worker whose interaction with the organizational system is expected to provide solutions to its deficiencies.

Consultants are hired for the sake of their expertise. They are expected to explore sometimes the most minute aspects of the organization, analyze the "chaos," and then, based on this analysis, devise solutions that will convert chaos into an orderly, organized whole. Such function implies a very significant interaction with the system, while Boyd's postulate clearly indicates that, with the increased interaction, the perception of disorder will also increase—a paradox as far as the concept of consultancy is concerned. However, it is also known that employment of consultants may not provide the expected relief or offer it only temporarily. Is it then possible that consultants spend too much of their effort on the analysis of detail and too little on the study of the functionality of the system as a whole? Possibly. If so, then the principal role of the consultant is that of an objective outsider, an observer whose main task is to determine how the system operates in relation to other similar systems, how it interacts with such systems, and also how it interacts with other, unrelated systems. By performing such analysis, the consultant uses the foundation of broad-based tacit and explicit knowledge and, through the extraction of the pertinent but hidden attributes of the observed systems, creates a new one that combines the previously chaotically arranged elements into a new, ordered, and functional structure. It follows then, that the consultant needs to be a generalist rather than a narrow specialist. The discord within one segment of operations may be, as a matter of fact, caused by problems created by a completely different and quite possibly seemingly entirely unrelated one. In medicine, such process is known as "differential diagnosis." Many diseases are characterized by deceptively similar or even identical symptoms. An experienced physician acts as an outside observer of the system—human body—and observes how its individual components (domains) interact, and what are the results of such interactions. Broad knowledge of anatomy, physiology, biochemistry, and often other non-medical fields (e.g., sociology, geography, or even history) allow objective restructuring through pharmacological, surgical, or even psychological interventions, and creation of a new, superior system—the cured patient. Thus, despite being a specialist—a surgeon, a neurologist, or a gastroenterologist—a good physician is also a generalist capable of looking beyond the realm of own specialty and of analyzing the underlying causes of disease from a variety of viewpoints. The process is based on the possession of broad-based knowledge, training in its use, experience, and the unique gift without which much of creation would be impossible—intuition.

Managing knowledge, whether at a personal or organizational level, is an exceedingly complex task consisting of many intricately interwoven elements. Yet, when performed properly, knowledge management is not only the instrument of knowledge classification—preparation for its practical applications—but also of creation of new knowledge. It is the task of knowledge workers and managers to perceive interrelationships and interdependencies of knowledge elements within and among individual domains. It is their task to extrapolate these relationships into new aspects of knowledge. And maybe sometime, one of these workers will be able to answer a simple question:

If Leonardo daVinci, a world-acknowledged painter, mathematician, aeronautical engineer, anatomist, architect, military engineer, urban planner, weapons designer, political advisor, teacher, and an eccentric applied for the position of CEO of a major international energy resource management company, would he be enthusiastically hired or would receive the following letter?

"Dear Mr. daVinci,

Thank you for your application for the position of CEO at Galactic SuperOil, Inc. We have received many applications from highly qualified candidates. After a careful selection, our review board determined that the lack of earned doctorate and the nature of your excellent qualifications as a generalist are not commensurate with the requirements of the present search. We thank you for your interest and, with your permission, will retain for future reference your curriculum vitae in our files. Galactic SuperOil, Inc. would like to wish you success in your search for the position that you so justly deserve.

Sincerely yours,
Paragon Moronus,
Head of the Search Committee
Galactic SuperOil, Inc."

It is a comfortable feeling to realize that neither Italian Renaissance princes nor the French king Francis I subscribed to the trends seen in the modern business employment practices. Had they done otherwise, we would not enjoy the creations of one of the greatest generalists of the world has known!

Key Success Factors for KM

The overall objective of any knowledge management initiative is to make knowledge "an integral part of the way in which we do business" so that the organization can gain a sustainable competitive advantage and be well positioned to do business in today's dynamic knowledge economy (Alavi & Leidner, 2001; Davenport & Grover, 2001). This is achieved by building knowledge management processes into proposals for new business as well as into existing delivery process (Davenport & Prusak, 1998). Incorporating all the components identified in Figure 1 is necessary but not sufficient to realize the full benefits of an organization's knowledge management initiative.

To any organization, the tangible benefits of considering implementation of knowledge management lie in the synergy derived from all knowledge management initiatives working together. The ensuing suite of services, coupled with the appropriate use of key tools, techniques, strategies, and processes, facilitates and focuses the activity of practice groups, cross-functional teams, and the individual knowledge worker (Hammond, 2001). Uncoordinated and disparate initiatives, while well meaning and individually successful, typically result in sub-optimization (Wenger, 1998). It is therefore necessary to emphasize a trivial but vital point: knowledge management is only truly effective when a firm-wide knowledge management process is robust and well organized; it should become a natural part of an enhanced business model, and blend readily into the institutional culture as depicted in Figure 1. Once such a state is attained, knowledge management can be perceived as an integral element of revenue generation and cost/efficiency management (Probst, Raub, & Romhardt, 2000).

The preceding considerations make it evident that it is critical for an organization to implement initiatives that leverage all knowledge management elements. The ensuing set of integrated tools (standard knowledge management practices, appropriate strategies, and relevant processes) constitutes a uniquely configured instrument that can be successfully employed in specific situations, as well as in the routine activities of work groups, cross-functional/cross-disciplinary teams, or individuals. It is important to remember that each unique configuration does not happen in vacuum but draws from the organization-wide infrastructure of people, processes, technologies, and content. The resulting "configuration management" approach (Davenport & Prusak, 1998) to deploying knowledge capital will permit all involved participants to take maximum advantage of the firm's investment in knowledge management, and also to contribute to its further development and to enhance its flexibility.

The following list of steps identifies the essential factors that facilitate successful development and subsequent implementation of the "configuration management" approach (Davenport & Prusak, 1998; Probst et al., 2000; Mahe & Rieu, 1998):

Step 1: Setting of Clear Objectives

In order to keep the objectives clear and simple; primary focus should be placed on supporting the firm's major business functions. Typical areas that should be considered at this step include:

1. Better and faster development of products, services, or solutions.
2. Rapid and efficient assembly and deployment of cross-functional teams.
3. Greater team productivity and efficiency as well as reduced costs by maximizing the knowledge capital available within and outside the firm.
4. Rapid assimilation of new team members.
5. Proliferation of the firm's knowledge capital and best practices to all knowledge workers.
6. Focus on making knowledge and content sharing "an integral part of the way in which we do business.

To achieve these objectives, there are several potential pitfalls that need to be identified and carefully scrutinized when deploying any firm-wide knowledge management initiative (Probst et al., 2000).

Step 2: Identification of Key Issues, Barriers, and Risks

In order to successfully deploy new and existing knowledge management initiatives into a configurable suite of knowledge management tools, the key issues, barriers, and risks must be recognized, understood, and addressed. It is useful to categorize these under the sub-components of the firm-wide architecture: people, processes, technologies, and content categories (Becerra-Fernandez & Sabherwal, 2001; Duffy, 2000, 2001; Martensen & Dahlgaard, 1999; Parent, Gallupe, Salisbury, & Handelman, 2000). Success requires coordination of these components within the firm's business model of acquiring, maintaining, and delivering products, services, or solutions.

1. People:
    *   **Sponsorship:** The progressive investment in organization-wide knowledge management solutions must have the active support of the company leaders. Likewise, the internal knowledge management team must understand the expectations the leaders have for knowledge management and its impact on the business model.

- **Perceived value from executives:** Lack of perceived value by executives can be a major barrier to success. Therefore, it is important for the senior management to understand not only the issues inherent to selling and delivering projects, but also the necessary integrated knowledge management solutions that address those issues. Creation of such understanding requires, in turn, that the internal knowledge management team is thoroughly familiar with and can easily communicate how the specific knowledge management initiative will in fact enable the achievement of tangible benefits.

- **Performance and rewards system:** The performance and rewards system for employees must be consistent with the firm's goals in sharing and leveraging its knowledge capital. This includes incentives, feedback, and training. Further, employees must not only know how knowledge management activities are related to their daily work activities, but also how such activities will enhance the outcomes of these daily activities.

- **Technical ability of employees:** Employees in general do not have the same level of technological sophistication as those who identify, build, and deploy such technologies. Therefore, the firm's internal knowledge management and IT professionals must see knowledge management and initiatives through the eyes of employee-users in order to configure and deploy solutions that make sense to the user. Once again, appropriate training (as discussed earlier in Section 3) should be implemented so that employees gain the skills needed to maximize the capabilities afforded to them by the technologies they have at their disposal.

- **Disincentives that work against incentives:** Resistance is expected when implementing a culture change that asks people to perform new tasks as part of their daily activity. Many knowledge management initiatives fail when implementers, typically unintentionally, introduce actions and policies that directly undermine incentives for change. For example, creating incentive systems for people to submit content into firm repositories can be wasted when simultaneous policies are put in place that refuse the very same submissions or add quality-enhancement steps that, through their complexity and redundancy, frustrate the target audience causing quality decline instead of the intended improvement.

- **Capabilities of knowledge management professionals:** Any major knowledge management initiative requires the staff of knowledge management professionals to either have an in-depth understanding of a key knowledge management component, or have an in-depth understanding of how those components can be configured to enhance the productivity of a variety of cross-functional teams.

2.   Processes:

- **Knowledge management and the firm's business model:** The knowledge management process must be designed within the firm's business model as depicted in Figure 1. This in turn will result in knowledge management solutions that are created contextually and thus, accepted by the user community.

- **The need to share within and outside the team:** Each cross-functional team should be able to share content within its own team as well as with others in the firm. This process must be made as seamless as possible to the user and utilize standard processes and technologies.

- **Packaging and deployment of knowledge management services and tools:** New and existing knowledge management initiatives have their individual value. However, the value is significantly enhanced when such initiatives also combine the enabling qualities of appropriate services and tools. For example, the drive to enhance automatization of a manufacturing process is a commendable initiative that may, potentially, reduce manufacturing costs. However, without incorporation of suitable technical support, relevant and tested computer software, process diagnostic tools, training, etc., the initiative will be bordering on expensive futility. Further, new and existing knowledge management tools, techniques, strategies, and processes need to be deployed to users in a contextual setting in order to optimize their implementation.

- **Quality standards:** While it is important to maintain quality standards, transforming the culture is of equal importance. Quite frequently this is also the most challenging obstacle to overcome. Therefore, creating a culture and environment that promote sharing and accept contributions of all content but have transparent filters for quality is necessary. It is important that the quest for quality however, does not dilute enthusiasm for sharing.

- **Confidentiality:** When open sharing is promoted, issues of confidentiality and its maintenance or relaxation demand to be addressed thoroughly. Policies and procedures that protect confidentiality are important features to any knowledge management initiative and process, and must be understood by all participants within the knowledge management process.

3.   Technologies:

- **User-friendly vs. complex technology:** The average employee-user has little patience with complexity in technology. Users prefer technologies that are fully transparent and simply help them to get their work done · faster and more efficiently. The unnecessary feature complexities offered by many technologies are wasted and often provide barriers to the users. Therefore, technology selection as well as changes and upgrades must be done with a strong understanding of user needs and their willingness to adapt to specific technologies.

- **Technology standards:** There are many competing technologies within the firm, where groups or individuals have purchased their own technical solution and therefore isolate themselves from the rest of the firm. This is common and generally is a direct result of ignorance of technologies available within the organization, ignoring the existing technology infrastructure and trying to leverage from it, and an opinion that "our needs are unique." This situation generally makes knowledge sharing more difficult and results in "silos" of various competing standards. Thus, it is imperative to have clearly articulated standards in place.

- **Depth and breadth of technical solutions:** It is also important to consider the depth and breadth of the technologies in which the firm invests. Individual technical solutions, by themselves, may seem like good investments. However, "technology overload" can occur when too much is acquired too fast. Additional technology features will always be available to append or replace the current status. Care must be taken to deploy only what is needed, and understand how this fits with the currently deployed suite of technologies as well as their future upgrades.

4. Content:

- **General and specific content:** Each cross-functional team or individual has needs for very specific knowledge capital as well as for general searching for new knowledge. It is important that users have the ability to easily find the required specific content as well as to perform more general searches without sifting through overwhelming amounts of irrelevant facts. The issue of balancing between general and specific searches must be as transparent as possible to the user. Hence, content must be stored in general and specific repositories.

- **Internal vs. external content:** Teams have a need for a mixture of content from internal as well external sources as well as secondary vs. primary ones. Since each team may deal with vastly dissimilar issues and circumstances, the sources available through the firm must be able to handle this breadth and depth. Internal repositories must be easily searchable and quickly take users to the useful content. Likewise, external sources must be readily available and searchable.

- **Repositories and taxonomies:** To assure optimal content searching, the repository structure and their imbedded taxonomies must be rooted within the firm's business model and project methods. The model must also consider the matrix of industry; service line, and technical areas encountered most frequently. Consequently, knowledge codification must be an important step in coordinating the volume, standards, and taxonomies of internal repositories.

- **Research and analysis:** Competent business research and analysis services are an important feature of a robust knowledge management process. Such services must cover not only the navigation within the knowledge management system but also how the application of key business intelligence and analytic tools can be utilized to provide value-added knowledge management services.

Step 3: Knowledge Management Processes to Support the Firm's Business Model

The building and subsequent deployment of a robust and useful knowledge management initiative demands the we use the organizational business model as the cornerstone, particularly those aspects of the model that relate to obtaining and delivering new products, services or solutions. Thus, it is essential that emphasis is placed on knowledge management processes that support the delivery of the firm's stated objectives within the realm of its business model. The relevant considerations must include issues related to new business acquisition, project set-up, and solution delivery to clients (Moore, 2000; Roberts, 2002; Silver, 2000; Spiegler, 2003; Srikantaiah, 2000; Stratigos, 2001; Swan Scarbrough, & Preston, 1999; Thorne & Smith, 2000; Wickramasinghe, 2003).

Implications for Knowledge-Based Enterprises

For knowledge-based enterprises, KM must not be considered a destination, rather a never-ending journey. The environment is dynamic and continuously changing, and organizations operating in this environment are going concerns, which must relentlessly evolve and adapt if they are to survive and thrive. The conceptualization of KM as a destination signifies a finite end. For an organization, this translates into the ceasing of operations or at least the ceasing of operating optimally and maximizing its knowledge assets. The need to view KM as an on going initiative is best illustrated by Boyd's OODA loop. Though the specific issue may changeover time, the principles of observation, orientation, decision and action must always be carried out effectively and efficiently if successful outcomes are to ensue. Furthermore, it is precisely because the environment is dynamic and complex that continuous calibration and re-evaluation is essential so that at all times the knowledge-based enterprise is best positioned to operate optimally and leverage its KM tools, techniques, and strategies.

Chapter Summary

Knowledge is a complex construct. Moreover, a solid theoretical understanding of KM while necessary is not sufficient for organizational success or the achievement of sustained competitive advantage. Consequently, in this chapter we have tired to emphasize that not only is management of knowledge becomes a complex task but requires numerous considerations to be made contemporaneously if success is to ensue.

Managing knowledge complexity requires the adoption of a multifaceted approach. In today's business world, it is imperative for organizations to be prepared for operations within a knowledge-based economy. To be "knowledge-prepared," it is necessary for organizations to develop a robust organizational knowledge management model. Such a model emphasizes a top down approach that combines the dynamics of the external environment with the organization's goals and business strategy necessary for the development of a sound knowledge management strategy. Then, in order to realize this strategy, the organization must focus on the four key steps of knowledge management. Central to the effective implementation of these steps is the need for a socio-technical perspective, the consideration of people, processes, and technologies. Finally, the four major steps of knowledge management can only be truly efficient if they are supported by the organization's knowledge infrastructure and architecture. For this to happen, these four key steps must be designed to leverage off the primary sub-components of the organization's infrastructure; namely, the business infrastructure, the technology infrastructure, and the organizational infrastructure.

Achieving this first step of "knowledge-preparedness" is a necessary but not sufficient condition for a successful knowledge management initiative. The second, and arguably more challenging stage, is becoming knowledge-ready. Readiness and the importance of being ready are best illustrated by examining warfare where disregard of pertinent information and thus the absence of pertinent (germane) knowledge have led to major military disasters. In contrast, preparedness coupled with readiness—the instantaneous ability to respond to a suddenly arising major crisis—consistently has lead to a desirable successful outcome.

The key question for organizations then becomes how to ensure a state of readiness once the organization is knowledge-prepared. Training, in particular simulation-based training provides the most suitable solution. From a knowledge management perspective, the key benefit of training is its facilitation of the acquisition and refinement of necessary tacit knowledge. Simulation-based training serves to build this stock of tacit knowledge in a most efficient fashion, since it puts the trainees through real world scenarios demanding real-time responses. The realism of simulation is currently the best tool to develop and refine key operational skills.

Two essential skills for knowledge workers operating in the fast changing world of knowledge-based economy are critical thinking and rapid decision-making, particularly in stressful, rapidly unpredictable evolving situations. Development of these skills is greatly assisted by the implementation of Boyd's OODA loop. The OODA loop cycles through four critical and interrelated stages: observation, orientation, decision, and then action. These cycles occur both in time and space. Observation and orientation stages of the loop are the critical aspects at which the plurality of implicit and explicit inputs determines the sequential decision and action stages. The deceptively simple loop represents the complexity of interactions and interrelationships involved in critical thinking and decision-making processes, and provides the basis for the subsequent implementation of appropriate action. It also provides predictive information on how the implemented action together with other, external, and new inputs, may affect the environment, and hence, the next revolution of the loop. Importantly, all actions within the loop are simultaneous—action does not interrupt observation nor decision does relieve from the need to orient. It is thus imperative that, in order to pursue a "winning strategy" one must act "within" the OODA loop followed by the opposition (hence the colloquial term "to be within the loop!") Speed of loop revolution is not necessarily the only factor. Other elements, such as more effective and comprehensive analysis of inputs, rapid rejection of irrelevant data, experience-based compression of response times, etc., may be of equally critical value in gaining advantage.

Combing the tools of simulation with Boyd's OODA loop creates a complementary tool set that facilitates training of knowledge workers. Practical implementation of such tools enhances the ability to perceive inter-domain relationships (sometimes referred to as double loop learning in learning organizations), a skill necessary to create new, germane knowledge that is, in turn, essential to solve key business problems of the future. Boyd's concept of destruction and creation is fundamental to the development of a generalist—the knowledge worker of the future, whose main attribute is the facility of inter- and intra-domain operations that will be required in order to solve increasingly more complex problems of the modern world.

In order to manage knowledge complexity successfully, and in addition to being knowledge prepared and ready, an organization must also be sure to address a number of key success factors:

- **People:** Requires executive sponsorship as well as the structuring of appropriate reward and consistent systems.
- **Process:** Knowledge should be shared across teams when necessary but confidentiality should be maintained where necessary.
- **Technologies:** Systems need to be user friendly and provide both breadth and depth of functionality.
- **Content:** Both general and specific knowledge content must be maintained.

It is imperative that consistency between these components are both developed and maintained so that they support and facilitate each other and in turn enable the success of the knowledge management initiative. As can be seen, the prescription for managing knowledge complexity is indeed multifaceted and detailed; however if such prescriptions are not adhered to, it is virtually certain the knowledge management initiative will fail and the consequences to the organization may be detrimental at best and catastrophic at worst.

References

Alavi, M. (1997). *KPMG Peat Marwick U.S.: One giant brain.* Harvard Business School, Case Study 9-397-1010.

Alavi, M., & Leidner, D. (2001). Review: Knowledge management and knowledge management systems: Conceptual foundations and research issues. *MIS Quarterly, 25*(1), 107-136.

Alexander, B. (2002). *How great generals win.* New York: W.W. Norton & Co.

Barnett, T. P. M. (2004). *The Pentagon's new map.* New York: G.P. Putnam's Sons.

Barber, N. (2003). *Sinister twilight: The fall of Singapore.* London: Cassell & Co.

Becerra-Fernandez, I., & Sabherwal, R. (2001). Organizational knowledge management: A contingency perspective. *Journal of Management Information Systems, 18*(1), 23-55.

Bloom, H. (2002). *Genius.* New York: Warner Books.

Boyd, J. R. (1976). Destruction and creation. In R. Coran (Ed.), *Boyd.* New York: Little, Brown & Co.

Boyd, J. R. (1987). In "Patterns of Conflict", unpublished briefing by Col. J. R. Boyd, USAF. See also "Essence of Winning and Losing" at http://www.d-n-i.net

Brandon-hall.com Staff. (2002). *E-learning simulations: Tools and services for creating software, business, and technical skills simulations.* Brandon-hall. com, Sunnyvale, CA. E-book retrieved from http://www.brandon-hall.com/ simulations.html

Chard, M. (1997). Knowledge management at Ernst and Young. Stanford University Graduate School of Business, Case Study M-291.

Conway's History of the Ship: The Shipping Revolution – The Modern Merchant Ship. (A. Couper, Consulting Editor). (1992). London: Conway Maritime Press, Conway Books, Ltd.

Davenport, T., & Grover, V. (2001). Knowledge management. *Journal of Management Information Systems, 18*(1), 3-4.

Davenport, T., & Prusak, L. (1998). *Working knowledge.* Cambridge: Harvard Business School Press.

d'Epiro, P., & Desmond Pinkovish, M. (2001). *Sprezzatura: 50 ways Italian genius shaped the world.* New York: Anchor Books/Random House.

Duffy, J. (2000). The KM technology infrastructure. *Information Management Journal, 34*(2), 62-66.

Duffy, J. (2001). The tools and technologies needed for knowledge management. *Information Management Journal, 35*(1), 64-67.

Hammond, C. (2001). The intelligent enterprise. *InfoWorld, 23*(6), 45-46.

Keil, M. (1988). Du Pont's artificial intelligence implementing strategy. Harvard Business School, Case Study 9-189-036.

Lary J. M., Pletcher, T., & von Lubitz, D. K. J. E. (2002). Developing mass medical readiness: A model for simulation-based, distributed training of geographically dispersed EMS and prehospital personnel. *Proceedings, SSGRR Conference on Internet, Business, Science, Education, and Medicine,* L'Aquila (Italy). http://www.ssgrr.it/en/ssgrr2003s/panel.htm

Mahe, S., & Rieu, C. (1998, October 29-30). A pull approach to knowledge management. *Proceedings of the 2nd International Conference on Practical Aspects of Knowledge Management,* Basel, Switzerland.

Martensen, A., & Dahlgaard, J. J. (1999). Integrating business excellence and innovation management: Developing vision, blueprint, and strategy for innovation in creative and learning organizations. *Total Quality Management, 10*(4/5), 627-635.

Moore, K. (2000). The e-volving organization. *Ivey Business Journal, 65*(2), 25-28.

Murray C. (2003). *Human accomplishment: The pursuit of excellence in the arts and sciences, 800 B.C. to 1950.* New York: Harper Collins.

Parent, M., Gallupe, R., Salisbury, W., & Handelman, J. (2000). Knowledge creation in focus groups: Can group technology help? *Information & Management, 38*, 47-58.

Probst, G., Raub, S., & Romhardt, K. (2000). *Managing knowledge: Building blocks for success*. Chichester, UK: John Wiley & Sons.

Richards, C. (2004). *Certain to win: The strategy of John Boyd, applied to business*. Philadelphia: Xlibris Co.

Roberts, J. (2000). From know-how to show-how? Questioning the role of information and communication technologies in knowledge transfer. *Technology Analysis & Strategic Management, 12*(4), 429-443.

Rouse, W. B., & Boff, K. R. (2005). *Organizational simulation*. New York: Wiley & Sons.

Silver, C. A. (2000). Where technology and knowledge meet. *The Journal of Business Strategy, 21*(6), 28-33.

Spiegler, I. (2003). Technology and knowledge: Bridging a "generating" gap. *Information and Management, 40*, 533-539.

Srikantaiah, T. K. (2000). Knowledge management for information professional. Information Today, Inc.: ASIS Monograph Series.

Stiglitz, J. E. (2003). *The roaring nineties: A new history of the world's most prosperous decade*. New York: W.W. Norton & Co.

Stratigos, A. (2001). Knowledge management meets future information users. *Knowledge Management Online, 25*(1), 65-67.

Strategy Dynamics. (2004). *People Express 2000*. Retrieved from http://www.strategydynamics.com/products/peopleexpress2000.htm

Swan, J., Scarbrough, H., & Preston, J. (1999). Knowledge management: The next fad to forget people? *Proceedings of the 7th European Conference in Information Systems*.

Thorne, K., & Smith, M. (2000). Competitive advantage in world class organizations. *Management Accounting, 78*(3), 22-26.

von Clausewitz, C. (1994). *On war*. New York: A. Knopf/Random House.

von Lubitz, D. K. J. E., Carrasco, B., Levine, H., & Richir, S. (2004). Medical readiness in the context of operations other than war: Development of First Responder readiness using OODA-loop thinking and advanced distributed simulation technology. *Proceedings of the International EMISPHER 2004 Conference*. Euro-Mediterranean Virtual Hospital, Istanbul, Turkey. Retrieved from http://www.d-n i.net/fcs/pdf/von_lubitz_1rp_ooda.pdf

Wenger, E. (1998). *Communities of practice*. Cambridge: Cambridge University Press.

Wickramasinghe, N. (2003). Do we practise what we preach: Are knowledge management systems in practice truly reflective of knowledge management systems in theory? *Business Process Management Journal, 9*(3), 295-316.

Yardley, R., Thie, H., Schank, J. F., Galegher, J., & Ripose, J. L. (2003). *Use of simulation for training in the U.S. Navy Surface Force*. Rand Corp. Retrieved from http://www.rand.org/publications/MR/MR1770/

Chapter IX

Learning Organizations

Introduction

The nations that will lead the world into the next century will be those that can shift from being industrial economies based upon the production of manufactured goods to those that possess the capacity to produce and utilize knowledge successfully (Porter, 1990). The focus of the economy of nations has shifted first to information-intensive industries such as financial services and logistics, and now toward innovation-driven industries, such as computer software and biotechnology, where competitive advantage lies primarily in the fostering and developing of unique ideas and maximizing the potential of the human resources of organizations. This represents a move from the era of standardization to customization, and the new organizational form found most helpful has been the network organization, which can respond rapidly to demands for new products and services. The new organizational form will rely on clusters of self-organizing components collaboratively investing the organization's know-how in product and service innovations for markets, which they have helped to create and develop. Such organizations can best be described as cellular, suggesting a living, adaptive organization, able to respond rapidly to new demands (Bukowitz & Williams, 1997; Nonaka, 1991).

In such a dynamic environment, the concept of a learning organization, one that continues to change and adapt to the demands of its environment, is critical if the organization is to survive and thrive (Popper & Lipshitz, 2000). Hence, greater attention needs to be given by organizations towards building learning organizations. Learning is connected with a company's ability to adapt to a rapidly changing environment. Essential to learning is the gaining of germane knowledge and the increasing of the existing extant knowledge base (Ellerman, 1999; Ellinger, Watkins, & Bostrom, 1999; Wickramasinghe & Schaffer, 2005). Through learning, organizations are better equipped to react faster and to fully exploit opportunities thereby placing themselves in a position of competitive superiority. Thus, no discussion of knowledge management is complete without reference to the important and allied areas of organizational learning, learning organizations and organizational memory. This chapter then is presented for completeness but does not in any way attempt to cover the breadth and depth of organizational learning. Rather, it is an attempt to show how strongly linked the area is to KM and that no KM initiative should proceed without some consideration of the implications of organizational learning and organizational memory (Sugarman, 1997).

Learning Organizations: Definitions

Learning is defined as acquiring new knowledge and enhancing existing knowledge (Huber, 1991). A learning organization is an organization that has an enhanced capacity to learn, adapt, and change (Levine, 2001). Learning takes place at two levels—individual and organizational. Learning within organizations, as with individuals, is evidenced through the change or growth of the extant knowledge base (Wickramasinghe & Schaffer, 2005). While organizations do not have brains per se, they have cognitive systems and memories that play a key role in organizational learning activities (Popper & Lipshitz, 2000). As individuals develop their personalities, personal habits, and beliefs over time, organizations develop their views and ideologies. Learning at both individual and organizational levels involves the transformation of data (un-interpreted information) into knowledge (interpreted, contextualized information). Individual learning and organizational learning share several similarities however organizational learning involves an additional phase, dissemination (i.e., the transmission of information and knowledge among different persons and organizational units) (Popper & Lipshitz, 2000). Without such a transmission, the benefits of organizational learning cannot be distinguished from individual learning and essentially the only learning that takes place is individual (Huber, 1991; Popper & Lipshitz, 2000).

A learning organization consists of employees who are continuously enhancing their capacity to learn in the corporate culture (Huber, 1991; Levitt & March, 1988). It is here that learning processes are analyzed, monitored, developed, and aligned with the organization's goals (Kapp, 1999). Most companies underestimate the importance of intangible assets such as knowledge, creativity, ideas, and relationships;

yet all these account for more value in a knowledge economy than the more easily measured and highly prized tangible assets (Probst, Raub, & Romhardt, 2000).

As we progress through the 21st century, the need for rapid access to relevant knowledge has never been greater. The business world is becoming increasingly competitive, and the demand for innovative products and services is continually increasing. Organizations are growing more knowledge-intensive in order to learn from past experiences and from competitors to reshape themselves and to change in order to survive and prosper. Organizations need to utilize knowledge across processes and functions, to become knowledge-driven organizations or learning organizations (Nevis, DiBella, & Gould, 1997). Hence, the organization that becomes a learning organization will have a significant advantage over its competitors because of its ability to learn faster and thereby adapt faster and more successfully to its environment. Learning organizations are generally described as those that continuously acquire, process, and disseminate knowledge concerning markets, products, technologies, and business processes (Roberts, 2000). This knowledge is often based on experience, experimentation, and information provided by customers, suppliers, competitors, and other sources (Ellinger et al., 1999; Senge, 1990, 1994).

In 1990, Peter M. Senge introduced the concept of the "learning organization" to the business world in his landmark book *The Fifth Discipline: The Art and Practice of the Learning Organization*. Such a learning organization represents a complex interrelationship of systems composed of people, technology, practices, and tools designed so that new information is embraced (Simon, 1999). Learning organizations are organizations that have embed institutionalized learning mechanisms into a learning culture (Popper & Lipshitz, 2000). Every organization has the potential to become a learning organization; some organizations learn explicitly, others implicitly. However, most organizations currently do not explicitly address both the learning and unlearning that is needed for keeping abreast with the changing dynamic reality of the business environment (Senge, 1990, 1994).

Learning organizations have to continually expand their capacity to be creative and innovative. The only way to sustain competitive advantage is to ensure that your organization is learning faster and more effectively than the competitor is. Organizations are realizing that their human capital (people power) and structural capital (databases, patents, intellectual property, and related items) are the distinguishing elements of their organizations.

Ultimately, despite all the advances in technology, it is the people within the organization that make the real difference. If an organization wishes to be successful, it must harness its workforce to use the tools and technologies as well as their own skills (Kapp, 1999; Srikantaiah, 2000).

Many significant benefits can be gained for an organization by shifting to a learning organization. Learning is the key competency required by any organization that wants to survive and thrive in the new knowledge economy. Learning provides the catalyst and the intellectual resource to create a sustainable competitive advantage (Cowan, 1995) and enables an organization to maximize the benefits of its KM initiative (Probst et al., 2000). A well-trained workforce will improve performance throughout the organization, which will then lead to an improvement in the competitive position of the industry in which it resides. Furthermore, training helps to support morale within the organization. All of these factors create a positive atmosphere that is present throughout the organization, both internally and externally making the organization attractive to unique and desirable prospective employees (Kapp, 1999; Srikantaiah, 2000).

Types of Learning

As with knowledge, organizational learning is not a homogenous construct. At its very simplest, there exist two types of learning (Argyris, 1977; Argyris & Schon, 1978, 1996; Huber, 1990):

1. **Incremental:** Learning that is characterized by simple, routine problem solving and that requires no fundamental change to your thinking or system.
2. **Radical:** Breakthrough learning that directly challenges the prevailing mental model on which the system is built.

Learning can be further classified as adaptive and generative learning (Argyris, 1977; Argyris & Schon, 1978, 1996).

Adaptive Learning and Generative Learning

The current view of organizations is dominated by the perspective of adaptive learning, which has its roots in biological sciences where organizations learn and adapt to survive in their environment (Huber, 1990; Senge, 1990). However, Senge (1990) notes that increasing adaptiveness is only the first stage; companies need to focus on generative learning or "double-loop learning" (Argyris, 1977). Generative learning emphasizes continuous experimentation and feedback in an ongoing examination of the very manner in which organizations set about defining and solving problems. In Senge's (1990) view, generative learning is about creating—it requires "systemic thinking," "shared vision," "personal mastery," "team learning," and "creative tension."

Generative learning, unlike adaptive learning, requires new ways of looking at the world.

In contrast, Adaptive Learning or single-loop learning focuses on solving problems in the present as they arise without examining the appropriateness of current learning behaviors. Adaptive organizations focus on incremental improvements, often based upon a past track record of success. Essentially, they do not question the fundamental assumptions underlying the existing ways of doing work nor do they look or think "outside the box."

A learning organization distinguishes itself, in particular, by a culture that encourages generative or double-loop (Argyris, 1977) learning in addition to possessing receptivity to adaptive or incremental improvement. Generative, or double loop learning, is thinking which challenges the dominant logic or assumptions that guide decision-making within an organization from the lowest level of operation to the CEO's office. It is, therefore incremental and transformational. Generative learning contrasts with adaptive learning; adaptive learning seeks improvements within the mental constraints of the prevailing assumptions of how an organization currently does or should conduct business (Morecroft & Sterman, 1994).

Generative learning, unlike adaptive learning, requires new ways of looking at the world. Generative learning requires seeing the systems that control events. When we fail to grasp the systemic source of problems, we are left to "push on" symptoms rather than eliminate underlying causes. The secret of the learning organization is to find the leadership, institutional arrangements, and cultural elements that result in generative learning as a continuous process. Table 1 provides the 10 steps of systems thinking that have been designed to support generative learning (Senge, 1990).

Table 1. Ten steps of systems thinking (Senge, 1990)

STEP	DESCRIPTION
1	How is the system defined?
2	What business or businesses is the corporation in?
3	How is the corporation organized?
4	How does the corporation actually operate?
5	What are the policies, practices, strategies and tactics currently in place?
6	What is the management style?
7	How has the corporation performed in the past and how is it performing now?
8	What/who are the corporations stakeholders
9	Who are the competitors
10	What are the laws and governmental regulations and how do these affect the corporation

One of the characteristics of a learning organization is that it moves beyond simple employee training to more of an environment that stresses problem solving, innovation, and learning. Organizations that embody the traits of such an environment consist of five areas, or disciplines, that make a learning organization what it is. These five disciplines, outlined in the book *The Fifth Discipline: The Art and Practice of the Learning Organization* by Peter Senge (1990), consist of personal mastery, mental models, shared vision, team learning, and systems thinking. These disciplines have already been described in Chapter IV but we summarize them here for completeness and also to underscore the fundamental connection between KM, organizational learning, learning organizations, and organizational memory.

- **Personal mastery:** This discipline allows people to clarify and focus their personal visions, focus energy, develop patience and see the world as it really is. Employees who possess a high level of personal mastery can consistently generate results, which are important to them through their commitment to lifelong learning.

- **Mental models:** These are internalized frameworks, which support our views of the world, beliefs in why and how events happen, and our understanding of how things, people, and events are related.

- **Building shared vision:** Developing "shared pictures of the future" together so that people are genuinely committed and engaged rather than compliant.

- **Team learning:** Teams as a vital element of a learning organization. Hence there is great significance in the ability of teams to learn (Price, 2000)

- **Systems thinking:** People in an organization are part of a system. Systems thinking is a discipline which integrates the other disciplines in a business. It allows the "whole" (organization) to be greater than the parts (people, departments, teams, equipment, and so on).

The five disciplines are connected to one another. By themselves, they do not provide guidance on how to build a learning organization. In order to transform an organization from a goods and services producer, for example, to one with a focus on integrating learning in their business practices of producing goods and services, a commitment must be made to establish a learning infrastructure. Learning must be institutionalized (Buhler, 1999; Dodge, 1991).

Boyd and Organizational Learning

From the perspective of Boyd, it is possible to conceptualize learning viewed as the creation of germane knowledge. According to Boyd, there are two main ways to approach creating concepts: (1) deduction and analysis—moving from general to specific or (2) induction and synthesis—moving from specific to general (Boyd, 1976, 1987). As time is traversed, be it at an individual level, organizational level or societal level, domains of knowledge are formed to represent observed reality. Destructive deduction is achieved by removing domain boundaries and the disassociation of the previously ordered domain constituents, thereby resulting in a state of chaos. Faced with such disorder the natural propensity is to regain the state of equilibrium and reconstruct order and meaning. The process of reconstituting such order requires induction, synthesis, and integration and ends in the construction of a new domain where new commonalities and orderly interrelationships govern the existence of previously disparate parts. The process reflects the fundamental essence of knowledge creation, and the forming of these commonalities and creation of a new domain constitute the principal force that drives increases in the extant knowledge base. However, since the original goal was to re-establish equilibrium, the new domain, and the new state of order that it both imposes and represents through the re-establishment of the state of equilibrium of all subcomponents also represents germane knowledge.

While the connecting threads that produce meanings are created by a mixture of the knowledge frameworks discussed earlier, they are insufficient to ensure the creation of germane knowledge. For this, creation of a new domain that re-establishes equilibrium is necessary. What is important to note here is that without the unstructuring of the existing domains, the creation of the new one (-s) cannot take place, and that the catalyst for the unstructuring is the change in the external environment. It is, however, the propensity to regain equilibrium that serves as the drive to create the new knowledge domain.

Boyd's approach to creation is rooted in mathematics and physics, a novel approach that may, ultimately, provide quantitative foundations for the learning process. Using Gödel's Theorem (Boyd, 1976) describing incompleteness and inconsistency of ordered systems Boyd demonstrates that "in order to determine the consistency of any new system we must construct or uncover another system beyond it" (von Lubitz et al., 2004). Like the Möbius strip, the process is continuous. However, the degree of intrusion into the system necessary for the construction of a new one is governed by Heisenberg's uncertainty principle. Hence, the uncertainty values not only represent the degree of intrusion by the observer upon the observed but also the degree of confusion and disorder perceived by that observer.

The entropy level of a system defines the system's capacity for doing work: high entropy implies a low potential while low entropy implies the reverse. Since potential for doing work can be equated with the potential for taking action, high entropy is associated with low capacity for taking action in the presence of a high degree of confusion and disorder, while low entropy is a state allowing the execution of order-imposing activities.

All natural processes generate entropy, and any closed system is characterized by a progressive increase of its entropy (i.e., chaos and disorder). Combining Gödel's theorem, Heisenberg's uncertainty principle, and the third law of thermodynamics, Boyd argues that any inward-oriented and continued effort to improve the match-up of concept with observed reality will only increase the degree of mismatch. Hence, we can expect unexplained and disturbing ambiguities, uncertainties, anomalies, or apparent inconsistencies to emerge with the frequency that is proportionate to our efforts to re-establish the order within the system. As a result, rather than reverting to the stability of equilibrium, we will impose an ever-increasing degree of confusion and chaos. Seen from a practical perspective of an organization wishing to survive and thrive in the dynamically changing environment of modern business, any attempt at introspective analysis of its operation that is limited to historical knowledge is doomed to failure and may be the main contributor to the doom of the organization itself. One solution available, and the solution that assures continuous progress is then that proposed by Boyd: a contiguous destruction of old domains, extraction of pertinent subcomponents, and recombination into new domains (Boyd, 1976). The solution also defines the role of the constructor—the more direct involvement in the destruction/creation process, the greater potential for inducing chaos. The creator needs to assume a superior position of providing overall guidance rather than participate in the details of the execution. Inadvertently, we have then arrived at the confirmation of one of the essential rules of operational conduct: micromanagement by superior entities of the organization is one of the most harmful forms of interaction that, rather than inducing order, produce chaos and loss of working potential. Consequently, the level and adequacy of the organization's germane knowledge will suffer and its decline will lead the organization to the rapidly steepening path of self-destruction.

Probably the best example of practical applications of Boyd's approach is the development of network-centric and joint force doctrine of warfare that transformed previously ponderous and top heavy command and control structure of the military into an organization capable of almost instantaneous response to new, emerging threats. Defining the mission, modern commanders break the domains of individual services and combine them into new, composite entities whose capabilities are suited to the individual tasks. At the same time, by leaving the details of mission execution to the initiative of the "on the spot" commanders, the superior levels of the chain of command reduce their chaos-inducing interference, and concentrate instead on the continuous evaluation and assessment of mission progress. The new approach provides greatly enhanced flexibility of action while, at the same time, greatly reducing the transparence of one's own responses to the enemy pressures—the necessary elements of the competitive advantage and the ability to survive on the modern, widely dispersed and continuously changing battlefield.

However, we note that double loop learning as defined by Argyris (1977; Argyris & Schon, 1978, 1996) is quite distinct from Boyd's OODA loop with respect to how the two models focus on the connection between knowledge and learning. The former is inextricably connected with knowledge transfer while the other focuses on a continuously evolving learning (observation stage)/knowledge building (orientation phase) process that involves incorporation of inputs from several, often entirely independent sources and may affect independent environments. Thus, while seemingly very similar, the concept of "double loop learning" and "OODA loop" differ significantly although both support Boyd's approach to destruction and creation and both can be viewed as its essential components.

Importance of KM for Learning Organizations

Knowledge management (KM) is inextricably linked with capitalizing on an organizations human skills, expertise, and intellectual assets (Duffy, 2001; Lee, 2000; Thorne & Smith, 2000). Taken together, these intangible assets including human capital (tacit knowledge and competencies), structural capital (intellectual property, methods, and policies), social capital (relationships), and organizational capital (customer relationships and agreements) provide an organization with its key unique strengths (ibid). Building on these unique strengths there are then two levels of organizational learning—the contribution level (where people learn, collaborate and innovate) and the multiplier level (where what comes from the contribution level is passed along to the rest of the organization through processes such as mentoring, networking and inspiring (Brown & Druid, 1991; Clegg, 1999; Davenport & Prusak, 1998).

To remain competitive, organizations must efficiently and effectively create, locate, capture, and share their organization's knowledge and expertise. Hence, the KM infrastructure is also essential to support learning organizations. It is indeed fair to say that a learning organization is one that has embraced a KM initiative and is moving towards becoming a knowledge-based organization. Thus, KM infrastructure (tools and technologies) provides the platform upon which learning can be built. As has already been discussed, the KM infrastructure includes repositories for unstructured data (i.e., document and content management), structured data (i.e., data warehousing, generation, and management), and groupware that supports the collaboration needed for knowledge sharing. It also includes tools like e-mail for other forms of interpersonal communication required for the efficient, time and location-independent exchange of information (Croasdell, 2001; Davenport & Prusak, 1997, 1998; Davenport, Jarvenpaa, & Beers, 1996; Duffy, 2001; Garvin, 1993). From the standpoint of a learning organization, it is the interaction of knowledge workers with the KM infrastructure that ensures that organization learning both single and double loop takes place (Davenport, 2005).

Organizational Memory

A core concept in technological support for knowledge management is the corporate memory. A corporate or organizational memory can be characterized as a comprehensive intelligent database, which captures a company's accumulated know-how and other knowledge assets and makes them available to enhance the efficiency and effectiveness of knowledge-intensive work processes. The successful development of such a system requires a careful analysis of established work practices and available information technology (IT) infrastructure. Organizational memory systems enable organizations to exploit knowledge that resides in the collective memories of their employees and is not found in any of the formal documents produced by the organization (Argyris, 1977; Argyris & Schon, 1978, 1996).

Information technology has enabled organizations to generate and retain vast amounts of information. Regrettably, many organizations are incapable of handling it. They have the information they need, but they do not know they have it. Or, knowing they have it, they can't find it. From the perspective of the organization, one method of managing its intellectual resources is to attempt to augment its organizational memory. Intuitively, we know that an organization of people should retain some knowledge of its past efforts and environmental conditions. If an organization learns, then the result should be available later. The standard connotation of organizational memory is essentially everything that can be captured in a written record, yet this is only one form of organizational memory. Other aspects include: information repositories such as corporate manuals, databases, filing systems, and even anecdotal information. Furthermore, individuals are significant sources for retention of the organization's knowledge. However, organizational memory can be retained in many other places, including organizational culture, processes, and structures (Walsh & Ungson, 1991). Hence, it is important to note that an organization's memory is actually made up of often very disparate components and becomes only truly powerful when all these components are integrated and analyzed using various KM tools and techniques so that learning might result.

Both organizational memory and knowledge management are concepts that dominate much of the recent literature. Furthermore, they have essentially the same main goal of trying to help organizations to cope with the following three changes in the business world: (1) An increasing complexity, dynamics, fragmentation and decentralization of knowledge or knowledge development, (2) An increasing complexity of organizational structures and the permanent need to change these structures, and

(3) An increasing quantity of non-traditional data to be managed (Maier & Lehner, 2000). However, organizational memory and knowledge management differ in that they suggest different methods and strategies to deal with these complexities and changes.

Organizational memory is concerned with the storing and subsequent accessing and replenishing of an organizations "know-how" which is recorded in documents or in its people (Ackerman, 1992; Maier & Lehner, 2000). Organizational memory systems enable the storing of knowledge as well as facilitating access to this knowledge and/or to the people who possess specific knowledge. However, organizational memory systems do not support sense-making knowledge creation activities (Wickramasinghe, 2003).

It is clear that there is an intersection or overlap between organizational memory and knowledge management and thus it is to be expected that organizational memory systems and knowledge management systems should share some similarities. Knowledge management is concerned with the management of the organization's knowledge and focuses on the stages of storing, retrieving, and distributing knowledge. However, a key component of knowledge management not addressed in the construct of organizational memory is the subjective aspect. Thus, knowledge management systems differ from organizational memory systems primarily because they support both the subjective and objective components of the knowledge construct (Wickramasinghe, 2003).

Organizational Learning vs. Learning Organization

Organizational learning and learning organization are terms that permeate much of the business literature and are often used interchangeably. However it is important to note that organizational learning is the ability of an organization to gain insight and understanding from experience through experimentation, observation, analysis, and a willingness to examine both successes and failures (Brown & Duiguid, 1991) and thereby a process. In contrast, a learning organization describes an organization that supports the process of organizational learning, has implemented KM initiatives and is or is transitioning to become a knowledge-based enterprise (Sharma, Wickramasinghe, & Gupta, 2004; Wickramasinghe, 2003). Figure 1 highlights these differences and the connection between KM and both organizational learning and the concept of a learning organization.

Figure 1. The fundamental elements for building a learning organization using knowledge management

Knowledge Management

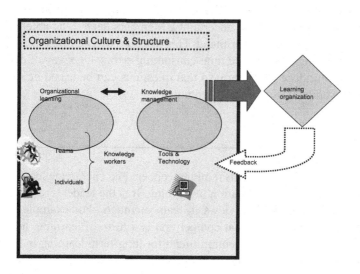

The Building Blocks of Learning Organizations

Before a learning organization can be implemented, a solid foundation must be established by taking into account the following (Kim, 1997; Levine, 2001; Morecroft & Sterman, 1994; Roberts, 2000):

Awareness

Organizations must be aware that learning is necessary before they can develop into a learning organization. Learning must take place at all levels, not just the management level. Once the company has accepted the need for change, it is then responsible for creating the appropriate environment in which the change can occur.

Environment

Centralized, mechanistic structures do not create a good environment. Individuals do not have a comprehensive picture of the whole organization and its goals. This causes political and parochial systems to be set up which stifle the learning process. Therefore a more flexible, organic structure must be formed. By organic, we mean a flatter structure which encourages innovations. The flatter structure also promotes passing of information between workers and so creating a more informed work force.

It is necessary for management to take on a new philosophy, to encourage openness, reflection, and accept error and uncertainty. Members need to be able to question decisions without the fear of reprimand. This questioning can often highlight problems at an early stage and reduce time-consuming errors. One way of overcoming this fear is to introduce anonymity so that questions can be asked or suggestions made but the source is not necessarily known.

Leadership

Leaders should foster the systems thinking concept and encourage learning to help both the individual and organization in learning. It is the leader's responsibility to help restructure the individual views of team members. For example, they need to help the teams understand that competition is a form of learning, not a hostile act. Management must provide commitment for long-term learning in the form of resources. The amount of resources available (money, personnel and time) determines the quantity and quality of learning. This means that the organization must be prepared to support all tenets of systems thinking.

Empowerment

Empowerment becomes significant when the focus of control shifts from managers to workers since workers become responsible for their actions while managers do not lose their involvement. They still need to encourage, enthuse, and coordinate the workers. Equal participation must be allowed at all levels so that members can learn from each other simultaneously. This is unlike traditional learning that involves a top-down structure (classroom-type example) which is time consuming.

Learning

Companies can learn to achieve these aims in learning labs. These are small-scale models of real life settings where management teams learn how to learn together through simulation games. By experiencing failure in a simulated environment or microcosm it is possible both to learn from mistakes and also be protected from the repercussion such costly mistakes might have brought. Furthermore, these lessons can then be applied to real life situations. These managers are then responsible for setting up an open, flexible atmosphere in their organizations to encourage their workers to follow their learning example. Anonymity has already been mentioned and can be achieved through electronic conferencing. This type of conferencing can also encourage different sites to communicate and share knowledge, thus making a company truly a Learning Organization (Richards, 1994).

Implementation Strategies

Any organization that desires to implement a learning organization philosophy requires an overall strategy with clear, well-defined goals. Once these have been established, the tools needed to facilitate the strategy must be identified.

Implications for Knowledge-Based Organizations

At both the individual and organizational levels, for a change in knowledge to occur learning must take place. Given the importance of knowledge assets to the knowledge-based organization, it is imperative that knowledge-based organizations are learning organizations and embrace the techniques of organizational learning. This will enable the knowledge-based enterprise to be confident that it continually builds on its extant knowledge base so that at all times the knowledge that resides within the organization is accurate, relevant, pertinent, and thus useful. It is important to note that the effective use of the knowledge in the knowledge base requires the appropriate application of the various KM tools and techniques discussed throughout this book. Hence, in practice it is not wise to separate organizational learning from knowledge management.

Chapter Summary

The concept of a learning organization that strives continually to develop its people and processes will be an accepted philosophy of all competitive organizations in the future. Within business, learning is a conscious attempt on the part of organizations to improve productivity, effectiveness, and innovativeness in uncertain economic and technological market conditions. The greater the uncertainties the greater the need for learning and hence learning becomes of even greater significance in complex and dynamic environments to enable organizations to develop quicker and more effective responses. In turn, effective learning is associated with increased information sharing, communication, and understanding. It is for these reasons the concept of "learning" is probably more pronounced in business than any other area.

There are essentially two key contributors that can create learning organizations—people and technology. It is the combination of these two factors with new business processes and business models that will underpin success in the next decade. The power of learning from customers, employees, and suppliers will provide considerable advantage to learning organizations and play a vital role in establishing and maintaining a competitive advantage. The importance of learning organizations and the dominant role of such organizations in a knowledge economy is only just being understood. However, what is of most significance is that it is not possible to have a learning organization without incorporating KM, it is not possible to support the process of organizational learning without KM nor is it possible to have a truly successful KM initiative without incorporating the processes of organizational learning or developing a learning organization. Hence, a knowledge-based business is also a learning organization.

References

Ackerman, M. S. (1992). The answer garden substrate: A platform for building organizational memory applications. *Proceedings of the Workshop on Information Technologies & Systems (WITS 92)* (pp. 104-113).

Argyris, C. (1977, September/October). Double loop learning in organizations. *Harvard Business Review*, 55(5), 115-25.

Argyris, C., & Schon, D. A. (1978). *Organizational learning: A theory of action perspective*. Reading, MA: Addison-Wesley.

Argyris, C., & Schon, D. A. (1996). *Organizational learning II: Theory, method, and practice*. Reading, MA: Addison-Wesley.

Boyd, J. R., COL USAF. 1976. "Destruction and Creation." In Coram, R. 2002. Boyd. New York: Little, Brown & Co.

Boyd, JR, 1987, in Patterns of Conflict, unpublished briefing by CO. J.R. Boyd, USAF. See also "Essence of Winning and Losing" at http://www.d-n-i.net

Brown, J. S., & Druid, P. (1991). Organizational learning and communities of practice: Toward a unified view of working, learning, and innovation. *Organizational Science*, 2, 40- 57.

Buhler, P. M. (1999). Managing in the 90's: Training 90's style: An organizational requirement. *Supervision*, 60(10), 14-16.

Bukowitz, W. R., & Williams, R. L. (1997, February-March). New metrics for hidden assets. *Journal of Strategic Performance Measurement*, 1(1), 12-18.

Clegg, S. (1999). Globalizing the intelligent organization: Learning organizations, smart workers, (not so) clever countries, and the sociological imagination. *Management Learning, 30*(3), 259-280.

Cowan, D. A. (1995). Rhythms of learning: Patterns that bridge individuals and organizations. *Journal of Management Inquiry, 4*(3), 222-246.

Croasdell, D. C. (2001). IT's role in organizational memory and learning. *Information Systems Management, 18*(1), 8-11.

Davenport, T. H., & Prusak, L. (1997). *Working knowledge: How organizations manage what they know.* Cambridge: Harvard Business School Press.

Davenport, T., & Prusak, L. (1998). *Working knowledge.* Cambridge, MA: Harvard Business School Press.

Davenport, T. H., Jarvenpaa, S. L., & Beers, M. C. (1996, Summer). Improving knowledge work processes. *Sloan Management Review, 37*(4), 53-65.

Dodge, B. (1991). Learning in an organizational setting: The public service context. Study prepared for the Canadian Centre for Management Development.

Duffy, J. (2000). The KM technology infrastructure. *Information Management Journal, 34*(2), 62-66.

Duffy, J. (2001). The tools and technologies needed for knowledge management. *Information Management Journal, 35*(1), 64-67.

Ellerman, D. P. (1999). Global institutions: Transforming international development agencies into learning organizations. *The Academy of Management Executive, 13*(1), 25-35.

Ellinger, A. D., Watkins, K. E., & Bostrom, R. P. (1999). Managers as facilitators of learning in learning organizations. *Human Resource Development Quarterly, 10*(2), 105-125.

Garvin, D. A. (1993, July 1). What makes for an authentic learning organization? *Management Update: Newsletter from Harvard Business School, 2*(6), 7-9.

Huber, G. (1991). On organizational learning: The contributing processes and literature. *Organization Science, 2*(1), 88-115.

Kapp, K. M. (1999). Transforming your manufacturing organization into a learning organization. *Hospital Material Management Quarterly, 20*(4), 46-54.

Kim, D. H. (1997). *Toward learning organizations: Integrating total quality control and systems thinking.* Cambridge, MA: Pegasus Communications.

Lee, J. Sr. (2000). Knowledge management: The intellectual revolution. *IIE Solutions, 32*(10), 34-37.

Levine, L. (2001). Integrating knowledge and processes in a learning organization. *Information Systems Management, 18*(1), 21-33.

Levitt, B., & March, J. G. (1988). Organizational learning. *Annual Review of Sociology, 14*, 319-40.

Maier, R., & Lehner, F. (2000). Perspectives on knowledge management systems theoretical framework and design of an empirical study. *Proceedings of the 8th European Conference on Information Systems (ECIS)*.

Morecroft, J. D. W., & Sterman, J. D. (1994). *Modeling for learning organizations*. Portland, OR: Productivity Press.

Nevis, E. C., DiBella, A. J., & Gould, J. M. (1997). *Understanding organizations as learning systems*. Cambridge, MA: MIT. Retrieved form http://learning.mit.edu:80/res/wp/learning_sys.html

Nonaka, I. (1991, November/December). The knowledge-creating company. *Harvard Business Review, 69*(6), 96-104.

Popper, M., & Lipshitz, R. (2000). Organizational learning: Mechanisms, culture, and feasibility. *Management Learning, 31*(2), 181-196.

Porter, M. (1990). *The competitive advantage of nations*. New York: Free Press.

Price A. (2000). *Principles of human resource management: An action-learning approach*. Oxford: Blackwell.

Probst, G., Raub, S., & Romhardt, K. (2000). *Managing knowledge building blocks for success*. Chichester, UK: Wiley & Sons.

Richards, G. (1994, December). Organizational learning in the public sector: From theory to practice. *Optimum, 25*(3).

Roberts, J. (2000). From know-how to show-how? Questioning the role of information and communication technologies in knowledge transfer. *Technology Analysis & Strategic Management, 12*(4), 429-443.

Senge, P. M. (1990, Fall). The leader's new work: Building learning organizations. *Sloan Management Review*, 7-23.

Senge, P. M. (1994). *The fifth discipline: The art and practice of the learning organization*. New York: Currency, Doubleday.

Sharma, S. K., Wickramasinghe, N., & Gupta, J. N. D. (2004). Knowledge management in healthcare. In N. Wickramasinghe, J. N. D. Gupta, & S. K. Sharma (Eds.), *Creating knowledge-based healthcare organizations* (pp. 1-13). Hershey, PA: Idea Group Publishing.

Simon, N. J. (1999). The learning organization. *Competitive Intelligence Magazine, 2*(2), 40-42.

Srikantaiah, T. K. (2000). Knowledge management for information professionals. Information Today, Inc.: ASIS Monograph Series.

Sugarman, B. (1997). *Notes towards a closer collaboration between organization theory, learning organizations, and organizational learning in the search for a new paradigm*. Cambridge, MA: MIT. BPR225 retrieved from http://learning.mit.edu:80/res/kr/Sugarman.html

Thorne, K., & Smith, M. (2000). Competitive advantage in world class organizations. *Management Accounting, 78*(3), 22-26.

von Lubitz, D., et al. (2004, September). Medical readiness in the context of operations other than war: Development of first responder readiness using OODA: Loop thinking and advanced distributed interactive simulation technology. *Proceedings EMISPHERE 2004 Symposium*, Istanbul, Turkey. Retrieved from http://www.d-n-i.net/fcs/pdf/von_lubitz_1rp_ooda.pdf

Walsh, J. P., & Ungson, G. R. (1991). Organizational memory. *The Academy of Management Review, 16*(1), 57-91.

Wickramasinghe, N. (2003). Do we practice what we preach: are knowledge management systems in practice truly reflective of knowledge management systems in theory? *Business Process Management Journal, 9*(3), 295-316.

Wickramasinghe, N., & Schaffer, J. (2005). Creating knowledge driven healthcare processes with the intelligence continuum. *International Journal of Electronic Healthcare (IJEH)* (in press).

Section IV

Realities for Knowledge-Based Enterprises

Chapter X

International
Case Studies

Introduction

The following case studies illustrate various instances of implementing and interacting with a specific knowledge management initiative. They are diverse both in terms of the industries in which the particular organisations are as well as the countries in which these organisations are located. This serves to highlight the universality, need, and benefit of knowledge management irrespective of macro and micro differences. Moreover, it underscores the need to approach the KM initiative in a holistic and systematic perspective as we have outlined in the preceding chapters of the book. Taken together, the case studies provide a useful compilation of lessons learned that can be applied to many KM project. In addition, they serve to emphasize the key challenges and benefits of any knowledge management initiative and how the transition to becoming a knowledge-based enterprise is neither easy nor painless. The most important factor is the unifying theme in all the case studies; the benefits the respective KM initiative brings to the firm and/or industry under consideration.

- **Case 1: IT platform for study and e-collaboration:** Discusses a Polish experience of implementing a knowledge sharing and e-collaboration environment.

- **Case 2: Distributed knowledge networks:** Construction industry modernization—a discussion of distributing knowledge in the construction industry in Denmark.

- **Case 3: Keller Williams Realty:** Consists of a discussion of framing a struc-ture for knowledge sharing in the U.S. real estate industry and has a follow up part B that discusses how Keller Williams Realty cemented these KM relationships.

- **Case 4: Contingency-driven knowledge management in palliative care:** Discusses the role and usefulness of KM in a generally considered "fringe" area of healthcare—palliative care.

- **Case 5: Managing knowledge in project-based organizations:** Discusses the critical role KM plays in project-based organizations in the UK.

- **Case 6: Knowledge Management in practice:** Discusses the need for the tools and techniques of KM in the semiconductor industry in Ireland.

Case Study 1[1]: IT Platform for Study and E-Collaboration

written by
Witold Abramowicz, Tomasz Kaczmarek, and Marek Kowalkiewicz
Poznan University of Technology, Poland

Introduction

At some stage, we stated that the particular part of a didactic process in our Depart-ment requires proper management, therefore the D-Leap project and its outcome—the D-Leap platform for knowledge sharing and e-collaboration. The rationale behind the project is that education technologies are recently expanding at an enormously rapid rate. However, instructional designers and curriculum developers have become captivated of the up-to-the-minute technologies without dealing with the underlying issues of learner characteristics and needs. By employing techniques that improve personalization, designers can boost e-learning systems' efficiency even more than by using new, experimental, teaching methods, keeping the deployment costs low at the same time. The D-Leap project attempts to implement new personalization features. The D-Leap research project, carried out at the Department of Manage-ment Information Systems, focuses on creating goal oriented e-learning system. The system incorporates e-marketplace technology in order to serve as a knowledge e-marketplace for dispersed buyers and sellers.

The prototype solution utilizes state-of-the-art Web portal technology and digital assets management system to provide consistent and common platform for system users to work, communicate, and share knowledge. It is currently used as a document repository for all electronic materials used in didactic processes, a platform supporting creation of research papers, and a tool used in day-to-day teaching. Both system components (that can be implemented as Web services) and data structures are designed to support collaboration between the users. The platform is aimed at sharing knowledge regardless of the topic this knowledge concerns. The D-Leap system introduces features realizing our vision of learning systems in individual dimension. The system is also a test platform for implementing knowledge representation structures for knowledge management purposes.

Didactic and Research Processes at MIS Dept.

The three main goals of the system can be enumerated as:

1. Explicit knowledge management,
2. Tacit knowledge management, and
3. Knowledge access protection.

Explicit Knowledge Management

The system is currently used to help students gain expertise in particular subjects. This goal is being achieved by managing the documents they provide. During the didactic process, students register into the system, then they gain access to knowledge created by their predecessors and to resources that can be used in their own study. The standard didactic procedure conducted at the Poznan University of Economics by students during their IT courses consists of gathering resource materials, preparing the practical project (if applicable), writing expertise document, and presenting the outcome to other students. All results, except practical implementations, are then published on the D-Leap platform.

Each new document, created by students, is undergoing approval process, and after a supervisor approves it, the document is made available to others. Apart from being stored in a specific folder, it is also introduced (with help of a student who publishes it) into the Topic Map structure, and thanks to that it can be linked with many other similar documents and categories. This is thanks to semantic network alike topic maps. Topic maps enable modelling and representation of knowledge in interchangeable form. At the same time, they make up a uniform framework for knowledge and information resources management. Topic maps present a model that is applicable by a wide range of industries. They are helpful in organisation and navigation of continuously growing information pools.

Tacit Knowledge Management

Our goal is to manage tacit knowledge itself without the need to convert it into an explicit one. Topic maps seem to provide too much limited instruments if we need to represent knowledge of each user (in this case, of each student). If we want to provide those users with mechanisms enhancing searching in knowledge repositories it turns out, that we need to extend Topic Maps technology by creating new structures for storing information about users, their knowledge and skills. Our proposed name for the structure is skill maps.

Protected Knowledge Access

The problem of trust in knowledge sharing is commonly overlooked in knowledge management implementations. Unfortunately, lack of trust can block attempts to get knowledge management to running. Knowledge owners are afraid, that their expertise will be used out of context, misapplied (blaming expertise originators), or it will be traded further without any notice of its original creator. The problem cannot be easily solved without an established and commonly accepted code of ethics.

Research of Connelly and Kelloway focused on trust in knowledge management. In this study, surveys have shown that respondents wanted to share knowledge only when they trusted the recipient. It is worth mentioning, that this specific trust was targeted toward individuals and coworkers. Obviously, this is relevant for peer-to-peer contacts while not facing the problem of trust in repository based systems. One can assume that in such case, the problem of trust targeted toward organization as a whole will be the problem. On the other hand, studies show that when one shares knowledge with others, his level of trust toward them increases. This leads to the conclusion that when first encouraged by the organization, the workers will share their knowledge it will finally lead to more spontaneous behaviors. Thus, interpersonal trust is not a crucial element when starting knowledge sharing. Instead, it can self-develop during the process.

One of the most important factors of the successful Knowledge Management solutions is adjusting them to the organizational culture. It is often described as "personality of the organization" and comprises the assumptions, values, norms, and behavioral signs of organization's members. Therefore, a short introduction into particular areas of the didactic and research process in the Department of Management Information Systems on the Poznan University of Economics would be in order.

The Department offers education in a field of business information processing.

We concentrate on information retrieval and filtering for MISs, data warehouses, workflow, e-marketplace, and mobile systems. Its members also conduct research on decision support systems for top-level management of a company and for investment activities. Moreover, our interests cover other fields of business information like personalization of internet services, knowledge management systems, customer relationship management systems, and more.

Several courses during the curriculum that our department is responsible for are taught using project method. Students, apart from having lectures and labs are due to collect valid material, write an essay, and prepare a presentation on the subject that they select shortly after the beginning of the semester. The subject topics vary from purely theoretical to very practical, including for example interviews in the selected company and the design of solution for particular case. The presentations of the projects are delivered at the end of the semester to the rest of students publicly.

Since this practice has been in use for a few years, the essay library has grown large—up to several hundred CDs. Such a library in its form has become unmanageable, and could not be efficiently used by students and departmental researchers. On the other hand, one should not underestimate the value of the library—thousands of documents chosen by potential experts in the field along with essays, most of them containing valuable knowledge.

On the other side of the fence, there was a research activity at the department that had, as we ascertained, similar requirements in terms of the support necessary to express tacit knowledge into an explicit form of the research paper. A number of researchers working on the paper, apart from communicating directly, had to document some of the thoughts and exchange the literature by means of electronic communication tools. As a number of such project team grows, e-mail communications becomes ineffective as it requires every member of the team to keep his own electronic project library, manage discussion threads, and to be up-to-date with e-mails, which is not always possible. The larger the team, the more troublesome it becomes and lots of effort is wasted on the work already done by somebody else. We draw from our experiences that even with the team as small as having four members, those effects become significant. On the occasions where ten or even more people work on the same subject at the same time, managing the communication and tracing changes in the documentation becomes so challenging that it even discourages less organized people or causes their exclusion from the work process.

At the end of the project, its outcome, the literature, and the documentation could be beneficial for the subsequent projects and other department members—if made available. This was rarely done prior to the introduction of the D-Leap knowledge management platform.

Need for Knowledge Management Solution

The shortcomings of the didactic and research processes previously described were lack of knowledge sharing and reuse by subsequent "generations" of students, constrained communication, and knowledge exchange among researchers. The explicit knowledge embedded in the presentations and essays was non-accessible. The potential of research papers corpus accumulated by students of several years laid idle, and students could not identify their older colleagues that possessed tacit knowledge gained in previous projects. Similar problems were present in the area of research work, which is summed up by a paper writing activity. The mutual knowledge of projects undertaken in the Department was limited not to mention poor idea exchange among scientists. Similarly, the exchange of interesting literature was problematic due to inconvenient means of distance communication. Maintaining project Web sites that would ease collaboration and could provide common storage place for project documents seemed too effortful. Such Web sites, even if they existed, were prone to become outdated. At the same time, tools to automate and integrate functionalities like forum, document storage, authentication, and access control were not readily available. Therefore, we stated that there exists a need for KM software solution that would encompass not-yet-integrated parts described above and could tackle our problems. This section is devoted to the particular needs that we identified in our environment and software tools that could be useful when dealing with them.

Requirements

The problems depicted were already addressed by various software packages; however, each piece of software covered the area only partially. We identified the following functions that were necessary and already present in the dispersed packages.

Technology should never be considered as a crucial element for building knowledge management solution. Nevertheless, by planning for appropriate technological mixture, one can more easily put the two remaining aspects (organizational culture and thoroughly planned solution) into practice. From the technological point of view, our proposed set of ingredients is as follows: network server, directory service, messaging server, instant messaging server, digital asset management system, and Web portal.

- **Network server:** The base for e-collaboration solution should be established on a network server, which can take advantage of organization's internal knowledge resources (presumably file servers, data warehouses, databases, and document repositories). Therefore, such a server should support at least TCP/IP protocol and other protocols used internally by an organization (such as IPX/SPX or NetBIOS). However, we opt for storing corporate knowledge in one place (we purposefully omit security considerations here), one format (or with standard metadata descriptions), accessible in the same way (by using the same network protocol). At the same time, the network server should be able to get through to external knowledge and information resources (structured and semi-structured) in order to respond to user requests. This should be done by using Web services features based on well accessible UDDI descriptions. Leading public retrieval systems provide Web service interfaces to their engines.

- **Directory service:** One should try to reuse most of existing data, and make new data, which is entered into the system, available to others. Hence, the e-collaboration solution should store all, or most of, user related data in well-known structures, such as standard directory services (Novell Directory Services, Active Directory, or Lightweight Directory Access Protocol, just to name a few). Apart from storing users' contact and configuration information, this should also include storing information about user groups, user rights, available services, etc.

- **Messaging server:** One of most important cooperation aids, even in relatively low dispersed environment is communication software. This includes e-mail server as well as more advanced newsgroup servers. Such complex systems are available for all major operating systems.

- **Instant messaging server:** It is often required that an individual contacts another to discuss some topic, exchange ideas or train each other. Instant messaging server can be helpful in such situation. This enables to create a one-on-one chat room, often sound and video enhanced. The typical instant messaging server alerts the user whenever somebody on her private list is online. Unfortunately, there is no standard protocol in messaging systems, and there are a large number of competing instant messaging systems.

- **Digital asset management system:** DAM is a central repository for organization's digital files (documents, images, streaming videos, etc.). This should also be a central point of storage for e-collaboration solution. There are many competitive technologies to be used such as relational databases, data warehouses, or specialized products offered by software vendors. The key characteristics when choosing the proper DAM are performance, flexibility, and open standards compatibility.

- **Web portal:** In order to provide a standard and well accessible user environment, one can decide to use Web portal technology. A standard Web portal offers such services as e-mail, search engine, forums, news etc. For that reason, authors believe that portal should also be used for e-collaboration purposes.

One of the assumptions of our model is that explicit knowledge is stored in documents. These are usually MSOffice, PDF, and HTML files. Therefore, we needed a system that is capable of storing and managing documents. After half a year of tests with some Content Management System, we decided to move our system entirely on Microsoft platform—SharePoint Portal Server. The reason for this was that content management capabilities of this application occurred less significant than our document management needs. We needed control over document creation process and access to the documents while they are already published. The Share-Point solution seemed ideal to us because it provided both document creation and storage control, and flexible, browser-based interface. Moreover, SharePoint fitted well assumptions and targets of our project. One of the initial goals was to create department's digital library. During years of scientific activity we gathered several hundreds of CD-ROMs of literature. These resources were unmanageable and, in fact, not used. The materials included conference proceedings, MSc and PhD theses, documents gathered from the Internet, from digital libraries, and prepared by students. The second goal was to create a system that would enable cooperation, sharing knowledge, and its creation (we wanted our library to grow). In our directory structure, we assigned separate places for students' workplaces and our Department projects—these are the places that contribute to library growth the most.

The former stores documents are prepared by students and gathered from external sources. These documents are described with subset of Dublin Core properties and placed in a directory prepared for each student per year, per class. The directories have assigned authors, approvers, and readers—these are users obtained from the Active Directory structure described next. Authors are able to submit new documents; approvers to allow publication (this are usually academic teachers). Before the documents are published (become publicly available to other system users allowed to read it), they undergo publication procedure that is implemented in the SharePoint Server environment. First, the document is checked in, then it may be approved or rejected. On both events, the author is notified via e-mail—we had to extend SharePoint functionality as it provides only notifications of acceptance by default. We had to extend SharePoint functionality by automating the process of creation of students' workplaces. We designed Web part for students to create directories for them. The student chooses the class, lecturer, and type of classes (lecture/labs) and after they are given a password, the workplace for him is created. The lecturer is given approver's privileges and the student is given author's privileges. When the classes end, the administrator can (again thanks to separate Web part placed on "Administration" dashboard) close workplaces, which revoke users privileges and makes documents available for public use. This model is extensible and allows creating project groups with a leader that would accept documents prepared and group members publishing their work.

In directories provided for our department projects, we store versions of scientific publications, resources collected to prepare them, and our internal documents. This part is administered manually because of lower administrative costs required.

Currently we are working on the mechanisms of automatic redundancy removal. We discovered that due to subjects (or classes) scope, many documents are resubmitted by users that do not know of them already being stored. If this is the case, the approver will be notified and he can reject the documents on that basis.

Solution Design and Implementation: Knowledge Management Experiences

After the earlier experiments with the content management software, we have settled on the Microsoft Sharepoint Server platform for the reasons previously indicated. However, the functionalities of this software had to be extended to fit our needs. During the design and implementation phase, we have adopted several of the knowledge management techniques. We split the programmers group (mainly students) into smaller teams and assigned them small tasks that emerged during the design phase. We provided good conditions to facilitate communication between teams, both verbal and electronic. For this purpose, we adopted the Web blogging technique—a single blog for the project was created. It served as a common storage for code pieces, links, and useful resources. We also tried to stimulate socialization and knowledge sharing among teams and team members throughout the exchange of team members and brainstorming sessions on harder questions. As for knowledge resources, we prepared some of them in advance, before the project began. We also performed knowledge localization, and identified useful resources on the Web such as portals with articles concerning our subject, useful newsgroups, and their archives. During the implementation phase, we have used our project management experiences obtained earlier. It occurred that it is a good practice to assign the hardest problems to the most skilled individuals. That provided the quickest solutions while the other team members could perform other tasks, not connected directly with the problematic one.

Daily Practice with New KM Solution

As literature indicates, introduction of novel information system (especially knowledge management related) into an organization is usually associated with changes to the organizational culture and processes. That was also the case with the D-Leap platform. Here changes to the didactic process had to be introduced, some of them intended, some arose as an outcome of the new possibilities generated by new information system. Those issues are discussed next from a point of view of system users.

The system was intended to facilitate collaboration and communication between students and lecturers and to become common storage for didactic and student knowledge resources. Therefore, it is focused on the processing of explicit knowledge—knowledge externalization, and acquisition processes, and to some extent on the socialization process. For students, new opportunities to interact with each other and with lecturers emerged. The new didactic process begins with the registration and creation of user accounts within the platform. Those accounts are activated by an administrator, then students can access the platform resources. Students obtain access to the resources that are associated with the classes that they attend. To minimize the administrative effort necessary to manage the access control, a password protection system was designed. Resources are grouped into subjects; each subject is accessible only for members of the assigned group. If a student wants to join the group, he or she has to give a password, which is usually delivered by a class lecturer at the beginning of the semester. After that, the workspaces for students have to be created. This process is partially automated but sometimes it is necessary to create the workspace manually (e.g., if it should be group, not personal workspace). A workspace has a form of folder with publication rights for the workspace owner and a small workflow attached which allows for interaction with a workspace supervisor, who accepts versions of documents published by students. An interaction is achieved by possibility of discussion about the published documents and by e-mail notifications that are sent to the supervisor if any change within a subscribed document occurs. A separate platform element is devoted to selecting assignment topics. Here the "first come, first served" policy is applied—a topic list is made available at certain time and students can reserve topics. The reserved topic becomes unavailable for the others. The students are required to prepare an essay and a presentation on selected topic. During the semester, they are free to use all the platform e-collaboration possibilities including versioning, discussions, and single storage space for resources. They can also use platforms' digital library and base their work on the documents gathered earlier by their older colleagues (in addition each document within a library is accompanied by information about its publisher, which may facilitate a socialization process among the students of different classes).

From a student point of view, the most important changes in the didactic process is its formalization: from registration, through topic selection, submission of assignment to its acceptation. There are no possibilities to extend deadlines; the student that is late for topic selection is left with less convenient subjects. The rules for publication and communication with lecturers are also more strict than they were previously. This leads to quite obvious conclusion that the introduction of knowledge management (or other) information system into organization formalizes some of the processes, makes them clear but also more demanding.

Students benefit greatly from the resources available within the digital library—that is the second important change and a suggestion for the knowledge management solution implementation. The knowledge gathered during organization life should be made explicit and saved for future use. The organization that looses knowledge also looses the competitive advantage. Historically, first knowledge management information systems aimed at preserving organizational knowledge and facilitating access to these resources. If a knowledge storage system is accompanied by integrated e-collaboration and e-communication means, it becomes a true knowledge management solution. An access to the explicit knowledge is important but an access to experts and search facilities is a next step toward successful exploitation of both tacit and explicit knowledge resources within the organization. On our platform, this is achieved through metadata about resource publisher (potential expert on the subject) and elements of e-collaboration integrated within a platform.

Lecturers and researchers also benefit from D-Leap a common storage place for the resources. It eases access to the documents through a single interface and embedded search engine, therefore improving knowledge acquisition. It is also simply convenient, which among the others saves time and effort. However, there is an extra burden imposed by the formalization of the processes indicated above. Some of the communication with students, previously done in an informal, verbal way, now has been moved to e-mail discussions and some additional activities like acceptation of resources published by students. Again, the introduction of knowledge management information system formalized the interactions and required more organized approach toward knowledge resources creation, management, and dissemination.

A knowledge management information system, as any other, requires certain administrative effort, which in our case consists of common maintenance procedures (backup, minor reorganizations of content) and user registration acceptation, which proved to be a good technique against user account clutter and potential security vulnerabilities.

The introduction of knowledge management platform in our Department allowed also for new didactic experiences. Inspired by modern organizational concept like matrix organization and management through projects, we introduced new type of assignments—matrix projects. The idea behind those projects is that students taking up different roles in their group projects should deliver two reports. One report from each group should consider project subject itself while the other should be a role report. For the second report, the motivation is that students that performed the same role in different project should share knowledge and experiences and try to summarize and generalize it. This is also a good exercise before students join real-world companies and begin to work in the project-driven organizations.

The processes previously described represent well-known processes of knowledge acquisition, externalization, socialization, and sharing. These processes are supported by the knowledge management information system, which delivers some necessary tools. For example, knowledge dissemination and sharing is assisted by system's search capabilities, which allow not only for full text search but also for the metadata search. Users may define queries that allow for retrieval of documents written by particular author or those that were assigned selected keywords. Carefully designed catalogue structure and document metadata ease browsing and finding relevant information according to topics and publication date. If someone is particularly interested in certain topic, he may use the subscriptions mechanism to be notified of changes in the content. All these support knowledge localization, acquisition and to some extent dissemination. Knowledge externalization is supported in the way that system enables storing documents and document versioning, which is crucial in cooperative work on single document.

The didactic process itself is aimed at knowledge development. We encourage making use of the resources created earlier. There are however, intellectual property rights issues here that have to be dealt with. We require that our students mark citations and explicitly reference the sources of information that they use. The publications, whose copyrights allow for copying and use for didactic purposes, are copied to the systems' digital library and attached as student's resources.

To at least partially protect ourselves against plagiarism we adopted the external anti-plagiarism system, which checks the documents to mark those that are composed, to large extent, from other, not, mentioned explicitly, documents.

Our experiences show that knowledge combination requires new and challenging topics to pursue. This may be easier to achieve in an organizational environment that is rapidly changing, but is much harder on the didactic field. The repetition or similarity of assignments topics is an outcome of the need to cover certain subject area designated for given class.

We would like to extend the systems' capabilities with group work environment in the future. This would be beneficial for distant students, but since the system is now used by stationary students mainly the e-collaboration means described were sufficient.

Conclusion

The implementation of the D-Leap system had two visible benefits. First, since students were involved in the development process from the beginning, they had significant influence on D-Leap's final form. While preparing the systems, many students gained expertise in implementing large-scale e-learning solutions. Second, the use of the system helps tutors to develop better and better lectures and laboratories, and gives students an opportunity to learn from older students' (indirectly, be studying their works).

The implementation of the platform taught us another important lesson—knowledge management initiatives never end. There is always a lot to do—from maintaining the repository to implementing new functionalities requested by users.

Discussion Questions

1. What are the key issues regarding knowledge management (KM) in this case study?

2. Identify the respective people/technology/process aspects of KM in this case study.

3. What should be done next with the D-Leap system?

4. What are the major lessons learned from this case study?

5. Map the critical issues of this case study in terms of Boyd's OODA loop. How does such a process centric KM perspective facilitate a superior understanding of the key issues?

6. What are the major barriers and facilitators with implementing the D-Leap system?

Case Study 2[2]:
Distributed Knowledge Networks:
Construction Industry Modernization:
Innovating a Digital Model for the
Construction Industry: A Distributed
Knowledge Management Approach

written by
Mogens Kühn Pedersen
Copenhagen Business School, Denmark

Abstract

How does a government achieve that the construction industry adopts a common digital model without the use of laws and regulations that might alienate many companies slowing adoption and if adopted by few would fail the objective of a higher productivity in the industry? The Danish digital construction model (DCM) provides an opportunity to study the application of a distributed knowledge management approach in a setting unfriendly to government intervention and at the same time subject to detailed (obligative) construction norms and expert based guidelines and recommendations. In this complex environment, adopting a distributed knowledge approach is suggested as a viable framework to apply in developing a common digital platform for the construction industry.

The Danish case of a digital model for the construction industry moves beyond digital models developed only for suppliers because it extends into the construction process and into the industry digital standards as a whole. The article presents a networked knowledge management model that purports to cover the knowledge management process of IT systems architecting and of data modeling in developing interdependent business systems thereby leveling company routines and creating transparency where previously only partial, custom solutions have been used. Expecting that a collaboration based on data interchange, process interoperability, and knowledge access and sharing, storage and retrieval will make an industry more efficient—how does this come about?

The government objective is to achieve significant productivity gains, fast. Reports both from government and from independent analysts prove that Danish construction industry insufficiently adopts better (best) practices and thus lags behind most other Scandinavian countries in productivity development and has done so in the last decades.

At first, the article presents a model of distributed knowledge management and how to understand its contribution to value added amongst participating companies. Secondly, the article presents the DCM case in a historical perspective of many trials and errors. The article is not a study in failures in ISD, it is a reasoned conjecture that is developing the platform for interdependent systems while preserving flexibility and mobility of all participants generates value-added to participants. The construction industry is now set on a path to innovate a common digital platform for the management of construction and the building processes. It is the claim here that adopting a distributed knowledge management approach to interoperable ISD makes it possible to achieve a set of viable systems. Conditions of success are not only to adopt a learning knowledge network principle and apply this conscientiously, but also to define an implementation process ensuring all significant actors are ready to move forward in concert.

We venture the proposition that innovative distributed knowledge networks are transformational of business practice if a wide adoption of new objects of knowledge interchange takes place based upon a transparent process of establishing common definitions and specifications of formats and application requirements enhancing participants" competence and forming peer-to-peer networks of innocuous knowledge interchange. Of course, the adoption of the distributed knowledge framework is no mechanical guarantee for the success of an innovative development process but it is a framework that explicitly identifies incentives and risks of interoperable business systems development. Though we are not that far in the empirical process now unfolding in Denmark, we venture characteristics on the basis of the three distributed knowledge models, thus accounting for development requirements on the basis of the framework and relate to some early observations of the unfolding of the digital construction model project in Denmark.

Introduction

Distributed knowledge management reflects the nature of knowledge: Incapable of being centralized it is bound to be distributed in nature. Already in the 30s, the British Economist Sir Frederic Hayek presented the axiom why centralized economic planning systems would fail to be as efficient as (distributed) market systems. The former had a cumbersome and unwieldy bureaucracy at its roots and the latter a less demanding knowledge structure, even bordering on an anarchic nature. Some critics suggested that if only we had large enough computers central planning would be superior to the market (Herbert A. Simon) though that position is heresy today for sound economic reasons.

Today, we would suggest that the challenge of the knowledge society is how we get the benefits of a common digital infrastructure ensuring interoperability at data, functional and process levels without having to succumb to a "benevolent" dictator, central planner, or a private monopoly.

In the vision of a distributed system, we have the embryonic idea of a synthesis of the need of a commons and the need for exercising the powers of initiative and innovation.

The Internet has proved the distributed market concept correct as far as any centralized market solutions are concerned. Even though telecommunication providers have had the centralized network power for generations, they have not been able to maintain that position since the Internet revolution. The decentralized, anarchic Internet was surely not in the economic interest of monopoly telecoms since highly profitable national and international traffic were cut short by local tariffs applying to the Internet concept bringing boom to data communication on e-mail and the information infrastructure of the world wide Web surpassing imaginations of any telecom manager.

Would a common digital construction model repeat the revolutionary impact on coordination and documentation requirements in the construction and building maintenance processes? We cannot yet determine the impact on the construction industry of common digital models as they are in the process of development. Here, we conjecture major requirements to a successful approach meeting the objectives of common digital models.

Theory of Distributed Knowledge Management

We present a model of knowledge management (Pedersen & Larsen, 2005) and its axioms of validity to set the scene for an interpretation of a case. We have had no influence upon the way the people and organizations in the case study have chosen their framework, meanings and interpretations of their "learning network" and other knowledge management and IS development tools. We do claim relevance in applying our framework to the case on the basis of the case organizations ways and structures of approach to developing common digital models.

We have previously argued that knowledge need to be understood from the basis of a distinction between knowledge acquisition and knowledge use as well as between situation-specific and non-situation specific knowledge (Pedersen & Larsen, 2001). It is our position that knowledge distinguishes itself from data and information by context, meaning that context provides signs, symbols, and other meaning systems with which to decode the intent of knowledge. Concisely, knowledge is context-rich whereas data are context-lean requiring further data to gain more context indications but it is only by transcending data can we obtain knowledge. However much data is added to data little do we know of context since context is a relational matter rather than an inventory of piecemeal data.

Figure 1 does not reveal what *distributed* knowledge is in contrast to "knowledge models" in general (Pedersen & Larsen, 2004). In the sense that "distributed" only reflects the fact that human beings form communities in society just as they are part and parcel of a language community, the concept would add nothing to knowledge. The adjective *distributed* to knowledge management means identifiable, active participants forming some kind of a network. There are different sorts of networks, some are peer-to-peer networks, others are hierarchically layered and others are centralized structures. Common to all networks are active, contributing members, differently contributing and committed over a period of time. *Distributed knowledge networks* refer to the intentional efforts by identifiable actors to establish and maintain conditions of interchange considered relevant and valuable to each actor over a period of time. The opposite of a network is people or the public as an amorphous structure of numerous, anonymous individuals. This category is not considered here.

Information systems are of particular interest to knowledge management because they may realize previous impossible knowledge collaboration, coordination, negotiation, and concurrence, thus building what has become known as communities of practice (Wenger, 1998). In our knowledge model, *acquisition* is distinct from *use* of knowledge motivating different information systems for each, as these processes are not necessarily synchronous. With information systems, a knowledge network may extend across time zones and continents as easily as across an urban district or a company site.

Knowledge interchange is the privileged way of verification and validation to held beliefs and judgments in all spheres of life. No community coherence and no group

Figure 1. A general knowledge model

Knowledge model		Contextual specificity		Domain specificity
		Location specificity	Time specificity	Epistemology
Individual knowledge production	Acquisition	Situated	Event	Learning (embedded)
		Epochal		
	Use	Grounded practice	Timely	Expertise (mobile)
		Opportune		
Social knowledge production	Peer to peer	Collaborative	Coordinate	Community of practice
	Hierarchical	Negotiate (command?)	Concurrent	

interaction can last without it. Just like information is a basic concept without an inclusive nominal definition so is the "unboundedness" of knowledge not subject to one all-inclusive conceptualisation but an ontological category in need of epistemological clarifications.

Further, knowledge interchange is determined as a socio-economic transaction. We have an acquisitive relation of proprietary knowledge while complementary knowledge is subject to a cluster relationship (Porter, 1998a, 1998b), and innocuous knowledge requires a peer-to-peer relationship (Benkler, 2002-3). These categories of knowledge are associated correspondingly to different networks that we call user-producer, cluster, and peer-to-peer.

Information systems owe its objectification of information to linguists that presented the view that a text only refers to itself and to other texts, thus staying within the universe of all texts. Reference to "the objective world" is also a text and does not merit a particular epistemological treatment. Likewise, information systems consists of data, data processing, and data interchange and do not need any external reference. An information system interpreted as data is a completely self-contained universe. Immersing knowledge in information systems brings in domain and contextual specificity to networking individuals extending their depth and scope of orientation (see Figure 1). The data level is superseded by social structures and processes enriched by knowledge contexts and domains that epitomize knowledge models corresponding to different distributed knowledge networks.

Across distributed knowledge networks we find three defining *parameters*: First, that product state models are constructed as (digital) objects; distributed competence as organizational learning (from espoused to theory-in-action) within (occupational) communities of practice embracing both individual and social knowledge production; and finally, networks that differ according to the nature of the knowledge interchanged; whether it is proprietary, complementary or innocuous knowledge that is transacted.

In the case of innocuous knowledge, the network takes on the form of peer-to-peer production that challenges proprietary knowledge as the only and the essential driving power of knowledge interchange.

Distributed knowledge is decisive to efficiency and innovative capacity building in today's business as it takes the form of competence building, product state model maintenance, and peer-production (Pedersen & Larsen, 2005). In differentiated networks (Nohria & Ghoshal, 1997), knowledge exchange generates performance advantages to the participants even where contractual knowledge exchange is unavailable as seen in peer-produced software in open source communities (Kogut & Metiu, 2001). Business advantages are leveraged by innocuous knowledge interchange (Pedersen & Larsen, 2005).

Each of the three types of distributed knowledge networks relate differently to the defining parameters of distributed knowledge, viz. object, competence, and networks of knowledge interchange.

The syntheses—distributed knowledge networks—take place across three factor sets. Information may have an orienting function on individuals, whereas distributed knowledge management systems are enacted by objects (artifacts), competence, and networks.

Objects

The first factor set is the digital object of product models. We derive from the analysis of these models the idea that distributed knowledge requires inter-operable specifications, digital interchange formats, or other means of bridging different semantic universes of product states. Another branch of research have changed focus from the product state to the boundary between actors and named the artifacts, boundary objects (Bowker & Star, 1999) and a third approach have focused on metaphors (Kanfer et al., 2000) finding them decisive to facilitation of inter-domain knowledge communication and innovation practice. When we move from product networks to services, we conjecture that the need for artifacts to leverage interchange is as important. We summarize this aspect as the *object* (an artifact) of distributed knowledge.

Competence

The second factor set considers competence. In a previous study, information specificity played a major role in explaining conditions of acquisition and use in terms of time and knowledge. The latter is easily translated into competence in regard to knowledge acquisition and use. Originating in information systems, competence seems an individualistic conception but we may take it into the organizational setting and add shared repertoires, practice as connection (in community of practice, Wenger, 1998), and work routines (new work patterns, Yates, Orlikowski, & Woerner, 2003) to the conceptual context. Competence enhancement (learning) also develops higher boundaries between insiders and outsiders reflecting a need for boundary spanning to cope with the inevitable discontinuities following competence enrichment (Wenger, 1998, p. 253). Competence structure therefore reflects a set of factors all associated with conditions of knowledge creation and communication. Employees in knowledge intensive organizations work across boundaries and use knowledge transformation mechanisms as identified by Yates et al. (2003).

Network of Knowledge Interchange

A third set of factors derives from knowledge in transactions. Therefore, we identify characteristics of both social interaction and knowledge interchange.

We may refer to a rich tradition of user-producer relationships characterized by knowledge flows without an extensive use of contracts but of other means of private knowledge appropriation (von Hippel 1988, 2001). Users are often taking a strong interest in improving their own performance, and being dependent upon equipment (technology) from key suppliers, they are willing to go to some length in providing knowledge that manufacturers may exploit in their design of products for the user. Since proprietary knowledge emerges, the social interaction though informal is strictly private to the participants.

Brown and Duguid (2000, p. 62) argue for the relation of complementarity between technology and humans rather than substitution as in actor network theory. This applies to networks in which human actors grant meaning, confidence, and trust in the artifacts (technology) to the extent other actors fulfill these expectations. In clusters, networks are defined by complementarity just as the specificity of distributed knowledge is complementarity.

Finally, as pointed out by Benkler (2002-3) "Peer production has an advantage over firms and markets because it allows larger groups of individuals to scour larger groups

Table 1. Distributed knowledge networks

Distributed knowledge networks	Product model	Boundary model	Peer model
Object	Product specifications	Boundary object	Metaphors and other artifacts
Competence	Company specific	Absorptive capacity	Transformative capacity
Network—social characteristic	Acquisitive relation	Cluster relation	Peer-to-peer relation
Network—knowledge characteristic	Proprietary knowledge	Complementary knowledge	Innocuous knowledge

of resources in search of materials, projects, collaborations, and combinations than do firms or individuals who function in markets. This is because when production is organized on a market or firm model, transaction costs associated with property and contract limit the access of people to each other, to resources and to projects, but do not do so when it is organized on a peer production model." Innocuous knowledge epitomizes the nature of this type of network.

In Table 1, we relate distributed knowledge network models to object, competence, and network and its associated knowledge characteristic as defining parameters. We identify the three distributed knowledge networks: Product, boundary, and peer model. Table 1 summarizes the analysis in the previous section.

Case: A Digital Construction Model Innovation Process

Since the mid-'80s, non-profit organizations have been working on digital models for the construction industry and in particular, for the adoption of interchange formats like IGES and STEP, both standards developed in the U.S. In spite of government funding and support, little has come from these initiatives over 20 years.

Government white papers on the construction industry in Denmark reveal low or even negative productivity development and an overall diminishing activity through the '90s. The digital construction model project has been cast as a lever for productivity growth and modernization of the industry that has seen foreign companies taking over major parts of Danish industry.

Government has now triggered the process of developing a digital construction model using purse (push) and whip (pull). Purse in the sense of funding a share of the costs of development, and whip in terms of announcing the obligation to use the digital construction model in public construction tenders as of 2006. A date that seems very tight considering that the projects were formed in 2003-4. Government acting both as political trigger and as demanding user frames the development and adoption processes exerting pressures on all major players in the construction industry. Opting out or stalling the process would bring at risk the very business of any major player in this very competitive industry thus having to forgo that option. We therefore see intense negotiations and pressures being exerted between players while taking part in a process they cannot afford to leave alone or to abandon completely.

In this context of pull and push, we look into how distributed knowledge networks of players in the construction industry at large emerge and unfold (i.e., including non-profit organizations for better construction practices, industry associations, real-estate funds, laboratories, and universities, etc.).

The government's push and pull policy and its project contracts have been instrumental in setting a scene for knowledge interchange between players that is contrary to custom in this industry.

We are thus researching an innovative process of development tied up with a process that envisions the adoption of a set of common digital models and formats supporting the construction process and the verification and validation of the delivered construction work and ensuing maintenance services.

A Digital Construction Scheme: Vision, Projects, and Processes

The National Building and Housing Agency in the Ministry of Economy and Commerce took the initiative to form a development scheme for a digital model for the construction industry (DCM) that government adopted granting a multi-million sum doubled by private foundations (10 millions and 20 millions DKK, respectively).

In contrast to previous initiatives, the digital construction model has the objective to enhance adoption and learning to use digital technologies rather than developing brand new technologies to the construction industry. Well aware of the long-term objective of one and only one digital construction model taking hand of both building elements and components and on the construction process is still a far away vision, the DCM scheme aims to build a foundation of consensus on classifications and taxonomies to make way for less ambitious partial construction models that should be compatible with the set of tools and guidelines developed by the scheme's projects.

The scheme on the DCM consists of four projects, three of which produce input to be implemented in DCM whereas the fourth project is a particularly interesting project from the point of view of distributed knowledge systems. The project is a "learning network" that supports the processes of debating and prioritizing taking place in the other three projects. It is a fully financed, integral part of the overall scheme. It is a contractual obligation of each of the three producing project groups to solicit workshops, drafts and other materials on the learning network and to use the network as complementary to workshops, hearings, and conferences.

After tenders, the government agency's steering group in which the industry is fully represented decided the selection of a consortium for each of the three projects.

The three producing projects are "Best Practice in Construction," "Builders' Requirements," and the "Digital Foundation."

The best practice project develops tools for the evaluation of impacts of IT investments in construction aiming to describe a set of best practice cases. The builders' requirements address four issues: Digital tenders, 3D visualization, a project Web, digital operations, and maintenance data delivery (an obligation to be effective when the DCM is implemented in June 2006). The digital foundation project focuses on standards, taxonomy, classifications, and long-term views on the digital foundation of construction.

One of the three projects in the scheme, "the digital foundation," has specification and definition of common standards, methods, etc., on the agenda. The vision is coherence between all processes in the construction value chain. That requires a use of a common taxonomy for description and exchange of data and for the proper ways of data maintenance and accessibility. If there exists national and international standards, they will be applied.

The project is scheduled to provide results that can be implemented by June 2006. Results will be in terms of terminology and classifications; 3D-work processes and interchanges, logistics and processes, maps for parts of the building helping those working on that part to extract relevant data. All require a conceptual clarity that needs to be coordinated within the overall scheme of the DCM and in particular with the project on builders' requirements. Public works are not included in the project on the digital foundation.

Like the other projects within the scheme of DCM, this project consists in a phase for idea generation and a project phase in-between, which consensus-building workshops are to take place. The idea generation phase resulted in a prioritized list of requirements recommended for the project phase and presented at a general hearing in May 2004.

The digital foundation project scheduled consensus workshops and a general hearing as their present input to a learning network.

The learning network, the fourth leg in the DCM scheme, circumscribes the three producing projects previously mentioned. This network is of particular interest as it is a vital facilitator of the development processes in the other projects. The learning net supports a way of working that will evolve reflecting the expected trend toward a consensus in the industry on the importance and impact of the DCM having a focus on an object oriented, process approach to digital construction.

The Danish construction industry is already accustomed to the use of Internet, e-mail, and digital building units and components catalogs and order processing systems. A digital infrastructure is in place. Presently, data is stored, unstructured in documents or in 2D CAD-files. Interchange of data (system to system) is rarely used (E&B, Det digitale Fundament, May 2004, 10-11). The digital foundation considers the present digital infrastructure a platform for a take-off of more advanced digital applications.

The four projects in the DCM scheme each contribute in a particular way to the overall objective. Even if there may be good use for more projects, it is within a manageable scale of complexity to try designing a common digital construction framework for the industry and the builders.

Value-added from digital objects to the construction industry players is considered in terms of enhanced coordination and in reduction of errors in order handling and data interchange and in an increase in quality of those data improving maintenance and operations in the long-term. In the best practices project, these expectations will be specified and the actual data operations will be measured creating a fund of knowledge on applications and organizations relevant to the industry.

In this chapter, we consider the deliverables from the three projects as resources for the industry. It varies to which extend these digital resources are new to the industry. The fourth project in the scheme is instrumental in encouraging and supporting a learning process of consensus creation on the essential elements of a digital model of construction.

How are these resources to be perceived in distributed knowledge networks? How is the learning network conceptualized in our model? In which ways are the distributed knowledge networks instrumental in providing explanation and guidance to the practice of a developing a common digital model for the construction industry?

Method of Research

The case study of the Danish construction industry illuminates how a distributed knowledge network may construct a range of digital objects in designing tools for managing distributed collaborative construction processes and for maintenance of buildings.

In the context of a common tool though, it is inclusion that matters since competing digital construction models would jeopardize the idea of a common collaborative platform in the industry, and it is as important to diffuse the DCM to all relevant actors in the industry.

Maintaining the DCM depends upon an effective market for the tools of DCM ensuring revenues for continuing the design and development of the DCM. If no adoption takes place, IT vendors will see no reason to continue developing the digital tools for the industry. Critical adoption rates are not explicitly part of the scheme but government has expressed intend to demand the use of DCM in public tenders after 2006.

In this phase of the DCM projects, we cannot conclude on sufficiency of diffusion into the industry. We can spot participation intensity and breadth in the workshops, hearings, and conferences. Of course, the large numbers of very small construction companies that consist of a handful of skilled and trained or unskilled workers are rarely seen present whereas consulting engineers, large entrepreneurs, and building companies are present. It seems clear that all types of partners in the construction industry take part in the process though indications (a minor survey) from the first half of 2005 are that small and medium sized construction companies rarely raise their voice.

The method of study has been to participate in some of the DCM events and interviewing key players during the first year of DCM development. We are at the starting phase in this study. Concluding on our propositions is not possible yet as the DCM projects are in the process of developing their products so that nothing has been taken into operations as of today. Adoption of the results of the projects is scheduled for July 2006. Today there are small-scale pilots on some of the partial models of the DCM.

Analysis and Findings

In a preliminary analysis of objectives and achievements until now, indications of which resources are generated will be highlighted.

On the basis of these data we will conduct an analysis of the prospects for the DCM in terms of the model of distributed knowledge networks that we previously presented.

We will use the model to increase our understanding of the opportunities and risks that the DCM projects are currently facing, taking conditions of success from our analytic model as a measure.

Taking departure in distributed knowledge networks, we identified three types of models. If we consider the general objectives of the DCM scheme, we can classify its deliverables into the model and compare it to presently available solutions.

The table reflects a vision of three stages of development envisioned by the distributed knowledge network models. In Denmark, the industry's point of departure is an infrastructure partly built on the Internet and partly based on VANS (for EDI interchange systems), yet mostly using proprietary applications with data and files formats not considered in terms of interchange and interoperability. The DCM will support the change into an interoperable and more interlinked set of digital resources but still lacking many standards and tools.

Finally, in the third phase of the DCM scheme, it is envisioned that the construction industry will take advantage of a highly developed set of digital objects, open standards, interoperable data, and file formats, and new applications supporting interlinked construction processes. This will occur during both building operations and in the phase of maintenance, and eventually in the demolition of the building if a lifecycle buildings model is finally adopted.

Our framework seems to structure the development of the digital construction model in accordance with the expectations expressed in the scheme for DCM in Denmark.

To consider if the learning network is instrumental in bringing about the shifts of phases of the digital infrastructure of the construction industry, we are hampered in an evaluation of this part of the scheme by inconclusive data. Though we have collected some data, they only form a fraction of the overall processes taking place at present. To judge from these data, we find it difficult to ascertain specific impacts from the learning network as there is no clear-cut picture of the use of the learning network across the projects. Considering the scope of such an analysis, we will reserve that for a paper reflecting the whole process that will be concluded in the summer of 2006.

Conclusion

Findings from this early study of a digital construction model in the Danish construction industry concerning objects, competence of absorptive, and transformative capacity, and knowledge network formation were insufficient to establish the odds of a successful—though implicit—application of a distributed knowledge network framework. A peer-to-peer network promising productive co-development relationships did not prove applicable at the present level of the development of DCM. It needs surely to be promoted as a framework endorsing visions expressed by some of the actors.

This calls for cautioning the management of the DCM processes to review progress and learning options already in this phase of the development. Postponing reviews and intervention to a later stage will increase risk of a breakdown in their development model.

It remains an exciting opportunity to research the complete process of development, adoption, and diffusion of the digital construction model in the Danish construction industry.

Table 2. Distributed knowledge networks of digital construction model phases

Distributed knowledge network model / Status of digital construction model	Product model: Pre-DCM status.	Boundary model: Intermediate phase of DCM.	Peer model: Mature phase of DCM.
Object	**Product specifications:** Ex. Digital proprietary catalog of building parts, 2D models, proprietary data, and file formats not using (open) standards.	**Boundary object:** Digital objects applying announced API and interchange data formats (XML) and Web services based on standards and vendor specific implementations.	**Metaphors and other artifacts:** Ex abstract digital construction models; objects based on open standards, open interchange data, and file formats, digital objects in open source code.
Competence	**Company specific:** In-house, consultant or vendor specific competence of digital model.	**Absorptive capacity:** Relating to users' existing platforms, new functions in applications, and introducing enhanced versions for "expert users" as trailblazers.	**Transformative capacity:** Users throughout the industry adapt their processes, adopting new digital objects, provide counsel to lesser competent firms to avoid bottlenecks.
Network	**Proprietary knowledge in acquisitive relation:** Users contribute data to vendors in prescribed format not available in user own applications or only in client application.	**Complementary knowledge in cluster relation:** Vendors participate in proprietary based implementation of standards to achieve interchange and interoperability.	**Innocuous knowledge in peer-to-peer relation:** Vendors and users apply open standards and open source digital objects, Web services on common frameworks, work process integration using open standards, open source applications (transparent).

Discussion Questions

1. What are the key issues regarding knowledge management (KM) in this case study?

2. Identify the respective people/technology/process aspects of KM in this case study.

3. What should be done next to ensure continuous improvement?

4. What are the major lessons learned from this case study?

5. What aspects of KM in this case might be applicable to other industries?

6. What are the major barriers and facilitators in implementing KM successfully in this case study?

7. How do the concepts of organizational learning apply in this context?

References

Argyris, C., & Schön, D. (1998). *Organisational learning*. Reading, MA: Addison-Wesley.

Badaracco, Jr. J. L. (1991). *The knowledge link*. Boston: Harvard Business School Press.

Barney, J. B. (1986). Strategic factor markets: Expectations, luck, and business strategy. *Management Science, 32*(10), 1231-1241.

Barney, J. B. (1991). Firm resources and sustained competitive advantage. *Journal of Management, 17*(1), 99-120.

Benkler, Y. (2002-3). Coase's Penguin or Linux, and The Nature of the Firm. In Yale L. J. 112 (3) (December 2002).

Bobrow, D. G., Cheslow, R., & Whalen, J. (2003). Community knowledge sharing in practice. Retrieved in 2003 from http://jonescenter.wharton.upenn.edu/Virtual Communities/whalen.pdf

Bowker, G. C., & Star, S. (1999). *Sorting things out: Classifications and its consequences*. Cambridge, MA: MIT Press.

Brown, J. S., & Duguid, P. (2000). *The social life of information*. Boston: Harvard Business School Press.

Chesbrough, H. W., & Teece, D. J. (1996). When is virtual virtuous? Organizing for innovation. *Harvard Business Review, 74*, 65-73, January-February.

Coase, R. H. (1937). The nature of the firm. *Economica, 4*, 386-405, November.

Cohen, W. M., & Levinthal, D. A. (1990). Absorptive capacity: A new perspective on learning and innovation. *Administrative Science Quarterly, 35*(1), 128-152.

Dyer, J. H., & Hatch, N. W. (2004). Using supplier networks to learn faster. *MIT Sloan Management Review, 45*(3), 57-63.

El Sawy, O. A., & Majchrzak, A. (2004). Critical issues in research on real-time knowledge management in enterprises. *Journal of Knowledge Management, 8*(4), 21-37.

Galbraith, J. R., & Lawler III, E. E. (1993). *Organizing for the future. The new logic for managing complex organisations.* San Francisco: Jossey-Bass Publishers.

Garud, R., & Nayyar, P. R. (1994) Transformative capacity: Continual structuring by inter-temporal technology transfer. *Strategic Management Journal, 15*(5), 365-385.

Granstrand, O., Patel, P., & Pavitt, K. (1997). Multi-technology corporations: Why they have "distributed" rather than "distinctive" core competencies. *California Management Review, 39*(4), 8-25.

Hayek, F. A. (1937). Economics and knowledge. *Economica, NS 4*, 33-54.

Kanfer, A. G., Haythornthwaite, C., Bruce, B. B., Bowker, G. C., Burbules, N. C., Porac, J. F., & Wade, J. (2000). Modeling distributed knowledge processes in next generation multidisciplinary alliances. *Information Systems Frontiers, 2*(3/4), 317-331.

Kellogg, K. C., Orlikowski, W., & Yates, J. (2002). *Enacting new ways of organizing: Exploring the activities and consequences of post-industrial work.* Presented at the Academy of Management Conference, Denver, Colorado, Published in the Academy of Management Best Paper Proceedings.

Kogut, B., & Metiu, A. (2001). Open-source software development and distributed innovation. *Oxford Review of Economic Policy, 17*(2), 248-264.

Kwok, J. S. H., & Gao, S. (2004). Knowledge sharing community in P2P network: A study of motivational perspective. *Journal of Knowledge Management, 8*(1), 94-102.

Larsen, M. H., & Pedersen, M. K. (2001). Distributed knowledge management in health care administration. In T. A. M. Spil & R. A. Stegwee (Eds.), *Strategies for healthcare information systems: Transformation of the healthcare chain in to the future* (pp. 182-197). Hershey, PA: Idea Group Publishing.

Levy, M., Loebbecke, C., & Powell, P. (2003). SMEs, co-opetition, and knowledge sharing: The role of information. *European Journal of Information Systems (EJIS), 12*(1), 3-17.

Majchrzak, A., & Wang, Q. (1996). Breaking the functional mind-set in process organisations. *Harvard Business Review*, 93-99.

Metcalfe, J. S., & James, A. (1998). Knowledge and capabilities: A new view of the firm. *CRIC mimeo.* University of Manchester.

Milgrom, P., Qian, Y., & Roberts, J. (1991). Complementarities, momentum, and the evolution of modern manufacturing. *American Economic Review, Papers, & Proceedings, 81*(2), 84-88.

Nohria, N., & Ghoshal, S. (1997). *The differentiated network. Organizing multinational corporations for value creation.* San Francisco: Josey-Bass Publishers.

Pedersen, M., Kuehn, & Larsen, M. H. (2001). Distributed knowledge management based on product state models: The case of decision support in health care administration. *Decision Support Systems (Special issue on Knowledge Management), 31*(1), 139-158.

Pedersen, M., Kuehn, & Larsen, M. H. (2004, January). Robustness of a distributed knowledge management model. *The 37ʰ Hawaii International Conference on System Sciences, HICSS.*

Pedersen, M., Kuehn, & Larsen, M. H. (2005). Innocuous knowledge: Models of distributed knowledge networks. In K. C. Desouza (Ed.), *New frontiers of knowledge management.* UK: Palgrave Macmillan.

Porter, M. E. (1998a). Clusters and the new economics of competition. *Harvard Business Review, 76*(6), 77-90.

Porter, M. E. (1998b). The Adam Smith Address: Location, clusters, and the "new" microeconomics of competition. *Business Economics, 33*(1), 7-13.

Prahalad, C. K., & Hamel, G. (1990). The core competence of the corporation. *Harvard Business Review,* 79-91.

Teece, D. J. (1987). Profiting from technological innovations: Implications for integration, collaboration, licensing, and public policy. In D. J. Teece (Ed.), *The competitive challenge.* Cambridge. MA.

Tsoukas, H. (1996). The firm as a distributed knowledge system: A constructionist approach. *Strategic Management Journal, 17,* 11-25.

Von Hippel, E. (1988). *Sources of innovation.* NY: Oxford UP.

Von Hippel, E. (2001). Innovation by user communities: Learning from open source software. *Sloan Management Review,* 82-86, Summer.

Wenger, E. (1998). *Communities of practice.* Cambridge.

Wernerfelt, B. (1984). A resource-based view of the firm. *Strategic Management Journal, 5,* 171-180.

Williamson, O. E. (1985). *The economic institutions of Capitalism.* New York: The Free Press.

Yates, J., Wanda J., Orlikowski, & Woerner, S. L. (2003). *Virtual organizing: using threads to coordinate distributed work.* Presented at the 36ᵗʰ Annual Hawaii

International Conference on System Sciences, Big Island. Published in the HICSS-36 Conference Proceedings. IEEE Press.

Case Study 3A[3]:
Keller Williams Realty: Framing a Structure for Knowledge Sharing

written by
Roberta Lamb
University of California, Irvine, USA

Introduction

Keller Williams Realty started like many other U.S. residential real estate firms did in the early 1980s—as a paper-based, two-man operation, located in a small local office in the heartland of middle America. Gary Keller, along with his co-founder Joe Williams, had gained hands-on experience by working for regional realty companies. Like others with drive and enthusiasm, Gary had begun to work his way up the organization. Unlike most other residential brokers, however, he had majored in insurance and real estate in college, and he had developed a radically different idea about how realtors could work together. His entrepreneurial approach would establish a basis for building a network of realtors to share profits, knowledge, and expertise.

Real Estate Industry Dynamics

In the U.S., state, county, and local zoning laws define the permissible use of a particular property, and building codes further restrict the improvements and structures that can be constructed on the site. Property may be publicly or privately owned. Depending on zoning laws and building codes, a private property may be classified as either residential, that is for use as a residence, or commercial, in which case it may be an office building, a shopping center, or an industrial manufacturing facility. When property owners wish to sell, they frequently retain a real estate agent. The agent brings together buyers and sellers, and she generally manages the details of the transaction. She may arrange for property inspections and appraisals, obtain title insurance, or perhaps facilitate lending arrangements. Most agents' brokers specialize in either residential or commercial properties. Keller Williams Realty focuses primarily on residential properties.

The residential real estate market is volatile. Property values escalate and decline based on a number of factors, such as interest rates, local economic conditions, and quality of living factors like traffic congestion or clean air. Real estate brokers track property value trends and try to predict what they will be next month, next year or five years from now. U.S. property markets expanded dramatically between the late 1960s and the late 1980s. However, the types of market expansion differed. Along the crowded coastlines, property values in attractive areas skyrocketed. In the Midwest, where more land is available, values rose more slowly, except in areas that had successfully mixed high-tech employment opportunities with a social and economic milieu that attracted new residents. This new urban form has been called "postsuburbia" (Kling, Olin, & Poster, 1991) or "edge cities" (Garreau, 1991) or "technoburbs" (Fishman, 1987), and Keller Williams Realty grew up in one of these postsuburban areas.

Over most of the past 30 years, U.S. residential properties have been good investments. In the midwest, property values enjoyed slow but steady growth, until the late 1980s brought a dramatic downturn (cf. FDIC, 1997). Businesses failed, borrowers defaulted on loans, savings institutions closed amidst accusations of improper lending practices and unreasonably risky investment schemes. Home prices plummeted as lenders dumped properties. Some of the defaults and failures can be traced to a nationwide economic downturn and to a savings and loan scandal that involved five senators, several banks, thousands of properties and tens of thousands of investors (Bode, 1993; Rowen, 1989) The decline of the manufacturing sector and a general decline in farm values also put downward pressure on regional economic growth as unemployment rates crept upward, while fluctuations in the oil industry added to housing market volatility in other Midwest locales. These conditions restrained the rise of Middle America's housing prices, even in the more prosperous technoburbs.

Throughout this turbulent decade, Keller Williams Realty continued to grow and in the early 1990s it began to expand throughout the U.S.—introducing a new organisational structure to the residential real estate industry and a new culture of sharing.

Sharing Structures

Many organizations that have tried to nurture a culture of knowledge sharing, know this is difficult to establish due to cognitive and motivational limitations (Hinds & Pfeffer, 2003). Cognitive limitations are related to the difficulties that experts in some domains have in making their tacit knowledge explicit, and the communication gap that needs bridging between novices and experts. Motivational limitations are largely structural, and they are more easily manipulated by the firm. Competitive environments, for example, present a clear disincentive for sharing; but they can be countered by programs that reward reciprocal exchanges. But what if the limiting structures are pervasive, entrenched, and industry-wide? The entire residential real estate industry is highly competitive; and competitive structures have become institutionalized at many levels--from the firm, to the regional office, to the individual real estate agent.

Profit Sharing

Keller Williams Realty is currently one of the largest U.S. residential real estate firms in North America, and it runs on a model that flies in the face of conventional competitive wisdom. The model is relatively simple, which makes it easy to communicate, and it has begun to dislodge the entrenched structures of the industry.

When Gary Keller designed Keller Williams' profit sharing approach in 1983, he wanted to establish a realtor-broker-firm relationship that lay somewhere between the models of two giants of the industry: the Century-21 employee-agent and the ReMax independent franchisee. "It bothered me that we had only two models: the dependent model, which is quasi-employment and [projects an attitude of], 'Hey, we're going to do everything for you,' to the other extreme, which is the 100 percent model [which says], 'We're not going to do anything for you.' What Keller Williams did was a natural revolution of the industry," Gary Keller maintains. "I saw things in both models that I liked" (Hawkins, 2004.) In the Keller Williams model, almost half of the company's profit goes to the agents, and each agent's share is determined by the number of productive agents he or she attracts to the company. As many as "25% to 30% of all agents are in the process of moving at any one time" (ibid), and Keller Williams has been structured to capitalize on that turnover. The formula promotes growth, and it also produces a more cooperative culture among the agents—they have a stake in the success of their associates.

There is a difference between a real estate salesperson, a Realtor®, and a broker, but the first two are commonly referred to as realtors or agents. According to the National Association of Realtors® (1985), a real estate salesperson is "a salesperson who is responsible to a real estate broker and who assists him in his business of buying, selling, exchanging, appraising, and managing property." A Realtor® is "a professional in real estate who subscribes to a strict Code of Ethics as a member of the local and state boards and of the NATIONAL ASSOCIATION OF REALTORS®" (NAR). A real estate broker is "any person, firm, partnership, co-partnership, association, or corporation which for a compensation sells or offers for sale, buys or offers to buy, negotiates the purchase or sale or exchange of real estate, leases or offers to lease or rents or offers to rent any real estate or the improvements on real estate for others as a whole or partial vocation" (NAR, 1985, p. 182). A real estate salesperson or a Realtor® must be associated with a broker, like Keller Williams Realty, to transact property exchanges.

The three industry models that Gary Keller identifies promote different degrees of sharing among agents. In the employee-agent model, a broker opens an office and hires people to work for him or her on a negotiated commission that may be anywhere from 20% to 50%. In the independent-franchisee model, agents keep all of their commissions but pay in a fixed amount of money each month to cover the firm's expenses. In contrast, Keller Williams' profit-sharing model establishes a norm of reciprocity, or a culture of sharing that knowledge management literature promotes, but which few firms that follow the other real estate business models can achieve, due to the structure of the U.S. residential real estate market. In that market, there are always two sides to every transaction: the buy and the sell. Thus, in a large regional firm, competition comes from other agents inside the office as well as outside. Likewise, an outside agent is very likely to supply a buyer for a firm listing. In this way, brokers and agents within a geographic region simultaneously cooperate and compete for real estate business; and they learn about each other and the market through these transactions.

Buy and sell agents of conventional brokers may agree to take on complementary roles within a particular territory, or agents may establish "farms" (i.e., particular neighborhoods) where they work exclusively, but on either side of the transaction. Among agents within the firm, these territorial claims are usually respected in "gentlemen's agreements"; but between firms, there are no territorial concessions. Because the competition within the firm is almost as intense as between firms, there is not much difference in agents' incentives to share between the two conventional models. Neither one creates any formal ties among agents. There are merely stronger or looser ties between the agent and the broker, as in the typical principal/agent relationships of "employee" and "contractor." In sharp contrast, the Keller Williams model connects agents in a "family tree"-like structure that fosters a sense of relatedness among agents of the same tree by establishing fiscal interdependence. This profit-sharing arrangement taps the well-spring of network ties that develop among agents in different firms as they put together the industry's two-sided transactions. Gary Keller expects his agents to bring their friends and valued colleagues into the firm, and in so doing they transform the agent-broker relationship into a profit-sharing *partnership*.

In 1991, Keller Williams Realty began franchising its offices, using the same interdependent model of profit sharing and recruitment it had developed for its own offices. By treating its 25,000-plus franchisees and associates as partners, it effectively shares its knowledge, policy control, and company profits on a firm-wide basis. The Keller Williams Realty approach lets agents choose flexible commission structures, and it encourages them to engage in profit-sharing partnerships to benefit from the related compensation features, which can vest and continue after retirement. About 20% of Keller Williams Realty agents participate in profit sharing. In 2001, $6.3 million was distributed in profit sharing, up from $4.2 million the year before, with profit sharing per recruited agent ranging from nothing to $1,000 (Hawkins, 2004).

This approach has been so effective in attracting agents away from other firms, that Coldwell-Banker developed a course for its brokers to help them combat the Keller Williams model.

Information Sharing

Keller Williams' profit sharing model sets the foundation needed to support the framework of a knowledge-sharing organization because profit-sharing financial records are open to everyone in the company. Top producers also can participate in running the company, and agent education is a priority (Hawkins, 2004). This framework has been constructed piece-by-piece and agent-by-agent through a multi-step, multi-year, interorganizational effort. Information and communication technology (ICT) systems are an integral part of that framework, and they help Keller Williams agents work together. But do ICTs really facilitate *knowledge sharing* at Keller Williams today? And if so, how did they come to be used in that way?

Like Hinds and Pfeffer (2003), managers are often "somewhat skeptical about the role of technology in facilitating the sharing of expertise... these systems generally capture *information or data* rather than *knowledge or expertise*. Information and information systems are extremely useful but do not replace expertise or the learning that takes place through interpersonal contact" (p. 21). Despite such doubts, it is obvious that two ICTs have radically reshaped the residential real estate industry in the last quarter of the 20th century by changing agent interactions: the multiple listing service (MLS) and the Internet. But have these ICTs had any impact on knowledge sharing?

The MLS

Brokers have traditionally been responsible for advertising the "listings" of properties they offer for sale on behalf of their clients. In some areas, they still share these as printed lists with other realtors and brokers. Most, however, have worked together with regional third-party providers to offer a single, comprehensive MLS for exclusive use by brokers and realtors within a geographic region. For a fee, the service helps brokers quickly exchange data about available properties without publishing that data broadly. Originally, the MLS was a printed booklet, but eventually it went online with broker listings and county recorded data.

This information cartel became an indispensable asset to real estate firms. Agents began to use their regional online MLS at least daily, and often hourly to monitor new listings, and to examine the historical data about local properties that they use in their price models. For many years, as one realtor reflected, only agents and brokers could mine this data. "Its been my experience 5 years ago even 10 years ago or 20 years ago, this thing called the MLS, the multiple listing service, was one of the most highly and closely held secrets [of the industry.] Real estate agents had access. Nobody else. There was no such thing as you being able to find out anything about property."

But that all changed with the Internet ... or did it?

The Internet

When the World Wide Web was introduced in the early 1990s, real estate agents seized upon it as an effective tool for advertising their listings and services directly to the general public. Early Web pages mimicked the newspaper advertisements or flyers that they had always used. More sophisticated Web sites then sprang up, allowing home buyers to shop online for the first time in history. For the most part, these sites served regional realtors, but it soon became apparent that the Internet would challenge those geographic boundaries and override local "gentlemen's agreements." By the late 1990s, realtors were afraid that giants, like Microsoft (**msn.com**) or even NAR's **realtor.com**, would dominate the Web and destroy local brokers the way "big box" retailers had decimated smaller retail stores. They also feared that the online shopping of local buyers would kill the two-sided transaction as buyers began contacting listing agents directly. In order to get into the transaction, buyer agents would have to "unbundle" their traditional real estate service packages, and offer cut rate deals to buyers who didn't need full service.

None of these dire predictions has come to pass—yet. One "stopper" is the transaction itself. In a real estate transaction, the listing agent has a fiduciary responsibility only to the seller. Even if a buyer contacts the listing agent directly, that agent is the seller representative, and must work to close a transaction that is favorable to the seller. "So," as Alex Goodman[4], a regional MLS manager, explains "smart people will get a buyer representative to negotiate with the seller representative." They do, and the two-sided transaction lives on.

Another source of protection is the MLS. Most regional MLS providers have moved their online access to the Internet. They allow local agents to download data and post it on their Web sites, as long as it is their own listing information, or listings from a broker who has a reciprocal agreement with their broker. In January 2002, the NAR mandated that all MLS providers must implement a broker reciprocity program for brokers who want to exchange listings and post them on regional or national Web sites. This agreement includes the industry giants, but the information in the MLS overnight feed to **realtor.com**, for example, is rather sparse. The same is true about the information that the MLS downloads to all public Web sites. Alex Goodman says that "We primarily have an intranet for the realtors. We do have an Internet for the public, [but] we give the public about 28 or 25 fields of information out of a possible 200. Plus, they don't get the confidential stuff like corporate commissions." His MLS effectively manages the boundaries in cyberspace to protect local realtors from outside groups, while at the same time expediting the exchange of published information. The MLS has helped maintain regional control of the market by extending proprietary information models of the past (i.e., incomplete transaction data and selective information sharing) while also maintaining dependencies on its service among a loyal clientele of regional brokers.

The MLS and individual agent Internet sites are clearly *information or data* sharing systems, rather than *knowledge or expertise* sharing systems. It is possible, however, that when ICT systems like these are widely shared, they can establish a model and a basis for sharing resources in more complex and interpersonal ways—particularly in an industry like residential real estate where barriers to entry are very low, and where information is a major component of the service. When brought within the organizational boundaries of the firm or of the network of trusted associates, these models could be adapted to support knowledge and expertise sharing activities.

Introducing Intranets

At Keller Williams Realty, intranets are coming to be used in ways that refit Internet and MLS information sharing models to the needs of Keller Williams' "families of agents." Like other agents throughout the country, they have been part of the explosive growth of Internet use among realtors, for which industry models are partly responsible. Many agents have several Web sites. For example, Chicago agent Karl Katzen has three sets of Web pages: one that uses his own name as the Internet domain (hosted by homes.com); one on the realtor.com host; and one on the Keller Williams-hosted site (which hooks into the regional MLS and the realtor.com pages). Agents explain this multiple-site approach by saying: "Well in real estate you're really marketing yourself." Because many broker sites are designed to brand the firm in a regional market, the agents need to develop alternative pages to brand themselves and to expand their market coverage. Keller Williams understands this need, and it is trying to help its agents develop better ways of pulling together industry, regional and local information sources to construct effective Web sites. In fact, a large portion of the Keller Williams corporate intranet is devoted to a suite of Internet page templates that agents can use as a Web kit to launch their own sites.

Other real estate brokers have introduced intranets to provide commonly shared resources like forms and firm directories to their agents. Many have also created downloadable page templates and hosting facilities for agents' Web pages. But few have also provided extensive training and responsive technical support to very busy, and sometimes, technology-challenged realtors. Instead, firms opt for either strict control of the Web pages or else *laissez faire* technical support.

Education is a key component of the Keller Williams model, and so it is not surprising that a good technology training program is in place to help agents use the Web, or that its corporate intranet contains a comprehensive array of course offerings and materials on a wide range of real estate business topics. What is surprising is the way in which the technology training and improvements to the IT infrastructure are funded. Keller Williams' realtors voted to pay for more IT themselves, at a rate of $10 per month per agent. As Keller Williams agent rosters grow, so does the fund to build the infrastructure and to provide adequate support and training.

The best-used portions of Keller Williams' corporate intranet are the profit sharing reports. Everyone uses them to track profit-sharing allocations, as well as sales volume and other statistics; to monitor growth among offices in terms of agents recruited, and to compare individual performance to that of other agents. They also use this data, the way buyer-agent Kim Alvarez does, to selectively connect with listing agents who can help them grow their business: "One of the things I use the intranet for [is] if there is a listing agent that happens to be a Keller Williams agent ... I can go and check to see what kind of production they're doing, because it's an open book company."

This "open book company" has also fostered a culture of local reciprocity among agents. Kim says that agents often copy other agents' materials with their full consent. "Let me just put it to you this way: [Susan Ito] gave anybody who wanted it, her entire buyers' packet by e-mail. Which means it was all in a Word document, so you could go and change it, put your name, from her name to your name..." Kim did this, and then passed the package on to another new Keller Williams agent. "If I can help him out, great. 'Cause I know he's going to turn around and help me out."

Helping people out is a recurrent theme at Keller Williams—even just by extending common courtesy. One of the more interesting intranet applications at the corporate facility is a simple but effective homegrown program called Lettuce. The name is derived from "Let Us," as in "Let us know where you are." People use it on a strongly encouraged but voluntary basis, to tell others if and when they will be coming into the office. It serves many of the same purposes that more complex online integrated calendaring systems do.

Sharing Knowledge and Expertise

When the goal is knowledge sharing, researchers have noted that facilitating ICTs are most effective if they are introduced *after* the network or community of practice has been established (Huysman & de Wit, 2003—e.g., Unilever). Keller Williams Realty's model has clearly established many tightly connected networks. As Keller Williams' Vice President of IT, Robert Bender, points out, however, when introducing ICTs "It's a very difficult and different environment with franchisees in the fact that you can't tell them what to do. You can consult with them. You can strategize with them. You can show them, but you can't tell them. Because, there's really very little that's prescribed in this relationship, particularly from a technology aspect."

Top down management styles do not work well with franchises—franchises run better on a consensus model. This limits what can be done with intranet development at the organizational level, and that is where most real estate firms stop. Few corporate IT management teams are comfortable supporting a proliferation of intranets at regional centers and local offices. But Bender and his team understand concepts about communities of practice and networks, and they realize that the "one-size-fits-all" approach to intranet development will not be the most effective one for Keller Williams Realty.

The interdependent, consensus-oriented business model, with its agent-based funding for IT infrastructure improvements, gives the corporate IT team a unique view of "user" and "developer" roles. IT salaries are paid in large measure by the agents' $10 monthly contributions and those agents are who the infrastructure has to support. Therefore, when regional market centers began to implement their own intranets using an intranet provider not affiliated with Keller Williams, the IT team did not try to shut down those grass roots efforts, as many IT teams in other industries do, but instead negotiated better contracts for all Keller Williams market centers who want their own intranets. In addition, the Keller Williams IT team has developed a program for support, training, and the co-learning that is needed to help groups work together with intranet technologies. As IT manager Jill Dubey remembers "Some market centers had already done their own intranets: San Francisco, Nashville, Tennessee; there were three offices in Arizona...The only ones that we were aware of, were folks that were using Intranets.com. So, they're going to stick with Intranets.com. ...So, we talked to Intranets.com for about two and a half months and put together an enterprise inside license to use the software for a very good price."

By early 2003, over half of Keller Williams Realty's regional market centers had implemented their own intranets with Intranets.com. Jill says that the three things reported to be of greatest value to the agents on these local intranets are: "the shared calendar, document management, keeping track of all these forms, and things that are used in real estate; and *shared contacts*...Not their client list, but the folks that they had better relationships with in the market center; and vendor, partners, whatever you want to call them nowadays."

It is difficult to say when sharing a document becomes sharing knowledge or when sharing contacts develops relationships for expertise sharing, in contrast to simple information or data sharing. However, communities, networks, common access, and reciprocity are fundamental to Keller Williams' models of operation and to models of knowledge sharing (Fulk & Monge, 2001); and the IT team has consciously tried to promote ICTs that will support the firm's communities of practice. In fact, unlike many IT executives who strive for ever tighter enterprise-wide integration, Bender has begun to think more expansively about the communities of practice that other intranets might serve, and how to make them effective. "We have the single consolidated intranet now, and, we're tearing it up." He plans to suggest some cross cutting community-based intranets by checking with the agents to "see if there's a need to establish intranets by role within a company. So, should there be a regional director intranet? Should there be an owner intranet? You know, MCA's [market center administrators] have got some right to operate the market centers. Should they have a repository on their own to share best practices?"

Preparing for Famine and Finding a Feast

Throughout the 1990s, analysts made dire predictions about the impending demise of the real estate agent. Those predictions were based on a steady 10-year downward trend in NAR membership from 822,935 realtors in 1989 to 718,483 in 1998, and from 1,954 local NAR associations in 1989 to 1,481 in 1998. (See NAR membership: http://www.realtor.org/libWeb.nsf/pages/fg003.) That decline, and the relatively flat real estate market of the 1990s, led industry analysts, as well as academic researchers, to speculate further about the ways in which the real estate industry would be transformed, and particularly how ICTs would soon completely disintermediate the realtor. A few researchers, however, foresaw some ways in which realtors might muster their social capital to salvage a modicum of profitability for the profession (Sawyer, Crowston, Wigand, & Albriton, 2003). Agents themselves generally accepted these bleak forecasts, and the Keller Williams model was attractive to them because it hedged against those expectations. Apparently, no one foresaw the dot. com bust, and the subsequent rush of capital to safe havens in real estate, nor the resultant economic downturn that would precipitate a change in Federal Reserve policy that eventually sent interest rates to their lowest levels in forty years. All these events came together, just as realtor numbers had begun to reach pre-1990 levels. By 2002, agents and the real estate market were back in full force. Instead of the spiraling decline of residential real estate jobs and profits that was predicted, there has been an unprecedented nationwide boom. Here are Keller Williams' own statistics on how it has grown over the past few years:

- Keller Williams Realty experienced a 53% increase in annual earned commissions to reach a total of nearly $800 million in 2003. This is a 105% increase since 2001. Projected earned commissions for 2004 are $1.34 billion.

- Profit sharing in 2003 grew by 111% and paid out over $13 million to Keller Williams associates. The projected payout for 2004 is $28.2 million—a 112% increase. Keller Williams' management says this phenomenal growth is a direct function of the firm's knowledge sharing feedback system.

- The number of agents grew exponentially by 49% in 2003 to over 25,000, which means the company has more than doubled in size during the past two years. By the end of 2004, they expect to have more than 38,000 agents.

- In 2003, the average size of Keller Williams Realty offices grew from 79 agents to over 85; with more than 300 offices located across the U.S. and Canada.

The firm is still expanding into new markets throughout North America and Hawaii.

Realtors may find it easy to share when everyone is doing well. If this real estate boom lasts long enough, a knowledge sharing culture may continue to evolve at Keller Williams; and if intranets are in place to support the appropriate communities of practice, then intranets may facilitate true knowledge sharing and provide a model for organizational knowledge management, in an otherwise fiercely competitive industry. Conversely, because the urge to share among Keller Williams's agents was based on an expectation of bad times, an unexpected boom could put cooperative approaches on the back burner. Robert Bender worries that the incentives that drove agents to band together with his IT staff to battle the threat posed by Microsoft, and others offering ICT-enabled alternatives to traditional real estate transactions, are no longer in place at Keller Williams Realty. In these flush times, realtors don't seem to take those threats quite so seriously. He knows that his team will not be able to push the firm's IT agenda forward without continued agent funding, and he wonders if the agents will change their IT strategy: "I mean, so, it's a fear-based strategy. And, that was great, except when that fear went away, why are we still together?"

Throughout 2005, Keller Williams Realty has continued to grow, but is the bubble about to burst? A simple graph of residential investment statistics compiled by the U.S. Department of Commerce looks ominous (see Figure 2). And if the housing bubble does burst, what can Keller Williams Realty and its agents do?

Figure 2[5].

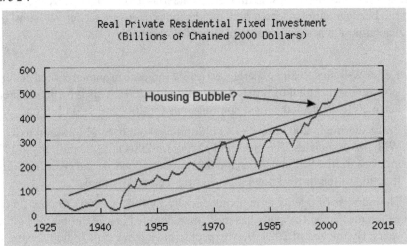

Source: U.S. Department of Commerce, Bureau of Economic Analysis

Discussion Questions

1. What are the key issues regarding knowledge management (KM) in this case study?

2. Identify the respective people/technology/process aspects of KM in this case study.

3. What should be done next at Keller Williams?

4. What are the major lessons learned from this case study?

5. Would the Keller Williams profit-sharing and knowledge-sharing model be applicable to other industries?

6. What obstacles might prevent more traditionally structured firms from adopting or adapting the Keller Williams model?

Acknowledgments

This study was funded by National Science Foundation, Information and Intelligent Systems, Computation and Social Systems Research Grant Awards #98-76879 and #00-96169 (1999-2003).

References

Bode, K. (1993). S and L Hell: The people and the politics behind the $1 trillion savings and loan scandal. *New York Times Book Review* (Sun, May 16, 1993):7.

FDIC. (1997). Survey of real estate trends. *Federal Deposit Insurance Corporation Report, January*. Retrieved September 1, 2004, from http://www.fdic.gov/bank/analytical/survey/1997jan/

Fishman, R. (1987). *Bourgeois utopias: The rise and fall of suburbia*. New York: Basic Books.

Fulk, J., & Monge, P. (2001). *Fostering intranet knowledge sharing: An integration of TransActive Memory and public goods approaches*. (CEO Pub. G 01-13 (403)). Los Angeles: Univ. of Southern California, Center for Effective Org.

Garreau, J. (1988). *Edge city: Life on the new frontier*. New York: Doubleday.

Hawkins, K. (2004). Profile. Gary Keller. *California Real Estate Magazine*, January/February. Retrieved April 1, 2004, from http://www.car.org/index.php?id=MzMyOTg=

Hinds, P. J., & Pfeffer, J. (2003). Why organisations "don't know what they know": Cognitive and motivational factors affecting the transfer of expertise. In M.

Ackerman et al. (Eds.), *Sharing expertise: Beyond knowledge management* (pp. 3-26). Cambridge, MA: MIT Press.

Huysman, M., & de Wit, D. (2003). A critical evaluation of knowledge management practices. In M. Ackerman et al. (Eds.), *Sharing expertise: Beyond knowledge management* (pp. 27-55). Cambridge, MA: MIT Press.

Kling, R., Olin, S., & Poster, M. (1991). The emergence of postsuburbia: An introduction. In R. Kling, S. Olin, & M. Poster (Eds.), *Postsuburban California: The transformation of Orange County since World War II*. Berkeley, CA; Los Angeles, CA: University of California Press.

(NAR) Realtors National Marketing Institute® of the National Association of Realtors® (1985). *Real estate sales handbook*, Chicago.

Rowen, H. (1989). The Lincoln mess: Let's say goodbye to Keating five. *Washington Post, 112* (Sun, Nov 19).

Sawyer, S., Crowston, K., Wigand, R. T., & Albriton, M. (2003). The social embeddedness of transactions: evidence from the residential real-estate industry. *The Information Society, 19*(2), 135-154.

Thornton, M. (2004). *Housing: Too good to be true*. Ludwig von Mises Institute. Retrieved September 1, 2004, from http://www.mises.org/fullstory.aspx?control=1533

Case Study 3B[6]:
Keller Williams Realty: Cementing the Relationships of Knowledge Management

written by
Roberta Lamb
University of California, Irvine, USA

Building on a Solid Foundation

By late 2004, Keller Williams Realty had become the fifth largest residential real estate firm in the U.S.; and its agent population continued to grow throughout 2005. In many parts of the country, the housing market boomed, with record sales prices and volumes making headlines.

Permanent IT Fee Renewal

Keller Williams' Vice President of IT, Robert Bender[7], had prepared the firm for this growth by putting together a sophisticated IT infrastructure with a flexible intranet development policy that reflected his broad-thinking technical view and the sharing culture of the firm's managers and agents. In 2003, CEO Joan Sanders asked agents to permanently renew their agreement to pay a $10 per month IT fee to maintain and grow the infrastructure; and they said "Yes!"

But even with agent rolls approaching 38,000 and commissions reaching a $1.34 billion rolling-12-month total by the end of 2004 (a 67% increase over 2003), the biggest IT challenge still remained: *usage*. This persistently lower-than-desired percent of use of "all this stuff" instigated some push technology initiatives, and some new training practices by Mark Madsen and his research and training team. Mark has worked in the real estate industry for 23 years, and he has been involved in strategy development at Keller Williams Realty for over 8 years. In that time, his team has repeatedly found that IT habits form within the first 6 months of the establishment of a new market center. There is now a launch support team that guides new offices through the process of setting up intranet reports; and during the center's "launch" phase, there is a conference call with Keller Williams headquarters every Thursday that purposefully integrates the use of local, regional and corporate intranets into routine communications and exchanges.

Intranets for All

Mark Madsen carefully studies the statistics of real estate industry models, and he knows how they work. The Keller Williams model doesn't work by means of top-down directives or forced enterprise-wide IT implementations. So when it comes to intranets, each market center is set up with its own local intranet that is sponsored by Keller Williams and hosted via Intranets.com, and the rest is "is all up to them," as Mark says. What he means is that Keller Williams expects intranet development to be "grass roots" in terms of use and leadership—the firm just sets up the initial structure. That structure now includes:

- Specific "user" intranets for each local office;
- An intranet where franchise owners can discuss ownership issues, like compensation plans, or how to find team leaders;
- Regional intranets for owners and Keller Williams' management;
- An intranet for all team leaders;
- One for market center administrators (MCAs).

There is also a new intranet for administrative assistants that Mark didn't know about until someone mentioned it at a sales meeting. "Who's running it?" he asked. "Some lady named Shirley," was the reply from the audience. "Oh," Mark responded, "I hope she's with our company." This very loose intranet control strategy is orthogonal to a carefully considered development plan that consciously tries to create a learning loop within Keller Williams, based on role-specific sharing. The management team and the education group tries to learn from the agents and their local administrators. For example, recruiting an agent from another company entails some problems in logistics—like switching all the agent's signs and advertisements over to Keller Williams' signage and logos. One of the local staff 'quarterbacks' developed a transition program (a series of intranet checklists) to facilitate the agent's move—now this is part of the corporate training program.

Intranet CBT

With all this growth, agents and staff desperately need training and expertise sharing. Keller Williams University (KWU) had been established a number of years earlier to serve this need, but it's delivery platform—road seminars—was just too slow to keep up with the rapid growth of the firm. Mark Madsen's team wanted to take KWU straight to its students with regular, modularized courses delivered via teleconference and internet-based training sessions. However, early pilot demonstrations of this synchronous approach showed that it was fatally flawed. Busy people won't sit and listen to phone seminars, like KWU's "Million Dollar Monday" one-hour broadcasts; and traditional online training sessions are simply boring. The demos showed Mark's team that they had the wrong platform. They needed to let agents and staff complete most of the training on their computer; but also provide a mix of other media, including "live" elements--and they had to let people do this on their own time. Now that they have the right platform, KWU's computer-based training (CBT) typically takes place over a period of 7-8 months.

Intranet CBT seems to work well for Maria Perez, a technology-savvy University of Southern California graduate, whose first job was to administer a new market center that launched in April 2003. Her story illustrates how a new office or market center becomes part of the firm. First, she attended "Operations Boot Camp" to learn how to set up an office. Then she continued her training on her own, via kw.com, for the next month. There was only one other California regional office when she started, and by participating in its MCA intranet, she learned about some documents and forms that her team could use. Her copier has a document server, so she obtained the files in that way, taking some of the pre-existing Texas documents, and customizing them for California. After about 6 months on the job, Maria felt ready to develop a local office intranet to support her role as the "middleman" and to "get stuff out to the agents." She says "I am totally dependent on it now."

Maria Perez has an impressive educational background, which gives her a good basis to evaluate KWU. She notes that other real estate companies in the area try to tell their agents that it isn't really a university—perhaps to keep them from switching firms. But Maria insists that it really *is* a university, and the intranet CBT is a big asset for her agents: "KWU is huge!"

Be Careful about What You Measure!

In order to help Maria and other new MCA's get a good start, it is important to know what makes one market center better than another, based on what they do. Without this kind of evaluation, intranets might actually facilitate sharing of the 'wrong' practice knowledge. Therefore, Keller Williams began using its corporate intranet to develop a balanced scorecard feedback system that ranks the offices on 25 metrics.

Scorecards

The scorecard system provides data on a monthly basis. The general card lists metrics that reflect office performance (e.g., number of agents, company sales dollars) with a rough peer group comparison to other franchises at the same level, and also a relative regional and international ranking.

The system fosters not only competition within the firm, it also gives agents and staff a way to ask for help. For evaluation purposes, each office is considered to be in one of three stages:

- A launch phase, which lasts about 18 months,
- A growth phase, from month 19 to month 48, or
- And an achievement phase, which extends beyond the fourth year.

An overall ranking on each of the metrics within each "stage" peer group allows for comparison across the entire firm. It's all about competition for those at the top of the list; but those in the lower slots use the rankings to measure their relative progress as they try to move up the list. The scorecard feedback helps offices focus their improvement efforts only on the metrics where they rank low. These metrics are discussed in meetings, and the education group explains what the metrics mean, and there is also a voice link on the intranet scorecard form that people can click on to remind themselves about the use of each metric.

All of the scorecard data and systems development is handled at corporate headquarters in Austin, Texas. The evaluations are funneled through database analyses into an enterprise reporting platform that triggers a push technology to send provocative messages to local managers that call attention to their office statistics. This suite of applications makes the corporate intranet a good education and office-level learning tool. There are currently no competitive/comparative reports on individual agents, but these are planned.

Before rushing into agent scorecard development, however, Keller Williams' strategists want to take time to absorb the lessons learned so far. Mark Madsen and his colleagues now know that, because scorecard feedback systems are high profile measurements, you have to be very careful about what you rank people on. When the firm averaged all 25 metrics to establish the rankings, the result was that some "weird" offices came to top—not ones that everyone thought to be the very best. Throughout 2003, the corporate group measured and refined the effectiveness of the scorecard, correlating the rankings with overall office performance, to determine which feedback really matters. Then they chose 6 metrics that seemed to be the most predictive and switched to this "20% scorecard" for comparative evaluations. Managers like Maria Perez use this Top 20 Scorecard to evaluate their office metrics, and to focus on areas for improvement. Now that her office has entered the growth phase, to improve its ranking, she will need to tap her knowledge networks for expertise on growth-related issues.

Knowledge, Culture, and Identity

Phenomenal growth. How has it affected Keller Williams' sharing culture? At the very least, it has given agents and staff more opportunities to share know-how and profits. With more than 300 offices located across the U.S. and Canada, the model still seems scalable; but managers have learned that they have to be more careful about the nature of the gathering that they are running.

By mixing online and offline elements in regional meetings and educational seminars, and by encouraging the growth of professional and personal networks within the firm, Keller Williams work environments have retained a close-knit "family" atmosphere. Online technologies, like scorecards and role-based intranets, allow agents and market center administrators to self-select whom they wish to learn from, whom they choose to identify with, and whom they want to emulate within the firm. The passive income aspects of the profit-sharing structure allow an agent to build a business-within-a-business that can continue beyond her retirement and can become a legacy to actual family members. Maria Perez, for example, was recruited to Keller Williams by her mother-in-law, and her husband is part of their team as well.

Mark Madsen and his corporate colleagues are pleased with their recent successes, but they remain philosophical about the volatile real estate market. Mark says that he thinks the Keller Williams model they have fine-tuned over the past 25 years will work best *when* the market crashes. Maria, on the other hand, knows that means the model will still work on a smaller scale—which may not include a role for her. She worries about having to find work in a different corporate environment, where more traditional working relationships and compensation structures might foster a less congenial culture.

Discussion Questions

1. What knowledge management (KM) issues become important in an expanding community?

2. Are there some KM "do's and don'ts" that can be learned from this case study continuation?

3. What could topple the Keller Williams profit-sharing and knowledge-sharing structures?

Acknowledgments

This study was funded by National Science Foundation, Information and Intelligent Systems, Computation and Social Systems Research Grant Awards #98-76879 and #00-96169 (1999-2003).

Case Study 4[8]:
Contingency-Driven Knowledge
Management in Palliative Care

written by
Graydon Davison
University of Western Sydney, Australia

Introduction

This chapter describes the management of knowledge in patient-based teams in palliative care organizations. These organizations are designed, configured and managed for dynamic response to uncertain, changing situations; to their contingencies. This response is knowledge based and contextualized by individual patient situations.

Three palliative care organizations in Sydney Australia have taken part in explanatory research into the management of their multidisciplinary teams—teams that are spontaneously innovative when necessary and capable of spontaneous knowledge creation and management across discipline boundaries. Members of these teams are grouped in disciplines for administrative purposes and allocated to patient-based teams as the need arises. Membership of patient-based teams is dynamic and often includes patients and whatever support mechanism is associated with them. Palliative care professionals are therefore often members of multiple dynamic teams simultaneously.

The majority of the contingencies described are derived from or related to the patients. These might be expected but can not always be predicted in terms of scope or impact and require the creation and recreation of knowledge specific to a patient's changing situation, at times spontaneously. The management of knowledge to best benefit the patient and patient-based careers (family and friends or other members of a patient's social support system) is primarily contingent upon the patient's situation, which can change without notice.

Background

Palliative Care

The palliative care environment is multi-disciplinary, team-based, people focused and systemically oriented, with a singular focus; an end of life experience for an individual and the members of any supportive social system that surrounds the individual. The role of teams in this environment is to establish and maintain a quality of life appropriate to each patient and the patient's requirements and to include within it people other than the patient who are willing to be included (McDonald & Krauser, 1996). A number of professions including nursing, medicine, pharmacology, physiotherapy, occupational therapy, social work, pastoral care, grief counseling, and administration attend this multifactored environment. Here people are the centre, not diseases, care results from understanding the causes of suffering and distress (Barbato, 1999) and multi-profession teams work collegiately so that the primary issue becomes and remains patient comfort (Meyers, 1997). The quality of life of people at the end of their lives is an issue of relief of suffering, whether the cause is physical, emotional, spiritual, known or unknown (Higginson, 1999; McDonald & Krauser, 1996). The patient is central in the ethics, philosophy, and practice of palliative care (McDonald & Krauser, 1996; Meyers, 1997). The patient's end-of-life state and central role in efforts to manage that state makes the patient a participatory member of the palliative care team and maintains a level of autonomy and control in relation to the other team members (McDonald & Krauser, 1996; McGrath, 1998).

The Case Study Organizations

Case Study 1, during involvement in the research, was conducted in a stand-alone palliative care organization that contained some 60 staff for inpatients and 35 inpatient beds. Additionally, there was ten dedicated staff for a community care program where patients were cared for at their homes. The organization's catchment was a population of some 350,000 and included hospitals, specialists, and general practitioners (family doctors). Multidisciplinary staffing consisted of the following disciplines: medicine, nursing, social work, spiritual care, physiotherapy, occupational therapy, and grief counseling.

Case Study 2, during involvement in the research, was conducted in a stand-alone palliative care organization that contained some 95 staff, including a team of 10 dedicated to the community care program where patients were cared for in their homes, and 50 inpatient beds. The organization's catchment was a population of some 320,000 and included hospitals, specialists, and general practitioners. Multi-disciplinary staffing consisted of the following disciplines: medicine, nursing, social work, spiritual care, physiotherapy, occupational therapy, and grief counseling.

Case Study 3, during involvement in the research, was a stand-alone palliative care organization that contained some 19 staff, 20 inpatient beds, and 10 day beds. The organization's catchment was a population of some 400,000 and included hospitals, specialists, and general practitioners. This case study organization did not contain a community care program but utilized such programs from hospitals within its catchment. Multidisciplinary staffing consisted of the following disciplines: medicine, nursing, social work, spiritual care, physiotherapy, occupational therapy, diversional therapy, and grief counseling.

Contingencies Driving Knowledge Management in Palliative Care

The contingencies that affect palliative care operations are uncertainty, patients, workforce, healthcare environment, and change (Davison, 2005). Of these, only the healthcare environment is not concerned directly with knowledge management in the multidisciplinary patient care teams.

Uncertainty

McCormick (2002, p. 128) described illness as containing uncertainty because it contained situations that included "ambiguous, vague, unpredictable, unfamiliar, inconsistent, and unknown factors" and proposed that uncertainty needed to be considered as a neutral concept, not driven by emotion. McCormick (2002, pp. 129-130) then proposed that uncertainty contained three attributes; probability—"...the core underlying the questions a patient may have...," temporality—"...how much time will be required until the ambiguity, unpredictability, or vagueness of a situation is clarified..." and perception—"...people perceive patterns of occurrences that they are not able to link to an existing frame of reference and that are contrary to their expectations."

Uncertainty can generate confusion and helplessness in cases of physical illness and disability; it is capable of immobilizing anticipatory coping and, therefore, the necessary decision-making for dealing with the uncertainty being faced. Uncertainty pervades the palliative care environment. The trajectory of the disease that brings a patient and patient-based-careers to palliative is commonly uncertain (Henkelman & Dalinis, 1998a; Rose, 1999). Symptoms, for example, pain, are not necessarily linked to obvious or certain causes (Lewis, Pearson, Corcoran-Perry, & Narayan, 1997; Rose, 1995). Reactions of patients and patient-based careers to the end of life process are uncertain (Henkelman & Dalinis, 1998a; Pierce, 1999). Membership of the group of patient-based careers can change during the end of life process. The reactions of palliative care professionals to the situations they will encounter during the end of life process of those in their care can be uncertain (Henkelman & Dalinis, 1998a; McDonald & Krauser, 1996). In addition, the range of palliation requirements occurs and is driven at the conscious and unconscious levels and the depth of experience at each level varies from patient to patient (Kearney, 1992).

Uncertainty plays a large role as an influencer. It is described in the palliative care literature as the driver of the need for multidisciplinary delivery of palliative care, pre-eminent in the considerations of individuals and teams, requiring dynamic complexity in team structures and in care delivery processes and as fundamental in the end of life process. Uncertainty in palliative care appears dynamic and manifold, varying in the level and intensity of its influence. This lack of uniformity in uncertainty appears to multiply the range of potential responses that multidisciplinary palliative care teams need to be able to offer.

The use of multidisciplinary teams is a response to uncertainty and to the range of palliation requirements that can be necessary for any given patient (McDonald & Krauser, 1996; Meyers, 1997). The dynamics of uncertainty bear directly on the way in which multidisciplinary patient care teams operate and the usefulness of multidisciplinary operations in palliative care is the opportunity provided for teams to mobilize and learn from each other's skills and experiences in patient care (Witt Sherman, 1999).

Patients

The persistence of uncertainty is evident in the constant changing of patients' situations, each of which is considered unique and requires constant re-assessment (Rose, 1995). Locating the majority source of uncertainty with the patient means also that the patient becomes the major informant of situational change (Henkelman & Dalinis, 1998b). The patient is described as a major informant of the trajectory of need and therefore the necessary direction of care (Henkelman & Dalinis, 1998b), followed closely at times by patient-based careers. This makes the palliative care professionals dependent on the ability of a patient and patient-based careers to explain what is changing, when and at what level, and requires that the professionals be able to enable and understand that explanation.

Changes in a patient's end of life can occur as a result of a change in any of the elements of the patient's life situation (Henkelman & Dalinis, 1998b), at multiple levels, sometimes in parallel, sometimes without obvious causes, sometimes without notice, sometimes without clear causal linkages between change and effect, sometimes consciously on the part of the patient or patient-based careers and sometimes not. This highlights the ability of a patient's situation to mediate that patient's care. Davison and Sloan (2003), in describing individual behaviors in palliative care teams, describe the patient's situation as the bridge between behaviors occurring in front of the patient and behaviors occurring away from the patient.

A better description might be that the patient's situation provides the bridge between a knowledge generating environment and an ability to manage and exploit knowledge.

This can be seen in Figure 3.

The opportunity to participate in decision-making is often valued by patients but the unpredictable nature of their illnesses means that participation does not guarantee successful consequences. Both decision-making and decision consequences require constant monitoring, particularly with regard to unsuccessful consequences. The patient's end-of-life state and central role in efforts to manage that state make the patient a participatory member of the palliative care team who maintains a level of autonomy and control in relation to the other team members (McDonald & Krauser, 1996; McGrath, 1998). There is also the issue of specific patient based contingencies such as history, family cultures, and language and the expression of symptoms and distress (Lobchuk & Stymeist, 1999). These are described as important contingent factors in the construction of meaning from the end of life experience and in the negotiation of symptoms between palliative care professionals, patients and patient based careers. Similar factors are described by Janssens, Zylizc, and Ten Have (1999) as contingent in shaping patient identity and the concept of self.

Figure 3. Understanding the patient's situation as a bridge between the establishment of a knowledge generating environment and ability to manage and exploit knowledge (Source: Davison, 2005)

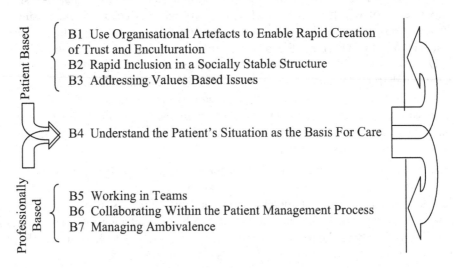

Workforce

Davison and Sloan (2003) identified that as well as being capable of dealing with levels of uncertainty and complexity, the palliative care workforce is required to utilize a number of behaviors; Using Organizational Artifacts to Enable Rapid Creation of Trust and Enculturation; Rapid Inclusion in a Socially Stable Structure; Addressing Values Based Issues; Understanding the Patient's Situation as the Basis for Care; Working in Teams; Collaborating Within the Patient Care Process; and Managing Ambivalence in the Team, while undertaking their discipline-based tasks in multi-disciplinary patient care teams. Successful utilization of these behaviors involved the application of a number of tools in the two different but sometimes overlapping communities, Patient Based and Professional: Trust; Openness; Dialogue; Double Loop Learning; Power Sharing; and Narrative (Davison, 2004).

A palliative care workforce must be able to utilize six organizational capabilities: managing knowledge; managing information; multidisciplinary operations; collaborative operations; managing technology; and managing change on a number of different fronts (Davison & Hyland, 2004). In the management of knowledge, the workforce needs to be able to effectively exploit dynamic career networks and discipline based networks formally and opportunistically. This is required for the creation, exchange, and utilization of knowledge (Cowling, Newman, & Leigh, 1999; Grantham, Nichols, & Schonberner, 1997; Heller, Oros, & Durney-Crowley, 2000). In the management of information, the workforce must be capable of those things mentioned with regard to managing knowledge. As well, given the essential role of information as a foundation of and vehicle for knowledge (Abell, 2000; Berman Brown & Woodland, 1999), the workforce must be able to exploit the diversity available in the palliative care environment as a rich source of information for innovation (Frambach, 1993).

The palliative care workforce must be able to utilize collaboration in four different ways; as an overarching ethos, as a capability available across the organization, as a behavior aimed at generating and transferring knowledge and information, and as a lever to influence behaviors that are situationally focused. The use of common languages at the interfaces between disciplines, between teams, between palliative care professionals and patients, and patient-based careers is also noted as important to the generation and transfer of knowledge and information (Duncker, 2001; Reese & Sontag, 2001). The fragmentation and paradigm conflicts described in the healthcare management literature by authors such as Mintzberg (1997), Oughtibridge (1998), and Newhouse and Mills (1999), would seem to obviate both collaboration and the generation and adaptation of common languages. Yet, if palliative care professionals are not recruited from within the palliative care community they would need to be recruited from the wider community of healthcare workers. The implication here is that, regardless of where palliative care organizations recruit staff; from within their own small community or from healthcare generally, the availability of appropriate workforce is an issue that mediates the delivery of care.

Healthcare Environment

McGrath (1998) makes the point that as hospice services are drawn back into mainstream healthcare services, they become increasingly complex due to increases in standardization and routinization demanded by healthcare funding bodies as they seek to "legitimize" palliative care as part of the mainstream. The result is s perceived and described by the palliative care professionals and volunteers in McGrath's (1998) case study as a diminution of the personalized, person-centered care that traditionally typifies palliative care.

The implication from the palliative care literature is that all disciplines involved in palliative care are expected to always behave collaboratively when necessary and be able to utilize any information and knowledge as required. This requirement appears at odds with the general healthcare management literature. In that, literature authors note the conflict and fragmentation of effort that is based in inter-professional barriers and the ability of discipline-based paradigms to reduce or nullify workforce flexibility and collaboration (Connelly, Knight, Cunningham, Duggan, & McClenahan, 1999; Firth-Cozens, 1999; Mintzberg, 1997; Newhouse & Mills, 1999). Yet the healthcare environment is the source of both patients and most staff for palliative care organizations.

The fragmentation and paradigm conflicts noted in the healthcare management litera-ture by authors such as Mintzberg (1997), Oughtibridge (1998), and Newhouse and Mills (1999) seem to obviate both collaboration and the generation and adaptation of artefacts or management levers such as common languages. The understanding and use of boundary objects as described by Albrechtsen and Jacob (1998) also seems to be limited in this climate. Yet, if palliative care professionals are not recruited from within the palliative care community, they will be recruited from the wider community of healthcare workers.

Change

Change is an important contingency in palliative care, impacting on a number of fronts. The first and obvious, already discussed as occurring inside the organization and a frequent part of palliative care, is change in the patient's situation. In addition, though, palliative care is noted in the literature as undergoing a number of changes being driven by agencies outside palliative care.

Changing demographics and increasing diversity of populations are also providing effects that needed to be managed. According to Witt Sherman (1999), the aging of the population provides changes to the nature and needs of the dying and there is a worldwide change of causes of death from acute conditions to chronic and progres-sive illnesses. Palliative care, while traditionally linked to cancer, has an applica-tion to other types of conditions such as HIV AIDS, end-stage cardiovascular and pulmonary disease and diabetes, diseases that have limited curative treatments. The growing diversity of populations served by palliative care organizations changes the nature and occurrence of illness and disease and requires that the populations of the palliative care professions and of the career networks change to accommodate the diversity in patient populations (Heller et al., 2000).

Managing Knowledge in Multidisciplinary Palliative Care Teams

This section of the chapter is a narrative description of the results of structured and semi-structured interviews carried out in management and workplace teams in the case study organisations.

Staff in the case study organizations are grouped by discipline for administrative purposes and are assigned to multidisciplinary teams that act as pools from which members appear to sometimes self-select for care of a particular patient. Some disci-plines, those in short supply like social work and perhaps physiotherapy, are shared between teams. Patient care teams are then formed from this pool of disciplines as the patient's apparent situation demands. Each patient has two permanent members of the care team—a doctor and a nurse. Apart from these two, membership of the individual patient care team is dependent on the patient's situation. A direct affect of this contingency-based team formulation is that the palliative care professionals belong to multiple patient care teams simultaneously. Some team members may also work at local hospitals and are therefore shared between institutions; becoming cross-institution patient care team members. The opportunity for high frequencies of informal communications exists in the common pooling of patient care team members in a larger group, the ward-team.

The environment for knowledge management in palliative care is one of change and uncertainty. This drives frequent informal communications within and between the multidisciplinary patient care teams. These teams also meet formally on a weekly basis and at these meetings; all patients under the care of all teams are discussed, as are situational changes and expectations of changes. A dedicated amount of time from this meeting is reserved specifically for articulating lessons learnt. However, a large part of knowledge management in palliative care occurs in front of the patient or as a result of changes in the patient's situation. This form of knowledge management, one could call it ad hoc knowledge management, is facilitated by informal communications that occur between team members and between disciplines. Often the progenitor of this informal communication is the common practice of members of disciplines observing across discipline boundaries. This practice is expected and encouraged and is said by members of this case study organization to be one of the things that discriminates work in palliative care from work in acute hospitals, aged care facilities and other parts of the healthcare environment.

Common languages are used between the disciplines to enable the reporting of observations. Informal reporting happens verbally and in written form. The disciplines themselves are used as conduits to access information and experience outside of the case study organization and the palliative care environment if necessary. This is a two-way exchange with the results of experiences within the case study organization being disseminated through the disciplines. In this case study organization, the majority of knowledge management that occurs is socially generated.

Knowledge management frequently occurs in real time, meaning that it frequently occurs without recourse to information management technologies. However, patients' notes are an open source of information, with all disciplines making their entries in the one set of notes so that all other involved disciplines have easy access to the information. Knowledge and information are not characterized or stratified by source. For example, knowledge created with a patient has the same value as knowledge created between multidisciplinary team members. Any source of relevant knowledge is utilized and knowledge creation and dissemination occur wherever and whenever they occur, not requiring specific times or spaces. Knowledge is seen as necessary, valuable, and worthy of resourcing. It is primarily tacit knowledge that is created, used, and managed.

The use of knowledge in response to contingencies generally occurs during the following events, although the occurrence is not necessarily linear. At administration of a new patient, the level of information accompanying the patient can vary greatly depending on where the patient is arriving from. Two interesting aspects of new patients are noted in the case studies; the level of information accompanying a new patient can depend on the personal relationship between palliative care staff and the originating organization; and, at times, patients have arrived not having been informed of the nature of a palliative care organization nor of the reason for their transfer. In most general circumstances, patients and patient-based careers attending or joining the palliative care network for the first time do so with some level of uncertainty about the future, the end of life process and the palliative care process itself. Palliative care staff must work quickly to build trust and include patients and patient-based careers in as stable a social environment as possible. Knowledge is a useful tool for these activities. Apart from the fact that the palliative care network needs to create a level of knowledge about new admissions that can be recorded and discussed, members of the network use knowledge to demonstrate competence and experience. The aim of this is to remove some of the uncertainty about the organization and the end of life process. Simple and fast applications of information can create knowledge with new admissions; explaining the reasons for a particular medication regime and explaining the medications themselves is a common way of doing this. Not only does this offer the patient a level of knowledge frequently not offered in other parts of the healthcare system it demonstrates that the patient will be trusted with information and knowledge. Another approach utilizing the volunteering of information to create knowledge is for palliative care staff to use narrative to indicate to new patients and patient-based careers that there is a discernable difference between palliative care and the general healthcare system and that staff have the experience to empathize with new admissions. These activities sometimes require repeated attempts to be successful and the level of success varies from patient to patient.

Addressing values-based issues is seen as an important enabler of the relief, or addressing, of distress in the end of life process. It is seen as an enabler of self-grieving in patients and patient-based careers. It is dependent on honest communication and all disciplines are involved persistently. The need to address these types of issues is one of the drivers of the informal communications that are used to build knowledge of patients and patient-based careers. Mentioned earlier, these communications often result from disciplines observing across the discipline boundaries and reporting observations as soon as possible. If it is not possible to report verbally then a book is kept for the purpose of recording observations so that the information is not lost. There are many examples of this cross-disciplinary observation; nurses observing or overhearing tensions in families; social workers observing pain that appears medically caused; doctors observing grief that needs counseling. A key word that is repeated in this case study organization, with regard to the frequent use of observations and informal communications is respect. This goes to credibility and this is another stated difference between palliative care teams and teams in other parts of healthcare, according to the team members. The fact that members of disciplines have credibility in other disciplines is an important factor in this ad hoc knowledge creation and management.

The use of trust, establishing the patient in a socially stable environment and the attempt to address values-based issues are preparations for understanding the patient's situation. Each time one of these activities is successfully carried out and knowledge is created, exchanged, and disseminated the team is a step closer to understanding the patient's situation and a step closer to dealing with that situation's inherent uncertainties. The creation of understanding is enabled by the previous activities. It provides direct input to formal and informal information and knowledge creation and management on a patient by patient basis and is utilized by all disciplines. The creation of this understanding can be seen as a collaborative effort that enables the creation of a whole picture that includes the patient and patient-based careers and is offered to them.

Away from the patient, knowledge of how the teams need to operate and what is required for individual patients is applied by team members to team maintenance. This arises as team members are cognizant of the need for optimum relationships within the teams. The fact that team membership is changeable during each patient's end of life experience multiplies both the difficulty and necessity of team maintenance. This maintenance is accomplished formally and informally and team members speak repeatedly of the value of speaking out about difficulties encountered in the teams operations.

Knowledge management in palliative care teams is driven by the contingencies of the operation. It often occurs informally in face-to-face encounters using narrative, dialogue and conversation, as the opportunity arises. It includes the patient and patient-based careers as primary sources and primary targets and can be an opportunistic process.

Future Trends

While the move to technologically-based knowledge management continues to gather pace, it would be difficult to relate this to managing knowledge in palliative care. Anthropocentrically based knowledge generation and dissemination that is contextualized by the situation "now" does not drive a search for certainty, for simplicity, or for predictability; it drives a constant and collective search to understand what is happening "now" in the patient's situation (Davison & Blackman, 2005). This provides a challenge for technologically-based knowledge management systems in that to be useful in this type of environment they must be capable of supporting the spontaneous creation and dissemination of tacit knowledge. In other words, it will not be until technologically based knowledge management systems are capable of supporting a processual perspective of knowledge (Newell, Robertson, Scarborough, & Swan, 2002) that they will be capable of offering advantage in operation to palliative care and other organizations with similar requirements for spontaneous knowledge based responses to the contingencies of the operating environment.

Conclusion

This case study offers a picture of organizations that undertake complex work involving heterogeneous teams of professionals that must maintain and exchange knowledge and information between disciplines in a workplace that demands collaborative effort be applied. Knowledge creation and dissemination can occur spontaneously and is managed collaboratively. These organizations persistently apply their capabilities for managing knowledge and information in multidisciplinary teams and commonly apply collaboration and change management as capabilities in the same teams. Resourcing, structure and capabilities are in place so that the teams are always available, can persistently work at generating trust and understanding a wide range of situational drivers surrounding and impacting each team's focus, the patient, and work collaboratively at these tasks utilizing high frequencies of ad hoc communications across disciplines, and through networks inside and outside the organization, to generate and exchange knowledge and information as a patient's situation changes or change in that situation is anticipated or detected. The purpose of this is to define, package and deliver whatever mix of care types is necessary to address an individual patient's situation. The patient can be a member of this team if so choosing. The mix of delivery style, as well as the mix of care type, can be new or not new as demanded by the patient's situation.

Discussion Questions

1.   What are the key issues regarding knowledge management (KM) in this case study?
2.   Identify the respective people/technology/process aspects of KM in this case study.
3.   What are the major lessons learned from this case study?
4.   What are the unique aspects of KM in this context?
5.   What are the major barriers and facilitators with implementing KM in this context and how might the barriers be addressed?

6.   By mapping the key case issues into Boyd's OODA loop, explain how a process centric KM perspective enables a superior understanding of the critical issues and thus leads to enhanced decision-making?

References

Abell, A. (2000). Skills for knowledge environments. *Information Management Journal, 34*(3), 33-41.

Albrechtsen, H., & Jacob, E. K. (1998). The dynamics of classification systems as boundary objects for cooperation in the electronic library. *Library Trends, 47*(2), 293-312.

Barbato, M. (1999). Palliative care in the 21st century: Sink or swim. *Newsletter of the New South Wales Society of Palliative Medicine*, May.

Berman Brown, R., & Woodland, M. J. (1999). Managing knowledge wisely: A case study in organisational behaviour. *Journal of Applied Management Studies, 8*(2), 175-198.

Connelly, J., Knight, T., Cunningham, C., Duggan, M., & McClenahan, J. (1999). Rethinking public health: New training for new times. *Journal of Management in Medicine, 13*(4), 210-217.

Cowling, A., Newman, K., & Leigh, S. (1999). Developing a competency framework to support training in evidence-based healthcare. *International Journal of Healthcare Quality Assurance, 12*(4), 149-160.

Davison, G. (2004). Managing knowledge on the run: Using temporary communication infrastructures for managing knowledge in the complex, dynamic, and innovative environment of palliative care. In N. Wickramasinghe, J. N. D. Gupta, & S. K. Sharma (Eds.), *Creating knowledge-based health care organizations*. Hershey, PA: Idea Group Publishing.

Davison, G. (2005). *Innovative practice in the process of patient management in palliative care*. Doctoral Thesis, University of Western Sydney

Davison, G., & Blackman, D. (2005). The role of mental models in innovative teams. Refereed journal article, *European Journal of Innovation Management, 8*(4), 409-423.

Davison, G., & Hyland, P. (2003). Palliative care: An environment that promotes continuous improvement. In E. Geisler, K. Krabbendam, & R. Schuring (Eds.), *Technology, healthcare, and management in the hospital of the future*. Westport, CT: Praeger Publishers.

Davison, G., & Sloan, T. (2003). Palliative care teams and individual behaviours. *Team Performance Management Journal, 9*(3), 69-77.

Duncker, E. (2001). Symbolic communication in multidisciplinary cooperations. *Science, Technology, and Human Values*, *26*(3), 349-386.

Firth-Cozens, J. (1999). Clinical governance development needs in health service staff. *British Journal of Clinical Governance*, *4*(4), 128-134.

Frambach, R. T. (1993). An integrated model of organisational adoption and diffusion of innovations. *European Journal of Marketing*, *27*(5), 22-41.

Grantham, C. E., Nichols, L. D., & Schonberner, M. (1997). A framework for the management of intellectual capital in the healthcare industry. *Journal of Healthcare Finance*, *23*(3), 1-19.

Heller, B. R., Oros, M. T., & Durney-Crowley, J. (2000). The future of nursing education: 10 trends to watch. *Nursing & Healthcare Perspectives*, *21*(1), 9-13.

Henkelman, W. J., & Dalinis, P. M. (1998a). A protocol for palliative care measures. *Nursing Management*, *29*(1), 40-46.

Henkelman, W. J., & Dalinis, P. M. (1998b). A protocol for palliative care measures: Part 2. *Nursing Management*, *29*(2), 36C-36G.

Higginson, I. J. (1999). Evidence based palliative care. *British Medical Journal*, *319*(720), 462-463.

Janssens, R. M., Zylizc, Z., Ten Have, H. A. (1999). Articulating the concept of palliative care: Philosophical and theological perspectives. *Journal of Palliative Care*, *15*(2), 38-44.

Kearney, M. (1992). Palliative medicine: Just another speciality? *Palliative Medicine*, *6*, 39-46.

Lewis, M., Pearson, V., Corcoran-Perry, S., & Narayan, S. (1997). Decision-making by elderly patients with cancer and their caregivers. *Cancer Nursing*, *20*(6), 389-397.

Lobchuk, M., & Stymeist, D. (1999). Symptoms as meaningful "family culture" symbols in palliative care. *Journal of Palliative Care*, *15*(4), 24-31.

McCormick, K. M. (2002). A concept analysis of uncertainty in illness. *Journal of Nursing Scholarship*, *34*(2), 127-131.

McDonald, K., & Krauser, J. (1996). Toward the provision of effective palliative care in Ontario. In E. Latimer (Ed.), *Excerpts from OMA colloquium on care of the dying patient.*

McGrath, P. (1998). A spiritual response to the challenge of routinisation: A dialogue of discourses in a Buddhist-initiated hospice. *Qualitative Health Research*, *8*(6), 801-812.

Meyers, J. C. (1997). The pharmacist's role in palliative care and chronic pain management. *Drug Topics*, *141*(1), 98-107.

Mintzberg, H. (1997). Toward healthier hospitals. *Healthcare Management Review*, *22*(4), 9-18.

Newell, S., Robertson, M., Scarborough, H., & Swan, J. (2002). *Managing knowledge work*. Basingstoke: Palgrave.

Newhouse, R. P., & Mills, M. E. (1999). Vertical systems integration. *Journal of Advanced Nursing, 29*(10), 22-29.

Oughtibridge, D. (1998). Under the thumb. *Nursing Management, 4*(8), 22-24.

Pierce, S. (1999). Allowing and assisting patients to die: The perspectives of oncology practitioners. *Journal of Advanced Nursing, 30*(3), 616-622.

Reese, D. J., & Sontag, M. A. (2001). Successful interprofessional collaboration on the hospice team. *Health and Social Work, 26*(3), 167-175.

Rose, K. (1995). Palliative care: The nurse's role. *Nursing Standard, 10*(11), 38-44.

Rose, K. (1999). A qualitative analysis of the information needs of informal careers of terminally ill cancer patients. *Journal of Clinical Nursing, 8*(1), 81-88.

Witt Sherman, D. (1999). Training advanced practice palliative care nurses. *Generations, 23*(1), 97-90.

Case Study 5:[9, 10]
Managing Knowledge in Project-Based Organizations: The Introduction of "Checkboards" at ConstructCo

written by
Jacky Swan, Anna Goussevskaia, and Mike Bresnen
University of Warwick, UK

Introduction

Project-based organizations are a potentially rich arena for the study of knowledge management (KM) because they are closely associated with product or process innovation and, yet, pose particular difficulties for the capture and transfer of knowledge and learning (DeFilippi & Arthur, 1998; Prencipe & Tell, 2001). Not only are there significant task discontinuities from one project to the next, which make the direct application of any "lessons learned" difficult, there are also potentially disruptive effects upon social groups and networks as project teams move on, disband and reform to pursue different projects with different objectives. Consequently, managing and sharing knowledge may be more difficult in project-based firms than in other types of organization. At the same time, KM is perhaps more vital for innovation in project-based organizations to avoid reinvention across projects (Bresnen, Edelman, Newell, Scarbrough, & Swan, 2003; Hansen, 1999, 2002). While there may be a significant amount of learning and innovation within a project (Newell, Robertson, Scarborough, & Swan, 2003), this can be difficult to capture and share across projects (i.e., from one project to another) or between the project and the wider organization (Prencipe & Tell, 2001). This apparent inability of organizations to benefit from project-based knowledge and learning has been described as a tendency to "re-invent the wheel" (Prusak, 1997).

In this case study, we explore how difficulties in managing knowledge in project-based organizations are a consequence, not only of the nature of project-based work itself, but also of the relationship between projects and their organizational context. As existing studies have identified, projects, are relatively autonomous, often sitting outside mainstream organizational structures and control mechanisms (Sahlin-Andersson, 2002). This suggests that the transfer of knowledge and learning generated within projects, either to other projects, or to other parts of the organisation, does not happen either smoothly or directly. There are often few, if any, formal or informal mechanisms through which the learning accumulated from projects can be assimilated as organisational knowledge (Ekstedt, Lundin, Soderholm, & Wirdenius, 1999). Therefore models of organisation learning and knowledge creation that depict learning smooth 'spiral' involving the conversion of knowledge from one type or location to another—for example, tacit to explicit or individual to collective (Nonaka, 1994)—may have limited applicability in project-based firms.

The case outlines an attempt to implement an organization-wide KM initiative in a large construction firm, ConstructCo. As we reveal, the importance of the organizational context suggests that KM in project-based firms needs to be viewed in terms of the relationship between organizational objectives, norms and practices and the norms and practices of particular projects (Bresnen, Goussevskaia, & Swan, 2004; Lindkvist, Soderlund, & Tell, 1998; Scarbrough et al., 2004). Indeed, in this case, misalignments between the interests and objectives of projects and the interests and objectives of the organization as a whole have a major impact on the success (or otherwise) of the KM initiative. The case described next is intended as a rich example of the kinds of complex organizational issues arising when KM is introduced in project-based firms.

The Organizational Context

ConstructCo is a major UK contractor company. The Building Division cuts across the company's three regional offices: Western, Central, and Eastern, the company's Head Office being situated in the Central region. The Building Division contributes a major part (about £160m) of the company's construction business annual turnover of around £360m (the company's total annual turnover was around £500m). The Building Division was formed at the beginning of 2003 and started to function fully as an autonomous unit from May 2005. Before then, each of the three regions had been responsible for both building and civil/process engineering projects. The restructuring of the organisation was intended to separate building from civil/process engineering and thus to integrate activity along product/divisional lines.

Each of the three regions of the Building Division differed in terms of the type of building work carried out. The Central region carries out most of its building work for the retail sector and in warehousing for the transport and distribution sector. Geographically, this region is positioned in a transport nexus (several major roads and rail-lines converge here), thus providing steady demand for this type of construction. As a result, the company implements a high volume of broadly similar projects, involving large project turnover, sizeable margins and low risk type of work. Because projects are fairly routine, performance is considered good and efficient. According to a head office director,

"...it would be foolish if anybody ever made a mistake because we have done so many [projects of this kind] we know how to put them together."

In contrast, Western region operated mostly in the office building sector. However, market saturation in office construction meant that the region had been forced to diversify into other areas (such as retail, industrial, and hotel building). As a result, projects were higher risk and less predictable than in the Central region. This was reflected in poor performance across many projects—some of which were rated by head office as *"of concern"* or even *"to be taken into care,"* according to performance reports.

Finally, Eastern region was also operating in difficult market conditions. General low demand meant that the region was basically taking on any kind of work it could get. Thus, almost all of the ongoing projects carried out in this region involved different types of work. Projects were characterized by low margins and, consequently, higher risk. Project performance in the Eastern region was also considered by senior management to be consistently poor. Table 3 summarizes these differences.

Table 3. Differences across regions

	Central	Western	Eastern
Context	Steady demand	Saturated market, fierce competition	Low demand
	High volume of similar jobs	Refocusing on new market sectors	Low volume one-off jobs
	Highest turnover and margins	Second highest turnover, narrow margins	Low turnover and margins
	Mature business	Mature business	Less mature business
Projects characteristics	Routinized	Moderately similar jobs	Higher degree of novelty
	Low risk	High risk	High risk
	Large project turnover	Medium project turnover	Small to medium project turnover
	Good performance (in terms of safety, quality, errors and delivery on time) consistently across projects	Variable performance from good to very poor across projects, though poor performance predominates	Poor performance consistently across projects

The Change Initiative: "Checkboards"

Scope and Application

Since the restructuring of the group in 2003 and, in the light of the performance problems noted above, attempts had been made to standardize processes and share best practice throughout the company. In particular, while performance problems were commonly acknowledged, it was unclear why projects, even similar projects in the same regions, were performing so differently. Senior management at ConstuctCo recognized, then, that poorly performing projects ought to be able to improve their project management practices by learning lessons from projects that were performing well. However, they also recognized that the information captured from projects was generally quite poor and that communication amongst project managers across regions, and between projects and regional management teams, was, at best, patchy. While management at ConstructCo did not explicitly attach a "knowledge management" label to these problems, essentially managing knowledge (i.e., about "best practice" in project planning and project improvement) across projects within regions, across regions, and between regions and Head Office was seen as the critical problem.

In October 2004, a firm of external consultants—Collate—were employed to carry out an audit in order to assess compliance to company standards and procedures across regions and projects. The audit identified a general lack of mechanisms for sharing knowledge across projects and for transferring best practice relevant to project planning. As a result, a new tool was recommended to improve the sharing of knowledge and information across regions, and between regions and HQ, about how projects were performing, how likely they were to complete on time, where performance problems existed, and how these were being solved. This tool would, it was hoped, enable the transfer of "best practice" project planning systems across the company, thus raising the level of competence (focusing on competence in project planning and project management) across projects in all regions.

The new tool introduced by the company was called "Checkboards." It was designed to enable project managers, and their site teams, to capture good practice and evaluate project performance in ways that were focused on future outcomes, rather than past performance. The major driver for this new initiative was concern about the increasing number of projects that were failing to deliver jobs on schedule and to quality. This would, it was thought, improve the capture and sharing of knowledge and information about project progress and performance, and ultimately enable project managers to anticipate, and deal with, likely future problems on the basis of information available within the tool.

"Checkboards" was developed with the help of Collate and consisted of several steps. First, the project managers, through weekly meetings with their teams, defined project success criteria. Each week, the list of criteria could be updated according to changing circumstances. Project progress was then monitored daily and scored weekly on each of the criteria. At the end of the week, the list of the criteria with their respective scores was to be shared amongst site teams and regional management. The role of regional management was to assess the teams, and provide feedback on their performance, and to ensure that examples of best practice were rolled out to other regions. The performance data were aggregated at regional level and forwarded to the Head Office, where the reports produced by the Checkboards would able to be used to support decision-making and share best practice amongst the regions. Thus, although the original problem had been conceived as a knowledge management one, in effect, the "Checkboards" initiative actually encompassed a number of key objectives: (i) a knowledge management objective (to improve project planning by capturing and sharing knowledge about project progress and performance); (ii) a performance management objective (to monitor and assess project performance); and (iii) a standardization objective (to standardise the project planning process across sites and regions). The conflation of these objectives ultimately proved extremely problematic for the implementation of "Checkboards," as is seen next.

Implementation

The roll out of "Checkboards" across the company began in January 2005. Figure 4 (top half) outlines the major phases and the time line of events associated with the roll out of the initiative. The introduction of the new tool began with a training program, which consisted of one-day workshops conducted by the external consultants for management and project teams over a three-month period. By the end of the training program, and with the strong encouragement of regional management, all project teams across all the regions had started to use "Checkboards." The Head Office began to review progress reports and "lessons learnt" on a weekly basis and give the teams and regional management feedback on the quality of the reports produced. This process carried on for 6 months and was part of what was described as an "educational program," aimed at coaching the teams on how to best use and exploit the information in "Checkboards."

The training program and coaching process had mixed effects. Generally, across the regions, it was felt that the teams received conflicting messages about what to consider as the key criteria to use for the "Checkboards." Whereas during the training programme, the tool was presented as designed to help project managers share best practice and do their job, feedback from Head Office indicated that other priorities—in particular those associated with performance monitoring—were to be reflected in the Checkboards. The disagreements between the project managers and the head office resulting from this ambiguity were eventually worked out through an interactive process comprising a number of, occasionally heated, meetings. However, this interaction with Head Office occurred differently across the regions and, therefore, had varying degrees of success across the teams. As one of the managers from the Head Office commented:

"While we were doing it, the feedback we were giving [the East] was not as good quality. The feedback we gave [the Western region] and [the Central region] was face to face every week. One of us would actually sit them down and say, why haven't you done this? Why that? And [we would] really have a debate about it."

In particular, the amount of attention received by the Eastern region reflected its low profile compared to other regions, as there were only a few projects going on in the

Figure 4. Time line of issues and events

	Jan 2005	Feb 2005	Mar 2005	Apr 2005	May 2005	Jun 2005	Jul 2005	Aug 2005	Sep 2005	Oct 2005	Nov 2005	Dec 2005	Jan 2006	Feb 2006	Mar 2006
Introduction of new management tool	▲														
Training programme	●——→														
Team report weekly to the head office			●————————→												
Weekly feedback from the head office			●————————→												
No commitment from the Eastern region	●- - - - - - - - - - - -→														
Repeated training in the Eastern region							●→								
Stop weekly feedback from the head office									▲						
Ownership of the tool attributed to the regions									▲						
Instances of the misuse of the tool									●- - - - - - - - - - - -→						
Problems in the Western region									●- - - - -→						
Renewed feedback in the Western region									●→						
Revision and simplification of the tool													●——→		
Sample of the Checkboards progress reports (managers' comments on the quality of the Checkboards produced)															
Central region	OK			OK			OK			OK			OK		
Western region	progress			improvement			no improvement			improvement			satisfactory		
Eastern region	no commitment			no commitment			poor quality			improvement			improvement		

Legend: ▲ decision taken; ●——→ action taken; ●- - - -→ issue arising during the period

East at the time. This poor feedback contributed to an increasing lack of commitment in the Eastern region to the new tool. As one project manager commented:

"[Feedback] was always done as [if] the Checkboard was not good enough. Not: how have you put your Checkboard together? Why have you put that in there? Or this is what you should be using it for. It was just: your Checkboard is not good enough."

And according to another project manager:

"I would get a call back on Monday afternoon: change it to this because it did not suit who was looking at it. That was when I lost heart in it. Because I thought it was important for my job [...] I just started thinking: hang on, it is just another reporting tool here. It is not really a knowledge management tool for day to day use; it is just another reporting tool."

By May 2002, it was recognized that the Eastern region was not going to succeed on the "Checkboards" without additional involvement from Head Office. Figure 1 (bottom half) illustrates an example of the kinds of reports on the quality of the "Checkboards" produced by Head Office. These reports indicated "no commitment" to the "Checkboards" from the Eastern region during the first 6-month period. As a result, Head Office decided to repeat the training program in the region.

The aim of the initial coaching program was to embed the new knowledge management tool within project teams across the company. At the end of the 6-month period, it appeared that the quality of the "Checkboards" produced by the regions had, in fact, reached satisfactory levels. The decision was then made to transfer the ownership and responsibility for the analysis of the "Checkboards" to the regions. Regional Managers" remit was to encourage project managers within their regions to share information relevant to project planning via the "Checkboards." This meant that project teams would no longer receive feedback from Head Office concerning their performance on the "Checkboards" and the quality of the actual "Checkboards" produced. Rather, the focus would be on actually using to share project planning ideas, progress, and best practice. However, at this point, soon after the completion of the coaching programme, some instances of the misuse of the "Checkboards" were identified by regional management. In some projects, it appeared, there was a mismatch between the performance reported on the "Checkboards" and actual performance of projects, which was measured according to financial targets and program for completion of scheduled work to target. The Operations Director recalled:

"Where people were applying the tool meaningfully they would set the key objectives and do it sensibly. And, if they missed them, they would score [that] they had missed it and they would reset the date. But for some of the teams getting a good score became more important than actually moving the job on. So they would set soft targets and then achieve them or if they did not achieve something they might

actually even say they had achieved it and were going to do it a day or two after-
wards. So the scores became...a game. So people were trying to look good with
the scores."

Thus, instead of capturing and sharing information about project progress, some
teams were treating "Checkboards" as a "scoring game"—a way of showing you
had outscored and outperformed other teams. These instances occurred across all
three regions. In other words, the performance monitoring and evaluation objectives
had overshadowed attention by project teams to the knowledge management objectives of the tool. In the light of these problems, Head Office restarted the feedback
process, but only for those teams that were seen as "problematic." This reaction of
head office resulted in, what was interpreted by some project managers as "heavy
interference" with their use of the "Checkboards." The attempts of Head Office to
overcome the effects of the scoring game, by putting more effort into the feedback
process, caused further resistance among some of the project teams. One project
manager from the Western region recalled:

"I have never had a real problem with the Checkboards—apart from...if you go
back to September/October of last year when there was what I would describe as
very heavy interference from Head Office as to what we should be doing on the
Checkboards. And, to be quite honest, I lost interest in the Checkboards for four
to five weeks."

In an attempt to improve the situation, head office intensified the support given to
the Western region for a period of time by trying to persuade the project managers
to use the tool accordingly to their recommendations. However, by now, resistance
of the teams to the (what was now perceived as) scoring system (that made them
"look bad") was so great across all regions that Head Office decided to exclude
the scorings altogether. From now on, performance on the project success criteria
would no longer be rated using a scoring system. The new approach would be to
use a color-coded scheme (green, amber, and red) to indicate progress made (good,
moderate, bad), coupled with the capture of ideas about how this progress was being made.

Outcomes

This case reported here covers a period of 18 months from the first introduction of
the "Checkboards" tool across the company. A number of projects were using the
tool at the end of this period and it was possible for the teams across the regions to
share and evaluate ideas regarding the contribution of the particular management

practices to project performance. The overall perception from project and regional managers the Western and Central regions was that the "Checkboards" had actually helped them to change project management practices for the better. The managers in these regions more readily recognized and accepted the benefits of the new tool. In contrast, in the Eastern region opinions remain ambivalent. One regional manager suggested:

"I think the sites have not seen the benefits yet. I don't think they see what it is doing."

Another manager in the same region explained:

"I think there is still a misunderstanding about what it is about. [...] There are still a lot of guys who are operating at too low a level. They are still using it as just a glorified action list."

Moreover, while knowledge sharing within regions was improved, at least within some regions, here was no evidence of significant interaction among the project managers across the regions. Usually, the project managers had only a very general idea about what was going on in the other regions in respect to the "Checkboards." This certainly reflected in the particular ways, in which the initiative was implemented and embedded in each of the regions.

Some project teams embraced the "Checkboards" initiative more readily than others. Variations in project managers' interpretations of the objectives of the KM initiative resulted in variations in deployment of the Checkboards tool, with some teams using scoring game. These variations were attributed, in part, to differences in the communication mechanisms used to support the introduction of the KM tool. Given the hierarchical power of Head Office over the regions, a crucial part of the communication process was the feedback to regions from Head Office. While Central and Western regions received face to face, intensive feedback, the Eastern region received much less attention. Moreover, given the Eastern region had been experiencing poorer performance, managers in this region were more likely to be both sensitive to, and defensive about, any initiative that could be seen as performance monitoring. These conditions led to a lack of understanding, and cynicism, regarding the espoused KM objectives of the tool, especially in the Eastern region. As one project manager in the Eastern region reported,

"I have never once had any feedback on what happens with the Checkboard information after I send it. We never know what it is used for."

Another important issue related to implementation was the support of regional management. Eastern region lacked the support and, most importantly, legitimization of the new tool by the regional management. The particular context in this region was manifested in negative attitudes toward the KM initiative amongst regional managers—attitudes that percolated down to the project teams. These issues are outlined further next.

Major Issues Concerning Implementation of KM

Regional Differences

The problems experienced in ConstructCo need to be understood in relation to the wider organisational context. Prior to the restructuring of the firm, the Eastern region had enjoyed the status of being the most independent part of the business with, what had been generally considered, to be the strongest management team. However, power relations changed with the restructuring of the group. As the operations director described:

"Now over the years we have broken down [regional] barriers but, in the East, it was more predominant than anywhere else."

The process of "breaking down barriers" involved reforming the regional management team in the east. In this region, of the three directors, two had joined Constructo after the restructuring and, so, were open to changes. A third, who had been with the company for several years, left following the introduction of the "Checkboards." According to Head Office, the removal of that individual was "necessary" for the region to embrace the changes. The person who took over had been with the company prior to the restructuring but was more open to changes, according to the operations director.

Another important feature of the organisational context concerned the nature of the projects undertaken across the regions (Table 3). Project teams that performed more routinized type of work (primarily in the Central and Western regions) tended to have fewer problems adjusting to the new standards and produced better quality information on "Checkboards" than teams (primarily in the Eastern region) that were undertaking more varied and novel types of work. The Central region, for example, had very few problems in applying the KM tool because, due to the repeat and predictable nature of projects, their criteria for success were well established "a priori" and, so, good practice was easy to capture. Western region performed more variable and less predictable types of project and this may have had some bearing on the problems reported here in the application of the tool. However, the major problems were experienced in the Eastern region. Here, project teams had to perform a wide variety of tasks and managers had difficulties adapting the "Checkboards" template to capture good practice for each new project. As one project manager reported,

"For instance, the job that I did [on the previous project] we had maybe 10 sub-contractors on it—quite straightforward job. Steel frame, ten or twelve subcontrac-tors, really basic and straightforward. Financially it was straightforward. It was a four-phase contract that we had done with the client, so financially it was quite straightforward. There was very little difficult detail in it where I am now we have got, I think, 75 subcontractors, [...] We have got a client that likes us and an archi-tect that hates us—a very difficult, strained relationship with the architect. A client who has not got a lot of money, so we are having to manage their budget and make sure they don't go off spending money they have not got. So, we have got completely different scenario on this site than we had on [the previous project]. So, different things are important on this site...And to try and convey that on the Checkboards for the [previous project] may have been easily [done], for all the salient points for the next five weeks, on one page. If I tried to do it for where I am now, it would run for pages and pages and pages."

This issue highlights a fundamental paradox associated with the use of formalized IT systems (such as "Checkboards") for KM. This paradox is that where teams have to deal with high uncertainty, novel tasks and problems (e.g., in the Eastern region), they arguably have the most to gain from sharing knowledge with, and acquiring knowledge from, other project teams that have encountered those problems. How-ever, precisely because of the highly varied, ambiguous, localized, and often tacit, nature of the knowledge involved, this is harder to capture in IT systems. In contrast, where projects are routine (e.g., in the Central region), knowledge relating to best practice is already well articulated and, therefore, easier to capture in IT systems. However, here, project managers have less to gain from KM initiatives because they already know much of what they need to know.

Alignment of the KM Initiative with the Existing Project Management Practices

Apart from the type of project and organisational context, the particular practices used by individual project managers also seemed to influence acceptance of the KM tool. Thus, a greater degree of resistance was observed in projects where individual project managers existing management practices were mismatched with the new procedures introduced by the tool. Common comments from the project managers included:

"We have got our contract programme. We have got at the moment a 6-week pro-gramme, we also have 2-week programme. For the actual production out on site those are good tools to manage that, for me. On that I have got indicated all the subcontractor notices that I have got and all that sort of stuff. So, what I need to know is all covered on there anyway. I don't see why I need another tool to do that."

As a consequence, in these instances little value was attributed to the new KM initiative, reducing it to a mere duplication of activities. As one project manager mentioned:

"... [it was] another reporting tool, another piece of paper coming in."

On the other hand, in projects where existing management practices were similar to the ones introduced by the "Checkboards," the benefits of the new tool were more readily recognised. Another project manager reported:

"It is just something that I feel has been with me for a long time. [...] Initially we were just doing weekly reporting. I would produce a report at the end of a week on a Friday and send it off to my MD. And that was fairly informal, albeit quite useful. Then we had what we used to call one and 5-week look ahead programmes. [...] And that worked very well for sharing ideas and it meant that when Checkboards literally came in and replaced these one and five week look ahead programmes I think I was better placed than most to be able to understand what was trying to be achieved. I have never had a real problem with the Checkboards."

According to regional managers, "good" project managers (those that they considered able to deliver projects on time and with acceptable margins) were also more resistant to using "Checkboards." This presented a dilemma, as Head Office had expected that "good" project managers would embrace the initiative more easily, because "they were doing it anyway." Hence, although the initiative was intended to achieve the transfer of "best practice" in project management across the company, those "good" managers that were actually delivering good practices were reluctant to use the tool, possibly because they felt they had little to gain.

In the case of "poor" performing managers, these teams scored poorly on the quality of their "Checkboards" reports and were more reluctant to accept the new processes. In these teams, capturing information about what they were doing, and what effects this had, and sharing this with others meant exposing weaknesses. As the senior commercial manager recalled:

*"When I saw the Checkboards and started going to this region, the first three jobs
I went to I was horrified. I could not believe how bad it could be."*

A final issue influencing the introduction of this KM initiative was the project life
cycle. Regional management observed that the quality of the information captured
in "Checkboards" by project teams deteriorated toward the end of the project life
cycle. The intensification of activities toward the end of a project meant that immediate priorities (hitting targets) tended to take over. Hence, at the end of projects,
where teams actually had more knowledge about what had worked and what had
not worked, they were less likely to share this via "Checkboards" due to increased
pressures on their time. Although end of project reviews were also conducted, these
were often delayed until some time after projects were completed, by which time
team members had either moved onto other projects or could not remember the
precise details around how they had solved problems.

Quite apart from the specific characteristics of their projects, the introduction of
the KM tool created tensions between the autonomy that project managers felt they
should have and the control that the tool was seen to represent. Project managers
appreciated the autonomy they were, as one project manager in the Eastern region
reported:

*"Me and all the other guys are responsible for everything on the site. The money, the
programme, quality, and safety and everything is down to the guys on the field."*

In many instances, however, the way in which the "Checkboards" were introduced
resulted in a perception that they were being used for purposes of control from head
office, rather than KM. According to a project manager in the Eastern region:

*"And that is when the Checkboards started to get really unwieldy. That is when it
started to get too complicated. So what tended to happen was that you had something that you knew was going to take you a long time to sort out [...] It was going
to look on your dashboard as if you had not sorted something out. So, you don't put
it on. It is just a waste of time, isn't it? [...] All that would happen was that people
would ring me up and say, "hey you have not sorted this out."[...] I was getting a
lot of grief from above saying you have not sorted this out yet, sort it out. I didn't
like this kind of transparency."*

This issue emerged strongly when project managers and Head Office management
disagreed about the criteria to use in the tool. Criteria that were seen as useful by
project managers might not be accepted by Head Office, because they were too de-

tailed and lacked a commercial perspective. The scoring system, introduced by Head Office (so it was claimed) to ensure that the information recorded in Checkboards was useful and relevant, was widely interpreted by project managers as reflecting lack of trust by Head Office. A project manager in the Western region commented:

"Although sometimes the level of control from the top is too much, Checkboards are great. It is when they try to interfere in how we put our Checkboards together. That is my biggest criticism."

Social Networks of Project Managers

Where "Checkboards" were successful as a KM tool, this relied heavily on formal and informal social networks amongst project managers. For example, the Western and Central regions held regular monthly, face-to-face, meetings among project managers, where issues related to the tool could be discussed. In contrast, project managers in the Eastern Region did not interact on a regular basis and, so, had little opportunity to see how the tool was used by other managers in the region. One project manager recalled,

"I have only ever seen other people's Checkboards by default when I had an e-mail that came to me that should not have. That is the only time I have seen anybody else's [Checkboards]. I got an e-mail from somebody who forwarded something instead of just sending it. And I got to see all the other sites and that is when I realised that the one [dashboard] I was doing was so totally different from what other people were doing."

In the case of the Western region, social networks also helped mobilise a collective response to the attempts of Head Office to interfere with the way the "Checkboards" were produced. Such a reaction eventually led to changes to the tool (elimination of the scoring system). In the eastern region, there were no established mechanisms for social interaction between project managers. The isolated resistance of the project managers did not lead to any concessions on the part of Head Office as to how information should be captured in "Checkboards." There was informal exchange of information among the project managers, but the patchy nature of this, merely served to convey a general feeling of dissatisfaction, interpreted as resistance by Head Office.

Conclusion

The ConstructCo case highlights that the problems incurred when the introduction of KM initiatives, and associated tools, conflate multiple, sometime competing, objectives (in this case, KM objectives, performance management objectives and standardisation objectives). In the context of project-based organisations, project teams work, very often, with significant autonomy in terms of how to plan their day to day operations, but with al, tight targets and deadlines, where the margins of error are extremely small (Lindkvist et al., 1998; Scarbrough et al., 2004). In such circumstances, as our case demonstrates, it is all too easy for KM to be perceived as an additional, peripheral administrative task rather than as a core operational activity—a perception that lowers commitment to KM and/or turns it into a "scoring game." For example, Keegan and Turner (2001) studied 18 project-based companies and found that all had "post-project review" practices in place and that a core aim of these reviews was to transfer knowledge and learning across projects. However, they also reported that *"In no single company did respondents express satisfaction with the process"* (p. 90). These authors highlighted the main problem as a lack of time, the implication being that, unless KM is viewed as a core operational activity (in the same way that project management is viewed as core), then it will not be prioritized, and its effects are likely to be limited.

Our case also suggests, however, that it is not simply time available that limits commitment to KM but also that the medium for KM is crucial. For example, project review practices (in this case, "Checkboards") often hinge upon the deployment of IT-based databases and/or intranets. Yet, research in KM suggests that while IT-based tools might facilitate knowledge sharing to some degree, they will only do so if supported by the development of social ties and networks, common interests (e.g., problem driven) among users, appropriate incentives, and a supportive organizational culture (e.g., Walsham, 2002).

In project-based firms, in particular, KM tools, where used, tend to focus on recording information on the content of the project and its deliverables (e.g., what the goals were, what was delivered, when key milestones or performance targets were met). In contrast, information about the processes used to achieve project outcomes and resolve any problems on the way tend not to be recorded in the databases (Newell et al., 2003). As seen in our case study, this emphasis on capturing content, as compared to capturing process, further confuses performance management objectives with KM objectives. For example, a reasonable KM objective might be to learn, not what, but *why* project successes and failures occurred, but this information is unlikely to be captured in a database where the information is also being used for performance monitoring or management (Williams, Ackermann, Eden, & Howick, 2005). Moreover, in project-based firms, each project tends to be seen by its members as unique, or novel, in terms of its content and deliverables. This means that, even though there may be valuable generic lessons to share regarding project and project management processes, the relevance of information about the content of the project per se is likely to be limited (or at least perceived as limited) from one project to the next (Newell et al., 2003).

Finally, our case suggests that, in project-based environments, managers' career progression, and the extent to which they are seen by others in the organisation as "good" managers, depends crucially on successful completion of their own particular projects. In other words, the edict in such organizations is that "you are only as good as your last project" (Robertson & Swan, 2003). This is, perhaps, another reason why it is so difficult to share knowledge across projects, as it is the project, and not the organisation, that is the major priority for project managers (Love, Fong, & Irani, 2005). In our case, for example, managers' interests and priorities were oriented mainly to their projects, rather than to the organization as a whole. At the same time the Central Head Office had limited power over regional managers, and individual project managers had significant autonomy over the particular practices they chose, or not, to deploy. Project practices, priorities and interests, therefore, did not align particularly well with organisational practices, priorities, and interests (Lindkvist et al., 1998). In such contexts, it is not surprising, then, that KM objectives have a tendency easily to become subsumed by project performance objectives.

This case has aimed, then, to highlight the issues and problems around sharing knowledge and introducing KM initiatives in project based environments. Of course, some of these problems also occur in other kinds of organization. However, in project-based organizations, the relative autonomy and localized nature of project work can make it even more difficult to introduce initiatives, such as KM, that are scoped in terms of their benefits to the organization rather than to the project. More specifically, our case illustrates the problems associated with the introduction of KM initiatives that: (1) conflate KM objectives with other management objectives (e.g., for performance monitoring and standardization); (2) fail to account for the nature of project work and, in particular, varied nature of localized tasks, management practices, and likely management responses, across the organization and; (3) rely overly on IT-based tools without attending, concurrently, to the development of social networks and incentives required to support the introduction of such tools. Such issues are particularly acute in project-based organizations and need close attention in the design of KM.

Discussion Questions

1. What are the key issues regarding knowledge management (KM) in this case study?
2. Identify the respective people/technology/process aspects of KM in this case study.
3. How can better goal alignment be achieved between regions?

4.   How can the social networks be used to enhance and support more effective KM creation, use, and sharing?

5.   What are the major lessons learned from this case study?

6.   By mapping the key elements of this case study to Boyd's OODA loop, identify why a process centric KM perspective is so essential?

7.   What are the major barriers and facilitators that impinge on successful KM initiatives in this context and how might these be addressed?

References

Bresnen, M., Edelman, L., Newell, S., Scarbrough, H., & Swan, J. (2003). Social practices and the management of knowledge in project environments. *International Journal of Project Management, 21*(3), 157-166.

Bresnen, M., Goussevskaia, A., & Swan, J. (2004). Embedding new management knowledge in project-based organisations. *Organisation Studies, 25*(9), 1535-55.

DeFilippi, R., & Arthur, M. (1998). Paradox in project-based enterprises: The case of filmmaking. *California Management Review, 40*(2), 125-40.

Ekstedt, E., Lundin, R. A., Soderholm, A., & Wirdenius, H. (1999). *Neo-institutional organizing: Renewal by action and knowledge in a project-intensive economy.* London: Routledge.

Hansen, M. T. (1999). The search transfer problem: the role of weak ties in sharing knowledge across organisational sub-units. *Administrative Science Quarterly, 44,* 82-111.

Hansen, M. T. (2002). Knowledge networks: Explaining effective knowledge sharing in multiunit companies. *Organisation Science, 13*(3), 232-48.

Keegan, A., & Turner, R. (2001). Quantity versus quality in project-based learning practices. *Management Learning, 32*(1), 77-98.

Lindkvist, L., Soderlund, J., & Tell, F. (1998). Managing product development projects: On the significance of fountains and deadlines. *Organisation Studies, 19*(6), 931-51.

Love, P., Fong, P., & Irani, Z. (2005). *Management of knowledge in project environments.* Amsterdam: Elsevier.

Newell, S., Edelman, L., Scarbrough, H., Swan, J., & Bresnen, M. (2003) "Best practice" development and transfer in the NHS: The importance of process as well as product knowledge. *Journal of Health Services Management, 16,* 1-12

Prencipe, A., & Tell, F. (2001). Inter-project learning: processes and outcomes of knowledge codification in project-based firms. *Research Policy, 30*, 1373-94.

Prusak, L. (1997). *Knowledge in organisations.* Oxford: Butterworth-Heinemann.

Robertson, M., Swan, J., & Scarbrough, H. (2003). Knowledge creation in professional firms: Institutional effects. *Organisation Studies, 24*(6), 831-857.

Sahlin-Andersson, K. (2002). Project management as boundary work. In K. Sahlin-Andersson & A. Soderholm (Eds.), *Beyond project management: New perspectives on the temporary-permanent dilemma* (pp. 241-260). Copenhagen: Copenhagen Business School Press.

Scarbrough, H., Swan, J., Laurent, S., Bresnen, M., Edelman, L., & Newell, S. (2004). Project-based learning and the role of learning boundaries. *Organisation Studies, 25*(9), 1579-1600.

Walsham, G. (2002). What can knowledge management systems deliver? *Management Communication Quarterly, 16*(2), 267-273.

Williams, T., Ackermann, F., Eden, C., & Howick, S. (2005). Learning from project failure. In P. Love, P. Fong, & Z. Irani (Eds.), *Management of knowledge in project environments.* Amsterdam: Elsevier.

Case Study 6[11]:
Knowledge Management in Practice: A Case Study in the Semiconductor Industry

written by
Brian Donnellan, Martin Hughes, and William Golden
National University of Ireland, Ireland

Abstract

Companies are constantly trying to establish and improve their competitive advantage in the market place. Many of them do this by differentiating themselves from their competitors through the products or services that they provide. In recent years, companies have been focusing on the knowledge of their employees as a key resource in the development of those products or services. The term "knowledge management" has come to be associated with efforts to harness the knowledge of employees for sustainable competitive advantage. Although the topic is maturing as a research specialization, there is scope for further empirical analysis to be done. This research was concerned with the development and implementation of a knowledge management initiative as part of an enterprise-level business process framework for New Product Development (NPD). The organizational context for this study was an NPD organization comprised of 430 staff members based in Ireland. The research method adopted for the work was action research (AR) and this paper describes the activities involved in the first cycle of a multi-cycle AR research project.

Introduction

The motivation for this study lay in the recognition that, on one hand, the role of knowledge management in supporting new product development (NPD) is an area that is of critical importance in today's competitive environment. On the other hand, there is a dearth of published empirical research in this area. The organizational context for the study is a new product development group based in Ireland and is part of a larger multi-national corporation. The corporation is a world leader in the design, manufacture, and marketing of high-performance analog, mixed-signal and digital signal processing integrated circuits (ICs) used in signal processing applications. Founded in 1965, it employs approximately 9,000 people worldwide. Its business is characterized by a high percentage of proprietary products with long design-in product life cycles, designed by very scarce engineering talent. Because of the knowledge-intensive nature of the development process barriers to market entry are extremely strong. The foundation of the company's success has been the research and development of new products, with a range of products being sold to thousands of customers in many different horizontal markets.

The purpose of the study was to analyze a knowledge management project in a multinational electronic design company using a method of inquiry based on action research. The project resulted in the creation of a knowledge management process for new product development and the introduction of information systems to support knowledge management. It was hoped that the research would increase our understanding of how to develop and implement knowledge management systems for new product development organisations.

A research method that has proven useful when research needs to be closely aligned with practice is action research (AR). Typically, an AR project is a highly participative activity where researchers and practitioners focus on a real business project or problem as a starting point. Thus, all the associated risk and unpredictability of a real organizational situation is factored in from the outset. The AR method recognizes that a research project should result in two outcomes, namely an *action* outcome and a *research* outcome. Taking each in turn: firstly, the action outcome is the practical learning in the research situation. Thus, a very important aspect of the research is the extent to which the organization benefits in addressing its original problem.

This serves to ensure the research output is relevant and applicable to practice. Secondly, the research outcome is very much concerned with the implications for the advancement of theoretical knowledge resulting from the project.

Action research was chosen as the research method of choice for this research and a framework for research methods devised by Braa and Vidgen as a mechanism for exploring possible research methods was a reference point for the choice of action research (Braa & Vidgen, 2000). The conceptual framework for the research design is based on two key elements: (a) an iterative participatory action research cycle based on work by Susman and Evered (1978) and (b) an action research operational model with five model parameters (paradigm, purpose, participants, process, and product) that was based on a contribution by Oates and Fitzgerald (2001).

Knowledge Management and New Product Development

Prior research has categorized some of the types of knowledge required by NPD processes. Table 4 lists the main contributors and their categorization of NPD knowledge types.

These types of knowledge are used in so-called "stage-gate" NPD processes (Cooper, 1994). A stage-gate process is a conceptual and operational road map for moving a new-product project from idea to launch. What differentiates stage-gate NPD processes from other NPD processes is that decision-making events follow each stage. Gates are meetings where the project undergoes a thorough examination and after which executive management decides whether to incur more R&D expense in the project or not. Product development teams complete a prescribed set of related cross-functional tasks in each stage before obtaining management approval to proceed to the next stage of product development. The gates represent control points where

Table 4. Knowledge needed in NPD processes

Researcher	NPD Knowledge Type
(Eder, 1989)	Prescriptive (know-how), Descriptive (know-that).
(Markus, 2001)	Shared work producers, shared work practitioners, expertise-seeking novices; knowledge producers.
(Nonaka, 1991)	Explicit and Tacit with four knowledge conversion processes: socialization, externalisation, combination and internalization.
(Orlikowski, 2000)	Knowing the organization, knowing the players in the game, knowing how to coordinate across time and space, knowing how to develop capabilities, knowing how to innovate.
(Rodgers & Clarkson, 1998)	Tacit, explicit, operative, substantive, heuristic, algorithmic, deep, shallow.
(Ullman, 1992)	Pre-project, product, and process design, manufacturing.

Figure 5. NPD stage-gate process

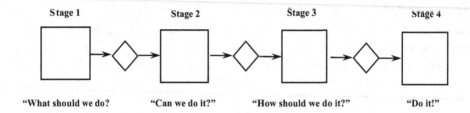

teams' plans are repeatedly re-assessed in the light of the additional information that emerges during the life cycle of the project. Researchers who have recognized that different phases of the NPD process may demand different KMS requirements include Adler, Mandelbaum et al., (1996), Scott (1996), and Yang and Yu (2002). The diagram in Figure 5 describes a typical NPD stage-gate process and indicates the critical decisions made at the different stages.

NPD processes provide challenges to knowledge management initiatives that attempt to capture and re-use knowledge that is created during the NPD process;

- In general, NPD processes have short product and process life cycles, which compress the available time window for recouping the expenses associated with product development. This places a premium on the ability to effectively capture knowledge created during the process so that it can be re-used in the next generation of products to reduce development time.

- Many current NPD projects involve cross-functional collaboration. For example, product development teams may span several geographical locations. This type of "virtual team" activity requires the merging of knowledge from diverse disciplinary and personal skills-based perspectives. The efficient management of virtual NPD teams provide significant knowledge management challenges. These challenges range from the "hard" technological barriers (networking, d/bases, intranets...) to "softer" challenges (cross-cultural issues).

- Cross-institutional collaboration is also becoming quite common in NPD processes. The need for this type of collaboration arises when organizations seek to collaborate with sources of knowledge, which are external to it. In such cases knowledge has to be combined from participants across multiple collaborating organizations.

- NPD teams are staffed with people who may possess much sought-after skills and expertise. Consequently, there can be high turnover rates in NPD organisations, as firms compete for staff with highly rated R&D experience. The resulting transient existence of teams results in a reduction in organisational knowledge. This can be mitigated by creating a repository for knowledge rather than a dependence on knowledge workers.

Ramesh and Tiwana (1999), and Macintosh (1997) have identified the detrimental effects of poor knowledge management on NPD organisation performance. Their research concludes that sub-optimum knowledge management in NPD teams can lead to situations where highly-paid workers spend too much time looking for needed information because essential know-how is available only in the hands of a few employees or else is buried in piles of documents and data. In addition, costly NPD errors are repeated due to disregard of previous experiences. Generally, there is an over-reliance on transmitting explicit rather than tacit design knowledge, leading to a lack of shared understanding and constant re-invention of solutions during product evolution. Skills that are developed due to collaboration may be lost after project completion because of an inability to transfer existing knowledge into other parts of the organisation. The end result is a gradual loss of tacit knowledge to the firm.

Some empirical work has been done on analyzing knowledge management in new product development processes. Anderson et al. (1993) look at the design activity in Rank Xerox and illustrate how collaborative, inter-actional, and organizational ordering are not addressed by the information technology infrastructure in the Design Dept. at Rank Xerox (Anderson et al., 1993). Adler et al. argue for a process-oriented approach to new product development and use a case study of a fictitious company, which represented a composite of a number of companies studied by Adler (1996). They claim that the process-oriented approach, which had cross-functional teams as a central element, led to the creation of best practice templates, which in turn led to greater efficiencies in product development. van de Ven and Polley empirically demonstrate how the early stages of product development projects can be accounted for by using principles drawn from chaos theory providing potential future insight into the front end of new product development efforts that traditionally have proven elusive (van de Ven & Polley 1992).

Peer Reviews as "Knowledge Events" in NPD Stage-Gate Processes

Each of the "gates" in an NPD process represents a peer review with a project "go" or "no go" outcome. Since the majority of costs are incurred in the latter stages of a project, and since companies do not want to "spend good money on a bad idea," the process should include a pause for reviewing all learning after each stage. The outcome of each gate is a critical decision to either continue or abort the process. This critical decision is illustrated in Figure 6.

Bergquist et al. (2001) draw attention to the potential offered by peer reviews as a mechanism for knowledge dissemination. In particular, they conclude from their

Figure 6. Decisions in a stage gate process (Adapted from Shake, 1999)

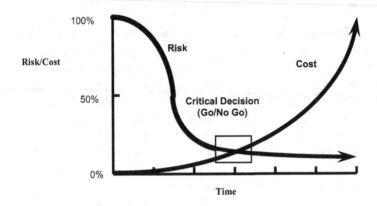

analysis of peer reviews in a pharmaceutical company, that the reviews "play an important coordination role in workers' daily knowledge activities." Furthermore, the collaborative effort involved in peer reviews has the effect of legitimizing new knowledge by "organizationally sanctioning it and thereby creating a platform for collective sense-making."

Previous researchers have applied process-oriented techniques to model KM initiatives in terms of four processes: creation, storage, distribution, and application. Nonaka (1991) proposes a comprehensive model that considers the *knowledge creation* process. Leonard-Barton (1995) proposes a detailed model that focuses on the *knowledge application* process. Other researchers have discussed certain specific aspects of *knowledge transfer* (e.g., Badaracco, 1991; Itami, 1987; Wikstrom & Normann, 1994). Other researchers have taken a broader perspective on KM and attempted to develop frameworks that describe the more general operating environment in which firms find themselves--and in particular, how knowledge could be managed in that competitive context (Davenport & Prusak, 1997). These models provide macro-level frameworks that can be used to aid in the management of knowledge management initiatives but lack the specificity of the process models. However, each model tends to study the impact of knowledge on organizations with different methods and at different levels of analysis and none of the models provide an adequate description of the full scope of KM phenomena.

The Research Method

Qualitative research using an interpretative paradigm is especially appropriate for research in knowledge management because a central concern of the research is the uncovering of facts in the everyday life of the individuals in the community under study. The uncovering of these facts will enable greater understand of the knowledge sharing behavior process. In addition, a better understanding of those needs will lead us to understand the role of knowledge management in the new product development cycle (Wilson, 2000).

The research design and execution is dependent on the researcher's conceptualization of the research problem. In this case, the management of knowledge to support new product development processes is perceived as a social process and the research sets out to understand it in practice from the participants' perspectives. This, therefore, implies the use of an interpretative research paradigm in which the world as seen as being socially constructed and subjective, and can therefore only be interpreted.

Action Research Frameworks

There is a large body of literature associated with the different approaches to action research. Whyte proposed the "professional expert" model of action research where an external professional expert plays a leadership role in driving an action research project (Whyte, 1991). The approach is similar to what is termed "diagnostic" (Chein et al., 1948). Susman and Evered (1978) stress the importance of the cyclical, iterative nature of action research. The intent is that, as the number of action research studies carried out on a topic grows, the resulting descriptive models can be integrated into more general and predictive models, and eventually lead to "grand theories" (Strauss & Evered, 1978). This is depicted in Figure 7 where the rectangles in the cycles represent each of the action research cycles where: "di"

Figure 7. Iterative action research (Adapted from Kock et al., 1997)

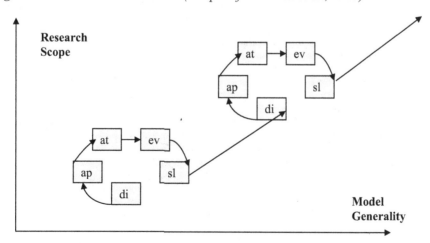

represents diagnosis, "ap" represents action planning, "at" represents action taking, "ev" represents evaluating and "sl" represents specifying learning.

Participatory Action Research (PAR)

PAR was initially formulated by Whyte and was primarily concerned with the alienation of some groups in society from the decision-making process and how they might empower themselves by changing some aspects of the community's structures or processes (Whyte, 1991).

PAR is characterized by the active involvement of members of a community in the research being conducted. Kemmis and McTaggart (1988, p. 5) define PAR as "collective, self-reflective enquiry undertaken by participants in social situations in order to improve the rationality and justice of their own social ...practices" and see PAR as requiring the participants in the study to be involved in every stage of the action research cycle. Argyris and Schon (1989, p. 613) put it thus: PAR is based on the Lewinian proposition that "causal inferences about the behaviour of human beings are more likely to be valid and enactable when the human beings in question participate in building and testing them."

Implementation of the Research Method

Lewin originally described the action research cycle as having four basic steps: diagnosing, planning, acting, and evaluating (Lewin, 1947). Lewin saw the process as a "spiral of steps, each of which is composed of a circle of planning action and

Figure 8. The action research cycle (Adapted from Susman & Evered, 1978)

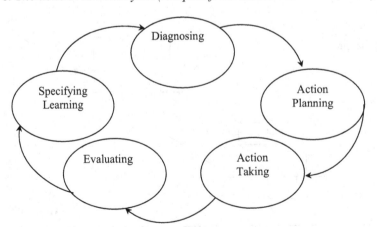

fact-finding about the result of the action" (p. 206). The most common action research description is to be found in Susman and Evered (1978) and sees the process as a five phase cyclical process containing the following discrete steps: diagnosis, action planning, action taking, evaluation, and learning (see Figure 8).

Steps in the Action Research Cycle

1. **Diagnosing:** This step involves the identification of the research themes. The step usually involves some collaborative work with the individuals situated in the content of the study.

2. **Planning:** This step evolves from the diagnosis of the problem and sets out the process to be followed during the project. Important aspects of the phase include the development of systematic data gathering and analysis mechanisms that engage with the actual experience of the community.

3. **Acting:** This step consists of the implementation of the plan.

4. **Evaluating:** Evaluation is based on the three fundamental questions: What happened during the research process? Who is the one to interpret what happened? In addition, what are the implications of these interpretations?

5. **Specifying Learning:** The knowledge gained in the action research can be directed to three audiences—those restructuring the organization norms to reflect the new knowledge gained by the organization during the research, those planning further action research interventions, and the academic community who may be interested in the success or failure of the theoretical frameworks that were proposed.

The general approach adopted for this research was

- Help to identify the primary problems that gave rise to the organization's desire to change.
- Work with stakeholders to specify organizational actions to address those primary problems.
- Collaborate with members of the organization to implement the planned action.
- Evaluate the outcome.
- Reflect on the new knowledge gained as a result of the research.

Oates and Fitzgerald (2001) describe how the action research process can be "operationalized" by using an implementation model with five parameters—paradigm,

Table 5. Operationalizing action research (Oates & Fitzgerald, 2001)

Parameter	Application of Parameter in the 1ˢᵗ Action Research Cycle of this Study
Paradigm	Interpretivist
Purpose	Develop enterprise-level model for knowledge management in NPD
Participants	researcher and new product development organization
Process	participatory action research
Product	A knowledge management business process suitable for use in NPD

purpose, participants, process, and product. These parameters map to five implementation steps in an action research project. The parameters and implementation
steps are shown in Table 5.

Data Gathering and Analysis

The centerpiece of an action research study is a story describing the sequences of
events that occurred during the research project. In this case, the story is created
chronologically around the phases of a participatory action research (PAR) project.
The research framework previously described shows the research design as being
based on a PAR model with four significant elements—planning, action, observation, and reflection. These elements are termed "PAR moments" (Seymour-Rolls
& Hughes, 2000). The data gathering methods used include surveys, interviews,
documentation reviews, observation, and focus groups. In this study, use was made
of interviews, documentation reviews, and observation.

Interviews are a suitable means of data gathering when a researcher wants to fully
understand individual's impression or experiences, or learn more about their answers
to questionnaires. Interviews give researchers an opportunity to get a comprehensive range and depth of information. They can also be tailored to suit individual
circumstances. However, they take longer to conduct and can be hard to analyze
and compare.

Documentation reviews can be an effective means of monitoring how a program
is progressing. They are a non-intrusive means of gaining insight. They can also
cover a wide range of data, depending on the amount of historical information and
the breadth of the documentation reviewed. They can, however, be a relatively
inflexible data gathering method because the researcher is restricted to the format
and content of the document being reviewed. Document reviews also need to be
clearly focused and carefully tailored to answer specific questions; otherwise the
reviews can be time-consuming and yield indeterminate results.

Observation is a common data gathering method used by PAR researchers because
it is a particularly appropriate method of gathering information about how a PAR

project actually progresses. The method enables the researcher to view events as they unfold and creates opportunities for the researcher to react to unforeseen events. The adaptive nature of the method is well suited to PAR projects because they are, by definition, conducted in social conditions where outcomes are uncertain and hard to predict. Interpretation and categorization of observed events can however, be problematic because of the complexities underlying human motivation and subsequent action. The very fact that a process is being observed can also influence that process, thereby adding an extra layer of difficulty in understanding and interpreting the process.

The Knowledge Management Initiative

In the previous section, a rationale for using action research was presented. This account focuses on the first action research cycle and uses the action research operationalization framework proposed in Oates and Fitzgerald (2001) to describe the research undertaken in this study. In that framework the operationalizing of action, research is comprised of five action research factors—paradigm, purpose, participants, process, and product.

Paradigm

The first cycle of the action research study is concerned with the development of a business process framework for an organisation engaged in product development and establishing a knowledge management process in that framework.

The underlying philosophical paradigm used in the action research cycle is interpretivist because the work is concerned with the act of clarifying or explaining the meaning of a phenomenon. The phenomenon in question is the creation of a business process map for a new product development organization and the implementation of knowledge management process in that framework. Interpretative research assumes meaning is "dependent on the subjective perspective of people as they interacted with others and the world" (Ridley & Keen, 2000) and is concerned with understanding phenomena through the meaning that people assign to them. This viewpoint is appropriate because the activity under study is concerned with how a group of people worked together to develop a business process map and created a process to cater for knowledge management. The starting point for interpretivist research, in general, and this cycle of action research in particular, is an assumption that access to reality is possible through social constructions such as language, consciousness, and shared meanings (Myers, 2000).

Purpose

The research goal of this action research cycle was the development of a knowledge management business process within an enterprise-level business process framework for new product development. A team was set up to propose a comprehensive framework that would take account of the overall business and the interdependence of the activities in the various business sub-units. It was hoped that the exercise would result in more focus on business process improvement that would incorporate subtle decision processes and make them more explicit. The position was summarized by the vice president of new product development, as follows: "We've been in operation for 25 years, so clearly we have our own very effective culture. We now need to update the value system, and core processes to complement the more complex business strategies and organization." It was felt that the company culture had, previously, tended to diagnose a problem or area for improvement, and the set goals, but typically did not spend enough time to be holistic, to set overall context and create links to critical business strategy. The sustainability of any improvement suffered as a consequence. Furthermore, the VP of NPD pointed out that there had been a somewhat fragmented approach to targeting market segments. He characterized the position as follows: "Our business model has been to have marketing/product development teams focused on market segments and lead customer clusters. Examples of target markets are consumer electronics like DVD, medical instrumentation, industrial automation, data networking, and PC motherboards. The issue became how do we get focused on the improvement process that leverages across these market/product line divides." The overall thrust of the initiative was to promote communication across market "segments" and lead customer "clusters" so as to maximize operational effectiveness, add sustainability to improvement processes by placing them in a holistic business context, establish balanced metrics for organizational performance, and create a basis for site leadership team activity. The purpose of this phase of the research was to treat the activity as the first cycle of a two-cycle action research project.

Participants

The participants in this phase of the action research were the researcher, a team of staff that was responsible developing the new business framework, and the product development organization that were the "customers" for the new initiatives. Having identified the problems previously described, it was decided that a team should be formed to build a core business process map. The team comprised 20 staff members in total. The process was facilitated by an external expert in core business process mapping.

Process

The research process chosen was a participatory action research model based on Susman and Evered (1978). The first step in the core business process team's work was a realisation that what was needed, initially, was a framework onto which the company's core business processes would be mapped. It was felt that the framework contained in the European Foundation for Quality Management (EFQM) business excellence model would be a good starting point for the work because it represented a body of work that had been built up over many years from the experiences of some of Europe's most successful companies. Consequently, some of the core business process team, including this researcher, went on intensive training courses to become familiar with how the EFQM business excellence model worked. A sub-group of the core business process team was formed to develop a "straw man" proposal for a core business process and present its findings to the wider core business process team for adoption and implementation. This sub-group met over a 6-month period and developed a core business process map for the organization.

Product

The first action research cycle had "action" outcomes and a "research" outcome. The "action" resulted in the development of a core business process map for the NPD organisation and a new core business process called "knowledge." The "research" outcome explores the implications of embedding knowledge management initiatives in NPD organizations and will be explored in the final section of this chapter.

"Action" Outcomes of the 1ˢᵗ Action Research Cycle

The Core Business Process Map

The map depicts a product development activity comprised of eight business processes and is shown in Appendix A. The map was developed with a deliberate structure in mind. The intent was to develop an image of an infrastructure with four cornerstones supporting a commercial "engine" that contained four processes. The four cornerstone processes were identified as people, technology, knowledge, and scorecard. These pivotal processes were seen as fundamental enabling processes whose role was to provide support for the four processes that comprise the commercial engine of the company viz. customer and market intelligence, strategic planning, portfolio management, and new product development. The people, knowledge, and technology and balanced scorecard processes were perceived to be enabling processes that had the potential to create the capability and expertise to enable new product development. The enabling processes were thus seen as pre-requisites that would constitute the four supporting pillars of a structure on which a systematic product development engine could be built. A process leader (and deputy) was assigned for each of the core processes.

During the creation of the core business process map there was considerable debate in the core process team about the potential role of a knowledge management process. There were two elements to the debate: (a) whether there should be a knowledge management process separate from the people and technology processes at all, given the feeling of some team members that all aspects of the knowledge management activity could be encapsulated in both the people and technology processes and (b) the team wanted to understand the specific projects that would be undertaken by a knowledge management process and how they would enhance product development.

The "Knowledge Management" Core Business Process

The company had been conscious for many years of the importance of organizational learning and the strategic management of intellectual assets. Seminal contributions by Stata had signaled the strategic importance of knowledge management before the term had become popular in management literature (Stata 1989, 1995). He predicted that in the future the only source of competitive advantage in knowledge-intensive industries would be the rate at which firms learn. This was well known to senior management and often quoted at internal company conferences. In Stata (1995), he stressed the importance of conversations and trusting relationships and went on to propose a model for improving the way people make and keep commitments as key enablers for any future jump in product development productivity. His focus on the achievement of productivity improvements through the "softer" aspects of knowledge management, rather than focusing on the "harder" technical aspects of the problem has similarities with Nonaka's emphasis of the importance of the socialisation and externalization phases in his knowledge creation model (Nonaka, 1991). Stata observed that in process improvement initiatives the soft stuff is actually more important than the hard stuff and much more difficult to master. This view—that many of the challenges associated with initiatives such as knowledge management, are not solely technical in nature—was shared by many of the leading thinkers in knowledge management (Davenport & Prusak, 1997; Nonaka & Konno, 1998; Snowdon 1999b).

Stata's thinking had been heavily influenced by the work of Flores (1997) who proposed the concept of "an atom of work" as the fundamental building block of all business processes. In Flores' model, most transactions between people in organizations are, in fact, requests and promises on one hand, and offers and acceptance on the other. Flores' assertion was, that what was often missing from these transactions was a clear understanding of the condition of satisfaction, including the requested response time. He also pointed to a lack of an explicit declaration of

Table 6. Phases in the development of the knowledge core process

Phase	Activity
A	Research into the State-Of-Art in KM and briefing of management team on current practice
B	Discussion on whether it is appropriate to establish knowledge as a "process"
C	Choice of the core business process name
D	Analysis of current knowledge management practices
E	Analysis of current practice vs. theoretical knowledge management models
F	Selection of knowledge process initiatives
G	Selection of knowledge metrics/indicators

the completion of a promise or a check to see if the performance was satisfactory to the customer.

The work of Stata had the effect of sensitizing senior management to the potential offered by successful knowledge management projects and his influence led to a relatively sophisticated understanding of organization learning among some members of the senior management team. This, in turn, culminated in a benign environment in which to launch a knowledge management initiative because senior management, in particular, was already well disposed to proposals that might lead to improvements in how knowledge is managed within the organization. The development cycle of the knowledge process involved the seven phases described in Table 6.

"Research" Outcomes of the 1st Action Research Cycle

There are two dominant approaches to describing knowledge management activities in corporations—the life-cycle model approach (e.g., Nonaka & Takeuchi, 1995 and the enterprise model approach—Wiig, 1993). When these approaches were applied to the NPD process, they were seen to have had some limitations. The life-cycle approach does not contain any guidance or mechanism for integrating a knowledge management initiative into the mainstream activities of the organization under study. The enterprise model builds on a functional view of the firm and attempts to identify the sources of knowledge in the organization so that those sources may be connected in a coherent manner to create an overall enterprise-wide knowledge management strategy. This perspective views knowledge as a somewhat static phenomenon and does not emphasize the dynamic nature of knowledge creation through a process of social interaction and externalization. In a distributed product development community, you have to have developed the capability to operate efficiently across the temporal, geographic, political, and cultural boundaries encountered in global operations (Orlikowski, 2000). The core process map represented a framework to promote a consciousness of KM in the organisation. The knowledge process was viewed in relation to this framework (Suen et al., 2000).

The choice of "knowledge" as a core business process and its positioning in a core business process map reflected a conscious, systematic attempt to overcome the limitations in existing knowledge management strategies. This viewpoint saw two distinct advantages to embedding a knowledge process in the activities of the product development organization. The primary perceived advantage was to raise the awareness among the product development community of value of articulating knowledge in a public forum so that a discursive dialogue might ensue and the process of knowledge "amplification" (Nonaka, 1991) would be triggered. There was a perceived weakness in the firm's current practices in that knowledge was being shared successfully within business units, but the process was breaking down at the business unit's organisational boundaries i.e. knowledge was not flowing from unit to unit and so knowledge amplification was being impeded rather than encouraged.

The second perceived advantage of a knowledge process was that—by positioning the process in a structured enterprise framework—it would be easier to leverage the benefits of knowledge creation across the organization and sustain these knowledge creation initiatives if they were part of an enterprise business model for the product development community. Up until that time there had been several successful knowledge-related activities, but since they were somewhat ad-hoc in their composition, they ran the risk of losing momentum over time because they were not linked to an established coordinated framework that had some long-term goals associated with it. Furthermore, some of those good practices in knowledge sharing were somewhat localized in separate business units and by elevating and linking them to a more holistic enterprise model, they stood a better chance of being replicated and disseminated throughout the organization.

The main thrust of the process was to stimulate knowledge creation and sharing by encouraging collaboration across organizational boundaries. Specifically, it was intended that the knowledge process would enhance product development effectiveness by:

- Promoting the use of "best practices" across product development teams.
- Preventing the waste of resources by learning from other groups in the company.
- Promoting innovation through combing ideas from different business units.
- Attracting and retaining key individuals by creating a learning environment.

Progress was made in each of the themes targeted by the knowledge process. Best practices were propagated across product development teams because of projects undertaken as part of the knowledge process. An example of such projects is the "Master Classes" initiative. These in-depth seminars address key technical topic during which talks are given by experts in the relevant subject area and the focus is on sharing problem-solving techniques across groups. Master classes were designed to identify and create best practice work routines, standardize those practices and diffuse them throughout the organization where applicable.

Learning from other groups in the company was encouraged by focusing on the detections of repeated occurrences of the same or similar mistakes. Such patterns would be an obvious indicator of a lack of systematic learning in an organization. One approach that was adopted to remedy this situation was to try to capture the criteria for major organizational decisions in some codified form that can subsequently be re-visited. The peer review process in the product development organization was re-engineered to be a forum for combining ideas from different business units. This initiative resulted in peer reviews evolving from a position where attendees were drawn solely from a single business unit to a point where peer reviews contained attendees from multiple business units across the organization.

Conclusions

Given the growing body of research encouraging a holistic approach to KM initiatives (Hofer-Alfeis, 2001; Hofer-Alfeis & Spek Van der, 2001; Lindroth, 2000; Spek Van der and Spijkervet, 1997), the knowledge process was developed after a thorough examination of the issues--both technical and socio-technical--relating to knowledge management. Furthermore, there was a conscious plan to embed the process in a bigger business framework to overcome the potential problems outlined in Spek Van der and Spijkervet (1997) and Lindroth (2000).

The underlying philosophical approach to the knowledge management initiative was that knowledge management should be integrated into the daily work of people in the organisation. A number of steps were taken in the development and implementation of the knowledge management process that were designed to promote the integration of the process into the daily working of the organization:

- **Focus:** Progress in the initiative was systematically monitored in a balanced scorecard that captured different facets of organizational performance.
- **Alignment:** The placing of the knowledge management process in a framework with other key business processes promoted alignment with those processes. Decisions were made on all the business processes in a collective manner with some mutual adjustment where necessary to achieve an overall consistency in strategic direction.
- **Instruments:** There were specific KM services and enabling technologies provided to promote and facilitate knowledge management. These included two specific KMS applications described elsewhere in this thesis.

- **Communities:** Communities-of-practice were set up which proved to be powerful mechanisms for disseminating knowledge across organizational boundaries.

Appendix A. Core Business Process Map

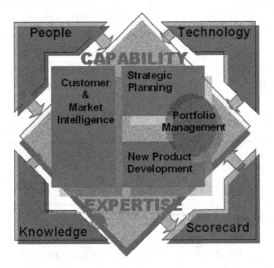

Discussion Questions

1.   What are the key issues regarding knowledge management (KM) in this case study?

2.   Identify the respective people/technology/process aspects of KM in this case study.

3.   What should be done next?

4.   What are the major lessons learned from this case study?

5.   How does a process centric KM perspective help to gain a better understanding of the key dynamics?

6.   What are the major barriers and facilitators impacting the KM initiative?

References

Adler, P. S., Mandelbaum, A., et al. (1996). Getting the most out of your product development process. *Harvard Business Review*, 134-152.

Anderson, B., Button, G., et al. (1993). Supporting the design process within an organisational context. *ECSCW'93*, Milan.

Argyris, C., & Schon, D. (1989). Participatory action research and action science compared. *American Behavioural Scientist, 32*(5).

Bergquist, M., Ljungberg, J., et al. (2001). Practising peer review in organisations: A qualifier for knowledge dissemination and legitimisation. *Journal of Information Technology, 16*, 99-112.

Braa, K., & Vidgen, R. (2000). Research: From observation to intervention. Planet Internet. K. Braa, C. Sorensen and B. Dahlbom. Lund, Studentlitteratur.

Brooks, A., & Watkins, K. E. (1994). *The emerging power of action inquiry technologies*. San Francisco: Jossey-Boss.

Chein, I., Cook, S., et al. (1948). The field of action research. *American Psychologist, 3*, 43-50.

Clark, A. (1976). *Experimenting with organisational life: The action research approach*. New York: Plenum Press.

Cooper, R. G. (1994). Developing new products on time, in time. *Product Innovation Management, 11*(5).

Davenport, T., & Prusak, L. (1997). *Working knowledge*. Boston: Harvard Business School Press.

Davis, L., & Valfer, E. (1976). *Controlling the variance in action research. Experimenting with organisational life: The action research approach*. New York: Plenum Press.

Drucker, P. F. (1988). The coming of the new organisation. *Harvard Business Review, 66*(1), 45-53.

Eder, W. E. (1989). Information systems for designers. *International Conference in Engineering Design*.

Elden, M., & Chisholm, R. F. (1996). Emerging varieties of action research: Introduction to the special issue. *Human Relations, 46*(2), 121-141.

Fairchild, A. M. (2002). Knowledge management metrics via a balanced scorecard. The *35th International Conference on System Sciences*, Hawaii.

Flores, F. (1997). The impact of information technology on business. The *50th Anniversary Conference of the Association for Computing Machinery*, San Jose.

Goodman, R., & Clark, A. (1976). The role of the mediator in action research. In A. Clark (Ed.), *Experimenting with organisational life: The action research approach*. New York: Plenum Press.

Hofer-Alfeis, J. (2001). Strategic management of the knowledge enterprise. The *6th APQC KM Conference--Next Generation Knowledge Management & Organisational Learning*, Houston, Texas.

Hofer-Alfeis, J., & Spek Van der, R. (2001). Knowledge Strategy Process and Metrics. Knowledge Management and Organisational Learning, London, Linkage International Ltd.

Kemmis, S., & McTaggart, R. (1988). *The action research planner*. Geelong: Deakin University.

Ketchum, L. D., & Trist, E. (1992). *All teams are not created equal*. Newbury Park, CA: Sage.

Kock, N. F., McQueen, R. J., et al. (1997). Can action research be made more rigorous in a positivist sense? The contribution of an iterative approach. *Journal of Systems and Information Technology, 1*(1), 1-24.

Leonard-Barton, D. (1995). *Wellsprings of knowledge: Building and sustaining the sources of innovation*. Boston: Harvard Business School Press.

Lewin, K. (1947). Frontiers in group dynamics *Human Relations, 1*(1).

Lindroth, T. (2000). May the force be with you: The force to implement KM organisational wide. *IRIS'23*, Laboratory for Interaction Technology, University of Trollhatten/Uddevalla.

Macintosh, A. (1997). Knowledge asset management. *AIring, 20*, 4-6.

MacIsaac. (1995). *An Introduction to Action Research*. Retrieved from http://www.phy.nau.edu/~danmac/actionrsch.html

Markus, M. L. (2001). Toward a theory of knowledge reuse: types of knowledge reuse situations and factors in reuse success. *Journal of Management Information Systems, 18*(1), 57-93.

McTaggart, R. (1991). Principles of participative action research. *Adult Education Quarterly, 41*(3), 168-187.

Myers, M. (2000). Qualitative research in information systems. ISWorld Net.

Nonaka, I. (1991). The knowledge-creating company. *Harvard Business Review, 69*(6), 96-104.

Nonaka, I., & Konno, N. (1998). The concept of "Ba": Building a foundation for knowledge creation. *California Management Review, 40*(3), 40-53.

Nonaka, I., & Takeuchi, H. (1995). *The knowledge-creating company*. Oxford: Oxford University Press.

Oates, B., & Fitzgerald, B. (2001). Action research: Putting theory into practice. *IFIP WG8.2 Organisations and Society in Information Systems (OASIS)*, New Orleans, Louisiana, USA.

Orlikowski, W. J. (2000). Knowing in practice: Enacting a collective capability in distributed organizing. *Organisation Science, 13*(3), 249-273.

Pace, L. A., & Argona, D. R. (1991). Participatory action research: A view from Xerox. In W. W. Whyte (Ed.), *Participatory action research*. Thousand Oaks, CA: Sage.

Raelin, J. A. (1997). Action learning and action science: Are they different? *Organisational Dynamics*, 21-33.

Raelin, J. A. (1999). Preface. *Management Learning, 30*(2), 115-125.

Ramesh, B., & Tiwana, A. (1999). Supporting collaborative process knowledge management in new product development teams. *Decision Support Systems, 27*(1-2), 213-235.

Reason, P. (1994). Three approaches to participative inquiry. In N. Denzin & Y. Lincoln (Eds.), *Handbook of qualitative inquiry*. Thousand Oaks, CA: Sage.

Ridley, G., & Keen, C. (2000). Epistemologies in use in information systems research: Divergent or change? *Information Research*.

Rodgers, P., & Clarkson, P. (1998). An investigation and review of the knowledge needs of designers in SMEs. *The Design Journal, 1*(3), 16-29.

Schein, E. H. (1995). Process consultation, action research, and clinical inquiry: Are they the same? *Journal of Managerial Psychology, 10*(6), 14-19.

Scott, J. E. (1996). The role of information technology in organisational knowledge creation for new product development. The *2nd Americas Conference on Information Systems*.

Seymour-Rolls, K., & Hughes, I. (2000). Participatory action research: Getting the job done.

Shake, S. (1999). Presentation "Articulating the New Product Development Process."

Snowdon, D. (1999b). Liberating knowledge: Introductory chapter. *CBI Business Guide*. Caspian Publishing. October.

Spek Van der, R., & Spijkervet, A. (1997). Knowledge management: Dealing intelligently with knowledge. In L. A. Wilcox (Ed.), *Knowledge management and its integrative elements*. CRC Press.

Stata, R. (1989). Organisational learning: The key to management innovation. *Sloan Management Review, 30*(3), 63-74.

Stata, R. (1995). A conversation about conversations. *Center for Quality of Management Journal, 4*(4), 15-20.

Strauss, G. I., & Evered, R. D. (1978). *Basics of qualitative research: Grounded theory procedures and techniques.* Newbury Park, CA: Sage.

Suen, L. T., Meng, Y. C., et al. (2000). Architecturing organisation consciousness for strategic advantage: Aligning knowledge management and organisation process. *ICMIT 2000.*

Susman, G. I., & Evered, R. D. (1978). An assessment of the scientific merits of action research. *Administrative Science Quarterly, 23,* 582-603.

Ullman, D. G. (1992). *The mechanical design process.* New York: McGraw-Hill.

van de Ven, A. H., & Polley, D. (1992). Learning while innovating. *Organisation Science, 3*(1), 92-116.

Whyte, W. W. (1991). *Participatory action research.* Thousand Oaks, CA: Sage.

Wiig, K. (1993). *Knowledge management foundation.* Schema Press.

Wilson, T. D. (2000). Recent trends in user studies: Action research and qualitative methods. *Information Research, 5*(3).

Yang, J., & Yu, L. (2002). Electronic new product development: A conceptual framework. *Industrial Management and Data Systems, 4*(102), 218-225.

Chapter Summary

What you read throughout this book is primarily theoretical. At times, some of the statements we make seem either trivial or entirely detached from the realities of life. Yet, if you were to look around closely, you would realize that you are immersed in an ocean of incidents that could be prevented had someone applied common sense and simple logic to the issue at hand. To be truly useful to organizations the tools techniques and strategies of KM must be utilized and actualized. This in turn necessitates a critical level of analysis and thought as the preceding case studies should have illustrated. However, knowledge management, as with anything else, has roots in common sense. It follows then, that business decisions based on knowledge management should also incorporate the element of common sense. But do they? Regrettably this is not necessarily so and we caution that KM implemented without thought and common sense is likely to cause more harm than good. Moreover, it is important to always remember that "knowledge is a process of piling facts; wisdom lies in their simplification" (Martin Fischer), hence KM is not a means to an end, but rather a vital link in enabling businesses not just to survive but to thrive in dynamic, complex and even unstable environments. Knowledge-based enterprises are organizations that not only have in place the essential KM tools but also know how to judiciously apply the techniques and strategies of KM to effect superior decision-making and enhanced, effective, and efficient operations. This is a continuous process that requires constant re-evaluation and calibration so that the organization is always prepared and ready to function at its optimal in its given environment.

Endnotes

1   This case study was written by Witold Abramowicz, Tomasz Kaczmarek, and Marek Kowalkiewicz, Poznan University of Technology, Poland for the basis of class discussion and not to illustrate effective or ineffective handling of an administrative situation.

2   This case study was written by Mogens Kühn Pedersen, Copenhagen Business School for the basis of class discussion and not to illustrate effective or ineffective handling of an administrative situation.

3   This case study was written by Roberta Lamb, Donald Bren School of Information and Computer Science at the University of California, Irvine for the basis of class discussion and not to illustrate effective or ineffective handling of an administrative situation.

4   This is a pseudonym, as are all individual names in this case, except Gary Keller and Joe Williams.

5   Figure in Thornton (2004).

6   This case study was written by Roberta Lamb, Donald Bren School of Information and Computer Science at the University of California, Irvine for the basis of class discussion and not to illustrate effective or ineffective handling of an administrative situation.

7   This is a pseudonym, as are all individual names in this case, except Gary Keller and Joe Williams.

8   This case study was written by Dr Graydon Davison for the basis of class discussion and not to illustrate effective or ineffective handling of an administrative situation.

9   This case study was written by Jacky Swan, Anna Goussevskaia, and Mark Bresnen for the basis of class discussion and not to illustrate effective or ineffective handling of an administrative situation.

10   The data for this case were collected from a research project conducted by Mike Bresnen, Anna Goussevskia and Jacky Swan at the University of Warwick. We are grateful to the support of the UK Engineering and Physical Science Research Council (EPSRC) and the Innovative Manufacturing Research Centre (IMRC) at Warwick for supporting this research. Company names have been changed.

     Data sources: 18 interviews, 3 meetings, internal documents, workshop presentation.

     Period of research: October 2001 – February 2004

11   This case study was written by Brian Donnellan, Martin Hughes, and William Golden, National University of Ireland, for the basis of class discussion and not to illustrate effective or ineffective handling of an administrative situation.

Appendix

Knowledge, Information, and Knowledge Systems:
Explaining the Conceptual Confusion

Elie Geisler, Illinois Institute of Technology, USA

Introduction

The following discusses human knowledge as a personal cognitive process. It challenges the information-knowledge progression of conventional thinking and serves to not only underscore that KM is a complex management technique but also an evolving field.

What is Knowledge?

Knowledge is a mental or cognitive state or phenomenon in which an individual has mastered a description of reality, a concept, or slices thereof. There is no knowledge but that which exists in the mind. The essence of the word "knowledge" is to "know something with familiarity gained through experience or association" as defined in the dictionary. Hence, experiences or associations are phenomena of cognition, which occur in the mind.

Does this focused definition of knowledge necessarily prescribe the doom of knowledge systems in organizations? Not in the least. There is ample room and compelling reasons for knowledge systems to exist. The purpose of this chapter is to clarify the confusion that seems to pervade the literature as to what constitutes knowledge and how it relates to information.

The assertion that knowledge, as we define it, exists only as a cognitive phenomenon has been previously addressed by those who considered the existence of "tacit" knowledge. Michael Polanyi coined this term and advanced the argument that there are two types of knowledge: (1) "tacit," which is knowledge contained in the person's mind, and (2) "explicit," which is knowledge that people externalize, share, and diffuse. Ikujiro Nonaka and his colleagues extended this typology of knowledge. They revealed the method used by successful Japanese companies to facilitate the sharing of knowledge by their members, thus turning "tacit" knowledge into "explicit" knowledge.

In this literature, both types of knowledge are considered as equal aspects of the phenomenon of knowing. The difference between them seems to be the locus of the knowledge. Tacit means it is embedded in the cognitive or mental enclosure and explicit means that the knowledge has already been diffused outside the individual's mind.

Here knowledge is defined *solely* as a phenomenon of the mind. Explicit, shared, or diffused knowledge is not *true* knowledge. Whatever the entity that floats in databases, information systems, or knowledge systems, it is not knowledge but the externalization of the processes of the human mind, which are the only constituent components of knowledge.

Human beings who live in societies must share what they know with others. The motives for this are survival, competitive pressures, and the need to grow and to add to our stock of skills, competencies, and capabilities. Add to these our need to cooperate to achieve complex tasks, and the result is the plethora of social, economic, organizational, and psychological reasons for the drive to share what we know and to tap the knowledge of others.

To do so, we devised means of communication, both nonverbal and languages. As philosophers such as Ludwig Wittgenstein and linguists such as Noam Chomsky have suggested, language allows us to exchange our description and understanding of reality—albeit in an imperfect mode. We are able to create linguistic artifacts, such as intellectual nuggets, which are statements about reality, as we know it *and* as we are able to share and to externalize it. Polanyi had even suggested that "tacit" knowledge is that knowledge which individuals are yet unable to externalize. But the issue is not the matter of where such sharing will occur, nor that all tacit knowledge may at some point become explicit. The issue is that, as individuals, we are bound by our ability to express our knowledge, to translate what we know into "shareable" quantities, and to externalize it via the communicative and linguistic tools we possess. Barring direct access by others to the crevices of our mind and a direct reading of our cognitive thoughts, we are limited in our ability to externalize what we know.

Externalized knowledge is not knowledge. It is a limited translation or, in graphic terms, a fuzzy picture of whatever knowledge we were able to share via the tools of human communication and language. What exists outside the mind is in the form of a collection of linguistic artifacts. These are "intellectual nuggets," which may be propositions, statements, formulae, symbols, or any other manifestation of human communication tools and devices.

This picture or projection of our reality (as we know it) is what we share and communicate to others. All such "explicit" projection of what we know is not only an incomplete and, to an extent, biased imprint of what we know, but it also is exposed to the tribulations of the shortcomings and barriers embedded in human communication.

What is Information?

What is this externalized form of what we know? As faulty and "non-knowledge" as it may be, this is a projection or representation of the reality as we are able to provide to others. Human interaction and our innate ability to communicate conjure to create a standardized mode of expressing this reality.

Once externalized, this description of reality (intellectual nuggets) loses its cognitive characteristics and its personalized format, which is the essence of knowledge. What is left is a collection of nuggets, standardized to a point where all who are versed in the "key" to deciphering this description are able to access and to absorb and comprehend its content.

Perhaps the term "information" is appropriate to describe and to identify this collection of externalized nuggets. The distinction made here is therefore not between "tacit" and "explicit" forms of knowledge, but between "knowledge" and a radically different form of description of reality, accessible to all, and residing outside the mind.

This distinction is not just a matter of semantic trifling. Rather, there are substantive differences between knowledge and what we may call "information." In addition to the different location of its existence, information is a "processed" description of reality, presented in a standardized form. Once acquired, interpreted, "read," or deciphered, this "information" is not knowledge—it remains the externalized projection of what we know.

For example, I *know* that upon my study of an organization, it is faltering and on a verge of collapse. I compose a report in which I detail this conclusion and how I arrived at it, my methodology, and my initial assumptions. This report contains intellectual nuggets, which are opinions, lessons, findings, conclusions, and descriptions of the organization and my exploration of its existence and its workings. The report is *not* knowledge. It contains "information" about the organization. The reader of the report does not *know* that the organization is on the brink of collapse, not because my conclusion is subjective, but because the projective "information" provided in my report needs to be absorbed by the mind of the reader and undergo the processes of generation of knowledge.

Here lies the crux of the differentiation between knowledge and information. As a cognitive phenomenon, knowledge is created when sensorial inputs are processed and clustered in the mind. Such nuggets are absorbed through the five senses and clustered as a cognitive phenomenon, thus generating knowledge. In a popular version, this would be equivalent to not "knowing" until one walks in another's shoes. Creating knowledge through sensorial inputs is to experience the reality about which we generate knowledge.

Challenging the Information-Knowledge Progression

The act of obtaining and absorbing information about the phenomenon is far from experiencing it via the clustering of sensorial inputs. Conventional thinking suggests that we have a progression: from data, to information, to knowledge, and to wisdom. Such a progression, in my view, is a conceptual and ontological fallacy.

The information-to-knowledge progression conveys the erroneous conception of how we can transform information into knowledge. To agree with this notion one must have an adequate theory that will explain *how* information is processed into knowledge. Such a theory is yet to be devised. A feeble excuse for the lack of such a theory is sometimes advanced on the grounds that the mental processes where information is transformed are the realm of consciousness and we are yet to unlock this amazing human ability.

However, if we approach this phenomenon with knowledge creation as the starting point, all that is needed is to establish whether the clustering in the mind is based on underlying concepts, as argued by some epistemologists, and what are the criteria for clustering and sensemaking. The creation of knowledge as a mental process is still a marvel to be unlocked, but there is no requirement in this approach to add a theory that attempts to explain how information is transformed within these cognitive processes.

What are Knowledge Systems?

When people externalize what they know, they do so within informal surroundings and they also do so within organizational boundaries. From times immemorial, humans externalized what they know to their kinfolk and to the members of their hunting parties. They raised their young and mentored them in the skills needed for survival and in understanding their environment.

As formal organizations emerged, there also arises the need to gather, to assemble, and to store the externalized knowledge of those who possess such knowledge. Initially, it consisted of a raw collection of skills (*how* to plow, sow, build bridges, ignite a fire, and make tools). Later, this need has evolved to more complex notions of *why* nature behaves as it does (why the seasons of the year, the flooding of the rivers, the frailty of the human existence, and the birth and death of living organisms).

Organizations thus became harbingers of the knowledge of their members, and a healthy trading began in such collections. In many instances, a ban was declared over revealing certain skills and competencies. The Philistines had such a ban on ways and means of forging weapons—a technology they possessed and kept as secretive as possible. Over the millennia of human civilization, organizations accumulated records of externalized knowledge ("information") for the purposes of conducting operations and for their performance and survival.

As harbingers of these records, organizations do not "know." They are repositories of whatever their past members were good enough to deposit and leave behind. Such records, containing a variety of topics of information, were used for training, operations, competition, and growth. Some of the information in these records was lost because of the unreadable form in which it was produced or stored, or other attributes of poor communication. Nonetheless, organizations became the key harbingers of whatever was shared by individuals after they departed the world of the living and could not themselves share their knowledge.

Knowledge systems and knowledge-based anything in the organization are therefore a misnomer. What is stored in organizational records is "information," since knowledge is solely defined as the cognitive activity in the individual's mind. However, the information stored in these records is the product of the attempts of countless individuals to externalize what they know. Hence the connection to the notion of knowledge.

In the final decade of the 20th century, we forcefully discovered the role that knowledge and its organizational systems play in the working, performance, success, and survival of the organization and its members. The notion of "knowledge workers" appeared and management scholars, such as the late Peter Drucker, emphasized their importance in the changing face of the global economy. What prompted this rush to identify and to be so laudably concerned with "knowledge-workers?"

As I suggested in my book *Creating Value with Science and Technology*, during the second half of the twentieth century there were three complementary phenomena. Massive investments by many nations, particularly the United States in publicly funded science and technology, complemented dramatic improvements in the education process. In much of the world, countries have invested in elementary and higher education to extents never before dreamed by previous governments. University education has become a popular rather than an elitist experience. Thirdly, dramatic improvements in sea and air transportation and the lowering of tariffs and several commercial treaties, plus the relative liberalization of economies, which previously had in place prohibitively defensive tariffs, have all contributed to the globalization of trade.

When the relative advantages of land, capital, and standardized workforce began to diminish or disappear, skills, competencies, and "knowledge" have emerged as crude yet powerful substitutes to the national economic toolkit. Because of the inherent difficulties in sharing and diffusing knowledge, the emphasis on this new element of economic power is gaining forceful momentum in both business and academic circles.

In global terms, as the literature on technology transfer has shown in its conclusive findings, the simple transfer and diffusion of "what we know" from country to country in a given area is highly insufficient to train a generation of "knowledge-able" people. Direct contact and mentoring are necessary so that which is shared by those who know may be absorbed by those who don't know to some degree of adequate use.

Within this trend of the focus on and the veneration of knowledge, organizations are increasingly creating and restructuring their "knowledge systems." These are collections of records deposited by individual members, past and present, who had knowledge about a topic, a given area, or an answer to a specific query. As they indulge in developing and using these systems, organizations are also becoming painfully aware of at least three problems. First, whatever they accumulate in their "knowledge systems" is only a fraction of what their members *actually* know. Secondly, members are very reluctant to share what they know and to deposit what they know in these systems. Thirdly, unlike libraries and traditional information systems, "knowledge systems" are a different type of repository. If a member of the organization needs to know how many people are employed by a competing company, she can find this item in a traditional information system, library, or depository. If, however, the member wishes to know what are the comparative advantages of the competing company in the commercialization of nanotechnology, such "knowledge" is not readily available nor is it accessible in the organization's systems. "Knowledge systems" are excruciatingly difficult to structure, manage, maintain, and utilize.

Why the Confusion?

If, as proposed here, all that is available in systems, records, and any medium *outside* the human mind is, at best, information—not knowledge—then we have some level of confusion between the concepts of information and knowledge. The issue, therefore, is *not* how to better and more fully extract "tacit" knowledge from organizational members. Rather, the issue is how to reconcile the coexistence of *information* (as the externalized mode of what we know) and *knowledge* (as the cognitive processes in the mind).

These two very distinct phenomena (*information* and *knowledge*) seem to not only coexist but also have some interaction, via the knower and the user of the externalized content. However we choose to name these phenomena, we have mental processes on the one hand and a collection of the externalized reflection or projection of these processes on the other. They are somehow connected, they are related, and they interact in the activities of organizational members.

We have therefore a gap between what we *know*, and the volumes of collected material from many individuals. This material is viewed as the externalization of what these other individuals had chosen to share and to deposit in the repository. The gap is conceptual: how do we transform one into the other? How do we make the interaction a successful event, when *knowledge* and *information* available in repositories are such different phenomena?

Consider a mundane example of a pedestrian skill. I gain access to a repository of information about tying the laces of shoes. I am exposed to text, graphics, and movies about how laces are tied. With all this information absorbed, I still do not know how to tie the laces of my shoes. I need to *see* the laces, *touch* them, try, fail, try again, and finally complete the cognitive process in my mind where the result is that I now *know* how to tie the laces of my shoes. Having access to the information about the skill does not make knowledge of the skill, nor of more complex forms of knowledge such as abstract notions and conceptual views of reality.

Explaining the Gap:
A Theory and Some Applications

To explain the gap between the phenomena of "knowledge" and its external projection as "information" we need a theory of the "interaction" between the two phenomena. This theory would attempt to explain: (1) how we externalize what we know in the form of intellectual nuggets, (This means how we translate our cognitive processes into communicative artifacts so that we may share our mental capacities with others), and (2) how we input "information" or the externalized communication artifacts and process them in our mind, as we do with clustering of sensorial inputs to create the mental capabilities we call knowledge.

The first question this theory would attempt to explain has been formidably addressed in studies of human communication, semantics, linguistics, and semiotics. The second question is the crucial task of this "theory of interaction." It deals with the difficult objective of explaining how we create knowledge not from the "raw material" of sensorial inputs, but from the assembly of regurgitated items of whatever others have externalized and communicated outside their minds. How do we input, process, and convert this material into "knowledge?"

There are cognitive, philosophical, and biological aspects to this theory. The mental processes in this case would perhaps be different from those that command the clustering of sensorial inputs. Consider, for instance, the biological function of generating energy in the body. Energy can be generated by digesting food, extracting its nutritional components, and transforming them into energy in the cells. This process is similar to the creation of knowledge from the mental "digestion" of sensorial inputs. Conversely, if we inject energy-producing agents directly into the cell, the process of generating energy will be quite different.

The philosophical aspect of this theory intersects with the problem of induction. Sir Karl Popper argued that, with his *conjectural knowledge*, he had solved the problem of induction by offering a good solution to David Hume's logical and psychological queries and to Bertrand Russell's struggle with this issue.

Hume's approach to induction was focused on the unique role of experience in shaping human reasoning. He argued that the generation of "general laws" or "expectations of regularities in nature" is a mental process based on our prior experiences. As we experience regularities in natural or other phenomena, we therefore project them to expectations and general laws (induction from the particular to the general). But Hume also suggested that humans associate ideas to create cognitive generalizations of phenomena in their surroundings—*in the absence of experience*. Hume justified such human attribution as a result of faith.

Popper combined what he described as Hume's logical and psychological problems of induction, and offered his solution. He proposed "conjectural knowledge" by which all universal laws or theories are conjectural and empirical explorations of these generalizations can be refuted but their "truth" cannot be established empirically.

The conjecture solution proposed by Popper greatly contributed to the philosophy of science and to scientific methodology. Donald Campbell relied on Popper's philosophical constructs when advancing his "evolutionary epistemology." But such advances in philosophy and methodology have not contributed to clarifying the gap between the sensorial impacts we gather from our world and the formation of knowledge as mental-cognitive processes.

Popper addressed this issue in his description of the "three worlds" of our perception of reality. The first world is the *physical*, the second the *mental*, and the third consists of *ideas* or *thoughts*. He believed that such entities of the "third world" are human discoveries and do exist outside the mind and apart from the physical world.

Although this is an elegant attempt to offer a solution to externalized knowledge, the ontological autonomy with which Popper endows human ideas and human conceptualization of reality is at best an egregious explanation. Human knowledge is more complex than ideas and universal laws. It contains skills, competencies, and capability to link, connect, assemble, and cluster disparate inputs. The externalization of, say, the theory of numbers (to use Popper's example) as a "man-made" conception of a certain reality does not make it ontologically independent from the mind which created such notions. The theory of numbers or the description of the evolution of biological systems or business corporations is not knowledge. Only when this "third-world" (in Popper's terminology) is combined with the human mind (the "second world") do we have knowledge. Ontologically such notions exist in records, documents, tombs of ancient kings, or supercomputers—but they are, for the purpose of knowledge, as "alive" or "knowing" as the paper, stone, or silicon chip in which they exist.

All this is different from what Popper termed the "bucket" vs. the "searchlight" approaches to knowledge, and the creation of *scientific* knowledge. The "bucket" approach argues that observations (experiences) precede hypotheses. In his approach to the methodology of *scientific* hypotheses, Popper suggested the "searchlight" approach, in which hypotheses precede observations and are thus tested by empirical observations. This methodological procedure for scientific exploration represents a focused view of how one should go about studying the world outside the mind. However, we go about it, the inputs to the human mind remain within the confines of the senses, which are then clustered to form higher-order knowledge such as concepts and theories. On the other side, the externalized form of such knowledge is re-absorbed by the human mind in a reverse process by which, I suggest, the externalized knowledge is "decomposed" into sensorial inputs and reassembled in the mind.

In summary, I suggest that the only possible process of cognition (and knowledge creation) is the mental process by which the neurons in the human brain cluster sensorial inputs. The belief (expressed by many philosophers and cognition scientists) that humans have the mental ability to produce, input, and process ideas, concepts, and theories is false. The process is as follows (Figure 1):

We are currently in the very preliminary stages of uncovering the process of (**A**) above—how sensorial inputs are clustered. Recent findings suggest that fewer neurons than we had believed are involved in clustering sensorial inputs such as images (vision) for the creation of knowledge about famous people's faces stored in our

Figure 1. Schematic of knowledge cognition process

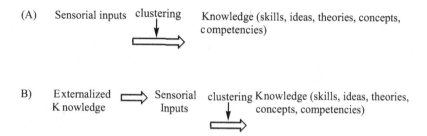

memory. We are beginning to gain insights into the *efficiency* or our brain, but we are still far from uncovering the processes described in (A) and (B) in Figure 1.

Some Implications

The view expressed here (that knowledge is narrowly defined with the knower, and all externalized forms are *not* knowledge) has some applications in the design of information and knowledge systems. If, as we are now discovering, our mental processes are very efficient and we need very few indicators, metrics, or sensorial inputs to create very complex concept, then the implication for knowledge and information systems is a call for efficient and very economical content in the design. As I had suggested in my book, *Knowledge and Knowledge Systems: Learning from the Marvels of the Mind*, a small number of sensorial inputs is sufficient to form complex mental notions. In addition, the cumulative impact of previously processed sensorial inputs and deposits in our mental memory contribute to an even more efficient, and certainly more effective processing of sensorial inputs to create knowledge in the form of complex notions, concepts, and theories.

Another implication is in the reassessment of the key concerns in the design and management of organizational knowledge systems. Currently we are mainly focused on the issues of tapping tacit knowledge, combining it with "explicit" knowledge, and learning by being embedded in external networks. A reassessment would change the problem from tapping tacit knowledge to designing a knowledge system in which the content deposited by organizational members will be in a form amenable to processing by other members or users of the system (per knowledge process B previously shown).

Finally, a key implication relates to the basket of incentives the organization provides its members to share their knowledge and to use its knowledge system. These incentives should be reformulated to fit the searching and processing behavior of the members. People do not search for externalized knowledge by assembling bits and pieces of information. Rather, their searching mode is focused on a topic, such as "What do we know about ____?" The reformulated incentives should compensate behavior that produces "quality," not "quantity." Members should not be compensated for the amount of use or deposits they perform with respect to the knowledge system in their organization. Rather, incentives should emphasize the content and its rate or power of absorption by other members of whatever members deposit in the knowledge system.

Conclusion

To know is the most laudable and the most painful of human capabilities. Much of our effort in organizations seems to focus on sharing, preserving, and diffusing what we know. The recent emergence of the nations of the "knowledge economy" and "knowledge workers" has helped to establish a disciplinary area of "knowledge management," beyond the realm of the management of information systems.

In this chapter, I have proposed a view of human knowledge as a personal cognitive process. Whatever we are able to externalize and share with others is but a collection of "information" which now should be absorbed and digested by other people to create knowledge in their minds. Knowledge cannot be externalized in the same form or power of its existence in the mind. This view would dictate some reassessment of the design and taxonomy of knowledge systems in organizations, and the type of incentives we give organizational members to use these systems.

Glossary

Adaptive Learning: Also known as single-loop learning, it focuses on solving problems in the present without examining the appropriateness of current learning behaviors.

Agrarian Age: Wealth was generated through agriculture so land was the key to wealth.

Application of Knowledge: The transformation of knowledge from a purely intellectual facet of life into a highly productive tool that is essential for the conduct of not only business, but practically any other meaningful human activity, providing its outcome is expected to produce tangible results.

Artificial Intelligence (AI): Using technology to simulate human intelligence such as reasoning and thinking.

Aspects of Knowledge: The four key aspects of knowledge that tend to transcend the boundaries of tacit, explicit, implicit, procedural, and declarative include Know-how, Know-why, Know-when (and -where), and Know-about.

Benefits of KM: Fosters innovation by encouraging the free flow of ideas, improves customer service by streamlining response time, and boosts revenues by getting products and services to market faster. Enhances employee retention rates by recognizing the value of employees' knowledge and rewarding them for it helps streamline operations and reduces costs by eliminating redundant or unnecessary processes.

Boyd's "Destruction and Creation": Creation of new knowledge can be attained only by the "destruction" of domain barriers and imaginative selection of suitable constituents belonging to the previously well-defined domains, followed by the reassembly of these constituents into an entirely new entity--the process of creation.

Business Process Re-engineering (BPR): Involves the fundamental rethinking and radical redesign of business processes to achieve dramatic improvements in critical, contemporary measures of performance, such as cost, quality, service, and speed.

Case-Based Reasoning (CBR): An AI technique that uses historical solutions to solve similar current problems.

Challenges of KM: Include getting employees on board, not allowing technology to dictate KM, having a specific business goal, having a dynamic not static approach to KM, identifying the correct information to turn into knowledge, identifying who should lead KM efforts, and identifying what technologies can/should support KM.

Change Management: Requires considering many aspects at both the macro level--taking an overall view of the organization, and the micro level--taking a view that considers individuals within a department or group.

Cluster Analysis: A data mining technique which uses in-group of undirected tools, with the purpose of finding the structure as a whole (i.e.. there are no target variables which are to be predicted but the clusters are formed and grouped together and then decision is made using decision tree or neural network).

Competitive Advantage and Value Creation: In trying to obtain a competitive advantage and thereby create value, three areas must be considered; namely, customer value, supplier value, and the value of the firm.

Competitive Forces: Porter's Competitive Forces model outlines the rules of competition and attractiveness of the industry in terms of five key forces: threat of new entrants, threat of substitutes, bargaining power of buyers, bargaining power of suppliers, and rivalry of existing competition.

Constructivism: Philosophy whose main proponents belonged to the Erlangen School and whose belief was that knowledge is constructed in our minds and thus is not objective.

Critical Rationalism: Philosophy whose main proponent was Popper and which stated that all knowledge must be open to empirical falsification before it can be accepted.

Critical Theory: Philosophy promoted by Habermas and Horkheimer, which used knowledge to integrate the tension between the reality of society and the real societal function of science.

Cross-Disciplinary Nature of KM: Knowledge management draws from: Cognitive Science, Expert Systems, Artificial Intelligence and Knowledge Base Management Systems (KBMS), Computer-Supported Collaborative Work (CSCW) and Groupware, Library and Information, Technical Writing, Document Management, Decision Support Systems, Semantic Networks, Relational and Object Databases, Simulation and Organizational Science.

Customer Relationship Management (CRM): A business strategy that integrates people, process, and technology to enhance relationships with customers, partners, distributors, suppliers, and employees to maximize revenue growth and market share.

Customer Value: Customers' willingness to pay for the firm's product or service, minus the asking price of the firm's product or service.

Data: Represents raw facts. In transforming data to information, the important 5Cs are: (1) contextualized, (2) categorized, (3) calculated, (4) corrected, and (5) condensed.

Data Mining (DM): A technology-driven framework for knowledge creation, consisting of various data operations such as sampling, partitioning, charting, graphing, associating, clustering, transforming, filtering, and imputing, with the ultimate goals of describing the existing data and predicting future variables.

Data Warehouse: Information technology infrastructure that supports access to knowledge by storing snapshots of operational data such as sales, inventory, and customer information.

Database: Information technology infrastructure that stores structured information and assists in the storing and sharing of knowledge.

Declarative Knowledge: Knowledge that is descriptive.

Deetz's Consensus/Disensus Perspectives: A framework designed to highlight the dual nature of knowledge: a consensus orientation toward knowledge seeks order and equilibrium as the natural state, while a dissensus orientation recognizes conflict and fragmented, divergent views and meanings.

Domain Expert: A person who is both experienced and knowledgeable in a particular domain or field.

Effectiveness: Doing something in the most suitable fashion.

Efficiency: Doing something as quickly as possible and incurring the lowest cost.

Empiricism: Philosophy whose main proponents, Locke and Russel, sustained that knowledge can be created from experiments and thus only mathematics and natural sciences can provide secure knowledge.

Enterprise Integration: We are currently observing the development of three distinct architectures for integrating e-commerce with ERP systems: the inside-out approach, the outside-in approach, and the open electronic cart.

Enterprise Resource Planning (ERP) Systems: A structured approach to optimizing a company's internal value chain.

Enterprise System: IC^2T that spans the whole organizations.

Enterprise Wide Portals: Require the integration of many technologies, including web modeling languages, data content, interface tools, content delivery tools, messaging technologies, etc., into one integrated storefront.

E-Readiness: Concerned with the physical information and communication technology infrastructure and the skills of the population to utilize this infrastructure.

Expertise: Another term for tacit knowledge.

Explicit Knowledge: Knowledge as a fact.

Externalization: The articulation of knowledge into tangible form through dialogue.

Generalist's Role in Knowledge Management, The: A specialist preoccupied with the contents of his own domain entirely misses the connections between domains, which are noticed by a generalist who, by combining several disciplines, is able to perceive the existence of functional relationships that appeared to be nonexistent by the observer capable of only a narrow view.

Generative Learning: Also known as "double-loop learning," it emphasizes continuous experimentation and feedback in an ongoing examination of the very way organizations go about defining and solving problems.

Generic Strategies: First embraced in business policy by the development of the SWOT (strengths, weaknesses, opportunities, threats) framework, its essential goal is to find a "fit" between the organization and its environment that maximizes performance.

Groupware: A class of software that helps groups of colleagues (workgroups) attached to a local-area network organize their activities.

Heuristics: Common sense knowledge drawn from experience "rule of thumb."

Implications of KM: Knowledge management is a multi-discipline approach that takes a comprehensive, systematic view to the information assets of an organization by identifying, capturing, collecting, organizing, indexing, storing, integrating, retrieving and sharing them. Such assets include (a) the explicit knowledge such as databases, documents, environmental knowledge, policies, procedures, and organizational culture; and (b) the tacit knowledge of its employees, their expertise, and their practical work experience.

Implicit Knowledge: Knowledge that can be either tacit or explicit but has not been articulated.

Incremental Learning: Learning that is characterized by simple, routine problem solving and that requires no fundamental change to your thinking or system.

Industrial Age: Wealth was generated through manufacturing and land was no longer the key to wealth. The Industrial age was about centralization and control.

Information: An understanding of relationships between data elements or the meaning of the data; i.e. what it stands for. When information is transformed into knowledge, the important 4Cs are: (1) comparison, (2) consequences, (3) connections, and (4) conversation.

Information Age: New technology and fast access to information are transforming the business landscape. The information age is about de-centralization and no/less control.

Information Society: A society that utilizes information, information technologies, and tools for day-to-day activities and business.

KM and the Strategic Vision: Knowledge management strategies should aim to set forth the criteria for choosing what knowledge a firm plans to pursue, and how it will go about capturing and sharing that knowledge.

KM Drivers: Include the shrinking cycle time for competency-base renewal, the urge to value intellectual capital, and the pressure for most organizations to cope with a massive flood of unstructured information.

Knowledge: Puts information into a context that enables shared meaning.

Knowledge Acquisition: The starting point of the organizational knowledge life cycle, which involves the capture of existing knowledge through activities such as knowledge transfer, knowledge sharing, observation, interaction, and self-study.

Knowledge Architecture: An integrated set of technical choices used to guide an organization in satisfying its business needs. The knowledge architecture recognizes the different yet key aspects of knowledge, such as knowledge as an object and a subject, and thus provides the blue prints for the design of an all encompassing knowledge management system (KMS).

Knowledge Discovery: The process consisting of the evolution of knowledge from data to information to knowledge, the types of data mining (exploratory and predictive), and their interrelationships.

Knowledge Discovery in Databases (KDD): A technology-driven framework for knowledge creation that focuses on how data is transformed into knowledge by identifying valid, novel, potentially useful, and ultimately understandable patterns in data. Primarily used on data sets for creating knowledge through model building, or by finding patterns and relationships in data.

Knowledge Economy (K-Economy): The term was coined by the OECD and defined as an economy, which is directly based on the production, distribution, and use of knowledge and information.

Knowledge Elicitation: Process to extract knowledge from expert.

Knowledge Life Cycle, The: The four key steps in the knowledge life cycle include: create/generate knowledge, represent/store, distribution/use/re-use, and knowledge application.

Knowledge Management (KM): A discipline that promotes an integrated approach to identifying, managing, and sharing all of an enterprise's information needs.

Knowledge Management Infrastructure: Consists of infrastructure for collaboration, organizational memory, human asset infrastructure, knowledge transfer network, and business intelligence infrastructure.

Knowledge Management Infrastructure Design: Choosing a knowledge management infrastructure, technological or organizational, should address the organization's process needs: generation of knowledge, access of knowledge, transfer of knowledge, representation of knowledge, embedding of knowledge, and facilitation of knowledge.

Knowledge Management Systems (KMS): The micro-level processes of assimilation and implementation of knowledge management concepts and techniques, systems that aim to facilitate the sharing and integration of knowledge.

Knowledge Workers: Own their means of production (i.e., knowledge, and are considered the most valuable human resource).

K-Readiness: About the ability of a country to create, access, share, and apply knowledge across a wide range of sectors, whether or not it involves the use of the e-technologies.

Leader: There are many roles that a leader must exhibit in any KM initiative and these include the following: being a creator of corporate culture, facilitator, coach, sustainer, change agent, pathfinder, empowering knowledge workers, and aligning key areas so that a consistent KM vision and strategy ensue.

Learning Organization: An organization that has an enhanced capacity to learn, adapt and change; a complex interrelationship of systems composed of people, technology, practices, and tools designed so that new information is embraced.

Learning: The process of acquiring new knowledge and enhancing existing knowledge.

Legacy Systems: Outdated and old computer systems.

Management of Knowledge Workers: To capture knowledge from experts, organizations use standard interview techniques including structured, semi-structured, and unstructured questions, posed to the expert in an attempt to extricate all critical knowledge.

Management Strategy: Incorporates: (a) external analysis of the market, (b) internal analysis of the market, and (c) what gives the firm its competitive advantage in order to design the firm's own competitive strategy.

Manager: Position in an organization that can entail various responsibilities at different levels of authority: senior managers focus primarily on long-term strategic decisions, middle managers focus on how to carry out the plans and goals of senior managers, while operational managers are concerned with monitoring the day-to-day activities of the firm.

McFarlan's Strategic Grid: A contingency model that underscores two key dimensions for determining the relative strategic positioning of an organization with respect to its competitors: (1) an assessment of a firm' business portfolio on the horizontal axis, and (2) the strength of a firm's IT portfolio on the vertical axis.

Multifaceted Knowledge Construct: Knowledge has more than one aspect: subjective and objective, declarative and procedural, implicit and explicit.

Necessary Factors to Create Knowledge-Based Organizations: Include widespread access of ICTs, a learning approach, continuous cycle of discovery, dissemination, intellectual capital, innovation and knowledge networks, learning organizations, and innovation systems.

Objective Aspect of Knowledge: When knowledge is grounded in the Lockean/ Leibnizian philosophy of convergence and compliance and thus can affect efficiencies of scale and scope.

OODA Loop, The: The OODA loop is based on a cycle of four critical and inter-related stages: observation, orientation, decision, and action.

Organizational Culture: The pattern of formal and informal codes of behavior, norms, rituals, stories about what happens within the organization, tasks and jargon in an organization.

Organizational Memory: A comprehensive computer system, which captures a company's, accumulated know-how and other knowledge assets and makes them available to enhance the efficiency and effectiveness of knowledge-intensive work processes.

Organizational Structure: Mintzberg identifies seven major typologies for organizations: (1) entrepreneurial, (2) machine, (3) professional, (4) diversified, (5) innovative, (6) missionary, and (7) political.

People-Oriented Perspectives to Knowledge Creation: Nonaka's knowledge spiral highlights four key perspectives to knowledge creation: socialization, transformation, externalization, and internalization.

Pertinent Information: Represents structured data, grouped into coherent categories that are easily perceptible and understood.

Pertinent Knowledge: Represents the ability to use pertinent information as the essential tool in interaction and response to the competitor's moves.

Porter's Value Chain Model: Identifies five primary functions and four secondary functions within a company. The five primary functions are inbound logistics, operations, outbound logistics, sales & marketing, and service. The four secondary functions are administration & management, human resources, technology, and procurement.

Positivism: Philosophy promoted by Comte, with the main idea that knowledge is gained from the observation of objective reality.

Pragmatism: Philosophy promoted by Dewey, which represented knowledge as a local reality based on our experiences.

Preparedness: The availability (pre-positioning) of all resources, both human and physical, necessary for the management of, or the consequences of, a specific event or event complex.

Procedural Knowledge: Knowledge that outlines activities or steps.

Radical Learning: Breakthrough learning that directly challenges the prevailing mental model on which the system is built.

Readiness: The instantaneous ability to respond to a suddenly arising major crisis that is based on the instantaneously and locally available/un-pre positioned and un-mobilized countermeasure resources.

Requirements to Overcome the Difficulties of KM: Enterprises need: to have an enterprise-wide vocabulary to ensure that the knowledge is correctly understood;

to be able to identify, model and explicitly represent their knowledge; to share and re-use their knowledge among differing applications for various types of users; and to create a culture that encourages knowledge sharing.

Reverse Value Chain, The: A method of information system development, which focuses on the marketplace as the "right" end of a value chain that weaves itself through the structure of a company and into the core business processes.

Significance of Knowledge Management Systems: In essence KM tools and technologies are the systems that integrate various legacy systems, databases, ERP systems, and data warehouse to help organizations to answer all questions "What Happened? Why Did It Happen? What Will Happen? What is Happening? and What Do I Want to Happen?"

Socialization: The process of creating new tacit knowledge through discussion within groups, more specifically groups of experts.

Socio-Algorithmic Approach to Knowledge Creation: Integrates the algorithmic approach (in particular data mining) with the psycho-social approach to knowledge creation (i.e., the people-driven frameworks of knowledge creation, in particular the knowledge spiral).

Sociology of Knowledge: Philosophy whose proponents Mannheim and Scheler encouraged the view of knowledge as a socially constructed reality.

Socio-Technical Perspective of KM: Means we must consider people, processes, and technology when we examine and analyze KM initiatives.

Strategic Knowledge: A term used by some to refer to what might be termed know-when and/or know-why.

Subjective Aspect of Knowledge: When knowledge is the center of discourse and shared meanings in the Hegelian/Kantian philosophical perspective.

Supplier Value: The bid price offered by the firm, minus supplier costs.

Supply Chain Integration: A business model in which customers and suppliers work together and form inter-organizational teams that facilitate improved communication between organizations and increase the rate of learning.

Supply Chain Management (SCM): Supply chain management (SCM) involves the adoption of strategies that enable the effective and efficient operation of the logistic network; i.e., the integration of suppliers, manufacturers, warehouses and customers both within and across industries.

Sustainable Competitive Advantage: From a KM point of view, a situation in which an entity positions itself in a state of information superiority relative to its environment.

Systems Thinking: The goal of systems thinking in business is to explore and analyze processes as wholes and understand the inter-relations and inter-connectedness of various processes and thus how they impact on each other, on the premise that the sum of the parts is indeed less than the whole.

Tacit Knowledge: Knowledge as gained from experience and "doing."

Technology-Oriented Perspectives to Knowledge Creation: Knowledge discovery in databases (KDD) (and more specifically data mining) approaches knowledge creation from a primarily technology-driven perspective.

Total Quality Management (TQM): Total quality management (TQM) is an evolving system of practices, tools, and training methods for managing companies to provide customer satisfaction by taking work requirements (inputs), putting them through an internal process that measures defect rates and cycle time, and producing an output that is of value to the client.

Training: A process that facilitates the proper use of knowledge as a solution to all forthcoming events based on extrapolation of a careful analysis of all pertinent characteristics of the evolving scenario, defining similarities to the past events, characterizing the differences and isolating entirely novel elements, visualizing all interrelationships among the individual subcomponents, and then making appropriate decisions.

Two Facets of KM: Knowledge management has two facets: (1) planning, capturing, organizing, interconnecting and providing access to organizational intellectual capital through such intellectual technologies as document markup, thesaurus construction or needs analysis and (2) directing or supervising such assets and those that are involved in these processes.

Understanding: The process by which one can synthesize new knowledge from previously held knowledge.

Value Chain: A group of high value-added internal activities of organizations and their core competencies, focused on core business processes, the "right" end of the value chain that weaves itself through the structure of a company and out into the marketplace.

Value Created by the Firm: Creating greater value of the firm is typically accomplished in three ways: (1) operating more efficiently, (2) providing greater benefits to customers by improving products and services, (3) developing innovative transactions that offer new value to the market.

Value-Driven Strategy: A method for choosing the appropriate goals and strategies by evaluating them based on whether or not they increase the firm's total value.

Value of Knowledge, The: Essentially knowledge assets are the knowledge regarding markets, products, technologies and organizations, that a business owns or needs to own and which enable its business processes to generate profits, add value, etc.

Value of the Firm: The difference between asking price, bid price, and cost of the firm's assets.

Wisdom: A uniquely human state, is the next step beyond knowledge: the process by which we also discern, or judge, between right and wrong, good and bad.

Yin-Yang Model of KM: Brings together the subjective and objective aspects of knowledge, thereby enabling a more holistic approach to knowledge creation.

About the Authors

Nilmini Wickramasinghe (PhD; MBA; GradDipMgtSt; BSc. Amus.A, piano; Amus.A, violin) researches and teaches in several areas within information systems including knowledge management, e-commerce and m-commerce, and organizational impacts of technology. Over the last 6 years, she has been instrumental in introducing courses on knowledge management at the graduate and undergraduate level in Australian, European, and U.S. academic institutions. She is well published in all these areas with more than 50 referred papers and several books. In addition, she regularly presents her work throughout North America, as well as in Europe and Australasia. Dr. Wickramasinghe is the U.S. representative of the Health Care Technology Management Association (HCTM), an international organization that focuses on critical healthcare issues and the role of technology within the domain of healthcare. She is the associate director of the Center Management Medical Technologies (CMMT), a unique research-oriented center with key research foci on knowledge management, healthcare, and the confluence of these domains and holds an associate professor position at the Stuart Graduate School of Business, IIT. In addition, she has been conferred as a visiting professor in knowledge management at Coventry University's BICORE (biomedical computing and engineering technology) HCKM group in the UK and is a visiting faculty member at the University of Cooperative Education BA, Heidenheim, Germany. Dr Wickramasinghe is the editor-in-chief of two scholarly journals: *International Journal of Networking and Virtual Organisations* (IJNVO) and *International Journal of Biomedical Engineering and Technology* (IJBET), both published by InderScience.

Dag von Lubitz, chairman and chief scientist at MedSMART, Inc. and adjunct professor at the College of Health Sciences at Central Michigan University, is the author of more than 120 peer-reviewed biomedical research papers, holder of prestigious international awards, and a frequent keynote speaker on management of medical technology, e-health, decision-making, and leadership in the dynamically changing environments. Working in the U.S. and Europe, DvL serves as a consultant on networkcentric healthcare and implementation of simulation and virtual reality in worldwide distance education and training of medical personnel, particularly in the rural/remote regions and in less developed countries. He also consults on management of complex disasters and decision-making in rapidly changing environments.

*   *   *   *   *

Witold Abramowicz is an associate professor and head of the Department of MIS. Prof. Abramowicz graduated in June 1979 from Poznan University of Technology, Poland, specializing in digital control systems. He received his PhD in economics from the Wroclaw University of Technology (Poland) in June 1985 and in March 1992—tenure at The Humboldt University, Berlin, Germany. His research interests include information management systems, information filters supplying information management systems, data warehouses supplied by information from the Internet, and workflow controlled by in-formation filtered from the Internet. He is author and editor of several dozens of books and articles in the in-formation systems and information processing; he also participated in numerous research projects and several EU-funded research projects within this area.

Mike Bresnen is a professor of organizational behaviour at the University of Leicester Management Centre. He holds a PhD from the University of Nottingham and has previously worked at Warwick Business School, Cardiff Business School, and Loughborough University. He is co-editor of *Organization* and a founding member of the Innovation, Knowledge, and Organizational Networking research unit (*ikon*) based at Warwick Business School, where he is also an associate fellow. He is the author of *Organizing Construction* (Routledge, 1990) and has researched and published widely on the organization and management of the construction process, as well as on inter-organizational relations, project management, leadership, and professionals. He is principal investigator on a number of recent EPSRC/ESRC projects investigating knowledge management and project-based learning in construction, manufacturing, and service sectors, as well as innovation in the biomedical field.

Graydon Davison joined the College of Law and Business at the University of Western Sydney in 2000, following careers in public and private sector management and in management consulting. Davison holds a Master of Technology Management degree and is a currently completing a PhD. He teaches organisational behaviour and management and decision-making. His PhD thesis, "Innovative Practice in the

Process of Patient Management in Palliative Care," is a non-clinical view of the management of innovation in a complex, dynamic environment where the results of innovation are social advantage, the care, and wellbeing of people.

Brian Donnellan is a lecturer in information systems in the National University of Ireland, Galway. His research interests lie primarily in the area of knowledge management systems, a broad area that encompasses the use of information systems to support knowledge management, innovation, new product development, and technology management. He has spent 20 years working in an industry where he was responsible for "KM" business processes and management of engineering computer services for new product development teams.

Eliezer (Elie) Geisler is a professor and associate dean for research at the Stuart Graduate School of Business, Illinois Institute of Technology. He holds a doctorate from the Kellogg School at Northwestern University. Dr. Geisler is the author of about 90 papers in the areas of technology and innovation management, the evaluation of R&D, science and technology, and the management of medical technology. He is the author of eight books, including *The Metrics of Science and Technology* (2000), and *Creating Value with Science and Technology* (2001). Dr. Geisler was founder and editor of the Department of Information Technology for the IEEE Transactions on Engineering Management, and is associate editor of the *International Journal of Healthcare Technology and Management*. He consulted for major corporations and for many U.S. federal departments, such as Defense, Commerce, EPA, Energy, and NASA. Dr. Geisler is director of IIT's Center for the Management of Medical Technology (CMMT). Dr. Geisler co-chairs the annual conference on the Hospital of the Future. His most recent books are *Installing and Managing Workable Knowledge Management Systems* (Praeger, 2003, co-authored with Rubenstein) and *Technology, Health care, and Management in the Hospital of the Future* (2003, with Krabbendam and Schuring). His forthcoming book is *The Structure and Progress of Knowledge: Applications in Databases and Management Systems* (M.E. Sharpe, 2004).

Michael J. Ginzberg is Chaplin Tyler professor of business at the Alfred Lerner College of Business and Economics, University of Delaware. From 2000-2006, Dr. Ginzberg served as dean of the Lerner College. Prior to coming to the University of Delaware, he served on the business faculties of Case Western Reserve University, New York University, and Columbia University. He has taught at SDA Bocconi in Milan, Italy, the International Management Center in Budapest, Hungary, and the Rotterdam School of Management, Erasmus Universiteit, The Netherlands. He received the PhD in management from the Alfred P. Sloan School of Management at MIT. Dr. Ginzberg's research has focused on the management and use of information technology in organizations and the management of technical professionals. His current research interests concern creating business value through investments in information technology and the impact of technology on corporate governance. He has published over 45 articles and chapters and edited a half dozen books and monographs in the fields of management and information systems. Dr. Ginzberg has held leadership positions in national and international professional and academic organizations, including the International Conference on Information Systems, the Association for Information Systems, and the Society for Information Management. He has served on the board of trustees of the International Management Center, Budapest, Hungary, the board of directors of Beta Alpha Psi, the international honorary society for financial information professionals, and as chairman of the board of trustees of the Sarajevo Graduate School of Business in Sarajevo, Bosnia & Herzegovina. He has also served on the advisory board of Environmental Consulting International, and as consultant to the board of directors of Quaker City Motor Parts Co. He currently serves on the preliminary review committee of the Delaware Board on Professional Responsibility and on the Business Leader Hall of Fame Committee of Junior Achievement of Delaware.

William Golden is a member of the Centre for Innovation and Structural Change and a lecturer in IS at NUI, Galway. He has held this position since 1991. He completed his doctorate on B2B electronic commerce at the University of Warwick, UK. He has presented papers at both national and international conferences. He has co-authored a book, contributed chapters to other texts and published papers in the areas of electronic commerce and information systems in *Omega, The International Journal of Management Science, International Journal of Electronic Commerce, Journal of Agile Management Systems, and Journal of Decision Systems.*

Anna Goussevskaia is a senior research fellow within a research centre, *Innovation Knowledge and Organizational Networks,* at Warwick Business School, The University of Warwick, UK, and a professor of innovation management at Fundação Dom Cabral, Brazil. Goussevskaia completed her PhD in management at Warwick where she was also involved in research and teaching. Her research interests include inter-organizational networks and collaboration, organizational knowledge and learning, and organizational change. She has published in related areas including articles in *Organization Studies* and *Building Research & Information,* and contribution to books including *Trust and antitrust in Asian business alliances* (Palgrave, 2004).

Martin Hughes is a lecturer in information systems at NUI, Galway, a position he has held since 2000. He is currently pursuing a PhD on e-business at the University of Bath, UK. His research interests include knowledge management, inter-organisational systems and risk, and e-commerce and the small firm. His work has been published in book chapters, leading international IS conferences and in the *Journal of End User Computing, the Journal of Electronic Commerce in Organisations, the Journal of Small Business, and Enterprise Development, and the Irish Marketing Review.*

Tomasz Kaczmarek, MSc research assistant and PhD candidate in the Department of MIS, graduated in 2002 from The Poznan University of Economics, specializing in MIS. His areas of interest include information retrieval and filtering systems (particularly time aspects of information), data integration, and electronic marketplaces. He authored several conference papers and articles in these areas.

Marek Kowalkiewicz, MSc research assistant and PhD candidate in the Department of MIS, graduated in 2002 from The Poznan University of Economics, specializing in MIS. His areas of interest include information retrieval and filtering systems, information extraction from the Web, content integration, electronic marketplaces, and e-learning systems. He authored numerous conference papers, book chapters, and journal articles in these areas.

Roberta Lamb is an associate professor of informatics in the Donald Bren School of Information and Computer Science at the University of California, Irvine. She conducts informatics studies of online technologies and socio-technical networks and she has recently completed a 4-year NSF-funded study of the development of organizational intranets, and the interorganizational relationships that shape intranet use. Papers from Lamb's studies have appeared in *Data Base*, *MIS Quarterly*, *The Information Society*, and other academic publications. Her research has won several grants and awards, including a Nokia-Fulbright Scholarship to lecture and conduct research in Finland.

Mogens Kühn Pedersen is head of the Department of Informatics at Copenhagen Business School. He conducts research in the theory of distributed knowledge management systems and in their use in healthcare, construction and other industries. Pedersen conducts studies in digital government (for business), governance of IT, and open source software and standards. Previously at Roskilde University, Pedersen has been with Copenhagen Business School since 1998 as a professor and director of the PhD School in Informatics (1998-2005) and head of the department (since April 2005). Pedersen has published IS research both nationally and internationally at all major conferences. Pedersen is an adviser to Danish government and boards (i.e., Open Source Software in eGovernment (2002)), on open source projects (2003-4); advanced eGovernment applications (2003-4), and open standards (2005-6). For more information, visit www.cbs.dk/staff/kuehn.

Jacky Swan is a professor is organizational behaviour at Warwick Business School, University of Warwick. She completed her PhD in psychology at Cardiff and formerly worked at Aston University. She is a founding member (and co-director) of IKON—a research centre in *Innovation Knowledge and Organizational Networks*—and conducts her research in related areas. Her current interests are in linking innovation and networking to processes of managing knowledge across different industry sectors and national contexts. She has been responsible for a number of UK Research Council projects on innovation and is currently working on projects investigating "Managing Knowledge in Project-Based Environments," and "The Evolution of Biomedical Knowledge for Interactive Innovation in the UK and U.S." She has published widely, including articles in *Organization Studies, Organization, Human Relations, Journal of Management Studies,* edited special issues, and the co-authored book, *Managing Knowledge Work* (Palgrave, 2002). She is currently a senior editor for *Organization Studies*.

Index